The Right to the Assistance of Counsel

The Right to the Assistance of Counsel

A Reference Guide to the United States Constitution

James J. Tomkovicz

Foreword by Yale Kamisar

REFERENCE GUIDES TO THE
UNITED STATES CONSTITUTION, NUMBER 1
Jack Stark, *Series Editor*

GREENWOOD PRESS
Westport, Connecticut • London

Library of Congress Cataloging-in-Publication Data

Tomkovicz, James J.
The right to the assistance of counsel : a reference guide to the United States Constitution / James J. Tomkovicz ; foreword by Yale Kamisar.
p. cm.—(Reference guides to the United States Constitution, ISSN 1539–8986 ; no. 1)
Includes bibliographical references and index.
ISBN 0–313–31448–9 (alk. paper)
1. Right to counsel—United States. 2. United States Constitution. 6th Amendment. I. Title. II. Series.
KF9646.T66 2002
345.73'056—dc21 2001058633

British Library Cataloguing in Publication Data is available.

Library of Congress Catalog Card Number: 2001058633
ISBN: 0–313–31448–9
ISSN: 1539–8986

First published in 2002

Greenwood Press, 88 Post Road West, Westport, CT 06881
An imprint of Greenwood Publishing Group, Inc.
www.greenwood.com

Printed in the United States of America

The paper used in this book complies with the Permanent Paper Standard issued by the National Information Standards Organization (Z39.48–1984).

10 9 8 7 6 5 4 3 2 1

To Vivian M. Tomkovicz, who showed me the worth of hard work, taught me the value of an education, nurtured me in every way, and encouraged me to aim high; and to the Honorable Edward J. Schwartz, a judge of unparalleled integrity, fairness, and compassion and a friend whose spirit lives on in those whose lives he touched.

The right of one charged with crime to counsel may not be deemed fundamental and essential to fair trials in some countries, but it is in ours.

—Justice Hugo L. Black, *Gideon v. Wainwright*,
372 U.S. 335, 344 (1963)

Contents

Series Foreword

One can conceive of the United States Constitution in many ways. For example, noticing the reverence in which it has been held can induce one to think of it as an equivalent of a sacred text, although unfortunately most of its devotees have had less knowledge and even less understanding of it than they have had reverence for it. It sometimes appears to be primarily a political document and on that basis has been subjected to analysis, such as Charles Beard's economic analysis of it. One can plausibly argue that the Constitution seems most astounding when it is seen in the light of the intellectual effort that has been associated with it. Three brief but highly intense bursts of intellectual energy produced, and established as organic law, most of the Constitution as it now exists. Two efforts that have been sustained over a long period of time have enabled us better to understand that document.

The first burst of energy occurred at the Constitutional Convention. Although some of the delegates' business, such as the struggle between populous and nonpopulous states about their representation in Congress, was political, much of it was about fundamental issues of political theory. A few of the delegates had or later achieved international eminence for their intellects. Among them are Benjamin Franklin, Alexander Hamilton, and James Madison. Others, although less well known, had first-rate minds. That group includes George Mason and George Wythe. Many of the delegates intelligently contributed. Although the convention's records are less than satisfactory, they indicate clearly enough that the delegates worked mightily to constitute not merely a polity but a rational polity that would rise to the standards envisioned by the intellectual ancestors who influenced the delegates. Their product, although brief, is amazing. William Gladstone called it "the most wonderful work ever struck off."

Despite the delegates' eminence and the Constitution's excellence, as seen from our place in history, its ratification was far from certain. That state of affairs necessitated the second burst of intellectual energy associated with that document: the debate over ratification. Soon after the convention adjourned, articles and speeches—some supporting and some attacking the Constitution—began to proliferate. A national debate about not only the document itself but also about the nature of the polity that ought to exist in this country commenced. Both sides included many writers and speakers who were verbally adroit and steeped in the relevant political and philosophical literature. The result was an accumulation of material that is remarkable for both its quantity and its quality. At its apex is *The Federalist Papers*, a production of Alexander Hamilton, James Madison, and John Jay that deserves a place among the great books of Western culture.

Another burst, which is not as impressive as the first two but highly respectable, occurred when the Bill of Rights was proposed. Some delegates to the Constitutional Convention had vigorously asserted that such guarantees should be included in the original document. George Mason, the principal drafter of the Virginia Declaration of Rights, so held, and he walked out of the convention when he failed to achieve his purpose. Even those who had argued that the rights in question were implicit recognized the value of adding protection for them to the Constitution. The debate was thus focused on the rights that were to be explicitly granted, not on whether any rights ought to be explicitly granted. Again many writers and speakers entered the fray, and again the debate was solidly grounded in theory and was conducted on a high intellectual level.

Thus, within a few years a statement of organic law and a vital coda to it had been produced. However, the meaning and effect of many of that document's provisions were far from certain; the debates on ratification of the Constitution and the Bill of Rights demonstrated that to be true. In addition, the document existed in a vacuum, because statutes and actions had not been assessed by its standards. After Chief Justice John Marshall, in Marbury v. Madison, asserted the right of the United States Supreme Court to interpret and apply the Constitution, both of those problems began to be attacked. Judicial interpretation and application of the Constitution, beginning with the first constitutional case and persisting until the most recent, is one of the sustained exertions of intellectual energy associated with the Constitution. The Framers would be surprised by some of those activities' results. References in the document to "due process," which seems to refer only to procedures, have been held also to have a substantive dimension. A right to privacy has been found lurking among the penumbras of various parts of the text. A requirement that states grant the same "privileges and immunities" to citizens of other states that they granted to their own citizens, which seemed to guarantee important rights, was held not to be particularly important. The corpus of judicial interpretations of the Constitution is now as voluminous as that document is terse.

As the judicial interpretations multiplied, another layer—interpretations of interpretations—appeared, and then it, too, multiplied. This layer, the other sustained intellectual effort associated with the Constitution, is the articles, most of them published in law reviews, and the books on the Constitution. That material varies in quality and significance. Some of it results from meticulous examination and incisive thought. However, some of it repeats earlier work or at great length applies a fine-tooth comb to matter that is too minute even for such a comb. Somewhere in that welter of tertiary material is the answer to almost every question that one could ask about constitutional law. The problem is finding the answer that one wants. The difficulty of locating useful guidance is exacerbated by the bifurcation of most constitutional scholarship into two kinds. In "Two Styles of Social Science Research," C. Wright Mills delineates macroscopic and molecular research. The former deals with huge issues, the latter with tiny issues. Virtually all of the scholarship on the Constitution is of one of those two types. A little bit of it is very general, and that category includes some first-rate syntheses such as Jack Rakove's *Original Meanings*. Most of the scholarship is molecular and, again, some fine work is included in that category.

In his essay Mills bemoans the inability of social scientists to combine the two kinds of research that he describes, to create a third category that will be more generally useful. This series of books is an attempt to do for constitutional law the intellectual work that Mills wanted done for social science. The author of each book has dealt carefully and at reasonable length with a topic that lies in the middle range of generality. Upon completion, this series will consist of thirty-seven books, each on a constitutional law topic. Some of the books, such as the book on freedom of the press, explicate one portion of the Constitution's text. Others, such as the volume on federalism, treat a topic that has several anchors in that text. The books on constitutional history and constitutional interpretation range over the entire document, but each does so from one perspective. Except for a very few of the books, as to which special circumstances dictate minor changes in format, each book includes the same components. Their major components are a brief history of the topic, a lengthy and sophisticated analysis of the current state of the law on that topic, a bibliographical essay that organizes and evaluates scholarly material in order to facilitate further research, a table of cases, and an index. The books are intellectually rigorous—in fact, authorities have written them—but, due to their clarity and to brief definitions of terms that are unfamiliar to laypersons, each is comprehensible to, and useful to, a wide audience, one that ranges from other experts on the book's subject to intelligent non-lawyers.

In short, this series provides an extremely valuable service to the legal community and to others who are interested in constitutional law, as every citizen should be at least to some extent. Each book is a map of part of the United States Constitution. Together they map all of that document's territory that is worth mapping. When this series is complete, each book will be a third kind of scholarly work that combines the macroscopic and the molecular. Together they will explicate all of the important constitutional topics. Anyone who wants assistance in understanding either a topic in constitutional law or the Constitution as a whole can easily find it in these books.

Jack Stark

Foreword

No right of the accused has been more highly praised than the right to counsel. It has well been called the right without which a person's "day in court" is "an idle expression."[1]

As Professor Tomkovicz points out, however, despite its stirring language, for many years Powell v. Alabama was viewed as holding that, absent special circumstances, *only* indigent state defendants charged with a capital offense were entitled to assigned counsel, "the linchpin of constitutional protection,"[2] "the most pervasive right" of an accused,[3] and "the master key" to all the rules and procedures designed to ensure the reliability of the guilt-determining process.[4]

To this list of praise one should add James Tomkovicz's own observations (p. 128):

> Without a lawyer's aid, it is quite unlikely that an accused will be able to enjoy the advantages of the other enumerated rights. Without counsel, there is little chance for a fair battle between equally able adversaries. Counsel's most basic role is to ensure that the confrontation between opponents contemplated by our Constitution actually does take place.

Such a monumental right deserves a monumental book. Happily, Professor Tomkovicz has written such a book.

Many will be surprised to learn that the great right had very humble beginnings, and Tomkovicz traces the right from its small beginnings to its present scope in a most illuminating way. Because the assistance of a lawyer for the defense was considered a major impediment to a successful prosecution, at one time in England those charged with serious offenses were not even allowed to *retain* counsel at their own expense. But the colonists rejected this grudging view of legal assistance, as did the Framers of the Bill of Rights. Thus, the Sixth Amendment provides that in "all criminal prosecutions, the accused shall . . . have the Assistance of Counsel for his defence."

However, as Tomkovicz points out, the Sixth Amendment guarantee most probably meant only the right to hire a defense lawyer, *not* the right to have a lawyer provided by the government if a defendant could not afford to pay for one. It was not until 1938—a century and a half after the adoption of the Sixth Amendment—that the Supreme Court read the amendment as entitling indigent *federal* defendants to government-furnished counsel (Johnson v. Zerbst). It was to take another twenty-five years before the Court ruled that the Constitution granted indigent persons charged with serious crimes in *state* courts a "flat" or "automatic" right to a lawyer at state expense (Gideon v. Wainwright, 1963).[5]

The overturning of Clarence Gideon's burglary conviction because, unable to afford a lawyer, he had to defend himself, and his acquittal of the burglary charge at a new trial (this time, with appointed counsel) mark the end of Anthony Lewis' prizewinning book, *Gideon's Trumpet*. But the story of the *Gideon* case is told early in Tomkovicz's comprehensive work. The reason is that *Gideon* raised many more questions than it answered—and Tomkovicz addresses these questions carefully and thoughtfully and answers them as clearly as they can be answered, such questions as:

- Does the right to appointed counsel extend to misdemeanor prosecutions? "Petty offense" cases?
- How early in the proceedings does the right to counsel come into play? Does it apply to the preliminary hearing? The bail hearing? The pre-trial lineup? Does it apply when the government uses an undercover agent posing as a friend or fellow-prisoner? If so, why? Is the Sixth Amendment guarantee of a lawyer's assistance in dealing with government efforts to elicit incriminating statements distinct from the better-known "right to counsel" included in the *Miranda* warnings?
- When does the right to appointed counsel end? Does it include a right to government-furnished counsel for indigent defendants on the first appeal of right? Or does it extend to every level of appellate review? If there is a right to appointed counsel on appeal, where does it come from? The Sixth Amendment? The Equal Protection Clause of the Fourteenth Amendment? The Due Process Clause of the Fourteenth Amendment?
- Even if the right to appointed counsel does not extend beyond direct appeal, should an exception be made for those on death row? Because of the need to provide greater protection to those charged with a capital offense and the emotional instability of inmates preparing themselves for impending death, should those on death row have a right to government-furnished counsel in order to pursue state collateral remedies?
- Is the "right to counsel" the right to *effective* counsel? If so, does counsel's performance fall short only when it can be called a "farce and mockery"? Or is the test more demanding? Does a woefully poor performance by a lawyer constitute a Sixth Amendment violation? Or must an accused also show how counsel's defective performance "prejudiced" his defense?

- Should a single lawyer be allowed to represent multiple criminal defendants charged with the same or related offenses? Does "multiple representation" *always* give rise to a conflict of interest? Or does such an arrangement engender only special dangers?
- Is a defendant entitled to "hybrid" representation, that is, an arrangement whereby a defense lawyer performs some functions and the defendant herself performs others? Should a claim for such combined representation be rejected on the grounds that it is likely to be too chaotic and too subject to abuse?
- Does an accused who chooses to be represented by a lawyer thereby surrender her authority to make all (or most) decisions regarding her defense? Can she still decide for herself whether to plead guilty? To take the stand in her own defense? To waive a jury?
- In addition to assuring the right to a lawyer, does the Sixth Amendment include its opposite—a right to dispense with a lawyer's assistance and conduct one's own defense? If the right to counsel is so vital, why should a layperson be allowed to represent herself—in effect, to shoot herself in the foot? Do the reasons for self-representation have the same force when a layperson seeks to represent herself on appeal?

As Tomkovicz shows so well, in the last 300 years the right to counsel has grown and been reshaped in various ways. There is no reason to doubt that the process will continue. But if one wishes to obtain an excellent grasp of the essence, the nature and character, and the scope of the right to counsel as of the year 2002, Tomkovicz's book is the one to read.

Yale Kamisar
Clarence Darrow Distinguished
University Professor
University of Michigan Law School

NOTES

1. William Beaney, *The Right to Counsel in American Courts* (Ann Arbor: University of Michigan Press, 1955). Compare Justice Sutherland's comments for the majority in Powell v. Alabama (1932): "The right to be heard would be, in many cases of little avail if it did not comprehend the right to be heard by counsel. Even the intelligent and educated layman has small and sometimes no skill in the science of law. . . . He requires the guiding hand of counsel at every step in the proceedings against him. Without it, though he be not guilty, he faces the dangers of conviction because he does not know how to establish his innocence."

2. Ronald J. Allen, William J. Stuntz, Joseph L. Hoffman, and Debra A. Livingston, *Comprehensive Criminal Procedure* (Gaithersburg, MD: Aspen Law & Business, 2001) 103.

3. Walter V. Schaefer, "Federalism and State Criminal Procedure," 70 *Harv. L. Rev.* (1956) 1, 8.

4. Yale Kamisar, "The Right to Counsel and the Fourteenth Amendment," 30 *U. Chi. L. Rev.* (1962) 1, 7.

5. As an original matter, the Sixth Amendment right to counsel, as well as the other provisions of the Bill of Rights, applied only to the federal government. However, shortly

after the Civil War, the Fourteenth Amendment to the Constitution was adopted. Among other things, this amendment prohibited any state from "depriving any person of life, liberty, or property without due process of law." This led the Supreme Court to struggle over the question whether the Fourteenth Amendment "incorporated" some or all of the Bill of Rights or included the "core" of some of these rights or, in effect, "selected" some of the most important ones in their entirety. Finally, the Court held, without a dissent, in the *Gideon* case that because it was so "fundamental and essential to a fair trial" the Sixth Amendment right to counsel (which by this time had been interpreted to entitle indigent *federal* defendants to government-furnished counsel in all serious cases) applied in its entirety to the states as well as the federal government by virtue of the Fourteenth Amendment.

Acknowledgments

I wish to express my gratitude to several research assistants who participated in the production of this text. Christopher McDonald deserves enormous credit for his painstakingly careful and thorough investigation and his coherent account of the history of the right to counsel. Christopher's input regarding this project was exceptional in every respect. In addition, Coree Smith, Justin Swaim, Cameron Sabin, Molly Loussaert, Jason Burns, and Kyle Kaiser made significant research, drafting, and editing contributions during the preparation and refinement of the manuscript. I am deeply indebted to all six for their outstanding dedication and remarkable diligence and for the high quality of the end product. This book truly is the fruit of our combined labors.

Moreover, I would be remiss not to mention the role played by Jack Stark. This important series of in-depth analyses of the provisions of the United States Constitution is his brainchild. From the start, Jack's support, assistance, and unflinchingly positive attitude have been evident. I am grateful to him not only for the invitation to participate in the series, but also for the indispensable feedback and encouragement that he has provided at every juncture.

Introduction

The Sixth Amendment grants seven fundamental rights to persons accused of crime. The last of the rights specified by that provision—but by no means the least—is "the right . . . to have the Assistance of Counsel for his defence." This constitutional right to counsel is "one of the safeguards of the Sixth Amendment deemed necessary to insure fundamental human rights of life and liberty" (Johnson v. Zerbst, 1938). This text begins with a brief history of the accused's entitlement to a lawyer's help. It then analyzes in considerable depth the nature, scope, and content of the constitutional entitlement to the assistance of counsel as interpreted and developed by the opinions of the United States Supreme Court. Together, these discussions provide a comprehensive basis for appreciating why the right to counsel is a "necessary" protection for "life and liberty" in the American scheme of criminal justice.

It should be noted at the outset that many of the opinions and doctrines discussed in this book are actually rooted in the Fourteenth Amendment mandate that states shall not deprive individuals of "life, liberty, or property without due process of law." The reason for that is simple. The constitutional rights found in the Bill of Rights govern only federal authorities (Barron v. Baltimore, 1833). Consequently, the Sixth Amendment right to counsel "applies only to trials in federal courts"; it does not restrict state officials (Betts v. Brady, 1942). States, however, are not free to deny defendants in their courts the right to a lawyer's assistance. According to the Supreme Court, any right that is fundamental and "necessary to [our] Anglo-American regime of ordered liberty" is protected against state infringement by virtue of the Fourteenth Amendment Due Process Clause (Duncan v. Louisiana, 1968). In determining which rights are "necessary to ordered liberty" and, thus, an essential part of due process, the Court has often found guidance in the specific safeguards of the Bill of Rights—the first ten amendments to the United States Constitution (Duncan v. Louisiana, 1968). As a result, almost every right guaranteed against the federal government by a particular Bill of Rights provision has been found within the protection of the Fourteenth Amendment promise of due process and made binding on the states. In 1963, the Court held that in our nation the right to counsel found in the Sixth Amendment is " 'fundamental and essential to a fair trial' " (Gideon v. Wainwright, 1963). Consequently, today the Fourteenth Amendment grants state court defendants the identical constitutional entitlement to the assistance of counsel that the Sixth Amendment affords federal court defendants. (For convenience, the discussions that follow ordinarily refer to both the Sixth and Fourteenth Amendment entitlements to counsel as the "Sixth Amendment right to counsel.")

Two subjects addressed in this text have foundations in provisions other than the Sixth Amendment Counsel Clause or the Fourteenth Amendment Due Process Clause. The right to represent oneself at trial derives part of its support from the Sixth Amendment right to counsel. Its constitutional roots also lie in the remainder of the text and entire structure of the Sixth Amendment (Faretta v. California, 1975). Moreover, the right to counsel on a first appeal of a criminal conviction in federal or state court grows out of both the Fifth and Fourteenth Amendment Due Process Clauses and those provisions' guarantees of "equal protection of the laws" (Douglas v. California, 1963; Evitts v. Lucey, 1985). These topics are included because they are integral to a complete understanding of the American right to counsel.

There are several recurring themes in this text. Perhaps the most significant is the ongoing debate and uncertainty over the fundamental nature and purposes of the right to the assistance of counsel. One perspective focuses on the *substantive* value of counsel's aid, stressing the positive effects that assistance has on the results of criminal proceedings. This view holds that the object of a lawyer's assistance is primarily, if not exclusively, to ensure that criminal prosecutions arrive at reliable, truthful resolutions. Another view does not deny that counsel's value is substantive but asserts that the *procedural* value of the right to assistance is also critical. The right to legal representation is seen as both a vital guarantee of fair results and an essential component of fair processes. This perspective maintains that excessive emphasis on the substantive contributions that defense lawyers make to the outcomes of proceedings is misguided and fails to account for the essential role that counsel plays in ensuring that those outcomes are achieved by means of fair procedures. As will be seen, the opinions of the Supreme Court do not provide unambiguous support for either of these positions. Some, particularly those handed down in recent years, emphasize the primacy of counsel's role in promoting reliable results. Others suggest that assuring a fair process is a significant goal of the counsel guarantee. Readers should be attentive to this basic conceptual tension and to the impacts that it has on right to counsel law.

Following this introduction, the history of the right to counsel is recounted. There is no room or reason to report every detail in that long history here. The goal is to explain the most important developments in England and America prior to the adoption of the Bill of Rights, to relate the historical events that led to the inclusion of the Sixth Amendment right to counsel in the Constitution, and to present the most germane developments in right to counsel law in the more than two centuries that have passed since the entitlement to assistance became a part of our fundamental law.

The heart of this text is the analysis that follows the historical account. The ultimate goal of the analytical sections is to depict the current status of the Sixth and Fourteenth Amendment rights to counsel. The first part discusses the nature and character of the right to legal assistance. More specifically, it explains the rationales for and functions served by counsel in our adversary system of criminal justice, the entitlement to retain counsel of choice, the indigent's right to have government-appointed counsel, and every defendant's right of self-representation. The second part addresses the scope of the right to counsel, particularly, the formal and informal pretrial stages to which the right extends, the core entitlement to assistance at the trial, and the rights to assistance in post-trial phases of the criminal process—sentencing, appeal, and collateral challenges to convictions. The final part, the longest and most important part of the analysis, considers the content of the right to counsel—the substantive components that are essential and integral to the right to a lawyer's aid. Included are the entitlements to adequate investigation and preparation, the promise of legal skill and expertise, the assurance of partisan advocacy, the right to consultation with counsel, the duty of loyalty and the entitlement to conflict-free representation, and the guarantee that counsel will provide professionally competent representation.

The concluding section of the text includes a bibliographical essay that describes and assesses an array of sources that contribute to our understanding of the various aspects of the right to counsel discussed in the historical and analytical portions of the text.

The Right to the Assistance of Counsel

Chapter 1

A History of the Right to Counsel

AN INTRODUCTION

"The right to counsel in Anglo-American law has a rich historical heritage" (United States v. Ash, 1973). The object of this part of the text is to accurately and concisely capture the richness of that history. The discussion sketches the historical facts, explains the evolution of the right, and explores the reasons behind particular developments in right to counsel law. The hope is that this historical account will provide a context and a foundation for the core of this text—analysis of the current understanding of the Sixth Amendment entitlement to counsel's assistance.

This account discusses both British and American legal history and is divided into four sections, each of which treats a particular phase in the development of the right to counsel. Because no history of the American right to counsel would be complete without an explanation of its roots in England, the first phase begins with early English common law traditions and continues through the end of the eighteenth century. The depiction of early English law reveals that the right to counsel had surprisingly modest beginnings. Originally, only those accused of minor offenses could be represented by counsel; those charged with serious offenses were denied the opportunity for legal representation. The monarch's refusal to permit counsel for those who stood to lose the most was rooted in fear that lawyers would prevent the successful prosecution and punishment of those whose acts most threatened the state's survival.

The second phase of development is the American colonial and Revolutionary period. The move from England to America was a significant event that brought about dramatic changes in the entitlement to counsel. While there was some variation, most of the colonies departed from the motherland's restrictive approach, acknowledging the fundamental importance of a criminal defendant's right to be assisted by a lawyer.

The third section of the account describes developments during a brief period beginning in 1787 and ending in 1791. The focus here is on the process of formulating and adopting our Constitution and Bill of Rights. The discussion addresses the Constitutional Convention, the absence of a declaration of rights from the proposed Constitution, the heated debate precipitated by anti-federalists' resistance to ratification because of this failure to guarantee fundamental liberties, and the eventual ratification and amendment of the Constitution.

The fourth and final phase extends from the birth of the Sixth Amendment right to counsel in 1791 through the Supreme Court's landmark 1963 decision in Gideon v. Wainwright. The discussion treats the significance of the adoption of the Fourteenth Amendment Due Process Clause and a small number of seminal United States Supreme Court decisions between 1932 and 1963—decisions that played critical roles in the evolution of the constitutional right to counsel in this country. Perhaps the most significant development during this thirty-year span is the Supreme Court's conclusion that criminal defendants who cannot afford to retain counsel have a constitutional right to have appointed, government-funded representation.

From the beginning to the end of this account, the history of the right to counsel is one of constant growth and expansion. In each phase, the steady progression was toward greater entitlements to the aid of a trained legal expert. Changes in the stability and security of the state, changes in the operation of the adversarial system of criminal justice, and changes in the community's sense of what is essential to a fundamentally fair trial all exerted pressures to grant criminal defendants more generous entitlements to counsel's aid. The brief summary of historical events recounted here explains how and why a right that was once completely denied to those accused of serious crimes has been transformed into the most prized, most fundamental constitutional entitlement of every person charged with a criminal offense.

HUMBLE BEGINNINGS: THE ENGLISH COMMON LAW RIGHT TO THE ASSISTANCE OF COUNSEL

The Early English Common Law Right to Counsel

An understanding of the right to counsel at common law during late-seventeenth- and early-eighteenth-century England requires an appreciation of the context in which the right operated—the criminal trial.[1] In general, a "criminal trial in those days was not unlike a race between the King and the prisoner, in which the King had a long start and the prisoner was heavily weighted."[2] Trials were exceedingly brief and informal. The presentation of evidence and return of a verdict lasted no longer than half an hour.

Ordinarily, criminal charges were not brought and prosecuted by a public prosecutor in the employ of the state.[3] Instead, a private party—usually the victim of the crime or a relative—would pursue charges against the defendant.[4] Occasionally, the victim employed a lawyer to prosecute the case, but ordinarily he prosecuted it personally.[5] The private prosecutor—the victim or a representative—would present his testimony and the testimony of other witnesses, and the accused, unaided by counsel, would respond to that evidence. The defendant, like the jurors, could ask questions of witnesses at any time simply by blurting them out. The result was a fairly chaotic proceeding.[6] The judge served as impartial referee between the two private litigants, managing the proceedings to guard against the use of illegal procedures. The judge also examined and cross-examined witnesses and answered questions of law but could not assist the accused in developing a defense.[7]

There were several impediments to a defendant's presentation of an effective defense to a criminal accusation. Ordinarily, an individual charged with a felony was confined until the time of trial.[8] He did not receive a copy of the indictment,[9] was not informed of the evidence against him,[10] and had no process for compelling witnesses to testify on his behalf.[11] For less serious crimes classified as trespasses or misdemeanors—offenses that could be punished only by incarceration or pecuniary loss—a defendant could employ a lawyer to present his defense.[12] An individual accused of a serious offense—a felony, such as murder, manslaughter, larceny, robbery, or rape, or treason or misprision of treason (concealment of treason by one not involved in its commission)—was at a much greater disadvantage. Until the middle of the eighteenth century, the British courts strictly adhered to a common law rule that prohibited those accused of these serious offenses from employing lawyers to assist in their defense.[13] Thus, defendants with the most at stake—those who traditionally could be punished by death as well as a forfeiture of their goods and land (a penalty ultimately suffered by the families of those convicted)—had to go it alone, without representation by counsel.

Judged by modern standards of criminal justice, the common law prohibition on counsel seems perverse and counterintuitive. A number of rationales have been offered in its defense. Some scholars have maintained that self-preservation was the core reason that the government denied counsel to those accused of the most serious crimes.[14] According to this view, "[t]he maintenance of a strong government was felt, and felt rightly, to be the only security for peace and order. But the government had no standing army and no force of police. It was exposed to intrigues from without and to sedition from within."[15] Threats to the government were so numerous and serious that "[t]he state was always in danger, the government always battling for its own life and the safety of society, the morrow always gloomy for the success of their cause."[16] In sum, the monarchy was unstable, ever in peril; its survival and the security of society were under constant threat.

Serious crimes and treason were prominent among the perils that jeopardized the very existence of the state. Felonies stirred social unrest and engendered disharmony. Treason and misprision of treason were direct assaults on the monarch. In serious criminal prosecutions, "[j]udges and jurors alike were engaged in the recognized task of the defence of the state."[17] Moreover, the common law at the time did not adhere to a presumption of innocence but, instead, subscribed to the contrary notion that those charged with offenses were assumed to be guilty. The "Government [was] not strong enough to be generous" and, therefore, could not "shut [its] eyes, to real probabilities" that suspects were guilty "in favour of a fiction" that presumed their innocence.[18] Because anyone brought to trial for a felony or for treason was thought to pose a real danger to the state, it was vitally important that he be prosecuted expeditiously and successfully.

The assistance of counsel was seen as an impediment to efficient and successful prosecution and punishment. By obstructing the criminal process and sometimes preventing convictions, counsel could interfere with the state's self-protective efforts. Moreover, because there were no professional police forces to gather the information and evidence necessary to sustain criminal charges,[19] the cases against those charged with felonies and treason were weaker than they might have been. The relatively weak evidence of guilt made it all the more likely that trained attorneys could hinder successful pursuit of the state's enemies.

Thus, the assistance of counsel posed a threat to the survival of the state. The common law rule prohibiting those charged with serious offenses from employing counsel was thought to be a necessary measure to ensure the monarch's preservation. By expediting the processes of justice and promoting successful prosecution, the common law rule aided efforts to combat threats to the government's stability and survival. The government could afford to permit those charged with minor offenses the protection of counsel, for they posed no meaningful threats to society.[20] For those whose offenses imperiled the state, however, a prohibition on retaining defense lawyers was critical to the government's ability to defend itself.[21]

Another explanation offered for the common law rule was that the assistance of counsel was "hardly necessary" because criminal proceedings were sufficiently simple for an accused—at least an innocent accused—to cope with by himself.[22]

> [I]t require[d] no manner of Skill to make a plain and honest Defence, which in Cases of this Kind [was] always the best; the Simplicity and Innocence, artless and Ingenious Behaviour of one whose Conscience acquits him, having something in it more moving and convincing than the highest Eloquence of Persons speaking in a Cause not their own.[23]

The notion that the relative simplicity of the process rendered trained, expert assistance unnecessary is a somewhat appealing but ultimately unconvincing explanation for the rule denying counsel to those accused of the most serious offenses. The ease of effectively defending oneself cannot logically explain why the common law permitted defendants to retain counsel in misdemeanor and trespass cases but denied assistance in felony and treason prosecutions. It seems clear that an accused would have been able to defend himself against a minor charge at least as well as he could have defended himself against a serious charge.

It has also been suggested that the common law denial of counsel was justified because the judge was able to safeguard the interests of both the private prosecutor and the defendant.[24] "[T]he court took charge of the proceedings and viewed indictors, prosecutors, jury, and prisoner with impartial distrust."[25] This theory holds that counsel was not necessary because accused felons received adequate protection from neutral trial judges. One authority even contended that *everyone* involved in a case was expected to ensure fair and just treatment for the defendant. The accused's interests were to be advanced not only by the judge but also by the victim or his paid private prosecutor.[26]

One of the reasons that neutral judges were thought capable of sufficiently safeguarding the accused's interests was that the opponent in a criminal case was usually an untrained private party, not an expert lawyer.[27] Ordinarily, the two sides were relatively equal in terms of legal training and skill. There was no great likelihood that a highly skilled prosecutor would take advantage of a less skilled defendant. There was no evident imbalance of ability that called for the remedy of trained defense counsel. As long as the prosecution was handled by laypersons, an impartial judge could adequately protect the interests of the lay accused.

The fact that the common law rule denying counsel's aid was later discarded at approximately the same time that trained, professional prosecutors became more prevalent in criminal trials furnishes some support for this explanation.[28] Nonetheless, there are reasons to doubt whether a judge could have adequately promoted and defended an accused's interests and to question whether a victim or his surrogate would really have sought fair treatment of the defendant.[29] The prosecutor had the advantage of an assumption that the accused was guilty. Because there was no release on bail, the defendant had to prepare a defense while incarcerated. The accused had no compulsory process to require witnesses to appear on his behalf, and private prosecutors were allowed to pursue convictions with vigor and zeal. Each of these facets of the criminal process seems to undermine the theory that counsel was unnecessary because a judge could adequately safeguard a defendant's interests. The fact that accused misdemeanants were allowed counsel casts further doubt on the "judicial protection" rationale for denying counsel to accused felons. If the supervision of impartial judges could render counsel unnecessary in felony trials, judicial supervision should have been more than adequate to ensure fair misdemeanor trials.

Blackstone, the most prominent and influential legal commentator of the time on both sides of the Atlantic, harshly criticized the common law's prohibition on the assistance of counsel in felony or treason cases. He considered the denial of counsel to be indefensible, asserting that the rule "seems to be not at all of a piece with the rest of the humane treatment of prisoners by the English law. For upon what face of reason can that assistance be denied to save the life of a man, which yet is allowed him in prosecutions for every petty trespass?"[30] Blackstone found the rule to be wholly unjustifiable, deeming it as contrary to enlightened principles of fairness and justice as a modern perspective would suggest.[31]

The Beginnings of an Entitlement to Counsel in Felony and in Treason Cases

The first formal modification of the common law rule came at the end of the seventeenth century. The Treason Act of 1695 declared that

> nothing is more just and reasonable, than that persons prosecuted for high treason and misprision of treason, whereby their liberties, lives, honour, estates, blood, and posterity of the subjects, may be lost and destroyed, should be justly and equally tried, and . . . should not be debarred of all just and equal means for defence of their innocencies in such cases.

The act, therefore, provided "that every person so accused and indicted, arraigned or tried for any such treason, . . . or for misprision of such treason . . . shall be received and admitted to make his and their full defence, by counsel learned in the law."[32]

This narrow legislative encroachment upon the common law rule was the Whigs' response to a decade of false treason charges leveled against its members by political opponents.[33] In treason prosecutions, the case for the Crown was presented by trained lawyers, often by the attorney general. The common law rule put defendants who were falsely accused of treason at a severe disadvantage in defending against those accusations. When the Whigs regained control of Parliament, they adopted the Treason Act provision for representation by counsel as a remedy for the imbalance of power and a safeguard against unjustified conviction. Despite the fact that it granted a quite limited right to counsel, the Treason Act was a watershed event in the history of the right to counsel, for it was the first statutory rejection of the common law rule.

Before long, the judiciary began to relax the common law tradition in *all* felony prosecutions.[34] By the 1730s, the evolutionary progress was noticeable as judges in an increasing number of cases allowed those accused of felonies to retain legal assistance. By the end of the eighteenth century, judges were frequently permitting those accused of felonies to be assisted by counsel, and defense lawyers were being allowed to perform most defense functions, except addressing the jury directly at the conclusion of the evidence.[35] The now-common appearance of defense counsel in felony proceedings proved that the

English right to counsel had undergone a dramatic transformation. The common law rule was on the road to extinction.

The courts' willingness to depart from the common law denial of counsel was rooted in the growing imbalance of power between the parties involved in felony prosecutions.[36] Over time, in an increasing number of serious cases, the defendant's opponent was no longer another private party. Instead, the opposition was a zealous lawyer hired by the state to prosecute.[37] Moreover, even when the government did not take charge, private parties frequently hired legal counsel to pursue criminal charges on their behalf. The reasons for this growth in the number of lawyers prosecuting criminal cases are not clear. The phenomenon was "almost certainly in part the result of the government's pursuit of its political enemies."[38] It may also have been the result of a broader governmental desire to effectively combat threats to the "public order" caused by the "violence and depredations" of "ordinary felons."[39] Whatever the reasons, it is clear that during the eighteenth century increasing numbers of prosecutors were trained, skilled experts in the law.

As a result, an accused was frequently overmatched by an expert adversary and overwhelmed by the criminal process. Judges were aware of the imbalance that existed and of the potential for unfairness that it created in felony prosecutions. The notion that criminal trials without defense counsel could be conducted fairly because the parties were equals was no longer realistic.[40] Because a defendant's need for counsel to safeguard his interests and prevent unfairness was considerably greater than it had been during the seventeenth and earlier centuries, judges started permitting defendants to retain lawyers to assist with their defenses.[41] The Treason Act of 1695, a legislative response to the imbalance and inequity in treason prosecutions, provided a precedent for this judicial innovation in all felony cases.

An additional reason that the courts were willing to depart from the restrictive common law rule was that the government had grown much more stable in the late seventeenth century.[42] The increased security of the state diminished the concern with self-preservation. Efficient and successful prosecutions were not thought to be as critical to the survival of society as they once were. Because the impediments posed by defense counsel were no longer considered a serious threat to the state, the government could afford to be more generous in allowing representation.

Although it was significant and transformative, the judicial expansion of the British right to counsel was both variable and less substantial than might appear. The extent to which defense counsel could participate in a proceeding varied from case to case and from court to court. The variation was caused by the fact that in all cases, except those governed by the Treason Act, the presiding judge had discretion to determine whether to allow counsel and how much participation to permit. There were no codified or uniform rules that dictated the scope of counsel's involvement in each case.[43] Judges tended to exercise their discretion to limit the roles that defense counsel could play. Typically, judges permitted attorneys for defendants to perform the tasks that the judge had performed under the traditional common law regime. Lawyers could examine and cross-examine witnesses and argue matters of law but were confined to those points of law that the accused suggested and were not allowed to argue matters of fact. Counsel could not speak to jurors on behalf of the defendant and could not offer a defense to the facts put in evidence.[44] The accused still had to perform these functions personally.

The explanation for restricting counsel's functions can be found in the nature of the criminal trial. Judges and juries had broad discretion with regard to both conviction and punishment.[45] The character of the accused was a critical factor in deciding whether to convict and in selecting an appropriate punishment. It was thought that judges and jurors needed to hear the accused speak for himself and answer the charges in order to make a sound evaluation of the credibility of the witnesses and the character of the defendant. In large part, the verdict depended on observing the accused answer the charges. Counsel was not allowed to speak to the jury directly[46] because the judge and jury needed to hear and see the defendant himself in order to perform their functions properly.

Blackstone considered discretionary judicial relaxation of the common law ban on counsel a step in the right direction but deemed it to be a sorely inadequate measure. In his view, the lack of legislative codification of the entitlement to counsel meant that the protection of the accused's interests hinged on the whims of individual judges. Some judges would allow counsel, while others would not. Some restricted counsel's role tightly, while others permitted counsel to perform a wide array of functions. To Blackstone, the need for counsel's assistance was "a matter of too much importance to be left to the good pleasure of any judge." Instead, it was "worthy the interposition of the legislature."[47] The assistance of defense counsel was a right that should be granted to all persons charged with serious offenses, not a privilege that could be arbitrarily denied by individual judges.

While British courts continued to relax the common law ban on counsel during the eighteenth century, at all times the decision to allow representation was in the hands of the judge presiding over a case. The sole exception was an exceedingly narrow legislative enactment in 1747—an act of Parliament that provided a right to counsel for those impeached by the House of Commons for high treason.[48] Thus, when the American Constitution was framed, England recognized a true *right* to retain counsel only for those accused of misdemeanors or high treason. For those accused of felonies, judges determined on a case-by-case basis whether they would enjoy the benefits of counsel's assistance and ordinarily restricted counsel's role in those cases where they did allow counsel. General statutory recognition of an entitlement to counsel for all accused of felonies did not arrive in England until long after the adoption of our Constitution and Bill of Rights. In 1836, Parliament enacted a law that allowed every defendant to enjoy the full assistance of counsel in presenting a defense.[49] Much later, in 1903, Parliament granted indigents the entitlement to appointed counsel.[50]

A DEPARTURE FROM THE BRITISH COMMON LAW RULE: THE RIGHT TO COUNSEL IN AMERICA PRIOR TO THE ADOPTION OF THE SIXTH AMENDMENT

The preceding section explored the development of the right to counsel in England during the seventeenth and eighteenth centuries. This section discusses the right to counsel in America during essentially the same period of time. The object is to explain the evolution of an accused's right to legal representation in the colonies and states and to accurately depict the status of that right in 1791, the year that the Bill of Rights was ratified.

As will be seen, most of the colonies departed dramatically from the restrictive approach to counsel of the British common law. To some extent during the 1600s and to an increasing degree during the 1700s, the colonies accorded constitutional and legislative recognition to the accused's right to an expert legal assistant. By the time the Sixth Amendment to the United States Constitution recognized a federal right to the assistance of counsel, at least eleven of the thirteen states had enacted, either by constitution or statute, a general right to be represented by counsel and one accorded the right as a matter of common law. Several had even recognized an entitlement to state-provided counsel in certain circumstances.

Criminal Procedures and Attitudes in Colonial America

During the early colonial period, the processes of criminal justice were like those that existed under the British common law. Trials were informal affairs and were prosecuted by private parties. For two reasons, defendants usually represented themselves in criminal prosecutions (Faretta v. California, 1975). First, well-trained lawyers were not widely available[51] (Martinez v. Court of Appeal of California, 2000). In addition, the colonists had an abiding distrust of lawyers and had little respect for the legal profession (Faretta v. California, 1975).

The colonists had inherited an accusatorial system from England. At the beginning of the eighteenth century, they modified that system by grafting onto it an institution that was part of the inquisitorial criminal justice systems of continental Europe—the public prosecutor.[52] Thus, while the prosecution of criminal cases in England remained largely in the hands of victims and their surrogates, by the time of the American Revolution all of the colonies employed professionally trained and state-funded lawyers to pursue criminal charges.[53] In addition, during the course of the colonial period the number of trained lawyers increased, making legal assistance for criminal defendants more widely available. Moreover, the public's attitude toward the legal profession changed. Respect for lawyers grew as the colonists came to recognize the critical roles that counsel could play in protecting individual rights and liberties against oppressive or overreaching government authorities. All of these changes fostered expansion of the right to counsel.

The colonists responded to the advent of public prosecutors by providing protections for criminal defendants that were deemed important to ensure fundamental fairness in the adjudicatory process. One of the safeguards granted was the right to the assistance of counsel. During the years leading up to the American Revolution, the ratification of the Constitution, and the adoption of the Bill of Rights, nearly every colony veered sharply away from the British common law rule[54] (Powell v. Alabama, 1932). The colonists recognized that the denial of representation by counsel was unfair and that a defense lawyer was a vital protection for those whose lives, liberty, and property were jeopardized by criminal accusations. At times, their words were remarkably similar to those used in modern times to express our reverence for and appreciation of the right to counsel. The discussions that follow briefly describe the specific developments in each of the thirteen colonies.

Constitutional Entitlements to the Assistance of Counsel in the Colonies and States

Prior to adoption of the federal constitutional right to counsel in 1791, several colonies and states had provided *constitutional* protection for the right to a lawyer's assistance. The Delaware Charter of 1701 granted to "all Criminals . . . the same Privileges of Witnesses and Council as their Prosecutors."[55] Delaware's 1776 Declaration of Rights and Fundamental Rules, drafted in response to the Declaration of Independence, stated explicitly that "in all Prosecutions for criminal Offenses, every Man hath a Right . . . to be allowed Counsel."[56] The Delaware Constitution of 1776 affirmed the fundamental status of the right to counsel, proclaiming that "[n]o article of the declaration of rights and fundamental rules of this State . . . ought ever to be violated on any pretense whatever"[57] and that the rights and privileges contained within the Constitution and Declaration of Rights could not be altered by the legislature.[58] Similarly, the Pennsylvania Charter of Privileges of 1701 granted defendants "the same Privileges of Witnesses and Council as their Prosecutors"[59] and the Constitution adopted by Pennsylvania in the wake of the Declaration of Independence accorded the accused "in all prosecutions for criminal offenses . . . a right to be heard by himself and his council."[60]

In addition, the New Jersey Constitution of 1776 provided "all criminals . . . the same privileges of witnesses and counsel, as their prosecutors are or shall be entitled to."[61] The 1776 Maryland Constitution stated that "in all criminal prosecutions, every man hath a right . . . to be allowed counsel."[62] The next year, the state of New York provided a constitutional entitlement to counsel. According to the New York Constitution of 1777, "in every trial on impeachment, or indictment for crimes or misdemeanors, the party impeached or indicted shall be allowed counsel, as in civil actions."[63] The 1780 Massachusetts Constitution extended to "every subject . . . a right . . . to be fully heard in his defence by . . . counsel."[64] Four years later, New Hampshire followed suit by providing an identical constitutional guarantee of counsel in 1784.[65]

Thus, before the Framers amended the United States Constitution in 1791 to provide that "[i]n all criminal prosecutions, the accused shall enjoy . . . the right to have the assistance of Counsel for his defence," seven states—Delaware, Pennsylvania, New Jersey, Maryland, Massachusetts, New Hampshire, and New York—had constitutional provisions that guaranteed criminal defendants a fundamental entitlement to representation by defense counsel. These states had established a clear and compelling precedent for incorporating a generous entitlement to legal assistance into our national charter.

Statutory Entitlements to the Assistance of Counsel in the Colonies and States

A number of colonies and states provided a statutory right to counsel in criminal cases prior to the birth of the Sixth Amendment. Four of these jurisdictions—North Carolina, Rhode Island, South Carolina, and Virginia—did not provide a constitutional entitlement to counsel at the time the Bill of Rights was ratified. Three others—Delaware, Massachusetts, and Pennsylvania—granted a statutory and a constitutional right to assistance prior to 1791. This section briefly describes the relevant legislative provisions, beginning with jurisdictions with no constitutional right to counsel before 1791 and concluding with those with a constitutional guarantee of assistance.

As early as 1660, the General Assembly for the colony of Rhode Island enacted a statute that made it "the lawful privilege of any person that is indicted, to procure an attornye to plead any poynt of law that may make for the clearing of his innocencye."[66] The act went well beyond the British common law rule. It entitled all defendants, including those charged with serious crimes, to retain representation. Judges had no discretion to deny a defendant the opportunity to receive representation by a lawyer.[67] Moreover, the statute allowed counsel to argue any points of law whether or not the accused suggested them. In prefatory language, the act explained that the colony was choosing to depart from the common law and grant a right to counsel because

> it doth appeare that any person inhabitting in this jurisdiction, may on good grounds, or through mallice and envie be indicted and accused for matters criminall, wherein the person that is soe [accused] may be innocent, and yett may not bee accomplished with soe much wisome and knowlidge of the law as to plead his own innocencye, &c.[68]

As early as the mid-seventeenth century, the inhabitants of Rhode Island understood that counsel was an important protection against the unjust conviction of innocent defendants who lacked legal skill and knowledge. Even though Rhode Island law did not provide constitutional sanction for the right to counsel, the residents of Rhode Island clearly had concluded, at an early date, that counsel was a vital safeguard for criminal defendants.

In 1731, the South Carolina legislature also acknowledged the critical importance of counsel in serious cases, observing that "many innocent persons . . . under criminal prosecutions ought to have proper assistance and all just and equal means allowed to defend their innocencys."[69] By statute, the lawmakers provided that "every such person . . . arraigned or tryed for any such treason, murder, felony, or other capital offence whatsoever as aforesaid, shall be received and admitted to make his and their full defense by counsel learned in the law."[70] Because South Carolina included no right to counsel in its constitution, this legislative provision for assistance was of vital importance to those accused of serious offenses.

Just after the American Revolution, North Carolina departed sharply from the British common law rule, according every accused individual the right to have a lawyer aid fully in the presentation of a defense. In 1777, the North Carolina legislature enacted a law specifying that "every Person accused of any Crime or Misdemeanor whatsoever, shall be entitled to Council in all Matters which may be necessary for his Defence, as well to Facts as to Law."[71] The state did not afford its citizens a constitutional right to assistance until 1868, almost 100 years later.

The colony of Virginia was strongly tied to the common law of England. For many years, while other colonies and states were abandoning the stingy British approach to counsel for serious offenses, Virginia recognized little, if any, entitlement to legal assistance beyond that permitted by the courts of England. In 1786, however, ten years after the Revolution but five years before the Bill of Rights was ratified, the Virginia legislature gave explicit recognition to a right to retain defense counsel. The simple, straightforward statutory language provided that "the court . . . shall allow [the defendant] counsel to assist him at his trial, if he desire it."[72] Without a constitutional provision for assistance, this statute seemed to afford significant protection for criminal defendants.

The Delaware and Pennsylvania Charters of 1701 both recognized entitlements to counsel. Subsequently, in 1709 in Delaware and in 1718 in Pennsylvania, both colonies also enacted statutory rights to assistance in capital cases.[73] Because many serious crimes were still capital offenses, these statutory enactments constituted significant acknowledgments of the vital need for legal assistance.[74] In addition, in 1777, three years before it adopted a much broader constitutional right to defense counsel, Massachusetts provided a statutory right to counsel for those accused or treason or misprision of treason.[75]

Significantly, a number of the statutory rights to counsel required the courts not simply to allow representation by retained counsel but also to provide lawyers for accused individuals who wanted legal representation. At least in some of these jurisdictions, perhaps in all, counsel was furnished only for those who could not afford representation.[76] The Pennsylvania provision of 1718 and the Delaware act of 1719 both provided for state-appointed counsel for capital defendants. South Carolina's 1731 enactment stated that

> in case any person or persons so accused or indicted shall desire counsel, the court before whom such person or persons shall be tryed, or some judge of that court, shall and is hereby authorized and required, immediately upon his or their request, to assign to such person and persons, such and so many counsel not exceeding two, as the person or persons shall desire, to whom such counsel shall have free access at all seasonable times, either before, at or after the said tryal.[77]

Finally, in 1791, the year that the Bill of Rights was ratified, New Hampshire statutorily required the appointment of counsel in cases where the offense was punishable by death.[78]

A Common Law Rejection of the British Rule

Prior to 1791, Connecticut granted neither a constitutional nor a statutory right to assistance of counsel in serious criminal cases. In fact, a constitutional entitlement to assistance was not recognized until almost thirty years after the Sixth Amendment was adopted.[79] Nonetheless, the colony had a profound common law commitment to the right to retain a lawyer in all cases, a commitment that sharply diverged from the prohibition on counsel inherited from the motherland.[80] The colonists of Connecticut "never admitted that cruel and illiberal principle of the common law of England, that when a man is on trial for his life, he shall be refused counsel, and denied those means of defense, which are allowed, when the most trifling pittance of property is in question."[81]

Adherence to the British Common Law Rule

As described in the first section of this historical account, the British common law at first denied the assistance of counsel to those accused of serious crimes. Over time, that absolute prohibition on legal representation evolved into a system in which judges discretionarily determined which defendants accused of serious offenses would receive representation by counsel. In 1791, when the Sixth Amendment to the United States Constitution was adopted, Georgia was the sole American jurisdiction that still adhered to the British approach.[82] The state of Georgia remained out of step with other American jurisdictions for another seven years, refusing to afford a broad entitlement to counsel until it adopted the Georgia Constitution of 1798.[83]

The Right of Self-Representation in America

From the earliest times, the ordinary practice in the American colonies in serious criminal cases was self-representation, not representation by counsel.

Apparently, self-representation continued to be the norm even when the colonies and states granted legal entitlements to assistance by counsel. One explanation offered for the prevalence of self-representation is the distrust of lawyers that flourished initially in the colonies (Faretta v. California, 1975). The self-representation norm has also been attributed to the fact that trained legal assistance was not generally available (Martinez v. Court of Appeal of California, 2000).

In accord with this tradition, some constitutional provisions for counsel adopted by the states specified that accused persons had not only a right to counsel but also a right to represent themselves. The Pennsylvania Constitution of 1776, for example granted the accused "a right to be heard by himself,"[84] and the Massachusetts Constitution of 1780 accorded the defendant "a right . . . to be fully heard in his defence by himself, or his counsel at his election."[85] While not all constitutional and legislative grants of counsel expressly recognized a right of self-representation, not a single one of those provisions denied the opportunity to conduct one's own defense. (This long tradition of self-representation, coupled with the absence of a single instance in which legal counsel was ever forced upon an accused, would later provide crucial underpinnings for the Supreme Court's holding that the Sixth Amendment contains an implicit constitutional right to represent oneself (Faretta v. California, 1975).)

In sum, by the time our nation was prepared to ratify a constitution, the states had dramatically departed from the restrictive English common law rule regarding retention of counsel in serious criminal prosecutions. The vast majority had concluded that counsel was an essential protection for those whose lives and liberties were in jeopardy and had granted criminal defendants the right to representation by a lawyer. In light of this American rejection of the grudging British attitude toward legal assistance and of the premises underlying that attitude, it is hardly surprising that the new nation's Constitution would be amended to include explicit recognition of the right to counsel.

THE FORMULATION OF A NATIONAL CONSTITUTION AND THE ADOPTION OF THE SIXTH AMENDMENT RIGHT TO THE ASSISTANCE OF COUNSEL

This section is concerned with the brief, but critical, four-year period between 1787 and 1791. The focus is on the specific events that prompted the inclusion of the Sixth Amendment right to the assistance of counsel in our Constitution. Because the history of the right to counsel is a part of the larger history of the Constitution and the Bill of Rights, the instant discussion is essentially a general account of the formulation and approval of those documents. Matters that bear specifically on the incorporation of the counsel guarantee are accorded special emphasis.

The Constitutional Convention and the Drafting of the United States Constitution

In the spring and summer of 1787, a delegation of fifty-five men representing the respective states gathered in Philadelphia. Thirty-one of them were lawyers. Their purpose was to amend the Articles of Confederation—a governing charter that had proven inadequate for the new nation's needs. The group soon determined that mere amendment would not suffice to "accomplish the objects proposed by the Articles of Confederation, namely 'common defence, security of liberty, and general welfare.' "[86] Consequently, the gathering became a Constitutional Convention with the purpose of devising an entirely new system of government for the country. To accomplish this goal, the men formulated an entirely new document—the Constitution of the United States.

At the time the Constitution was being drafted, all of the state constitutions included some sort of declaration of rights that limited the power of the state and preserved citizens' liberties. It was somewhat surprising, therefore, that the participants in the convention spent very little time discussing such liberties and that the document framed in Philadelphia contained very little language devoted to the preservation of fundamental freedoms. Proposed drafts included few protections for those accused of crime. Some of them specified a right to trial by jury and preserved the privilege of habeas corpus (a judicial writ whose object is to secure release from unlawful custody), but not a single proposal included a right to the assistance of counsel.

There are two apparent reasons for the Framers' lack of attention to provisions detailing the rights of those charged with criminal offenses. First, the wide variation in procedures among the states made it seem unlikely that consensus could be reached regarding the rights that should be included in the national charter.[87] Second, it was anticipated that state criminal justice systems would handle the bulk of criminal prosecutions.[88] Because those charged with federal offenses would be a relatively small class, there was less reason to be concerned about their rights.

The omission of a declaration of rights from the proposed Constitution did not go unnoticed. Many of the delegates were deeply troubled by the failure to include provisions limiting the government's power to deprive the citizenry of fundamental liberties.[89] The potentially extensive powers of the newly created federal government—granted in provisions such as the "necessary and proper" clause—gave rise to particular fears of serious official encroachment on valued freedoms. As the convention was coming to an end, George Mason of Virginia expressed a wish that "the plan had been prefaced with a Bill of Rights" and suggested a motion to that effect.[90] In response, a motion was made to add a Bill of Rights to the Constitution. Without debate or comment, the proposal was emphatically rejected by all ten states that voted on the question.[91] Five days later, on September 17, 1787, the Constitution was signed.

George Mason was so angered by the developments that he "returned to Virginia with a fixed disposition to prevent the adoption of the plan if possible. He consider[ed] the want of a Bill of Rights as a fatal objection" to ratification of the Constitution.[92] While Mason was one of the first to attack the proposed document for failure to include a declaration of rights, he was not the only one to oppose the Constitution on that ground. Sixteen of the fifty-five delegates to the convention refused to sign the document as it was and left Philadelphia determined to prevent approval by state ratifying conventions. The words of a commentator who wrote under the pseudonym Brutus reflect the sentiments of these opponents:

> [A]t a time when the pulse of liberty beat high and when an appeal was made to the people to form constitutions for the government of themselves, it was their universal sense, that such declarations should make a part of their frames of government. It is therefore the more astonishing, that this grand security, to the rights of the people, is not to be found in this constitution.[93]

The Debate over Ratification: Eventual Agreement on the Need for a Bill of Rights

Those who objected to the omission of a declaration of liberties from the new Constitution expressed their views clearly and fervently. Richard Henry Lee, whose "Letters from the Federal Farmer" are thought to be the most significant anti-federalist writings against ratification of the Constitution,[94] complained that "there is no restraint, in form of a bill of rights, to secure . . . that residuum of human rights which is not intended to be given up to society, and which, indeed is not necessary to be given up for any social purpose."[95] He maintained that there

> are certain unalienable and fundamental rights, which in forming the social compact, ought to be explicitly ascertained and fixed—a free and enlightened people, in forming this compact, will not resign all their rights to those who govern, and they will fix limits to their legislators and rulers. . . . These rights should be made the basis of every constitution.[96]

Lee suggested that there was "a very strong argument" that a people who "cannot agree in ascertaining and fixing" those rights should not "attempt[] to form one entire society, [or] to live under one system of laws only."[97] Moreover, he objected that the inclusion of some rights in the text of the Constitution—in particular, the entitlement to writs of habeas corpus and the bans on bills of attainder (special legislative acts declaring specified persons to be guilty of serious offenses and imposing capital punishment without trial or conviction according to ordinary procedures) and ex post facto laws (laws enacted after acts have occurred that either retrospectively declare noncriminal acts to be crimes and prescribe punishment or retrospectively increase the punishment for acts already declared criminal)—proved that it was necessary to include other protections. He argued that "the establishment" of these rights would "evince that we could not claim them without it" and that "the omission of" other rights—such as the "right to have council"—would imply that "they are relinquished, or deemed of no importance."[98]

The federalists attempted to answer the concerns of the Constitution's critics. Alexander Hamilton, in *The Federalist No. 84*, opined that a bill of rights was not necessary because "the Constitution is itself, in every rational sense and to every useful purpose, a Bill of Rights."[99] Oliver Ellsworth maintained that declarations of rights were needed against kings who "claimed all power and jurisdiction" but were not needed when "government is considered as originating from the people, and all the power government now has is a grant from the people. The constitution they establish with powers limited and defined, becomes now to the legislator and magistrate what originally a bill of rights was to the people."[100] Hamilton went further, suggesting that a Bill of Rights "would even be dangerous. [It] would contain various exceptions to powers not granted; and, on this very account, would afford a colourable pretext to claim more than were granted. For why declare that things shall not be done which there is no power to do."[101] James Wilson, a member of the Pennsylvania delegation to the convention, explained that a Bill of Rights had not been included in the Constitution because it was "impracticable . . . to enumerate all the rights of the people[.]" Moreover, "if the enumeration [was] not complete, everything not expressly mentioned [would] be presumed to be purposely omitted."[102]

A part of the debate focused on the specific liberties that ought to be included in a declaration of rights. Many proposals incorporated protections for those accused of crime. Some of them listed the assistance of counsel as one of the rights that should not be left out of the Constitution. Brutus (an anti-federalist pseudonym), for example, noting that "most of the states [had] declared" that a defendant should "be fully heard by himself or counsel,"[103] maintained that the right to retain legal assistance was "as necessary under the general government as under that of the individual states."[104]

Eventually, the anti-federalist position prevailed. It became clear during the ratification debates that the Constitution would not be ratified in the state conventions without a bill of rights. As the Supreme Court would later observe,

> so strong was the sense of the country of the importance [of a declaration of rights], and so jealous were the people that these rights highly prized might be denied them by implication, that when the original Constitution was proposed for adoption it encountered severe opposition; and, but for the belief that it would be amended so as to embrace them it would never have been ratified. (Ex Parte Milligan, 1866)

The lesson of history is clear. A fervent desire for and commitment to the assurance and preservation of fundamental rights—including an entitlement to the assistance of counsel—played a central, influential role in the process that led to the approval of our Constitution.

Ratifications of the Constitution and the Bill of Rights: The Sixth Amendment "Right to the Assistance of Counsel" Is Born

Once it was settled that the Constitution would be amended, two questions remained. The first was a question of timing: When would the amendments be made? The second was a question of substance: What amendments were needed to ensure protection for the guarantees thought by the people to be essential? One view held that the document should be amended *prior to* ratification. Elbridge Gerry argued that amendment could "be better attained before a ratification." He questioned whether "a *free* people [should] adopt a form of Government, under conviction that it wants amendment[.]"[105] Agrippa (an anti-federalist pseudonym) opined that he could "hardly conceive that it should seriously be made a question" whether the charter should be amended before it was adopted.[106] Samuel Chase noted that "no wise people ever gave power over their liberties with a view of getting back the power."[107] Luther Martin observed that "almost every one agrees the Constitution, as it is, to be both defective and dangerous" and maintained that "every principle of reason, common sense, and safety would dictate" that "the necessary amendments [should be] made . . . while we have the liberty of acting for ourselves, before the constitution becomes binding upon us by our assent." It was his view that acceptance of the Constitution without amendment would reduce the people "to a level with [their] own slaves, with this aggravating distinction, that [they] once tasted the blessings of freedom."[108]

These potent arguments, however, proved unavailing. Despite objections to approval of the Constitution before it was amended, the states proceeded with the process of ratifying the Constitution in the form proposed, a process that reached fruition in 1789. Article VII of the proposed Constitution provided that the "Ratification of the Conventions of nine States, shall be sufficient for the Establishment of this Constitution between the States so ratifying Same." At its convention held June 21, 1788, New Hampshire became the ninth state to ratify the Constitution.[109] The Congress received New Hampshire's ratification letter on July 2, 1788.[110] On the same day, the nine ratifications were sent to a committee to "examine the same, and report an act to Congress for putting the said Constitution into operation."[111]

On July 14, 1788, the committee reported an act to Congress that would implement the new Constitution in the following year—1789.[112] The Congress debated the merits of the act until September 13, 1788, deciding that the election of government officials would be held early the following year and that the "first Wednesday in March next be the time . . . for commencing proceedings under the said Constitution."[113] The new government was established, and on April 30, 1789, George Washington was inaugurated as first president of the United

States.[114] By mid-1790, all thirteen states had ratified the Constitution and joined the new government.[115]

Although the states completed the process of ratifying the Constitution before it was amended, the need for modification did not go entirely unnoticed or unmentioned during that process. Six states—Delaware, Pennsylvania, New Jersey, Connecticut, Georgia, and Maryland—transmitted their ratification letters to Congress without proposed amendments or declarations of rights.[116] Seven states included in their transmission letters either declarations of rights or specific proposed amendments. Both Massachusetts[117] and New Hampshire[118] proposed amendments, though neither made mention of a right to assistance of counsel. South Carolina proposed amendments, but they were more of a structural nature; the proposals included neither the right to counsel nor other individual liberties.[119] The four remaining states—New York,[120] Virginia,[121] North Carolina,[122] and Rhode Island[123]—each drafted and conveyed to Congress a declaration of rights that, among other things, provided for the right to representation by counsel.

While he had campaigned for approval of the Constitution, James Madison had pledged to support a Bill of Rights. Understanding that his constituents in Virginia had approved the document with an expectation that the amendment process would be undertaken immediately, he quickly turned his energies toward the task. On June 17, 1789, Madison proposed a draft of amendments to Congress. The proposal consisted of nine propositions to be inserted at appropriate places in the body of the Constitution. The fourth proposition contained protections in the criminal process and did specify that "in all criminal prosecutions, the accused shall enjoy the right . . . to have the assistance of counsel for his defence."[124]

In July, Madison's proposals were submitted to the Committee of Eleven, which consisted of one delegate from each state that had ratified the Constitution at the time. (North Carolina and Rhode Island had not yet ratified the document.) After only one week of work on the language of the amendments, the committee forwarded them to the House. In late August 1789, having made no changes to the provisions forwarded by the committee, the House passed the amendments. It referred them to a Committee of Three. The sole responsibility of this committee was to arrange the amendments to conform with the House's decision to make them additions to, rather than insertions into, the Constitution.[125] On August 24, the committee reported to the House a slate of seventeen amendments. The amendments were forwarded to the Senate the same day.[126]

After one week of deliberations, the Senate returned the amendments to the House with several changes and a request for a conference of managers. The conference met for several days, ultimately reducing the number of amendments from seventeen to twelve. The right to counsel appeared in the eighth of these proposed amendments. In compliance with Article V of the Constitution, the twelve amendments were then sent to the states for ratification.[127]

The states rejected the first amendment (which would have regulated the number of representatives in the House) and the second amendment (which addressed the compensation of senators and representatives), ratifying ten of the twelve proposed Bill of Rights provisions.[128] The proposed eighth amendment, including its declaration that "[i]n all criminal prosecutions, the accused shall enjoy . . . the right to the assistance of counsel for his defence," was agreed to by all ten of the states that sent in returns regarding the proposed amendments.[129] (Connecticut, Massachusetts, and Georgia did not send in returns.) In 1791, that provision became the Sixth Amendment to the United States Constitution.[130]

For those seeking a window into the intentions of those who formulated and approved the Sixth Amendment right to counsel, the historical record is a disappointment. While many other rights were the subjects of considerable discussion during the congressional formulation of and the states' ratifications of the Bill of Rights, there was very little mention of the right to counsel. The record contains no real insights into the particular intentions of those who framed, proposed, and approved the Sixth Amendment right to counsel. Thus, historical guidance regarding the original meaning of the constitutional entitlement to representation is quite limited.

Despite this dearth of evidence concerning the precise understanding of those responsible for the provision, the background of the right to counsel raises "considerable doubt that the Sixth Amendment . . . originally . . . contemplated any guarantee other than the *right* of an accused in a criminal prosecution . . . *to employ a lawyer* to assist in his defense" (Scott v. Illinois, 1979) (emphasis added). It seems quite likely that the Sixth Amendment was designed to "secure those rights which by ancient rules of the common law had been denied to them; but it was not contemplated that this should be done at the expense of the government" (United States v. Van Duzee, 1891).

A number of reasons support the conclusion that the Framers meant to provide a right to retain a defense lawyer but not a right to government-appointed assistance. First, the constitutional text does not even allude to any entitlement to appointed assistance. Second, the colonial and state provisions for government-furnished counsel that did exist at the time were all statutory. No state constitution included such a guarantee. Finally and perhaps most persuasively, while the Sixth Amendment was under consideration, Congress passed the Federal Crimes Act of 1790, which provided that for treason and other capital offenses

> every person . . . shall . . . be allowed and admitted to make his full defence by counsel learned in the law; and the court before whom such person shall be tried, or some judge thereof, shall, and they are hereby authorized and required immediately upon his request to assign to such person . . . counsel.[131]

A statutory right to appointed counsel would have been superfluous if the Sixth Amendment already contained such a guarantee. This congressional enactment, therefore, strongly indicates—although it does not conclusively prove—that those who were intimately involved with the development and adoption of the

Sixth Amendment did not understand that provision to mandate appointed assistance.[132] It seems highly probable that the Sixth Amendment was designed to grant a right to retain a legal representative of one's choosing but no right to have counsel provided by the government.

THE HISTORY OF THE RIGHT TO COUNSEL AFTER RATIFICATION OF THE SIXTH AMENDMENT

This final section of the history of the right to counsel addresses significant developments subsequent to the adoption of the Sixth Amendment. It begins with the period following the ratification of the Bill of Rights in 1791 and ends with the Supreme Court's landmark 1963 decision in Gideon v. Wainwright. The main events during this period are the adoption of the Fourteenth Amendment Due Process Clause in 1868 and the Supreme Court's decisions in five seminal right to counsel cases between 1932 and 1963. The opinions in each of those cases are also considered at appropriate points in the analysis of the constitutional right to counsel that follows this historical account. The discussions of the opinions in the analysis chapter explore the contributions that each makes to our current understanding of the right to counsel. In this section, the Court's decisions are described to complete the historical backdrop against which the modern law of counsel must be understood.

The Adoption of the Fourteenth Amendment to the United States Constitution

In 1833, the Supreme Court made it clear that the provisions of the Bill of Rights were limitations upon the power of only the federal government and had no application to state authorities (Barron v. Baltimore, 1833). Consequently, the Sixth Amendment right to the assistance of counsel "applie[d] only to trials in federal courts" (Betts v. Brady, 1942). It did not guarantee those accused in state criminal proceedings a right to the assistance of counsel for their defense. Because the vast majority of criminal prosecutions were brought by the states, the Sixth Amendment entitlement to counsel had a relatively limited practical significance. It afforded a right to legal representation only in the very small percentage of criminal cases that involved federal offenses.

In 1868, following the Civil War, the Constitution was amended to include the Fourteenth Amendment. In pertinent part, that provision declares that "[n]o State shall . . . deprive any person of life, liberty, or property without due process of law." This generous assurance that states must afford "due process" furnished a constitutional predicate that the Court would later rely upon to extend the right to counsel to the legions of defendants facing criminal accusations in state courts. It is not overstatement, therefore, to regard the adoption of the Fourteenth Amendment as a watershed event in the historical expansion of our constitutional right to counsel. It is undoubtedly the most significant right to counsel development subsequent to the ratification of the Bill of Rights.

The relationship between the Due Process Clause and the fundamental liberties contained in the Bill of Rights has been the subject of considerable dispute.[133] Some Supreme Court Justices have taken the position that the Due Process Clause made the guarantees of the Bill of Rights directly and specifically applicable to the states (Betts v. Brady, 1942 (Black, J., dissenting); Gideon v. Wainwright, 1963 (Douglas, J., concurring)). According to their understanding, when the Fourteenth Amendment was made a part of our Constitution in 1868, the states were thereby obligated to afford criminal defendants the identical entitlement to legal representation that the Sixth Amendment required the federal government to ensure. The view that the Due Process Clause was designed to "incorporate" the *entire* Bill of Rights, however, has never commanded a majority of the Court (Gideon v. Wainwright, 1963 (Douglas, J., concurring)). The prevailing view has been that the guarantee of due process commands states to abide by all procedures that are essential to "fundamental fairness." In the context of state criminal cases, this conception of the Due Process Clause has required the Supreme Court to explore and expound upon the relationship between "fundamental fairness" and the assistance of defense counsel.

As will be seen, the Supreme Court ultimately concluded that the Fourteenth Amendment guarantees the same entitlement to legal representation in state prosecutions that the explicit terms of the Sixth Amendment guarantee in federal cases. During a thirty-year progression toward that conclusion, the Court's opinions provided numerous and invaluable insights into the nature and underpinnings of the right to the assistance of counsel promised by the Sixth Amendment. In sum, the Fourteenth Amendment mandate of "due process of law" has afforded state defendants a generous right to counsel, and the cases explaining that right have enhanced our understanding of why the entitlement to a lawyer's assistance is fundamental and necessary in American criminal justice systems.

Powell v. Alabama: A Due Process Right to Retained and Appointed Assistance in State Court[134]

The first significant United States Supreme Court opinion concerning the right to counsel was not rendered until 141 years after the ratification of the Sixth Amendment and almost sixty-four years after the adoption of the Fourteenth Amendment. In Powell v. Alabama—a case that attracted considerable attention—the Supreme Court addressed several defendants' claims that they were constitutionally entitled to the assistance of counsel in state rape trials.[135] The Court agreed with their contentions.

The facts that gave rise to *Powell* involved a fight between black youths and white youths who were riding a freight train through Alabama.[136] After all but one of the white youths had been tossed from the train, a message was sent ahead to the next train station, reporting the fight and asking that the black youths be removed from the train. When the train arrived at Painted Rock, a sheriff's posse seized several of the black youths.[137] The posse took the young men and two white girls, who had also been on the train, to Scottsboro, which was the county seat. The girls claimed that they had been raped. The young men asserted that they had not even seen the girls before the train was stopped.[138]

The youths "were met at Scottsboro by a large crowd." While there apparently was no serious threat or danger of

> mob violence[,] . . . the attitude of the community was one of great hostility. The sheriff thought it necessary to call for the militia to assist in safeguarding the prisoners. . . . [T]he proceedings, from beginning to end, took place in an atmosphere of tense, hostile and excited public sentiment. . . . [M]ost, if not all of [the blacks] were youthful. . . . They were ignorant and illiterate. All of them were residents of other states, where alone members of their families or friends resided.

The assaults had allegedly occurred on March 25, 1931. Six days later, on March 31, seven of the young men were indicted for rape, an offense with a potential punishment of death. "[I]mmediately upon the return of the indictment defendants were arraigned and pleaded not guilty. Apparently they were not asked whether they had, or were able to employ, counsel, or wished to have counsel appointed." Later, the judge would assert that he had appointed "all the members of the bar" to represent the defendants at the arraignment and that he "anticipated [that the members of the bar would] continue to help [the defendants] if no counsel appeared."

At the state's request, the defendants' trials were severed into three separate groups. When the proceedings began, "six days after the indictment," no counsel "appeared to represent or defend" the defendants. After a fairly lengthy colloquy, the trial judge appointed two attorneys to represent the defendants—Mr. Roddy, a Tennessee lawyer who had been contacted by "people who were interested" in the case, and Mr. Moody, a local lawyer who had expressed a willingness to assist. Thus, "until the very morning of the trial no lawyer had been named or definitely designated to represent the defendants." The "three trials were completed within a single day. . . . The juries found the defendants guilty and imposed the death penalty upon all." On appeal, the Alabama Supreme Court affirmed the judgments.

The Supreme Court began its consideration of the case by analyzing whether the defendants had in fact received the assistance of counsel. Because the trial judge's appointment of the entire bar at the arraignment "was little more than an expansive gesture, imposing no substantial or definite obligation on any one," the Court concluded that "during perhaps the most critical period of the proceedings . . . , from the time of their arraignment until the beginning of their trial, . . . the defendants did not have the aid of counsel in any real sense." Although two lawyers were appointed to represent the defendants on the first morning of trial, their appearance in the case at that late juncture did not "accord[ ] the right of counsel in any substantial sense. To decide otherwise," the Court opined, "would simply be to ignore actualities." In sum, the Court had no doubt that the defendants did not receive meaningful legal assistance at any relevant point in the criminal process.

The critical constitutional question was "whether the denial of the assistance of counsel contravene[d] the due process clause of the Fourteenth Amendment to the federal Constitution."[139] The Court began its answer to that question by reviewing the history of the right to counsel in England and America. It described the restrictive English common law rule, deeming it "so outrageous and so obviously a perversion of all sense of proportion that the rule was constantly, vigorously, and sometimes passionately assailed by English statesmen and lawyers." The Court noted that the common law "rule was rejected by the colonies" and described the constitutional, statutory, and common law developments in America. Its review of the relevant history led the Court to conclude that by the end of the eighteenth century twelve of the thirteen colonies accorded some recognition to the right to counsel in prosecutions for serious offenses and that most of the colonies granted it "in all criminal prosecutions." The colonists' rejection of the British common law and their general legal recognition of the importance of the right to the assistance of counsel provided a solid foundation for the Court's conclusion that the denial of counsel in a serious criminal case was inconsistent with the American conception of due process.

The *Powell* Court, however, did not rely on history alone. One "compelling consideration" in deciding whether a right found in the Bill of Rights is an essential part of due process is whether it "is of such a character that it cannot be denied without violating those 'fundamental principles of liberty and justice which lie at the base of all our civil and political institutions' " (Quoting Hebert v. Louisiana, 1926). According to the Court, "the right to the aid of counsel is of this fundamental character." There can be no doubt that "notice and hearing" are preconditions for due process. Moreover, both "[h]istorically and in practice, in our country . . . [a hearing] has always included the right to the aid of counsel when desired and provided by the party asserting the right." In a famous passage that would be quoted frequently in later right to counsel opinions, the Court explained that the

> right to be heard would be, in many cases of little avail if it did not comprehend the right to be heard by counsel. Even the intelligent and educated layman has small and sometimes no skill in the science of law. . . . He lacks both the skill and knowledge adequately to prepare his defense, even though he have a perfect one. He requires the guiding hand of counsel at every step in the proceedings against him. Without it, though he be not guilty, he faces the danger of conviction because he does not know how to establish his innocence. If that be true of men of intelligence, how much more true is it of the ignorant and illiterate, or those of feeble intellect.

These premises led the Court to conclude that the Fourteenth Amendment Due Process Clause contains an entitlement to *retain* counsel in state criminal trials. "If in any case . . . a state . . . court were arbitrarily to refuse to hear a party by counsel employed by and appearing for him, it reasonably may not be doubted that such a refusal would be a denial of a hearing, and, therefore, of due process in the constitutional sense." Based on the facts of *Powell*—in particular, the ignorance, illiteracy, and youth of the defendants, the public hostility, the imprisonment and surveillance by the military, the distance of friends and families, and "above all that [the defendants] stood in deadly peril of their lives"—the Court concluded that "the failure of the trial court to give [the defendants] reasonable time and opportunity to secure counsel was a clear denial of due process." Their constitutional entitlement to retain legal representation had not been honored.

The Court proceeded to assume that the defendants would not have been able to secure their own lawyers. If so, there could not have been a denial of the right to retain representation. It concluded, nonetheless, that the defendants had still suffered constitutional deprivations, for "under the circumstances just stated, the necessity of counsel was so vital and imperative that the failure of the trial court to make an effective appointment of counsel was likewise a denial of due process." According to the Court, "[i]n a case such as this, . . . the right to have counsel appointed, when necessary, *is a logical corollary of the constitutional right to be heard by counsel*" (italics added). In the Court's view, if due process guarantees a hearing, and if a meaningful hearing requires the aid of a lawyer, an accused who cannot secure representation and, therefore, is tried without counsel is denied due process. Although some of the Court's language was far-reaching, suggesting a general right to appointed counsel in *all* cases, the opinion's holding regarding the right to appointed assistance was carefully restricted to the facts of the *Powell* case. Stating that "we need not determine" whether due process would be denied by a failure to provide a lawyer "under other circumstances," the Justices decided that the state must provide counsel in "a capital case" in which "the defendant . . . is incapable of making his own defense because of ignorance, feeblemindedness, illiteracy or the like."

Powell v. Alabama is a major landmark in the evolution of the constitutional right to the assistance of counsel. It recognized that at least for some defendants in state prosecutions due process includes both the right to retain a lawyer and the right to have a lawyer furnished by the state. Moreover, the Court's opinion contained expansive suggestions that due process might afford rights to retained and appointed counsel in most, if not all, state prosecutions.[140] The Court's explicit confinement of its holdings to the extreme facts of the case before it, however, meant that the details of the relationship between the Due Process Clause and the right to counsel would have to be developed in future cases.[141]

Johnson v. Zerbst: A Sixth Amendment Right to Appointed Assistance in Federal Court[142]

In 1938, six years after *Powell*, the Court considered whether the Sixth Amendment's explicit right to counsel includes a right to government-furnished assistance for indigent federal defendants.[143] As already observed, the probable intent of the Framers of the Bill of Rights was to abrogate the British common law restriction on the employment of counsel for serious charges and to create a right to retain assistance in all criminal prosecutions. In Johnson v. Zerbst, with no mention of that likely intent, the Court easily concluded that the Sixth Amendment encompasses a generous right to government-appointed legal representation.

In *Zerbst*, two enlistees in the Marine Corps, Johnson and Bridwell, were charged in a federal court in South Carolina "with feloniously uttering and passing four counterfeit twenty-dollar Federal Reserve notes and possessing twenty-one such notes." ("Uttering" is the criminal offense of offering or putting into circulation a forged or counterfeit instrument.) Both men "lived in distant cities in other states," had no "relatives, friends, or acquaintances" in South Carolina, "had little education[,] and were without funds." After their arrests, they "were kept in jail due to inability to give bail." Indictments were handed down on January 21, 1935. Two days later, on January 23, they were first notified of the indictments, then "arraigned, tried, convicted and sentenced . . . to four and one-half years in the penitentiary." The defendants had been "unable to employ counsel for their trial. Upon arraignment, both [had] pleaded not guilty, said they had no lawyer, and—in response to an inquiry of the court—stated that they were ready for trial. They were then tried, convicted and sentenced, without assistance of counsel." Applications for appeal, filed five months later, were denied on the ground that they were too late. Both men collaterally attacked their convictions, seeking writs of habeas corpus. (A "collateral attack" is a "civil" process outside the direct channel of appeal. When direct appellate relief from a conviction is no longer available, prisoners pursue collateral attacks in order to obtain release from confinement based on allegedly improper convictions.) After the writs were denied, the Supreme Court granted review.

The Court began by quoting the Sixth Amendment language that guarantees the assistance of counsel. It then characterized the right to assistance as "one of the safeguards of the Sixth Amendment deemed necessary to insure fundamental human rights of life and liberty" and as one of the "essential barriers against arbitrary or unjust deprivation of human rights. The Sixth Amendment stands as a constant admonition that if the constitutional safeguards it provides be lost, justice will not 'still be done' " (Quoting Palko v. Connecticut, 1937). According to the Court, the right to counsel provision

> embodies a realistic recognition of the obvious truth that the average defendant does not have the professional legal skill to protect himself when brought before a tribunal with power to take his life or liberty, wherein the prosecution is presented by experienced and learned counsel. That which is simple, orderly and necessary to the lawyer, to the untrained layman may appear intricate, complex, and mysterious.

After quoting Powell v. Alabama's explanation of why " 'the guiding hand of counsel' " is necessary to preserve " 'the right to be heard,' " the Court concluded that the Sixth Amendment does more than extend a right to retain assistance to those accused of crimes. It also "withholds from federal courts, in all criminal proceedings, the power and authority to deprive an accused of his life or liberty *unless he has or waives the assistance of counsel*" (italics added). This means that unless an accused makes a valid waiver, he must be represented by a lawyer whom he has secured or, if he cannot retain legal assistance, by one that the government has appointed.

After discussing the constitutional standards for a valid waiver, the Court reinforced and clarified the implications of its opinion. Because "the Sixth Amendment constitutionally entitles one charged with a crime to the assistance of counsel, compliance with this constitutional mandate is an *essential jurisdictional prerequisite to a federal court's authority* to deprive an accused of his life or liberty." If a defendant does not relinquish the right and "is not represented by Counsel . . . the Sixth Amendment stands as a jurisdictional bar to a valid conviction and sentence depriving him of his life or his liberty."[144] The Sixth Amendment, therefore, requires a judge "to complete the court . . . by providing counsel for an accused who is unable to obtain counsel." Because it was not clear whether the defendants had validly waived their entitlement to the assistance of counsel, the Court remanded the case to the district court for a waiver determination.

The clear message of the *Zerbst* decision was that the Sixth Amendment mandates an entitlement to counsel for every defendant in federal court who does not waive that right. For those who can afford counsel, the Constitution grants a right to retain assistance. For those who cannot, the Constitution affords an entitlement to appointed representation. Moreover, the Sixth Amendment rule announced by the Court was apparently intended to apply to every case. Unlike the holding in *Powell*, the conclusion in *Zerbst* was not limited by the specific nature of the charges, the individual inadequacies of the defendants, or the particular jeopardy that they faced.[145]

Betts v. Brady: A More Limited Due Process Right to Appointed Counsel in State Court[146]

The reasoning of Johnson v. Zerbst, coupled with the premises underlying the *Powell* opinion, could have supported a holding that the Due Process Clause affords indigent state defendants a right to appointed counsel coextensive with that granted by the Sixth Amendment to federal defendants. The logic that led the Court to find an unqualified right to government-supplied assistance in federal court could have been invoked to sustain a similar right in state trials. Just four years after *Zerbst*, in 1942, the Court had an opportunity to address the breadth of the due process entitlement to counsel in a state case involving an indigent defendant. In Betts v. Brady, the Court rejected the contention that the guarantee of due process included a right to appointed counsel equivalent to the federal right secured by the Sixth Amendment. It decided, instead, that the Fourteenth Amendment provides a more limited right to appointed representation[147] (Betts v. Brady, 1942).

Betts involved a man indicted by Maryland for robbery. He informed the judge at his arraignment that he could not afford counsel and "requested that counsel be appointed for him." The judge denied the request, noting that in the county where he was charged the practice was to appoint counsel for indigents only in murder and rape cases. The defendant pleaded not guilty and waived his right to a jury. He called and examined his own alibi witnesses, cross-examined the government's witnesses, and chose not to take the stand and testify in his own behalf. The judge found him guilty and imposed an eight-year sentence. After state petitions for writs of habeas corpus were denied, the Supreme Court granted review of his contention that he was denied a constitutional guarantee of counsel.

At the outset, the Court made two points clear—that the Sixth Amendment did not govern the state court case before it and that the Fourteenth Amendment "does not incorporate, as such, the specific guarantees found in the Sixth Amendment." While a state's denial of a right listed in the Bill of Rights can violate the assurance of due process, that

> concept [is] less rigid and more fluid than those envisaged in other specific and particular provisions of the Bill of Rights. Its application is less a matter of rule. Asserted denial is to be tested by an appraisal of the totality of facts in a given case. That which may, in one setting, constitute a denial of fundamental fairness, shocking to the universal sense of justice, may, in other circumstances, and in light of other considerations, fall short of such denial.

Mr. Betts contended that the Court's prior decisions had established that the promise of due process includes a "rule . . . that, in every case, whatever the circumstances, one charged with crime, who is unable to obtain counsel, must be furnished counsel by the State." According to the Court, each of its earlier decisions was distinguishable. In particular, Powell v. Alabama involved a statutory entitlement to counsel for the offense charged, and the Court's holding, which rested on the compelling circumstances of that case, reserved the question of whether appointment was necessary in other settings.

Having found no controlling precedent, the Court turned directly to the question presented—"whether due process of law demands that in every criminal case, whatever the circumstances, a State must furnish counsel to an indigent defendant." According to the Court, the requirement of appointed counsel for indigent defendants is "obligatory upon the States" only if it "expresses a rule" that is "fundamental and essential to a fair trial." To determine whether that was the case, the Court first turned to history, finding "great diversity in respect of the right to have counsel in criminal cases" in the "Constitutions of the thirteen original States, as they were at the time of federal union." While some had no right to counsel, most did include such a guarantee, although they expressed it in a variety of ways. According to the Court, the meaning of these colonial and state provisions for counsel could be found in the restrictive common law practice inherited from England. The entitlements to representation were merely "intended to do away with the rules which denied representation . . . by counsel in criminal prosecutions" and "were not aimed to compel the State to provide counsel for a defendant." States that afforded appointed counsel did so by means of statute, and their legislation exhibited a "great diversity of policy." In sum, history showed that the right to appointed counsel was not considered a fundamental right at the time our nation was born.[148]

With one exception, the state constitutions extant at the time of the *Betts* decision included a right to counsel's assistance. Most used language indicating that only a right to employ counsel was contemplated, and most had not been interpreted to require appointed assistance for indigents. Thus,

> in the great majority of the States, it [was] the considered judgment of the people, their representatives and their courts that appointment of counsel *is not a fundamental right, essential to a fair trial.* In the light of this evidence [the Court was] unable to say that the concept of due process incorporated in the Fourteenth Amendment obligate[d] the States . . . to furnish counsel in every such case.

Maryland's practice of appointing counsel only when accused individuals were "at a serious disadvantage by reason of the lack of counsel" but not in cases like *Betts*, gave "point to the principle that the States should not be straitjacketed . . . by . . . the Fourteenth Amendment." Because *Betts* involved a bench trial, it was "much more informal" than a jury trial and put the judge "in a better position to see impartial justice done."[149] A robbery had unquestionably occurred. The state's evidence identified the defendant as the perpetrator, while the defendant sought to prove "an alibi." He called and examined witnesses to establish that he was elsewhere when the crime was committed. The "simple issue" in the case was the veracity of the witnesses, and the accused was a forty-three-year-old "of ordinary intelligence and ability to take care of his own interests on the trial of that narrow issue." He had some experience with and knowledge of the criminal process. In the totality of these circumstances, a trial without the assistance of counsel was not fundamentally unfair.

In concluding, the Court evinced real concern with the costly implications of a contrary holding. If due process contained a general requirement of counsel, states would have to furnish assistance "without distinction between criminal charges of different magnitude." They would be obliged to pay for lawyers for indigents accused of small crimes—even traffic offenses—and would even have to furnish "counsel in civil cases involving property."

In sum, while "the Fourteenth Amendment prohibit[ed] the conviction and incarceration of one whose trial [was] offensive to the common and fundamental ideas of fairness and right, and while want of counsel in a particular case [might] result in a conviction lacking in such fundamental fairness," the Court could not "say that the Amendment embodie[d] an inexorable command that no trial for any offense, or in any court, [could] be fairly conducted and justice accorded a defendant who [was] not represented by counsel." Instead, case-by-case analysis was necessary. When the circumstances—the complexities of the case, the abilities of the accused, and the jeopardy posed by the charges—demonstrated that a trial would not be fair unless the accused had expert assistance, the Constitution demanded that states appoint counsel. When the relevant factors indicated that an unaided defendant could adequately conduct the defense—that is, where a fair trial was possible without counsel—due process did not demand state-provided representation.

The *Betts* Court's conclusion that due process afforded a considerably more limited grant of appointed assistance than the Sixth Amendment rested on four premises. First, under the Constitution the states had retained more freedom to experiment with criminal processes than the federal government. The Due Process Clause was meant to be flexible and was not meant to constrain state criminal justice systems as stringently as the more specific provisions of the Bill of Rights constrained the federal system. Second, the assistance of counsel at trial is not always vital to a fair process and fair results. Some cases and trials were simple enough to be handled by laypersons. Third, it was possible to accurately identify those cases in which counsel was needed and those in which fundamental fairness did not require legal assistance. The case-by-case, "special circumstances" approach did not deny counsel to any who truly needed help, whereas a *per se* counsel requirement would provide protection for some who needed none. Finally, in cases where a fair trial would take place without defense counsel, the provision of counsel would impose substantial, unnecessary costs on state governments.

Chandler v. Fretag: An Ample Right to Retained Counsel in State Court

As a result of the *Betts* decision, indigent state court defendants enjoyed a much narrower entitlement to appointed representation than indigent federal court defendants. It was logical to wonder whether the right to representation by retained counsel under the Due Process Clause was also more limited than the expansive right to retained counsel guaranteed by the Sixth Amendment. In 1954, in Chandler v. Fretag, the Court answered that question.

Mr. Chandler, a middle-aged black man with limited education, was indicted in Tennessee for "housebreaking and larceny, an offense punishable by a term of three to ten years." The total value of the items that he allegedly stole was three dollars. He was released on bail and appeared for trial without a lawyer, intending to plead guilty. He did not believe that a lawyer would be of assistance on the pending charge. "When his case was called for trial, he was orally advised by the trial judge that he would also be tried as a habitual criminal because of three alleged prior felonies. He was informed that conviction under the Tennessee Habitual Criminal Act carrie[d] a mandatory sentence of life imprisonment with no possibility of parole." At that point, the defendant requested a continuance "to obtain counsel on the habitual criminal accusation." The judge summarily denied his request, "a jury was impaneled, and the case proceeded immediately to trial."

The accused pleaded guilty to housebreaking and larceny, and the prosecutor introduced corroborating evidence. The judge then asked the jurors "to raise their right hands if they accepted" the guilty plea and "approved of a three-year sentence." They did so. He next instructed them to raise their hands again "if they found [defendant] to be a habitual criminal." Again, all hands went up. "The entire proceeding—from the impaneling of the jury to the passing of sentence—consumed between five and ten minutes."

After serving the three-year sentence for housebreaking and larceny, the defendant sought state habeas corpus relief from the mandatory life sentence that was based on the "habitual criminal" finding—that is, he pursued a collateral attack in the Tennessee state court system. The Circuit Court denied relief, upholding the mandatory life sentence, and the Tennessee Supreme Court affirmed. The defendant then took his challenge to the United States Supreme Court.

The Court thought it "clear beyond question that petitioner did not waive counsel on the habitual criminal accusation." The Tennessee attorney general maintained, however, that under Betts v. Brady, the defendant had no "federal constitutional right to counsel." He asserted that because counsel was not essential to a fair trial, Mr. Chandler's right to due process had not been violated. The Supreme Court emphatically rejected the state's contention, stating that the *Betts* "doctrine has no application here" because the defendant had not asked for appointed counsel but, rather, had asked for a continuance to secure a lawyer on his own. "Regardless of whether petitioner would have been entitled to the appointment of counsel, *his right to be heard through his own counsel was unqualified*" (italics added). The Court quoted the reasoning of Powell v. Alabama at length. It placed particular emphasis on the *Powell* Court's conclusion that a court's refusal in any case to hear retained counsel would deny an accused due process. According to the Court, by denying the defendant "any opportunity whatever to obtain counsel on the habitual criminal accusation, the trial court [had] deprived him of due process of law as guaranteed by the Fourteenth Amendment."

The *Chandler* Court discerned a clear distinction between the scope of the due process entitlement to retain representation and the scope of the due process right to have counsel appointed, concluding that every defendant has an absolute Fourteenth Amendment right to retain representation. The guarantee of fundamental fairness obligated the states to allow defendants to be represented by retained counsel no matter what the circumstances of the case. It required the states to appoint counsel for indigents only when the totality of the circumstances established that counsel was essential to a fair proceeding.

Gideon v. Wainwright: A Dramatic Expansion of the Right to Appointed Counsel in State Court Proceedings[150]

No history of the right to counsel could be complete without a discussion of Gideon v. Wainwright—one of the best-known and most significant right to counsel decisions rendered by the Supreme Court. The Warren Court's landmark 1963 opinion in *Gideon* revisited the issue confronted twenty years earlier in Betts v. Brady—the scope of an indigent defendant's constitutional entitlement to government-provided assistance in state court. The *Gideon* Court's straightforward, unanimous holding constituted the last major step in the historical expansion of the constitutional right to counsel in America. Its forceful reasoning elevated the status of the right to counsel to new heights, giving it an honored place as the most fundamental of all rights guaranteed to the accused.[151]

Mr. Gideon was charged with the felony of breaking and entering a poolroom with the intent to commit a misdemeanor. He appeared in court without an attorney. Because he could not afford to retain a lawyer, he requested that the judge appoint counsel. The judge denied the request, informing him that Florida law permitted appointed counsel only in capital cases. In the trial that followed, Gideon made an opening statement, cross-examined government witnesses, called his own witnesses, declined to testify, and made a short closing argument. The jury found him guilty, and he was sentenced to five years in prison. The Florida Supreme Court denied a petition for a writ of habeas corpus. To reconsider the issue resolved in Betts v. Brady, the Supreme Court granted review.

The Court first observed that the facts of *Betts* and *Gideon* were so similar that the holding of *Betts*, if still good law, would require rejection of *Gideon*'s contention that he had a due process entitlement to appointed counsel. The Court then declared, however, that after reconsidering the *Betts* holding, it had decided that it "should be overruled." The *Betts* Court had been correct in the perception "that a provision of the Bill of Rights which is 'fundamental and essential to a fair trial' is made obligatory on the States by the Fourteenth Amendment." Its fatal error was "in concluding that the Sixth Amendment's guarantee of counsel is not one of these fundamental rights."

According to the *Gideon* Court, the fundamental nature of the right to counsel had been established in Powell v. Alabama—ten years before *Betts* was decided. Although the *Powell* Court had limited its holding to the particular circumstances of the case, "its conclusions about the fundamental nature of the right to counsel [were] unmistakable." Moreover, in subsequent cases, including Johnson v. Zerbst, the Court had made it clear that the assistance of counsel was " 'necessary to insure fundamental human rights of life and liberty.' " By failing to acknowledge that the assistance of counsel is *always* essential for a fair trial and concluding that the " 'appointment of counsel is not a fundamental right,' " the Court's opinion in Betts v. Brady "made an abrupt break with its well-considered precedents." In so doing, it had erred.

Precedent was not the only reason to declare *Betts* misguided. "[R]eason and reflection" also led to the "obvious truth" that "in our adversary system of criminal justice, *any person* haled into court, who is too poor to hire a lawyer, *cannot be assured a fair trial unless counsel is provided for him*" (italics added). After all, the government deems it essential to have lawyers prosecute criminal cases, and few criminal defendants who can afford them "fail to hire the best lawyers they can get." These are "strong[] indications . . . that lawyers in criminal courts are necessities, not luxuries." From the start, American law has put "great emphasis on procedural and substantive safeguards designed to assure fair trials before impartial tribunals in which every defendant stands equal before the law. This noble ideal cannot be realized if the poor man charged with crime has to face his accusers without a lawyer to assist him." As the *Powell* Court had observed, the right to be heard would mean little if it did not include the right to be heard through counsel. Even intelligent laypersons lack the legal skill and knowledge required to adequately defend against accusations. Although they may in fact be innocent, they may well be convicted because they do not know how to demonstrate their innocence.

According to *Gideon*, the *Betts* Court had "departed from the sound wisdom" of *Powell*. Its decision was " 'an anachronism when handed down,' " and its holding that the Fourteenth Amendment right to appointed counsel belongs to only some state court defendants was a misinterpretation of the Constitution. Like the Sixth Amendment right to counsel, the Fourteenth Amendment guarantee of due process bestows upon *every* indigent state defendant a right to state-provided representation. (As explained in the analysis chapter, in a post-*Gideon* opinion, the Court has held that the right to appointed assistance does *not* extend to *every* indigent criminal defendant. Construing *Gideon* as guaranteeing the right to appointed counsel to all indigent persons charged with *felonies*, the Court has concluded that those accused of *misdemeanors* are constitutionally entitled to appointed counsel *only* if they are sentenced to serve some time in jail.)

As observed at the outset, *Gideon* was a landmark ruling. While the Court's characterization of *Betts* as an opinion that disregarded well-settled precedents is highly questionable, in other respects the constitutional reasoning in *Gideon* is defensible and consistent with statements made in earlier opinions. Not a single Justice dissented from the conclusion that due process mandates a general entitlement to appointed representation in state trials. In addition to the reasons proffered by the Court, a number of other factors probably motivated the decision to overturn the Betts v. Brady doctrine. First, in the twenty years following *Betts*, the Supreme Court's own decisions had, in substance, abandoned the "special circumstances" approach to deciding whether counsel was required in state cases. "In truth," by the time of *Gideon*, "the Betts v. Brady rule [was] no longer a reality" (Gideon v. Wainwright, 1963 (Harlan, J., concurring)). Many state courts, however, had not recognized that the *Betts* doctrine was a dead letter. By explicitly overruling *Betts*, the *Gideon* Court sought to remove all doubt about the status of the "special circumstances" approach.

In addition, *Gideon* was decided during the 1960s, a time of increasing sensitivity to civil rights deprivations and the inequalities of American society. The Supreme Court was well aware that those who were being denied assistance under the *Betts* rule were not only the poor. A disproportionate number of them were members of minority groups. The recognition of an unqualified right to appointed counsel was a means of ensuring equal justice for all. In this respect, *Gideon* was not an isolated decision. It was one of a number of rulings by the Warren Court aimed at promoting equality for criminal defendants and others who were socially and legally disadvantaged.

Finally, the *Gideon* Court was probably skeptical of two fundamental premises underlying the *Betts* decision—that there were a sizable number of cases in which unaided defendants could receive fair trials and that those cases could be identified accurately. Because virtually all defendants were in fact incapable of conducting their defenses, and because it was exceedingly difficult to isolate the few instances in which that might not be true, a blanket guarantee of counsel for all was the only way to assure fairness for all.[152]

SUMMARY REFLECTIONS ON THE HISTORY OF THE RIGHT TO COUNSEL

This brief account of the historical development of the right to counsel began with an exploration of the status of that right in seventeenth-century England. It ended with a depiction of the character of the entitlement to counsel in mid-twentieth-century America. One consistent trend has been evident from start to finish—the history of the right to counsel has been one of constant, almost relentless expansion.[153]

In England, the common law initially granted only a right to retain counsel. Moreover, it granted that right only to those charged with minor offenses—misdemeanors and trespasses. Defendants who had the most to lose—those charged with felonies and treason, crimes that carried the penalty of death—were prohibited from being represented by counsel. Eventually, the law of England grew somewhat more generous. By statute, those charged with treason were allowed to retain lawyers. More important, judges relaxed the common law rule, exercising discretion to permit limited use of counsel in other cases involving serious crimes.

In the American colonies, the law quickly departed from this restrictive common law approach. By constitution, statute, or common law, almost all of the original thirteen states afforded criminal defendants a right to retain counsel to defend against accusations of serious crime. Some even made provision for state-assigned counsel in certain cases. Moreover, the movement was consistently toward broader entitlements. At no point did any jurisdiction step backward, restricting rights to counsel that had already been recognized. By the time the federal Constitution was amended in 1791 to include the Sixth Amendment right to the assistance of counsel, the vast majority of states recognized a generous right to retain legal assistance.

The document produced by the Constitutional Convention of 1787 and submitted to the states for ratification specified very few liberties. The federalists defended the absence of a declaration of fundamental liberties, while the antifederalists campaigned fervently against adoption of a fundamental charter that did not include a Bill of Rights. After much debate, it became clear that the Constitution would not be ratified if it were not amended to specify fundamental freedoms that the government could not abridge. The states ratified the Constitution with the clear understanding that it soon would be amended. Shortly after ratification, the process of formulating amendments began. Of the twelve amendments submitted to the states for approval, ten were accepted. Among them was the Sixth Amendment, which provided, in part, that "[i]n all criminal prosecutions, the accused shall enjoy the right . . . to have the assistance of Counsel for his defence." Thus was the right to counsel made an integral part of the fundamental charter of our nation.

Expansion of the right to counsel in America did not stop with the adoption of the Bill of Rights. The Sixth Amendment guarantee was probably intended to create only a right to retain counsel. Moreover, it bestowed that right only on defendants charged with federal offenses. The basis for a constitutional right to counsel in state trials did not become a part of our Constitution until adoption of the Fourteenth Amendment Due Process Clause in 1868. Over time, the command that "[n]o State shall . . . deprive any person of life, liberty, or property without due process of law" would become the foundation for a broad entitlement to legal assistance in state court proceedings.

From 1868 to 1963, expansions of the right to counsel resulted from the Supreme Court's interpretations of the Sixth and Fourteenth Amendments. The first significant judicial step in development of the right to counsel occurred in 1932. In Powell v. Alabama, the Court held that at least in certain circumstances—capital cases involving disadvantaged defendants—due process granted both a right to retain a lawyer and a right to appointed counsel for those unable to retain counsel.

In 1938, the Court turned its attention to the express Bill of Rights grant of counsel. In Johnson v. Zerbst, the Court concluded that the Sixth Amendment provides more than a right for the criminally accused to employ lawyers to represent their interests. It also accords indigent federal defendants an entitlement to government-appointed counsel.

In 1942, Betts v. Brady held that some, but not all, state court defendants had a due process right to appointed assistance. If an indigent could receive a fair trial without a lawyer's representation, the promise of due process did not require a state to afford it. Although the Supreme Court would later brand *Betts* as a retrogressive step that had narrowed the right to counsel in state courts, it seems more accurate to view *Betts* as an incremental step forward in the expansive tradition of right to counsel law (*Gideon* v. Wainwright, 1963 (Harlan,

J., concurring)). The actual holding of *Powell* had announced a due process entitlement only in cases of extreme need and severe jeopardy. The *Betts* Court, while denying an entitlement to appointed assistance on the particular facts of the case before it, did acknowledge that the Due Process Clause afforded state-furnished assistance whenever fairness required it. After *Betts*, it was apparent that the right first recognized in *Powell* extended beyond capital cases involving woefully deficient defendants.

In 1954, in Chandler v. Fretag, the right to counsel in state courts was extended further. The Court held that, unlike the right to appointed assistance, the due process right to retain a lawyer was absolute. No matter what the circumstances, a court had to permit an accused to be represented by a lawyer whom he could retain.

The most significant expansion of the entitlement to counsel occurred in Gideon v. Wainwright, the decision that ushered in the modern era of right to counsel law. In that 1963 landmark opinion, the Warren Court held that the Due Process Clause affords poor state defendants the same absolute right to appointed counsel that the Sixth Amendment grants to indigents in federal court. The Court held that the right to counsel is a fundamental requisite for a fair trial. Consequently, the Constitution commands states to provide a lawyer for a defendant who wants assistance but cannot afford to pay for it.

For over 300 years, the history of the right to counsel was one of consistent growth. As the recognition of counsel's importance in ensuring fair processes and just outcomes increased over time, the entitlement to legal assistance expanded. Although it is appropriate to end the historical section of this text with *Gideon*, and to turn at this point to analysis of the current law, it bears mention that the right to counsel has continued to evolve during the nearly four decades since *Gideon*. As seen in the analysis that follows, the expansionist trend came to a halt sometime during that span. During the 1960s and early 1970s, a number of Supreme Court opinions endorsed liberal constructions of the right to legal assistance. Several decisions during the last twenty-five years of the twentieth century, however, betrayed a grudging attitude and announced narrowing interpretations of the Sixth and Fourteenth Amendment guarantees. At the beginning of the twenty-first century, it seems quite unlikely that the constitutional right to counsel will undergo noticeable expansion in the foreseeable future.

NOTES

1. For a thorough treatment of the history of English criminal law, see generally James Fitzjames Stephen, *A History of the Criminal Law of England* (London: Macmillan and Co., 1883). See also J.M. Beattie, "Scales of Justice: Defense Counsel and the English Criminal Trial in the Eighteenth and Nineteenth Centuries," 9 *Law & His. Rev.* (1991) 221; J.M. Beattie, *Crime and the Courts in England, 1660–1800* (Princeton, NJ: Princeton University Press, 1986).

2. 1 Stephen, *A History of the Criminal Law of England* 397.

3. John H. Langbein, "The Origins of Public Prosecution at Common Law," 17 *Am. J. Leg. Hist.* (1973) 313, 316–17.

4. Beattie, *Crime and the Courts in England* 271, 342; Beattie, "Scales of Justice," 221; Langbein, "The Origins of Public Prosecution at Common Law," 317–18; 1 Stephen, *A History of the Criminal Law of England* 418–19.

5. Beattie, "Scales of Justice," 221, 222; Beattie, *Crime and the Courts in England* 353.

6. Beattie, "Scales of Justice," 222.

7. Beattie, "Scales of Justice," 222–23.

8. Beattie, *Crime and the Courts in England* 281–83; Beattie, "Scales of Justice," 223.

9. Francis H. Heller, *The Sixth Amendment to the Constitution of the United States: A Study in Constitutional Development* (Lawrence: University of Kansas Press, 1951) 10.

10. Beattie, *Crime and the Courts in England* 271.

11. Beattie, "Scales of Justice," 223.

12. William M. Beaney, *The Right to Counsel in American Courts* (Ann Arbor: University of Michigan Press, 1955) 8; John H. Langbein, "The Criminal Trial Before the Lawyers," 45 *U. Chi. L. Rev.* (1978) 263, 308 (offering a partial rationale for allowing counsel in misdemeanor prosecutions).

13. 1 Stephen, *A History of the Criminal Law of England* 397; 5 William S. Holdsworth, *A History of English Law*, 7th ed. (London: Methuen & Co., 1956) 192; Beattie, "Scales of Justice," 221; Edward Powell, *Kingship, Law and Society: Criminal Justice in the Reign of Henry V* (Oxford: Clarendon Press, 1989) 78; Beattie, *Crime and the Courts in England* 352–53.

14. Heller, *The Sixth Amendment to the Constitution of the United States* 10 (stating that " 'the manner in which the accused was either deprived of or hampered in his liberty of defense was not only tolerated but even applauded by a large body of public opinion because the government was so weak and its enemies so strong that it was felt, not without reason, that it must take every advantage of its enemies' ") (quoting W.S. Holdsworth, *A History of English Law* 196).

15. 5 Holdsworth, *A History of English Law* 189–90.

16. 5 Holdsworth, *A History of English Law* 190 (quoting John Pollock, *The Popish Plot, A Study in the History of the Reign of Charles II* (Cambridge: Cambridge University Press, 1944) 267.

17. Pollock, *The Popish Plot*, 286–87.

18. 1 Stephen, *A History of the Criminal Law of England* 355; see also Beattie, *Crime and the Courts in England* 340–41.

19. Powell, *Kingship, Law and Society* 65.

20. Beaney, *The Right to Counsel in American Courts* 8 (arguing that the state's interest in convicting for minor offenses was so slight it could afford to be considerate toward defendants).

21. Beaney, *The Right to Counsel in American Courts* 11.

22. Theodore F. Plucknett, *A Concise History of the Common Law*, 4th ed. (London: Butterworth & Co., 1948) 410; Beaney, *The Right to Counsel in American Courts* 11; Beattie, *Crime and the Courts in England* 356.

23. Beattie, "Scales of Justice," 223; see also Beattie, *Crime and the Courts in Eng-*

land 271–72 (stating that trial procedure was established so that jury could watch reaction of defendant and to test the force and sincerity of his denials).

24. Beaney, *The Right to Counsel in American Courts* 11; Beattie, *Crime and the Courts in England* 345–46; Langbein, "The Criminal Trial Before the Lawyers," 263, 307–8; but see Beattie, *Crime and the Courts in England* 358 (noting that advanced opinions at this time scoffed at the notion that judges could preserve the interests of the accused because judges were more interested in serving their paying client, the king); Langbein, "The Criminal Trial Before the Lawyers," 309 (same).

25. Plucknett, *A Concise History of the Common Law* 410.

26. Roland Knyvet Wilson, *History of Modern English Law* (London, Oxford, and Cambridge: Rivingtons, 1875) 107–8 ("[T]he counsel for the prosecution (and still more of course the judge) [was] supposed to be as much concerned to present to the jury the points of law in his favour as those against him.").

27. Langbein, "The Criminal Trial Before the Lawyers," 282.

28. Beattie, "Scales of Justice," 224 (observing that judges relaxed the common law rule because of the perception "that the balance in the courtroom between defendant and prosecutor was shifting, and shifting to the detriment of the defendant").

29. Thomas M. Cooley, *Treatise on Constitutional Limitations* (Boston: Little, Brown, and Co., 1868) 333 n.2 (doubting whether a judge could effectively protect the defendant's interests).

30. 4 William Blackstone, *Commentaries on the Laws of England* (Oxford: Clarendon Press, 1769) 49.

31. See also Beattie, *Crime and the Courts in England* 358 (quoting criticism of common law prohibition of defense counsel by Sir Robert Atkyns, a judge during the reign of Charles II).

32. 7 Wm. III, c. 3 (1695).

33. Beattie, *Crime and the Courts in England* 357–59 (briefly summarizing the history surrounding the enactment of the Treason Act of 1695); Beattie, "Scales of Justice," 224.

34. Beattie, *Crime and the Courts in England* 359 (observing that Treason Act of 1695 was crucial but that the stimulus for judicial modification of the common law rule was pressure within courts to respond to growing inequity between professional prosecutor and accused).

35. Beaney, *The Right to Counsel in American Courts* 10.

36. Beattie, "Scales of Justice," 224.

37. Beattie, "Scales of Justice," 224–25; Beattie, *Crime and the Courts in England* 353–62.

38. Beattie, "Scales of Justice," 225; see also Beattie, *Crime and the Courts in England* 353.

39. Beattie, "Scales of Justice," 225; Beattie, *Crime and the Courts in England* 352–55.

40. Beattie, "Scales of Justice," 224.

41. Beattie, *Crime and the Courts in England* 356–57.

42. Heller, *The Sixth Amendment to the Constitution of the United States* 10 (observing that not "until after the revolution of 1688 did the stability of the government enable it to become more generous, and counsel was then permitted to appear on behalf of persons accused of treason").

43. Beaney, *The Right to Counsel in American Courts* 10 (noting that the absence

of statutory basis for practice resulted in wide variety of applications); Beattie, *Crime and the Courts in England* 359 (increased use of counsel was allowed by judicial "sufferance" and developed unevenly); Langbein, "The Criminal Trial Before the Lawyers," 313 (stating that degree of participation allowed by lawyers varied greatly among the courts until 1836, when legislation eliminated remaining restrictions on use of counsel).

44. Beattie, "Scales of Justice," 231; see also Stephen Landsman, "The Rise of the Contentious Spirit: Adversary Procedure in Eighteenth Century England," 75 *Cornell L. Rev.* (1990) 497, 534–42; David Fellman, "The Constitutional Right to Counsel in Federal Courts," 30 *Neb. L. Rev.* (1951) 559, 560.

45. Beattie, "Scales of Justice," 231.

46. Beattie, "Scales of Justice," 231–32.

47. 4 Blackstone, *Commentaries on the Laws of England* 350.

48. 20 George II, c. 30 (1747).

49. 6 and 7 W.4, c. 114, s. 1,2 (1836).

50. 3 Edw. 7, c. 38 (1903).

51. Beaney, *The Right to Counsel in American Courts* 15.

52. Heller, *The Sixth Amendment to the Constitution of the United States* 21; see also Randolph N. Jonakait, "The Origins of the Confrontation Clause: An Alternative History," 27 *Rutgers L.J.* (1995) 77, 101 n.112 (stating that the origins of the public prosecutor system are unclear, although one theory is that the concept of a public prosecutor was imported from France or Scotland).

53. Heller, *The Sixth Amendment to the Constitution of the United States* 21; Jonakait, "The Origins of the Confrontation Clause," 99.

54. Jonakait, "The Origins of the Confrontation Clause," 108–12 (concluding that the Sixth Amendment was the final embodiment of growing American resentment of common law procedures).

55. Del. Charter of 1701, § V.

56. Del. Declaration of Rights and Fundamental Rules, para. 14 (1776).

57. Del. Const. of 1776, art. 30.

58. Del. Const. of 1776, art. 25.

59. Pa. Charter of Privileges of 1701, § V.

60. Pa. Const. of 1776, Declaration of the Rights and Inhabitants of the State of Pennsylvania, para. IX.

61. N.J. Const. of 1776, para. XVI.

62. Md. Const. of 1776, A Declaration of Rights, para. 19.

63. N.Y. Const. of 1777, para. XXXIV.

64. Mass. Const. of 1780, Part the First, art. XII.

65. N.H. Const. of 1784, Part I, art. I, para. 15.

66. 2 John R. Bartlett, *Colonial Records of Rhode Island and Providence Plantations in New England* (Providence: A. Crawford Greene and Brother, state printers, 1857) 239.

67. Beaney, *The Right to Counsel in American Courts* 18.

68. 2 Bartlett, *Colonial Records of Rhode Island and Providence Plantations in New England* 239.

69. Act of Aug. 20, 1731, para. XLIII, 3 S.C. Stat. 274, 286 (1731).

70. Act of Aug. 20, 1731, para. XLIII, 3 S.C. Stat. 274, 286 (1731).

71. An Act for establishing Courts of Law, and for regulating the Proceedings therein, para. XCIV, 1777 N.C. Laws 296, 317, reprinted in *The First Laws of the State*

of North Carolina, John D. Cushing, editor (photo. reprint, Wilmington, DE: Michael Glazier, 1984) (1791).

72. 12 Hening's Va. Stat. 340, 343 (1779).

73. An Act for the Advancement of Justice, § 4, 1 Del. Laws 64, 66 (1719); An Act for the Advancement of Justice, § 3, 3 Pa. Stat. 199, 201 (1718) (providing for assigned counsel).

74. Beaney, *The Right to Counsel in American Courts* 16.

75. Act of Feb. 1, 1777, § 10, 5 Mass. Acts 615, 617 (1777).

76. Beaney, *The Right to Counsel in American Courts* 16, 21.

77. Act of Aug. 20, 1731, para. XLIII, 3 S.C. Stat. 274, 286 (1731).

78. Act of Feb. 8, 1791, 5 Metcalf's N.H. Laws 596, 599 (1791).

79. Conn. Const. of 1818, art. I, § 9.

80. Beaney, *The Right to Counsel in American Courts* 16 (noting that by 1750 judges in Connecticut appointed counsel for the accused when the accused requested it and appointed counsel for the accused when the accused did not request it but appeared to be laboring under some handicap).

81. 2 Zephaniah Swift, *A System of the Laws of the State of Connecticut* (New York: Arno Press photo. reprint 1972) (1796) 398–99.

82. Beaney, *The Right to Counsel in American Courts* 16.

83. Ga. Const. of 1798, art. III, § 8 (providing that "no person shall be debarred from advocating or defending his cause before any court or tribunal, either by himself or counsel, or both").

84. Pa. Const. of 1776, Declaration of the Rights and Inhabitants of the State of Pennsylvania, para. IX.

85. Mass. Const. of 1780, Part the First, art. 12.

86. 1 Jonathan Elliot, *The Debates in the Several State Conventions on the Adoption of the Federal Constitution as Recommended by the General Convention at Philadelphia in 1787* (Photo reprint, Buffalo, NY: William S. Hein & Co., 1996) (Philadelphia: J.B. Lippincott & Co., 1881) 150.

87. Heller, *The Sixth Amendment to the Constitution of the United States* 24.

88. Open Letter from Roger Sherman (Dec. 8, 1787), in Supplement to Max Farrand's *The Records of the Federal Convention of 1787* (New Haven, CT, and London: Yale University Press, 1987) 288.

89. Heller, *The Sixth Amendment to the Constitution of the United States* 25–28.

90. 2 Max Farrand, *The Records of the Federal Convention of 1787* (New Haven, CT: Yale University Press, 1966) 587.

91. 2 Farrand, *The Records of the Federal Convention of 1787*, at 582, 587–88.

92. 3 Farrand, *The Records of the Federal Convention of 1787*, at 135–36.

93. Open letter from Brutus to the Citizens of the State of New York (Nov. 1, 1787), in 2 Herbert J. Storing, ed., *The Complete Anti-Federalist* (Chicago: University of Chicago Press, 1981) 374.

94. Most scholars attribute the Letters from the Federal Farmer to Richard Henry Lee. There has been some doubt raised about the correctness of this attribution. See generally 2 Herbert J. Storing, ed., *The Complete Anti-Federalist* 214–17; 2 William W. Crosskey, *Politics and the Constitution* (Chicago: University of Chicago Press, 1953) 1299–1300; Gordon S. Wood, "The Authorship of the Letters from the Federal Farmer," 31 *Wm. & Mary Q.* (1974) 299.

95. 1 Elliot, *The Debates in the Several State Conventions* 503.

96. 2 Storing, *The Complete Anti-Federalist* 231–32.
97. 2 Storing, *The Complete Anti-Federalist* 231.
98. 2 Storing, *The Complete Anti-Federalist* 328.
99. The Federalist No. 84, at 264 (Alexander Hamilton) (Roy P. Fairfield ed.) (Baltimore: The Johns Hopkins University Press, 1981).
100. The Letters of a Landholder (Dec. 10, 1787), in 2 *The Roots of the Bill of Rights* (Bernard Schwartz ed.) (New York: Chelsea House Publishers, 1980).
101. The Federalist No. 84, at 263 (Alexander Hamilton) (Roy P. Fairfield ed.).
102. 3 Farrand, *The Records of the Federal Convention* 144.
103. Open Letter from Brutus to the Citizens of the State of New York (Nov. 1, 1787), in J.R. Pole, *The American Constitution: For and Against* (New York: Hill and Wang, 1987) 40.
104. Open Letter from Brutus to the Citizens of the State of New York (Nov. 1, 1787), in Pole, *The American Constitution: For and Against* 41.
105. Letter from Elbridge Gerry to New York Legislature (Oct. 18, 1787), in 2 Storing, *The Complete Anti-Federalist* 7.
106. Letter from Agrippa to Massachusetts Convention (Jan. 22, 1788), in 4 Storing, *The Complete Anti-Federalist* 111.
107. Samuel Chase, Notes of Speeches Delivered to Maryland Ratifying Convention (Apr. 1788), in 5 Storing, *The Complete Anti-Federalist* 88.
108. Letter of Luther Martin to the Citizens of Maryland (Mar. 28, 1788), in 3 Schwartz, *The Roots of the Bill of Rights* 502.
109. 1 Elliot, *The Debates in the Several State Conventions* 325.
110. 1 Elliot, *The Debates in the Several State Conventions* 332.
111. 1 Elliot, *The Debates in the Several State Conventions* 332.
112. 1 Elliot, *The Debates in the Several State Conventions* 332–33.
113. 1 Elliot, *The Debates in the Several State Conventions* 333.
114. 1 Elliot, *The Debates in the Several State Conventions* 333.
115. 1 Elliot, *The Debates in the Several State Conventions* 335.
116. 1 Elliot, *The Debates in the Several State Conventions* 319–25.
117. 1 Elliot, *The Debates in the Several State Conventions* 323.
118. 1 Elliot, *The Debates in the Several State Conventions* 325–26.
119. 1 Elliot, *The Debates in the Several State Conventions* 325.
120. 1 Elliot, *The Debates in the Several State Conventions* 328.
121. 3 Elliot, *The Debates in the Several State Conventions* 658.
122. 4 Elliot, *The Debates in the Several State Conventions* 243.
123. 1 Elliot, *The Debates in the Several State Conventions* 334.
124. 1 *Annals of Congress* 435 (1789).
125. Nelson B. Lasson, *The History and Development of the Fourth Amendment to the United States Constitution* (Baltimore: The Johns Hopkins Press, 1937) 101.
126. See Heller, *The Sixth Amendment* 30–31, for a summary of the developments described in this paragraph.
127. See Heller, *The Sixth Amendment* 31–32, for a summary of the developments described in this paragraph.
128. 1 Elliot, *The Debates in the Several State Conventions* 339–40.
129. 1 Elliot, *The Debates in the Several State Conventions* 339–40.
130. 1 Elliot, *The Debates in the Several State Conventions* 340.
131. 1 Statutes at Large 112, 118 (1790).

132. Alexander Holtzoff, "The Right to Counsel Under the Sixth Amendment," 20 *N.Y.U.L.Q. Rev.* (1944) 1, 7–8; see also Heller, *The Sixth Amendment to the Constitution of the United States* 110–11.

133. See generally Charles Fairman, "Does the Fourteenth Amendment Incorporate the Bill of Rights? The Original Understanding," 2 *Stan. L. Rev.* (1949) 1; Stanley Morrison, "Does the Fourteenth Amendment Incorporate the Bill of Rights? The Judicial Interpretation," 2 *Stan. L. Rev.* (1949) 140.

134. For further discussion of Powell v. Alabama, see generally Beaney, *The Right to Counsel in American Courts*; Heller, *The Sixth Amendment to the Constitution of the United States*; Holtzoff, "The Right to Counsel Under the Sixth Amendment." See also James Goodman, *Stories of Scottsboro* (New York: Pantheon Books, 1994).

135. See Goodman, *Stories of Scottsboro* 1–23, for a more complete account of the facts surrounding the Scottsboro rape trials.

136. Unless otherwise indicated, the facts reported in quotation marks and otherwise are taken from the Court's opinion in Powell v. Alabama, 1932.

137. Goodman, *Stories of Scottsboro* 4.

138. Goodman, *Stories of Scottsboro* 5.

139. Heller, *The Sixth Amendment to the Constitution of the United States* 121–25 (discussing the legal obstacles preventing the Court from finding that the defendant's rights had been violated and how the Court circumvented those obstacles); Beaney, *The Right to Counsel in American Courts* 149–57 (discussing in detail the social, legal, and political ramifications of the *Powell* decision).

140. Alfredo Garcia, *The Sixth Amendment in Modern American Jurisprudence: A Critical Perspective* (Westport, CT: Greenwood Press, 1992) 4–6.

141. See Beaney, *The Right to Counsel in American Courts* 157–60 (discussing some of the cases arising immediately after *Powell*).

142. For further discussion of Johnson v. Zerbst, see generally Beaney, *The Right to Counsel in American Courts*; Heller, *The Sixth Amendment to the Constitution of the United States*; Holtzoff, "The Right to Counsel Under the Sixth Amendment."

143. Heller, *The Sixth Amendment to the Constitution of the United States* 110–11 (noting that although the Court had not decided the issue, many lower courts had already begun the practice of assigning counsel in grave, even noncapital cases).

144. Heller, *The Sixth Amendment to the Constitution of the United States* 112 (noting that the jurisdictional language was necessary because the case had originated as a petition for a writ of habeas corpus, and doctrine at the time limited habeas corpus review to jurisdictional defects).

145. Garcia, *The Sixth Amendment in Modern American Jurisprudence* 6 (discussing the rationale of *Zerbst*, particularly the waiver standard).

146. For further discussion of Betts v. Brady, see generally Beaney, *The Right to Counsel in American Courts*; Heller, *The Sixth Amendment to the Constitution of the United States*; Holtzoff, "The Right to Counsel Under the Sixth Amendment."

147. Beaney, *The Right to Counsel in American Courts* 160–64 (discussing *Betts* and the limited nature of its holding); Garcia, *The Sixth Amendment in Modern American Jurisprudence* 8 (noting that the Court reached a counterintuitive result given the broad rationales of prior cases).

148. Holtzoff, "The Right to Counsel Under the Sixth Amendment," 7–8; see also Heller, *The Sixth Amendment to the Constitution of the United States* 110.

149. Beaney, *The Right to Counsel in American Courts* 163 (noting that some have

taken the position that the *Betts* decision was influenced by the fact that the trial judge was known to be of upstanding character and very fair in the pursuit of justice).

150. For further discussion of Gideon v. Wainwright, see generally Anthony Lewis, *Gideon's Trumpet* (New York: Random House, 1964).

151. Garcia, *The Sixth Amendment in Modern American Jurisprudence* 8–11 (discussing the dynamics and lobbying within the Court and the rationale and impact of the *Gideon* decision).

152. Garcia, *The Sixth Amendment in Modern American Jurisprudence* 8–11 (noting that *Gideon* attempted to achieve fairness by equalizing the strength of the adversaries in criminal litigation and that even though the balance is not equal, it is more fair than prior to *Gideon*).

153. David Fellman, *The Defendant's Rights Today* (Madison: University of Wisconsin Press, 1976) 208–18 (concluding that the right to counsel has expanded consistently since the colonial era).

Chapter 2

Analysis

THE NATURE AND CHARACTER OF THE RIGHT TO THE ASSISTANCE OF COUNSEL

The Sixth Amendment provides "the accused" with a number of rights considered critical to constructing an effective defense against a criminal prosecution. Among them are the right to a speedy and public trial, the right to trial by an impartial jury, the right to be confronted with the witnesses against him, and the right to have compulsory process for obtaining his own witnesses. Each of these constitutional safeguards makes a significant contribution to the fairness of trials in the American adversary system of criminal justice. None make a more important contribution, however, than the right that appears last in the Sixth Amendment's litany—"the right [of the accused] . . . to have the Assistance of Counsel for his defence."

From humble historical origins in England and relatively modest beginnings in this country, the right to counsel has developed into the most vital of all the protections guaranteed to criminal defendants by the United States Constitution. The right to a lawyer's assistance in a criminal prosecution is thought to be "fundamental to our system of justice" (United States v. Morrison, 1981) and "necessary to insure fundamental human rights of life and liberty" (Johnson v. Zerbst, 1938). It is a safeguard of "special value" to the accused, by far the " 'most pervasive' " of all the constitutional entitlements granted to a person charged with committing a criminal offense (United States v. Cronic, 1984). The assistance of a defense attorney is no less than "indispensable to the fair administration of our adversary system of criminal justice" (Brewer v. Williams, 1977).

A clear, meaningful appreciation of the nature and character of the right to counsel and of why counsel is so critical to the fair operation of the system requires an understanding of the stage on which defense lawyers perform. Consequently, this part of the analysis begins with a brief exploration of the adversarial character of American systems of criminal justice and of the reasons that counsel is essential to the functioning of those systems. It then discusses the qualified constitutional right to retain counsel of one's choice and explains the right of indigents to have government-appointed assistance. The analysis continues with a consideration of the ability, indeed, the entitlement, to waive counsel's assistance and the constitutional right to represent oneself. This part concludes with a treatment of the constitutional allocation of decision-making authority between the accused and the defense attorney.

The Reasons for and Roles of Counsel in the Adversary System[1]

The United States has chosen an adversary system of criminal justice (United States v. Nixon, 1974).[2] In both state and federal American criminal justice schemes, the prosecution establishes an adversarial relationship with an individual suspected of crime by leveling a formal accusation against that individual (Kirby v. Illinois, 1972). From that point in the process forward, the two sides—the government, as the representative of society, and the individual accused of crime—engage in a contest, a battle, a competition. The prosecution zealously strives to secure a conviction, limited only by the mandates not to engage in unfair methods or pursue an unjust outcome (United States v. Ash, 1973).[3] The defendant actively resists the prosecutor's efforts, seeking to gain an acquittal. Each side challenges the opponent's claims, arguments, and evidence; each seeks to defeat the other side and emerge as the victor. In pursuing a guilty verdict, the government's lawyer is supposed to " 'strike hard blows' " (United States v. Ash, 1973 (quoting Berger v. United States, 1935)). In trying to avoid that result, defense counsel is expected to promote and safeguard " 'the undivided interests of his client' " (Polk County v. Dodson, 1981 (quoting Ferri v. Ackerman, 1979)).

Judges and jurors preside over the contest. While judges alone resolve questions of law, judges or jurors decide questions of fact, observing the two sides' presentations and determining whether the state has sustained the constitutionally imposed burden of proving the accused's guilt beyond a reasonable doubt.[4] As neutral arbiters of the competition, judges and jurors have no bias or interest in the outcome and may not help either side prevail. Moreover, they are entirely dependent on the two adversaries to present the facts and arguments upon which resolution of the dispute will depend. Judges and jurors may not undertake independent inquiries into the merits of a case in order to determine where the truth lies and what the most just result would be. While there are procedural, evidentiary, and even constitutional rules that restrict what the parties may and may not do and others that mandate what the parties must or must not do, within those constraints, the battle that unfolds is shaped by the strategic and tactical decisions and maneuvers of the parties.[5]

The Sixth Amendment is premised upon and reflects an acceptance of the adversarial method of resolving criminal accusations. It contains "a compact statement of the rights . . . [that are] basic to our adversary system of justice" and "constitutionalizes the right in an adversary criminal trial to make a defense as we know it" (Faretta v. California, 1975).[6] The Framers of the Bill of Rights contemplated a legal confrontation between adversaries in which each side would have a full and fair opportunity to present its own case and subject the opponent's case to a rigorous testing process (United States v. Cronic, 1984). According to the Supreme Court, under our Constitution a "fair trial" is a trial "in which evidence subject to adversarial testing is presented to an impartial tribunal for resolution of issues defined in advance" (Strickland v. Washington, 1984). The Sixth Amendment provides the rights necessary to have such a trial.

One of the primary reasons that our nation has chosen an adversarial approach to resolving criminal charges is an abiding conviction that it is the best method of ascertaining the "truth."[7] Proponents of the adversary system hold it as an article of faith that when the state accuses one of its citizens of a criminal offense, a contest between committed opponents is the method that will most accurately and reliably determine the merits of that accusation. According to this view, " '[t]ruth . . . is best discovered by powerful statements on both sides of the question' " (United States v. Cronic, 1984).[8] The "very premise of our adversary system of criminal justice is that partisan advocacy on both sides of a case will best promote the ultimate objective that the guilty be convicted and the innocent go free" (Herring v. New York, 1975). An adversarial system of criminal adjudication may not always reach the factually correct result, but those who support it believe that it is more likely to do so than the available alternatives.

The ascertainment of truth is a fundamental justification for the adversarial design of our criminal justice systems, but it is not the sole rationale.[9] Another reason for an adversarial approach is the assurance that it provides that accusations will be resolved by means of fundamentally fair processes. A legal battle between opponents before a neutral arbiter according to prescribed rules gives society a meaningful chance to vindicate its interest in prosecuting and convicting those who have committed criminal offenses. Moreover, it gives the accused a full and fair opportunity to fend off the government's efforts to impose criminal sanctions.[10] The adversary system is believed to be the method of adjudication that reaches the most just results by means of the fairest processes (Polk County v. Dodson, 1981). Of course, the mere fact that a method of adjudication is adversarial in nature does not mean that its processes will necessarily be the fairest. Without adequate procedural safeguards, an adversarial approach might be quite disadvantageous to criminal defendants. The belief that the adversary system is preferable because it ensures a fair method of adjudication rests only in part on the fact that it depends upon opposing parties to contest the merits of cases. It also rests on the array of procedural mechanisms and protections afforded by the systems that have evolved in American jurisdictions.

From time to time, members of the Supreme Court have been troubled by aspects of the adversary system, criticizing what they characterize as the "sporting theory" of criminal justice. In their opinion, criminal trials should not be seen as sporting contests (Mathews v. United States, 1988 (White, J. dissenting)).[11] To the extent that athletic competitions are frivolous exercises designed to entertain, this criticism seems appropriate. Nonetheless, wholesale rejection of the sporting contest analogy seems misguided. The adversary system's devotion to achieving fair, balanced processes produces undeniable similarities to sporting events, similarities that are not at all undesirable. As in athletic contests, the opponents in criminal trials are both committed to attaining a victory. Moreover, each must adhere to prescribed rules established before the contest begins, rules that are enforced by neutral, disinterested arbiters. The controlling rules are designed to promote fair play, evenhanded treatment of the adversaries, and an unbiased determination of the merits. Like a sporting contest, an adversarial criminal trial is designed to produce the best outcome by means of a process that affords opportunities to both sides but favors neither of the combatants.

The primary alternative to the adversary system of adjudication is the "inquisitorial" approach to criminal justice employed by continental European countries. The "inquisitorial process is firmly committed to the search for material truth." The central player in this quest for truth, the one around whom the "entire adjudicatory process revolves," is the judge. In contrast to adversary system judges, those in inquisitorial systems are charged with both investigating the facts and examining the witnesses. Their freedom "to conduct the inquiry" is broad, for the proceedings are "informal" and are regulated by few evidentiary or procedural rules. Because the guiding object is truth—the accurate resolution of disputes—inquisitorial system judges are entitled "to ask for virtually any sort of information"—except that protected by privileges. The centrality of judges means that juries of laypersons "are not favored." Moreover, because the parties' control over the "proceedings is minimized, . . . [l]awyers play a far less important role than they do in the adversary system."[12]

By rejecting an inquisitorial approach and adopting an adversarial model of adjudication, our nation made the parties important players in the adjudicatory process and ensured that lawyers would play critical roles in the operation of that process. In the adversary systems that have evolved in America—systems in which lawyers are "necessities, not luxuries"—counsel for the accused is "fundamental and essential to a fair trial" (Gideon v. Wainwright, 1963). A contest between adversaries cannot possibly be fair if there is a substantial disparity in skill and knowledge between the opposing parties. Fairness requires the two sides to be at least roughly equal in strength and ability.[13] Laypersons accused of crimes are in no sense the equals of the state. They are presumptively incapable of coping with the skillful maneuvers of the legally trained, professional, and experienced prosecutors who are charged with furthering the government's interest in securing a conviction. They are woefully unequipped to understand and function within the substantive and procedural legal system that faces them (Powell v. Alabama, 1932). Unaided, legally ignorant defendants are also quite unlikely to take advantage of any of the constitutional and other legal rights that ensure fair trials and just outcomes (Johnson v. Zerbst, 1938). In sum, if an accused had to go it alone, "without counsel, the right to a trial itself would be 'of little avail' " (United States v. Cronic, 1984). The government could prevail not because of the merits of its position but simply because superior resources and strength would enable it to overpower its defenseless opponent. Both truth and fair play would be the casualties of such imbalanced confrontations.

The adversarial process is designed to produce a fair contest between the opposing sides, not the "sacrifice" of an inferior accused to a superior accuser (United States v. Cronic, 1984). The core reason for the constitutional right to "the Assistance of Counsel for [one's] defence" is to "equalize" the status of the criminal defendant in the battle with the state. In the adversarial battle, the defense lawyer serves as both an offensive "sword" and a defensive "shield" for the defendant.[14] The professional skill and knowledge furnished by counsel guarantee a fair, balanced clash of adversaries, rather than a sacrifice of the defenseless accused.[15] By subjecting the prosecution's case to real adversarial testing, counsel ensures that the government will carry its constitutional burden of proving guilt beyond a reasonable doubt. Counsel ultimately enables the criminal defendant to enjoy the most basic of rights—the right to "a meaningful opportunity to present a complete defense" (California v. Trombetta, 1984).

More specifically, a defense attorney affords the legal expertise necessary to counter the trained, professional prosecutor's strategic and tactical maneuvers (Strickland v. Washington, 1984; United States v. Ash, 1973). She provides the training and knowledge necessary to cope with the intricacies of the substantive law and procedural system (Strickland v. Washington, 1984; United States v. Ash, 1973). The assistance of a lawyer enables the accused to protect and exercise all the other rights that are vital components of a fair adversarial trial (Kimmelman v. Morrison, 1986; United States v. Cronic, 1984).[16] Counsel, for example, confronts government witnesses, calls defense witnesses, guards against efforts to compel the accused to incriminate himself, and ensures full enjoyment of the entitlement to trial by jury. "The Sixth Amendment recognizes the right to the assistance of counsel because it envisions counsel's playing a role that is critical to the ability of the adversarial system to produce just results" (Strickland v. Washington, 1984). The role that counsel plays is equally critical to the ability of the adversary system to promote our profound commitment to fair treatment and fair play and to demonstrate our enduring respect for the dignity of individual citizens. By providing a legal champion to vigorously safeguard the accused's interests, the Sixth Amendment makes it possible to achieve the two fundamental objectives of the adversary system of criminal justice—

truthful, just outcomes and fair methods of adjudication. In sum, "[t]he right to counsel . . . assures the fairness, and thus the legitimacy of our adversary process" (Kimmelman v. Morrison, 1986).

The Right to Retained Counsel of Choice

The Nature of Legal Assistance

While the nature of the "Assistance of Counsel" that is guaranteed is not described in detail by the terms of the Sixth Amendment, interpretations of that provision have made a number of things clear.[17] The constitutional guarantee accords criminal defendants the right to a legally trained assistant, that is, to the aid of a qualified attorney who is a member of the bar (Caplin & Drysdale v. United States, 1989; Wheat v. United States, 1988). Although an accused may personally prefer to form a relationship with and be assisted by a layperson who has abilities and talents as an advocate and counselor, the Constitution does not include an entitlement to such assistance.[18] The Sixth Amendment promises only the right to a *lawyer's* aid.

This limitation is consistent with the apparent intent of the drafters of the Bill of Rights—to provide *legal* assistance to those prosecuted for crimes. It is also entirely consonant with the reason that those accused of criminal offenses are accorded a right to such assistance. The Sixth Amendment right to counsel is not granted to accused individuals "for its own sake" but, rather, to ensure that trials are fair (United States v. Cronic, 1984). While it is conceivable that representation by a layperson could enhance the fairness of a trial, it is highly unlikely that an individual without legal training would be able to compete competently with the lawyer representing the government or to understand and cope adequately with the complexities of the legal system. A defendant might derive personal satisfaction and comfort from representation by an untrained layperson of his choice, but in the vast majority of cases, he would be little better off than if required to stand alone. The substantive aid provided by a lay assistant could not produce the equality necessary for a fair adversary system trial.[19] Consequently, lay representation would not yield the reliable outcomes and the fair processes contemplated by the Sixth Amendment. Moreover, the orderly administration of justice would likely be hindered, perhaps severely, by the participation of an individual who is unschooled in the intricacies and requirements of the legal system. The efficiency of the trial process would undoubtedly suffer costly delays and disruptions if a layperson were in charge of the defense.

The Right to Retain Counsel

The constitutional right to counsel created by the Framers of the Sixth Amendment was intended to provide the accused with a *right to retain a lawyer* to help in presenting an effective defense against a criminal charge (Scott v.

Illinois, 1979).[20] "[T]he Sixth Amendment guarantees a defendant the right to be represented by an otherwise qualified attorney whom that defendant can afford to hire, or who is willing to represent the defendant even though he is without funds" (Caplin & Drysdale v. United States, 1989). This right to use one's own resources—financial or otherwise—to secure representation by a defense attorney has never been seriously questioned. When occasions have arisen, the Supreme Court has consistently and resoundingly affirmed its solid constitutional foundation. Indeed, at a time when the Court still subscribed to the view that only a limited class of indigent defendants was constitutionally entitled to government-appointed counsel, it pointedly held that every defendant who could retain legal representation was entitled to do so because the "right to be heard through [one's] own counsel [is] *unqualified*" (Chandler v. Fretag, 1954) (italics added).

The accused's right to be represented by privately retained counsel means that ordinarily the government cannot prohibit a defendant from using her own resources to secure a lawyer and cannot prevent a retained lawyer from representing a defendant. In addition, a judge cannot "arbitrarily . . . refuse to hear a party by counsel, employed by and appearing for him" (Powell v. Alabama, 1932) and must afford the accused "a reasonable opportunity to employ" a lawyer (Chandler v. Fretag, 1954).

The Qualified Right to Counsel of the Accused's Choice

The Constitution includes not merely a right to retain counsel but a personal right to choose the particular representative who will assist the accused in making a defense. The Supreme Court has clearly recognized that "the right to select and be represented by one's preferred attorney is comprehended by the Sixth Amendment" (Wheat v. United States, 1988). Majority opinions that have acknowledged this implicit right to choose one's representative have not elaborated upon its underlying rationales. Individual Justices have, however, offered helpful, sensible insights into the reasons that a constitutional right to choose is an implicit and essential part of the Sixth Amendment guarantee.

Justice Marshall has suggested that the constitutional right to the assistance of counsel must include an entitlement to counsel of choice because "a primary purpose of the Sixth Amendment is to grant a criminal defendant effective control over the conduct of his defense." According to his reasoning, a "critical aspect of making a defense is choosing a person to serve as an assistant and representative." Moreover, allowing the accused to select defense counsel promotes the objectives of the Sixth Amendment by enhancing the "fairness and integrity of criminal trials" (Wheat v. United States, 1988 (Marshall, J., dissenting)).

Justice Blackmun has offered additional reasons for finding "choice" to be an inherent part of the constitutional entitlement to legal assistance. According to him, vesting the right to select an attorney in the accused promotes "trust" and "confidence" in defense counsel. Trust and confidence are necessary to ensure that "the attorney [will] be a truly effective advocate," to foster a belief by the accused that the trial has been conducted fairly, and to enhance the chances that the accused will be willing to accept the outcome of the proceedings. Furthermore, granting the defendant the right to be represented by an attorney whom he prefers "serves to assure some modicum of equality" with the government. A lawyer chosen by the defendant himself is more likely to provide a "truly equal and adversarial presentation of the case" than counsel not selected by the accused. Counsel of choice, therefore, furthers the proper operation of the adversary system, guarding against imbalanced contests and unjust verdicts. Finally, in Justice Blackmun's opinion, a right to "privately chosen and compensated counsel" safeguards against undesirable "socialization" and standardization of criminal defense services and helps preserve defense counsel independence (Caplin & Drysdale v. United States, 1989 (Blackmun, J., dissenting)).[21]

The meaning and scope of the "right to retain counsel of [one's] choosing" (Caplin & Drysdale v. United States, 1989) have not been fully developed or explained by the Supreme Court. It is clear, however, that the Constitution does not include an "absolute" entitlement to representation by the lawyer whom one prefers.[22] The "presumption in favor of . . . counsel of choice" means that, as a general rule, a defendant must be allowed to be represented by an attorney whom she has been able to retain (Wheat v. United States, 1988). However, because there are countervailing interests that justify depriving an accused of the counsel whom she has chosen, this general rule is qualified by a number of "limitations."[23]

The particular circumstances that justify denial of a defendant's choice have not been exhaustively catalogued. A number of them, however, have been identified. An accused, for example, may not choose a lawyer who is not a member of the bar, may not demand representation by a lawyer whom she cannot afford or by a lawyer who declines to serve as defense counsel, and does not have a constitutional right to representation by an attorney who has a prior or current relationship with her opponent (Wheat v. United States, 1989). The right to counsel of choice probably requires judges to grant reasonable requests for postponements of proceedings if time is needed to enable a defendant to secure the assistance of a particular lawyer (Morris v. Slappy, 1983 (Brennan, J., concurring in the result); see also Chandler v. Fretag, 1954). However, if representation by an attorney preferred by the accused would require an unreasonably long continuance (i.e., a postponement of the proceedings) or a delay that would interfere with significant interests in securing a conviction or administering justice, a court could undoubtedly refuse to postpone a trial without running afoul of the constitutional entitlement to choose (Ungar v. Sarafite, 1964).[24]

A trio of decisions involving interesting claims of improper governmental infringement upon the Sixth Amendment right to counsel of choice offers additional insights into the legitimacy of restrictions on the constitutional right to select one's own attorney. In Wheat v. United States, an accused sought to be represented by a private lawyer who was also representing his codefendants.

Such joint representation of multiple codefendants by a single attorney frequently engenders conflicts of interest (i.e., situations in which the attorney's zealous, effective representation of one client's interests precludes or interferes with zealous, effective representation of another client's interests). To allay concerns that the lawyer whom he desired might be placed in a "conflicted" position, the defendant in *Wheat* offered to "waive" (that is, to relinquish) his constitutional entitlement to conflict-free representation. Because he preferred to have the advantages of assistance provided by a particular attorney, the accused was willing to risk the obstacles to effective representation that could result from competing, inconsistent duties and loyalties owed to his codefendants. Moreover, both codefendants were amenable to the arrangement; they also were willing to waive their rights to unconflicted assistance from counsel. The prosecution, however, objected to the proposed joint representation, arguing that the defense attorney would have serious conflicts that would threaten the integrity of the proceedings. The trial judge agreed with the government's contention and refused to permit Mr. Wheat to have the assistant whom he had chosen.

Upon review, a majority of the Supreme Court upheld the trial judge's decision. That decision was proper because the Constitution permits a judge to reject a waiver of the entitlement to unconflicted assistance and to deny counsel of choice whenever there is a showing of either an "actual conflict of interest" or "serious potential for a conflict" (Wheat v. United States, 1988). In either of those situations, the institutional interests in ensuring lawyers' compliance with ethical standards, in preserving the appearance of fairness, and in promoting the "rendition of just verdicts" counterbalance an accused's interest in choosing a particular lawyer and justify limitation of the Sixth Amendment right to choose. While members of the Court were divided over whether the facts of *Wheat* justified a denial of the defendant's choice of counsel, *all* agreed that there are situations in which actual or potential conflicts of interest justify a refusal to permit defendants to be represented by the particular lawyers whom they prefer.[25] In sum, the Supreme Court unanimously agreed that the institutional interests identified in *Wheat* are substantial enough to outweigh a defendant's interests in choosing a specific representative and to limit the constitutional entitlement to counsel of choice.

The year after its decision in *Wheat*, the Court decided Caplin & Drysdale v. United States and United States v. Monsanto (Caplin & Drysdale v. United States, 1989; United States v. Monsanto, 1989). In *Caplin & Drysdale*, a majority of the Court held that a federal statute authorizing the government to seek the forfeiture of assets that an accused wishes to use to compensate a retained attorney does not "impermissibly burden[]" the Sixth Amendment right to counsel of choice. The first premise for the Court's conclusion was that the federal forfeiture statute did not explicitly or directly prevent an accused from hiring a chosen attorney or disqualify any attorney from serving as counsel. In addition, while the statutory forfeiture provision did place some burden on an accused's choice of counsel, that burden was "limited." Any assets that were not subject to forfeiture could still be used to retain counsel. Moreover, some lawyers would be willing to represent a defendant despite the risk that all the resources to be used to pay their fees might be forfeited upon conviction.

The *Caplin & Drysdale* Court acknowledged that in some cases the threat of asset forfeiture would mean that a defendant who otherwise would be able to hire a particular lawyer would be "unable to retain the attorney of his choice" but concluded that this restriction of the constitutional entitlement to counsel of choice is justified. According to the majority, forfeitable property in fact becomes the property of the government at the time that the criminal act that is the basis of forfeiture is committed, and it is clear that a defendant has no right to use a third party's property to retain counsel.[26] The "strong governmental interest in obtaining full recovery of all forfeitable assets . . . overrides any Sixth Amendment interest in permitting criminals to" use those assets to pay for defense counsel (Caplin & Drysdale v. United States, 1989).

In United States v. Monsanto, a companion case to *Caplin & Drysdale*, the Court addressed the statutory authority to "freeze" potentially forfeitable assets, that is, to prevent defendants from transferring them to counsel or anyone else prior to a forfeiture determination. Under the statute, assets could be frozen by means of a pretrial restraining order issued on the basis of probable cause to believe that the assets were subject to forfeiture. A majority of the Court held that the provision for freezing assets prior to forfeiture also was compatible with the constitutional right to counsel of choice. The reasoning supporting this conclusion was terse. Because post-trial forfeiture that prevents an accused from using assets to pay an attorney does not violate the right to counsel of choice, no constitutional deprivation can result from an order that effectively prevents an accused from frustrating the government's legitimate interests in obtaining forfeited assets by barring him from "dissipating [those] assets prior to trial" (United States v. Monsanto, 1989).[27]

In sum, the Sixth Amendment includes a right to retain a trained member of the bar whom the accused has chosen to assist in defending against criminal charges. Although that right is not absolute, there is a "presumption" in favor of the defendant's choice of counsel. That presumption means that the defendant's choice must be honored unless there are adequate reasons to preclude or restrict representation by a particular defense attorney.

The Indigent's Right to Appointed Counsel

Indigent criminal defendants—those who do not have the financial means to retain private legal assistance—are constitutionally entitled to have the government appoint and pay for counsel to represent them.[28] As will be seen, while every indigent accused of a felony is entitled to government-provided counsel, not all of those charged with misdemeanor-level offenses are entitled to lawyers furnished by the state. The fact that the state selects and compensates an indigent's defender does not alter the duties and obligations of counsel.[29] An indigent's appointed lawyer is expected to play the same adversary system roles as privately retained counsel (Polk County v. Dodson, 1981). Her essential functions are to ably, loyally, and zealously promote and defend the interests of the accused in confrontations with the prosecutors and the legal system.[30]

The Evolution of Indigents' Right to Appointed Counsel in Federal and State Courts

The original intent of the Sixth Amendment was apparently only to grant accused individuals the right to retain legal assistance (Scott v. Illinois, 1979).[31] Over time, however, the Supreme Court recognized that some defendants who are financially unable to pay for legal representation nonetheless have a constitutional entitlement to assistance. The state may not prosecute and convict those defendants unless it provides representation for them. This constitutional right to government-furnished counsel developed incrementally over the course of a critical thirty-year span during the twentieth century.

The first important recognition of the entitlement to appointed assistance occurred in 1932, in Powell v. Alabama, a landmark case involving a state trial for a capital offense.[32] The Court first concluded that the Fourteenth Amendment Due Process Clause required the trial judge to give the defendants "reasonable time and opportunity to secure counsel" and that the judge had failed to afford them an adequate opportunity. The Court then proceeded on the assumption that the defendants did not have the means to secure counsel on their own. It found a distinct constitutional violation, holding that the trial court's failure "to make an effective appointment of counsel was likewise a denial of due process" (Powell v. Alabama, 1932).

The significance of the *Powell* decision was undeniable, but its meaning was subject to multiple interpretations. On the one hand, statements in *Powell* could be read broadly to signify that *all* state court defendants charged with *serious* offenses had a due process right to government-appointed assistance. Alternatively, it could be understood to grant a more limited right to state-provided counsel only in all capital cases.[33] Indeed, because the Court specifically restricted its holding regarding the right to appointed counsel to the specific facts of the *Powell* case—a capital charge against young black men who were ignorant and illiterate and far from home—it was arguable that the due process right to counsel in state court was exceedingly narrow, extending only to those extreme cases that involve identical or substantially similar facts.

Six years later, the Supreme Court held that the explicit right to counsel granted by the Sixth Amendment "withholds from Federal Courts, in *all criminal proceedings*, the power and authority to deprive an accused of his life or liberty unless he has or waives the assistance of counsel" (Johnson v. Zerbst, 1938) (italics added). According to *Zerbst*, unless a defendant has the assistance of counsel or validly waives his right to assistance, a court lacks jurisdiction to impose a conviction. For accused persons who want but cannot afford to have counsel, the *federal* government must furnish a lawyer. Unlike the rule announced in *Powell*, the rule endorsed by the Court was clearly one of widespread application. The Sixth Amendment entitlement to appointed assistance identified in *Zerbst* did not hinge on the particular facts of a case—the nature of the charges or the deficiencies of the defendant.[34]

Just four years later, in 1942, the Court returned to the question of a state court defendant's entitlement to appointed assistance. After first observing that "the Fourteenth Amendment [Due Process Clause] does not incorporate, as such, the specific guarantees found in the Sixth Amendment," the Court rejected a claim that due process "demands that in every criminal case, whatever the circumstances, a state must furnish counsel to an indigent defendant" (Betts v. Brady, 1942). The Court ruled, instead, that the due process right of indigent state defendants to appointed assistance extends *only* to those whose trials would be *fundamentally unfair* in the absence of counsel. Whether a trial without counsel would be fundamentally unfair depended on all the facts of a case, including the complexity of the issues, the abilities of the accused, and the consequences of conviction. According to the *Betts* Court, the Constitution required a state to provide counsel for the accused only when an individualized determination, based on the specific facts of a case, established that legal representation was necessary to guarantee a fair trial.[35]

Twenty-one years passed before the Court revisited the issue of appointed counsel in state trials. The result was probably the most significant and best-known decision in the history of American right to counsel law—Gideon v. Wainwright. In this landmark 1963 ruling, the Supreme Court concluded that its earlier decision in *Betts* was " 'an anachronism when handed down' " and unanimously decided that it should be overruled. The Court agreed with the basic premise of *Betts*—that due process requires states to respect all provisions of the Bill of Rights that are "fundamental and essential to a fair trial." It concluded, however, that the Sixth Amendment's guarantee of counsel "is . . . one of these fundamental rights." Consequently, the broad right to appointed counsel that is granted by the Sixth Amendment is also included in the Fourteenth Amendment. Whenever an accused would be entitled to appointed assistance in a federal criminal proceeding, that same defendant has a due process right to appointed counsel in a state trial.[36]

In all three decisions recognizing a constitutional right of indigents to have government-appointed representation, the reasoning underlying the Court's conclusions was similar. That reasoning rests on the critical roles played by lawyers in the proper functioning of the adversary system and is best captured by two classic passages from those opinions. In Powell v. Alabama, Justice Sutherland observed that

> [t]he right to be heard would be, in many cases, of little avail if it did not comprehend the right to be heard by counsel. Even the intelligent and educated layman has small and sometimes no skill in the science of law. If charged with crime, he is incapable, generally, of determining for himself whether the indictment is good or bad. He is unfamiliar with

the rules of evidence. Left without the aid of counsel he may be put on trial without a proper charge, and convicted upon incompetent evidence, or evidence irrelevant to the issue or otherwise inadmissible. He lacks both the skill and knowledge adequately to prepare his defense, even though he have a perfect one. He requires the guiding hand of counsel at every step in the proceedings against him. Without it, though he be not guilty, he faces the danger of conviction because he does not know how to establish his innocence.

In *Gideon*, Justice Black asserted that

reason and reflection require[d the Court] to recognize that in our adversary system of criminal justice, any person haled into court, who is too poor to hire a lawyer cannot be assured a fair trial unless counsel is provided for him. This seems to us to be an obvious truth. . . . Lawyers to prosecute are everywhere deemed essential to protect the public's interest in an orderly society. Similarly, there are few defendants charged with crime, few indeed, who fail to hire the best lawyers they can get to prepare and present their defenses. That government hires lawyers to prosecute and defendants who have the money hire lawyers to defend are the strongest indications of the wide-spread belief that lawyers in criminal courts are necessities, not luxuries. The right of one charged with crime to counsel may not be deemed fundamental and essential to fair trials in some countries, but it is in ours. From the very beginning, our state and national constitutions and laws have laid great emphasis on procedural and substantive safeguards designed to assure fair trials before impartial tribunals in which every defendant stands equal before the law. This noble ideal cannot be realized if the poor man charged with crime has to face his accusers without a lawyer to assist him.[37]

Nothing in the *Zerbst* or *Gideon* opinions restricted the right to appointed assistance to indigents charged with particular kinds of offenses. However, both cases did involve prosecutions for felonies, that is, offenses with potential sentences in excess of one year in prison. In subsequent opinions, the Court has refined and clarified the law. Today, the categorical Sixth and Fourteenth Amendment rights to government-appointed counsel announced in *Zerbst* and *Gideon* govern *only* felony prosecutions (Nichols v. United States, 1994; Scott v. Illinois, 1979). For misdemeanor charges, the constitutional entitlement to appointed assistance is more limited.

The Right to Appointed Counsel in Misdemeanor Prosecutions

By the terms of the Sixth Amendment, the right to the assistance of counsel extends to "*all* criminal prosecutions." According to one view, this language unambiguously indicates that the right to appointed counsel extends to *every* indigent criminal defendant prosecuted for a crime, no matter the nature of the charge or circumstances of the case (Scott v. Illinois, 1979 (Brennan, J., dissenting)).[38] The Supreme Court, however, has rejected that literal interpretation of the Sixth Amendment's terms. According to a majority of the Court, the recognition of any right to appointed counsel was itself a departure from the original intent of that guarantee—to grant to accused persons an entitlement to retain legal assistance in criminal prosecutions. Because the Framers used the word "all" in a provision designed to afford a right only for *those with means to retain* assistance, the plain meaning of that term cannot dispositively answer the question whether all *indigents* have a constitutional right to *appointed* counsel (Scott v. Illinois, 1979). Guidance—and an answer—had to be found beyond the literal words of the Constitution.

In interpreting the reach of the entitlement to state-appointed legal assistance, a number of possibilities emerged. Each of them assumed first that every person accused of a felony had a right to appointment. They differed over the breadth of the right to government-provided counsel for those accused of misdemeanors. One extreme position was that the Constitution affords appointed assistance only to those charged with felonies and not to any indigents accused of misdemeanors. Another view was that the right to state-provided aid extends to misdemeanor proceedings that would be fundamentally unfair in the absence of counsel. An individualized determination would have to be made based on the facts and circumstances of each case. Other possibilities were that those charged with misdemeanors that carry imprisonment as an "authorized" penalty or those charged with "serious" misdemeanors—misdemeanors that could result in sentences greater than six months of imprisonment—are entitled to government-furnished lawyers. Finally, it was possible that only indigents who suffer actual imprisonment as a result of a misdemeanor trial and conviction have a constitutional right to have the state provide representation.

Several of these interpretations of the Constitution gained support from individual Supreme Court Justices. Justice Powell, for example, espoused an individualized, case-by-case approach that would determine whether fundamental fairness required appointed counsel for one accused of a misdemeanor (Argersinger v. Hamlin, 1972 (Powell, J., concurring)).[39] Justice Brennan contended that an "authorized imprisonment" approach made the most sense; whenever prison was a possibility, an indigent person accused of a misdemeanor would receive assistance (Scott v. Illinois, 1979 (Brennan, J., dissenting)).[40] Justice Blackmun asserted that the right to state-furnished legal aid ought to extend to any charge for which more than six months in prison was an authorized penalty—to serious misdemeanors—and to any lesser charge that resulted in actual imprisonment (Scott v. Illinois, 1979 (Blackmun, J., dissenting)). None of these views, however, could attract sufficient support to prevail. Instead, a majority coalesced around the "actual imprisonment" dividing line—that is, that the Constitution guarantees state-funded legal assistance only for those convicted of misdemeanors and sentenced to serve actual time in jail (Scott v. Illinois, 1979).

Historically, those accused of felonies had a less generous entitlement to legal assistance than those accused of misdemeanors (Argersinger v. Hamlin, 1972; United States v. Ash, 1972).[41] Today, the opposite is true. Indigents charged with misdemeanor-grade offenses—typically, those offenses with authorized punishment of no more than one year in prison—are constitutionally entitled to have lawyers appointed to represent them if, but only if, the result of the proceeding is a term of actual imprisonment. In misdemeanor prosecutions, both "the Sixth and Fourteenth Amendments . . . require only that no indigent criminal defendant be sentenced to a term of imprisonment unless the State has afforded him the right to assistance of appointed counsel in his defense" (Scott v. Illinois, 1979). Any amount of imprisonment will suffice to trigger the right, but if the sanction imposed upon conviction is a fine, a term of probation, or any other penalty that does not involve "actual" jail time, an indigent accused has no constitutional entitlement to appointed representation.

Scott v. Illinois, the case that fixed the dividing line at "actual imprisonment," involved an indigent man who was charged with theft based on a shoplifting incident. The charge was a misdemeanor punishable by a $500 fine or one year in jail or both. After the judge denied a request for appointed counsel, the defendant was convicted and sentenced to pay a $50 fine. The Supreme Court rejected the argument that he had a constitutional right to counsel, concluding that for misdemeanor charges, only "actual imprisonment" required the state to appoint counsel. The "central premise" of the Court's holding was that "actual imprisonment is a penalty different in kind from fines or the mere threat of imprisonment." While incarceration is "so severe a sanction that it should not be imposed as a result of a criminal trial unless an indigent defendant ha[s] been offered appointed counsel to assist in his defense," other penalties are not sufficiently onerous to require the government to furnish a legal assistant. Sanctions that do not involve incarceration can be imposed based on trials conducted without appointed counsel (Scott v. Illinois, 1979).

In essence, the Court decided that the core objective of both the Sixth and Fourteenth Amendments—fundamental fairness—can be achieved without providing an indigent with legal aid if the consequence of conviction is something less "severe" than prison time. Even though risks are present whenever an untrained layperson confronts a prosecutor and the legal system, if the state does not send the accused to jail upon conviction, those risks do not compromise the fairness of the trial. According to this view, the nature of the sanction imposed upon the defendant is a critical variable in determining whether a proceeding is fundamentally fair. A greater risk of error in the verdict and a less balanced trial process are constitutionally acceptable *if* the state forgoes the "severe sanction" of incarceration. Some have explained the *Scott* holding as resting on the premise that "the concern over *reliability* raised by the absence of counsel is tolerable when a defendant does not face the deprivation of his liberty" (Nichols v. United States, 1994 (Souter, J., concurring)) (italics added). Although a majority of the Court has not explicitly endorsed the "reliability" rationale, it does provide a constitutionally defensible foundation for the *Scott* Court's conclusion.

The actual imprisonment criterion for appointed assistance is rigid and absolute. No matter how brief the sentence of imprisonment for a misdemeanor, appointed counsel is required. On the other hand, apparently no other kind of sentence entitles any indigent defendant to a lawyer's aid. Not even the most ignorant, ill-equipped defendant has a constitutional right to appointed assistance if the state refrains from putting him behind bars. Even if the legal and factual issues in the case are exceptionally complex, the result is the same. Moreover, the magnitude of the nonimprisonment penalty does not alter the outcome. Large monetary penalties do not trigger the constitutional right. Restrictive probation conditions do not dictate a different result. (However, a violation of those conditions that leads to the revocation of probation cannot result in jail time.) Demanding community service obligations do not require the appointment of defense counsel. Only actual imprisonment matters. With it, appointed counsel must be offered. Without it, an indigent accused must go it alone.

The decision to so limit the constitutional right to government-funded representation for misdemeanor accusations has not gone unchallenged. Some believe that most, if not all, misdemeanants should be constitutionally entitled to appointed counsel for the same reasons that fairness in the adversary system demands appointed counsel for felony prosecutions.[42] They contend that some penalties are more burdensome than a short time in jail and are simply too onerous to be imposed based on a trial whose reliability is compromised by the absence of defense counsel. They maintain that the stigma of any criminal conviction and that the collateral consequences of a criminal record for a person's life and future are unjustifiable absent a process that includes counsel.[43] In addition, they argue that some misdemeanor prosecutions are so complex that the absence of counsel fatally undermines the reliability of the process and result (Argersinger v. Hamlin, 1972 (Powell, J., concurring in the result)). A misdemeanor conviction based on such a grossly imbalanced contest is fundamentally unfair, no matter how light the sanction. One concern that motivated a majority of the Court to reject these and other arguments was a belief that a more expansive entitlement to appointed counsel would impose untoward financial burdens on governments. The costs that states would have to sustain if they were constitutionally required to provide counsel to all or most indigents accused of misdemeanors factored into the *Scott* Court's analysis.[44]

One oddity of the constitutional standard chosen by the Court is that trial judges who are deciding whether to appoint counsel must make a preliminary sentencing determination before misdemeanor trials. Some contend that this puts the cart before the horse—sentence first, trial later (Scott v. Illinois, 1979 (Brennan, J., dissenting)). In essence, a judge must at least decide whether it is possible that she will want to sentence a particular defendant to jail time upon conviction.[45] If so, to preserve that option, she must appoint counsel. Otherwise, a jail sentence will be foreclosed. The only sentences available upon conviction will be those that do not entail incarceration, for if an indigent defendant is denied counsel and convicted, a sentence of imprisonment is constitutionally invalid and must be vacated.

Scott held that the state need not *appoint* counsel for indigents in misdemeanor cases not resulting in imprisonment. The Court's conclusion had no direct bearing on the entitlement to retained counsel. The right to retain assistance in misdemeanor cases that do not lead to imprisonment has not yet been challenged in the Supreme Court. One could argue that an accused with the means to secure private representation has no constitutional right to retain an attorney in any case where an indigent is not entitled to appointed assistance. Logically, the basic premise underlying *Scott*—that an uncounseled misdemeanor trial is sufficiently fair if a defendant is not incarcerated—could support the conclusion that a defendant with funds has no entitlement to representation at a misdemeanor trial if conviction is not sanctioned by time in jail. Nonetheless, based on the 1954 holding that a defendant has an "unqualified" due process right to retain counsel (Chandler v. Fretag, 1954) and the Sixth Amendment's original intent to grant a right to retain assistance in "all criminal prosecutions," it seems likely that the Court would conclude that both state and federal defendants have a right to retain legal assistance in every criminal case.[46]

A number of federal and state statutes provide for increases in the classification of and the sentences for offenses based on past convictions. A "recidivist" statute, for example, might provide that a misdemeanor offense punishable by no more than one year in prison is elevated to a felony offense punishable by up to three years in prison if the state proves a prior conviction for the same offense. (For an illustration, see Baldasar v. Illinois, 1980.) Alternatively, a sentencing scheme might provide that a prior conviction of some sort elevates an accused into a "criminal history" category that authorizes a period of imprisonment two years greater than would have been permissible without that conviction (Nichols v. United States, 1994). One question that arose in the wake of *Scott* was whether an uncounseled conviction that was valid because the accused was not sentenced to imprisonment at the time could properly be used later to enhance a sentence imposed upon conviction for a subsequent offense.[47]

In 1980, just one year after it decided *Scott*, the Supreme Court addressed the issue of whether an uncounseled misdemeanor conviction could be used to increase a sentence under a recidivism provision. In Baldasar v. Illinois, a badly divided Court reversed a lower court ruling that had permitted enhancement use of a misdemeanor conviction. While five members of the Court approved of the result, there was no rationale upon which all of them agreed (Nichols v. United States, 1994). For fourteen years, the significance of the result and opinions in *Baldasar* were much debated by the judiciary. Some lower courts concluded that the decision meant that an uncounseled conviction could never be used to increase a period of confinement for a subsequent offense. Others concluded that the constitutional restriction imposed by *Baldasar* was quite narrow and that valid, uncounseled misdemeanor convictions often could be used to increase later sentences of imprisonment.

In 1994, in Nichols v. United States, the Court settled the dispute. After concluding that the meaning of the *Baldasar* opinions was unclear, a majority overruled the decision and held that under the Sixth and Fourteenth Amendments "an uncounseled misdemeanor conviction, valid under *Scott* because no prison term was imposed, is also valid when used to enhance punishment at a subsequent conviction." According to the Court, enhancement statutes, no matter their nature, "do not change the penalty imposed for the earlier conviction" but merely rely on the earlier conviction to determine what the appropriate punishment is for the present conviction. The limited holding of *Scott* is *only* that an uncounseled misdemeanor conviction cannot *itself* be punished with imprisonment. *Scott* does not prevent the government from using such a conviction to justify the magnitude of the sentence that a defendant deserves for a subsequent conviction. The apparent message of *Nichols* is that if a conviction is initially valid under *Scott*, any future use of that conviction against the accused is constitutionally permissible.

The *Nichols* majority reasoned, further, that enhancement of a sentence based on a prior, uncounseled misdemeanor conviction not only was consistent with the principles underlying *Scott* but was also "consistent with the traditional understanding of the sentencing process." As a general rule, sentencing judges may increase sentences on the basis of a wide variety of factors. They may rely on both prior convictions and prior criminal conduct that has not even resulted in a conviction. For sentencing purposes, prior criminal conduct has to be proven only "by a preponderance of the evidence"—that is, it only needs to be established that the defendant more likely than not committed the criminal act. If it is proper to increase a sentence based on proof of conduct by a preponderance of the evidence, then it must also be proper to increase a sentence based on criminal conduct proven *beyond a reasonable doubt* at an uncounseled misdemeanor trial.

Not all on the Court agreed with the reasoning or conclusion in *Nichols*. Three dissenting Justices would have barred enhancement of a sentence based on a prior, uncounseled conviction. They contended that a prohibition on enhancement was the only result that could logically be reconciled with the reasoning that supported the Court's holding in *Scott*. In their view, a conviction after trial without counsel cannot lead to imprisonment because it is simply too *unreliable*—too likely to be an inaccurate reflection of the accused's criminal past—to support "the severe sanction of incarceration." In their view, if a conviction is not reliable enough to justify jail time initially, it is not reliable enough to support additional jail time for a subsequent offense.

The Right to Choose Appointed Counsel, the Meaning of Indigency, and the Recoupment of Costs from Indigents

Unlike those who retain their own counsel, indigents do not have a constitutional right to choose the lawyer who will represent them (Caplin & Drysdale v. United States, 1989).[48] As long as appointed counsel performs her duties adequately, a defendant cannot succeed with a claim that he would have preferred representation by a different government-provided lawyer. One likely rationale for this limitation is that an attorney who is not the choice of the defendant can still play the role contemplated by the Constitution and ensure a fair trial. Moreover, honoring a presumption in favor of choice for indigents could generate unacceptable administrative burdens and costs in criminal justice systems already taxed to their limits.[49]

The constitutional right to appointed counsel hinges on "indigency."[50] Because the demand to appoint counsel is constitutional in nature, the question of who qualifies as indigent must ultimately be answered by the Sixth and Fourteenth Amendments. The Court has never confronted that question directly.[51] As a result, the constitutional indigency standard is uncertain. We do not know what level of resources separates the indigent from the nonindigent or whether certain assets that can be liquidated must be counted in deciding whether an individual qualifies for state-provided assistance. In the absence of definitive constitutional guidance, answers to these questions have been dictated by statute.

A state may attempt to recover the costs of providing defense to an indigent without running afoul of the Sixth Amendment. At least some "recoupment" provisions are valid.[52] Fuller v. Oregon involved a state provision that allowed a judge to require a convicted defendant to repay the costs of providing him a legal defense. The obligation to repay the expenses could be imposed only on defendants who were or would be able to pay them. Defendants with no likelihood of obtaining sufficient funds to pay back the costs could not be put under even a conditional obligation to repay them. Moreover, those with conditional obligations to repay could be subjected to collection procedures only if their indigency had ended and if no "manifest hardship" would result from requiring them to pay. In sum, "the obligation to repay the State accrue[d] only to those who later acquire[d] the means to do so without hardship" (Fuller v. Oregon, 1974).

In *Fuller*, an indigent defendant pleaded guilty to a sex offense and was sentenced to five years of probation. His probation was conditioned, in part, on repayment to the county of the fees and expenses of the attorney and investigator who had been provided to him. He challenged the Oregon recoupment provision, claiming first that it violated the Equal Protection Clause of the Fourteenth Amendment. The Court concluded that the statutory distinction that allowed imposition of an obligation to repay only on those *convicted* of an offense did not violate equal protection principles because it created a "noninvidious" and rational classification. The defendant also contended that the recoupment provision unconstitutionally "chilled" an indigent's exercise of his right to appointed assistance. A defendant might be deterred from requesting or accepting appointed counsel by the prospect of a future obligation to repay the state. The Court also repudiated this argument, finding that the state's effort to recoup expenses was fully consistent with Gideon v. Wainwright's promise of legal assistance for those unable to afford it. According to the Court, Oregon's law complied with the constitutional command to provide counsel to all indigents; an accused's knowledge that he may someday have to repay the costs of legal services "in no way affect[ed] his eligibility to obtain counsel." Moreover, the statute was "carefully designed to insure that only those who actually become capable of repaying the State [would] ever be obliged to do so." In sum, recoupment statutes that provide for repayment by convicted indigent defendants who later become able to pay the costs of their appointed attorneys without hardship are fully consistent with the Sixth and Fourteenth Amendment rights to appointed counsel.

Waiver of the Right to Counsel and the Constitutional Right of Self-Representation

This section addresses two significant topics pertaining to the nature of the constitutional right to counsel—waiver of that right and the constitutional right to represent oneself in a criminal trial. The subjects are addressed together because they are inextricably related. One who chooses to waive the right to legal representation will, of necessity, engage in self-representation. Moreover, an acceptable choice to exercise the right of self-representation requires a valid waiver of the Sixth Amendment right to assistance.

Waiver of the Right to Counsel

Like almost all constitutional rights, the right to the assistance of counsel can be waived (Johnson v. Zerbst, 1938). An accused individual does not have to exercise the entitlement to a retained or appointed lawyer. Rather, a defendant has the power to choose to forgo all the benefits associated with this most fundamental right. Thus, while the Sixth Amendment provides counsel as an essential guarantee of fundamental fairness in the adversarial criminal process, "the Constitution does not force a lawyer upon a defendant" (Adams v. United States *ex rel.* McCann, 1942).

The critical nature of the right to the assistance of counsel requires judges to presume that defendants have not decided to waive that right (Johnson v. Zerbst, 1938). The burden of overcoming that presumption falls upon the government (Michigan v. Jackson, 1986). The state must establish that an accused has validly chosen to surrender the entitlement to equalizing assistance (Godinez v. Moran, 1993). The standards for judging waivers are clear. A waiver is constitutionally acceptable only when it constitutes "an intentional relinquishment or abandonment of a known right or privilege" (Johnson v. Zerbst, 1938).[53] Moreover, an accused must be mentally "competent" to waive the right and must actually make a "knowing and voluntary" waiver of counsel's assistance (Godinez v. Moran, 1993).

The requirement of an "intentional relinquishment" means that the accused must have made a purposeful decision to surrender the entitlement to legal representation. A mere failure to demand or request assistance does not constitute a waiver. At a minimum, there must be evidence showing that a failure to obtain or ask for representation reflects a conscious, deliberate decision to forgo the right to a lawyer's help (Brewer v. Williams, 1977). A determination of whether an accused is competent to waive the right to counsel requires an inquiry into the accused's "mental capacity." The general question is whether the defendant "has the ability to understand the proceedings." More specifically, an accused is competent if he " 'has sufficient present ability to consult with his lawyer with a reasonable degree of rational understanding' and [has] 'a rational as well as factual understanding of the proceedings against him' " (Godinez v. Moran, 1993 (quoting Dusky v. United States, 1960). This competence standard is identical to the standard used to determine a defendant's mental competence to stand trial at all. One need have only *competence to waive* the assistance of counsel. Competence to conduct one's defense ably or to defend one's interests adequately is not necessary. In fact, the ability to represent oneself effectively "has no bearing upon . . . competence to" waive counsel (Godinez v. Moran, 1993).[54]

To be valid, a waiver must be sufficiently "knowing" (Faretta v. California, 1975). An accused who wishes to surrender the right to counsel "should be made aware of the dangers and disadvantages of self-representation, so that the record will establish that 'he knows what he is doing and his choice is made with eyes open' " (Faretta v. California, 1975 (quoting Adams v. United States *ex rel.* McCann, 1942)). The question here is whether an accused who is competent to understand actually does understand the significance and consequences of the decision to forgo an equalizing assistant (Godinez v. Moran, 1993). Adequate awareness and comprehension of the existence and nature of the Sixth Amendment right to assistance are essential for a waiver to be acceptable (Von Moltke v. Gillies, 1948 (plurality opinion)).[55] It is often said that a waiver must also be "intelligent" (Faretta v. California, 1975; Johnson v. Zerbst, 1938). The use of this term is potentially misleading and confusing. A waiver never has been deemed unacceptable because it was not a smart or wise decision under the circumstances. If surrenders of the right to representation had to be "intelligent" in that sense, it is doubtful that many would survive, for in all but the rarest of cases wisdom militates against waiving the fundamental right to counsel. The term "intelligent" is probably best understood as a shorthand expression for the requirement that the defendant must have sufficient cognizance and understanding of the character of the right being relinquished.

The precise things that an accused must be aware of and the depth of comprehension required are both uncertain. Four members of the Court once opined that a valid waiver requires "an apprehension of the nature of the charges, the statutory offenses included within them, the range of allowable punishments thereunder, possible defenses to the charges and circumstances in mitigation thereof, and all other facts essential to a broad understanding of the whole matter" (Von Moltke v. Gillies, 1948). A majority of the Court, however, has refrained from prescribing the specific knowledge necessary. There is no approved catalogue of the "dangers and disadvantages" of which an accused must be aware, no guiding explanation of how "open" the defendant's "eyes" must be. As a consequence, there has been considerable debate in the lower courts about the nature and quantity of the "knowledge" needed to validly waive counsel.

The "voluntariness" demand for a valid waiver is satisfied when the decision to forgo assistance is "uncoerced" (Godinez v. Moran, 1993). Thus, a waiver is "involuntary" and invalid only if it is the product of "coercion." In the "involuntary confession" and *Miranda* contexts, the Supreme Court has endorsed the identical definition of voluntariness—a confession or waiver of *Miranda* rights is voluntary only when it is the result of official coercion or pressure brought to bear on the suspect (Colorado v. Connelly, 1986). There is no reason to believe that the Court intends voluntariness to have a different meaning in the waiver of counsel setting. Consequently, a surrender of counsel is voluntary unless it is the product of undue pressures brought to bear by government officials—pressures that "overbear the will" of the defendant. A decision to forgo counsel that is the product of purely subjective, internal forces that induce an accused to act against his will qualifies as voluntary. Thus, for example, even though an accused has a severe mental illness that prevents his decision from being a free and rational one, his waiver is still voluntary. An accused's individual vulnerabilities and weaknesses do factor into the voluntariness equation, but a waiver is invalid because it is involuntary only if there is sufficient external, government-generated pressure to break the particular defendant's will.

Waiver determinations are governed by a "totality of the circumstances" standard. This means that in making the essential determinations—actual relinquishment, mental competence, adequacy of knowledge, and voluntariness—all of the particular facts and circumstances of the case, "including the background, experience, and conduct of the accused," must be taken into account (Johnson v. Zerbst). When deciding whether the government has proven a valid waiver by "a preponderance of the evidence" (Colorado v. Connelly, 1986), a judge must take into consideration any information that is logically relevant to each of these required and discrete inquiries.

A significant question regarding waiver of the right to counsel is whether a trial court must follow any particular procedural steps in order to ensure that the accused has made a constitutionally acceptable choice to forgo assistance. As will be seen later, the Sixth Amendment provides a right to assistance at various stages of the criminal process—at informal and formal pretrial stages, at trial and sentencing, and on appeal. A waiver of any of these entitlements to counsel is possible. Moreover, the same substantive standards govern the validity of all surrenders of the Sixth Amendment right—the defendant's choice must be a knowing and voluntary relinquishment. At least in informal pretrial settings—government efforts to elicit incriminating statements or to secure eyewitness identifications of an accused—there is no need for officials to provide detailed information or conduct an extensive inquiry (Patterson v. Illinois, 1988). For waivers of the right to assistance of counsel *at trial*—and quite possibly for waivers of the right in formal pretrial settings (e.g., preliminary hearings) and on appeal—the Constitution demands more process.

In Johnson v. Zerbst, the Court observed that because the duty to protect the vital right to counsel's assistance imposes on trial judges the responsibility of determining whether a valid waiver has been made, it is "fitting and appropriate for that determination *to appear upon the record*" (Johnson v. Zerbst, 1938) (italics added). Ten years later, four members of the Court would have saddled trial courts with the "solemn duty" to make a "thorough inquiry." Those Justices asserted that trial judges have obligations to "investigate . . . long and . . . thoroughly" and to conduct "a penetrating and comprehensive examination of all the circumstances" to ensure that a constitutionally acceptable choice has been made (Von Moltke v. Gillies, 1948). In Faretta v. California, a majority of the Court opined that the accused "*should be made aware* of the dangers and disadvantages" of trial without counsel "*so that the record will establish* that 'he knows what he is doing and his choice is made with eyes open' " (Faretta v. California, 1975 (quoting Adams *ex rel.* McCann, 1942)) (italics added). These opinions provided the foundation for the later declaration, in Patterson v. Illinois, that a waiver of the right to trial assistance "require[s] a more searching or formal inquiry." According to the Court, there are "rigorous restrictions on the information that must be conveyed to a defendant, and the procedures that must be observed, before" a waiver of the "right to counsel at trial" is acceptable (Patterson v. Illinois, 1988). The *Patterson* Court clearly understood the *Faretta* and *Von Moltke* opinions as mandates that a certain amount of process is a prerequisite for a valid waiver of trial counsel.

The Court has never specified the particular steps that a trial judge must take to ensure that a waiver is acceptable. It has not prescribed the "information that must be conveyed to the defendant" or the "procedures that must be observed." This failure to prescribe the nature of the "searching or formal inquiry" that is "require[d]" has prompted a difference of opinion in the lower courts. Some have concluded that trial courts have the obligation to recite prescribed litanies of the dangers and disadvantages of forgoing counsel and are duty-bound to inquire into certain pertinent matters in every case. Although these courts do not agree on the particular information that must be conveyed to the accused or the specific questions that a judge must ask, they do agree that a waiver is invalid if the necessary steps are not taken. Other courts have decided that a waiver can be constitutionally acceptable even if a trial judge does not provide the accused with detailed information or inquire extensively about his understanding. In their view, as long as the record includes evidentiary bases for finding the essential components of a valid waiver, a failure to adhere to a particular process will not invalidate a waiver of trial assistance.[56]

The latter view seems inconsistent with the *Patterson* Court's conclusion that a "searching or formal inquiry" is "require[d]." The *Patterson* Court acknowledged that there is a constitutional obligation to furnish a certain amount of information to a defendant and to clear certain procedural hurdles. Unfortunately, the Court neglected to specify either the nature of the information that has to be conveyed to an accused or the particular procedures that have to be observed. In the absence of more detailed guidance, the lower courts will undoubtedly continue to disagree over the character of the process that the Sixth Amendment demands for a valid surrender of representation at trial.

Because there has been no dispute over the constitutional propriety of allowing an individual accused of even the most serious of crimes to waive the right to counsel, there has been almost no discussion of the reasons for allowing a defendant to forgo this critical right. Perhaps the best explanation of why an accused is permitted to relinquish so fundamental a protection is that the alternative—a prohibition on waivers and insistence that an accused exercise the right to counsel—would "imprison a man in his privileges and call it the Constitution" (Adams v. United States *ex rel.* McCann, 1942). Like the other vital adversary system safeguards contained in the Sixth Amendment, the entitlement to counsel is a tool for self-defense offered to those accused of crimes for their own benefits. It is not an invariable prescription of how our society will conduct trials. Those subject to prosecution may accept the advantages of counsel if they wish. There is nothing constitutionally offensive, however, about empowering them to choose whether they wish to "enjoy" or forgo the benefits of legal representation. To categorically reject informed, free choices by mentally competent individuals to relinquish the protection granted by the Constitution would convert "rights" into "obligations." That approach would be paternalistic and contrary to American notions of freedom.

The Constitutional Right of Self-Representation

The fact that an accused is *able* to waive a constitutional right ordinarily does not mean that he is *entitled* to waive that right, that is, that he has a constitutional "right" to relinquish the particular protection (Faretta v. California, 1975). While the Constitution does not require an accused to exercise his rights and permits the government to accept waivers, it does not require the government to allow or accept surrenders of those rights. Thus, the state may permit a defendant to waive the entitlement to trial by jury but also may reject an accused's effort to forgo jury trial and may insist on trial before a jury. A defendant has no constitutional right to waive the entitlement to a jury and to demand the opposite, trial before a judge (Singer v. United States, 1965).

The right to counsel, however, is dramatically different from other constitutional rights, for the Sixth Amendment provides not only an entitlement to be represented by a lawyer but also an affirmative right of self-representation. Put otherwise, an accused has a constitutional entitlement to dispense with the assistance of a lawyer—to waive counsel—and to conduct the defense personally (Faretta v. California, 1975).[57] The terms of the Sixth Amendment do not explicitly provide a right of self-representation. In Faretta v. California, however, a majority of the Supreme Court agreed with a defendant's claim that a trial judge's refusal to allow him to conduct his own defense had violated the implicit constitutional right to serve as his own representative.[58] The Court proffered many reasons to support this landmark interpretation of the Sixth Amendment.

First, federal and state laws reflected a "consensus," a "nearly universal conviction, on the part of our people . . . that forcing a lawyer upon an unwilling defendant is contrary to his basic right to defend himself." Moreover, that consensus "is soundly premised" in the "structure of the Sixth Amendment." The Sixth Amendment contains a compact statement of the rights necessary to make a full defense in our adversary system. Significantly, it extends these rights specifically to criminal defendants themselves, granting "*to the accused personally* the right to make his defense. . . . [T]he right of self-representation—to make one's own defense personally—is thus necessarily implied by the structure of the Amendment" (italics added). The explicit right to counsel "supplements" this general Sixth Amendment "design." A lawyer is provided as an "assistant." Like the other tools contained in that provision, counsel was meant to be an "aid to a willing defendant—not an organ of the State interposed between an unwilling defendant and his right to defend himself personally." Forcing a lawyer upon an accused violates the logic of the Sixth Amendment by making counsel a "master" and stripping the right to make a defense of its "personal character." Unless a defendant desires legal representation, the defense that he receives is "not the defense guaranteed by the Constitution for it is not his defense."[59]

According to the *Faretta* majority, the American consensus about self-representation is also deeply rooted in British and American legal history. With one anomalous exception—the infamous Star Chamber—the British never imposed counsel on criminal defendants. The common law practice was predominately self-representation, not representation by trained counsel, and the clear rule was that a person charged with an offense could not be forced to have a lawyer represent him. Americans fervently insisted on self-representation from the start and forged the Constitution in an atmosphere of appreciation for the virtues of self-reliance and distrust of lawyers. Even after they came to recognize the fundamental importance of counsel, the general practice continued to be self-representation. No state or colony ever required defendants to be represented by lawyers, and both federal and state laws explicitly recognized the right to conduct one's own defense.

One reason for concluding that the Sixth Amendment does not include a right of self-representation is that the text of that provision does not explicitly mention self-representation. Perhaps the most persuasive reason for disagreeing with the *Faretta* Court's conclusion, however, is the evident tension between that right and the premises of the landmark Supreme Court opinions that have deemed counsel to be fundamental and indispensable to the fair operation of our adversary system. The *Faretta* Court admitted that a personal right to conduct one's own defense cuts sharply "against the grain" of "decisions holding that the Constitution requires that no accused be convicted and imprisoned unless he has been accorded the right to the assistance of counsel." The "basic thesis of" those decisions is "that the help of a lawyer is essential to assure the defendant a fair trial." Indeed, in a recent decision, the Court observed that even though the right to represent oneself is " 'fundamental' in nature . . . experience has taught us that 'a *pro se* defense is usually a bad defense, particularly when compared to a defense provided by an experienced criminal defense attorney' " (Martinez v. Court of Appeal of California, 2000 (quoting Decker, "The Sixth Amendment Right to Shoot Oneself in the Foot: An Assessment of the Guarantee of Self-Representation Twenty Years after *Faretta*," 6 *Seton Hall Const. L.J.* 483, 598 (1996)). (*Pro se* literally means "for himself." In this context, it refers to a defense conducted by the accused himself without the assistance of counsel.) Arguably, it would have been irrational for the Framers of the Constitution to grant one right that is essential to a fair trial and, in the very same provision, provide another right that poses serious threats to the fairness of the proceeding.[60]

The *Faretta* Court concluded that despite the tension between self-representation and the right to counsel, it was not at all illogical for the Framers to include the right to represent oneself in the Sixth Amendment. According to the majority, the Framers did so because "they understood the inestimable worth of free choice." The Sixth Amendment, as a whole, reflects their belief that the accused "must be free to decide how to defend" and that her "choice must be honored out of that respect for the individual which is the lifeblood of the law.' " In essence, self-representation can logically coexist with a fundamental entitlement to counsel because the right of self-representation is rooted in and safeguards values distinct from the interest in conducting fair trials. Those values—individual freedom, dignity, and autonomy—rank higher than society's or the defendant's interest in ensuring the fairness of a trial.[61] Furthermore, the Court believed that the advantages of having a lawyer would be realized imperfectly, at best, if the accused did not want assistance and that there are rare instances in which self-representation will yield the "best defense" for an accused.

The right of self-representation is ample, but not absolute. An accused can exercise the right only if he "knowingly and intelligently forgoes his right to counsel" and if "he is able and willing to abide by rules of procedure and courtroom protocol" (McKaskle v. Wiggins, 1984). A defendant who cannot or will not provide a waiver that satisfies the standards for a valid surrender of counsel may not represent himself. On the other hand, if the accused is mentally competent and willing to provide a knowing and voluntary waiver, a judge cannot deny the choice of self-representation because the accused lacks legal skill, expertise, or experience. A defendant's "technical legal knowledge, as such, [is] not relevant to an assessment of his knowing exercise of the right to defend himself" (Faretta v. California, 1975).

The intent of conditioning the entitlement to self-representation on a defendant's ability and willingness "to abide by rules of procedure and courtroom protocol" is not entirely clear. Certainly, those who deliberately engage in "serious and obstructionist misconduct" in the courtroom need not be permitted to represent themselves (Faretta v. California, 1975). If there are others encompassed by the "unable or unwilling to abide" standard, others who can be denied the choice of self-representation, the Court has not specified who they are.

While a judge may not insist that a defendant be represented by a lawyer, in any case where a defendant has chosen to go *pro se*, the judge may appoint a lawyer to serve as "standby counsel" (Faretta v. California, 1975). Standby counsel can assist defendants who want help in constructing and presenting their defenses. Standby counsel can also step in and take over the defense of a case when termination of the right of self-representation is justified.

Because the Sixth Amendment requires a judge to allow an accused to conduct his own defense if he provides a valid waiver and is able and willing to abide by the rules, outright denial of a request to represent oneself clearly violates the Constitution. In addition, because the core of self-representation is the right to have one's voice heard, a defendant who is conducting his own defense "must be allowed to control the organization and content of his own defense, to make motions, to argue points of law, to participate in [jury selection], to question witnesses, and to address the court and the jury at appropriate points" (McKaskle v. Wiggins, 1984). Unjustified restrictions on an accused's efforts to make his voice heard are as constitutionally unacceptable as a total denial of the self-representation option.

In addition, the Sixth Amendment guarantees the accused "a fair chance to present his case in his own way," and the right of self-representation serves two purposes—it gives the accused "actual control" over the case that he chooses to present and affirms the accused's "dignity and autonomy." Consequently, the right of self-representation also includes protection against competition from standby counsel. Thus, a standby lawyer "must generally respect a defendant's preference to go it alone," and excessive, unwanted participation in the trial by standby counsel can violate the right to represent oneself. Counsel's participation is constitutionally objectionable if it either deprives the accused of control over the case or destroys or severely undermines the accused's appearance before the jury in the status of one representing himself (McKaskle v. Wiggins, 1984).

There is no "categorical bar," however, on undesired participation by standby lawyers. Participation is forbidden *only if* counsel's intrusions interfere with the accused's control or damage the accused's appearance, in jurors' eyes, as one who is representing himself. Moreover, some participation by standby counsel can never infringe upon the right to represent oneself. Even if unrequested, assistance "in overcoming routine procedural or evidentiary obstacles to the completion of some specific task" and help in ensuring that the accused complies with "basic rules of courtroom protocol and procedure" are constitutionally tolerable. In addition, if a defendant requests standby counsel's assistance, he cannot plausibly contend that the participation that he requested violated his *Faretta* rights. Furthermore, unless the accused makes it clear that he does not want further aid, a request for assistance from standby counsel will severely undermine claims that subsequent, unrequested actions by the lawyer violated the entitlement to self-representation (McKaskle v. Wiggins, 1984).[62] All of these limitations upon the fundamental right to self-representation rest on the fact that "the government's interest in ensuring the integrity and efficiency of the trial at times outweighs the defendant's interest in acting as his own lawyer" (Martinez v. Court of Appeal of California, 2000).

While an accused has independent rights to counsel and to self-representation and a judge may permit both rights to be exercised simultaneously, the Constitution does not afford a "hybrid" right to both counsel and self-representation (McKaskle v. Wiggins, 1984).[63] Put otherwise, a defendant has no Sixth Amendment entitlement to insist on partial representation by counsel and partial self-representation. A trial judge, therefore, may require the accused to choose one of the two entitlements and to forgo enjoyment of the other.

Logically, because the Sixth Amendment provides accused persons with the right to make their own defense personally and affords counsel as a supplement to this scheme, it is arguable that combined representation should be part and parcel of the constitutional entitlement. The best defense may involve trained counsel performing some functions and the lay accused performing others. The *McKaskle* Court did not offer reasons in support of the conclusion that such "hybrid" representation is not a constitutional entitlement.[64] One possible basis is a dearth of historical support for combined representation. Another is the fear that hybrid representation could be chaotic and contrary to the orderly administration of justice. A third concern may be that an accused could abuse the hybrid option. A defendant might in fact enjoy the full assistance of counsel, employing the facade of self-representation to make arguments that, in essence, would be "testimony" that could not be subjected to cross-examination by the prosecution. Finally, it has been suggested that it is demeaning to lawyers to be relegated to the role of co-counsel with an accused, called upon by the defendant to appear as needed.

A final, possible limitation on the *Faretta* right is a requirement of timely assertion. On the one hand, it is arguable that the autonomy interests that undergird the right to represent oneself require that a defendant be entitled to opt for *pro se* representation at any time before or during a trial. On the other hand, it is arguable that an accused should not be able to wait until the commencement of trial to assert the entitlement to self-representation unless he has good reason to do so. When a request is not made sufficiently ahead of time—how long before trial is uncertain—it may be constitutional to force the defendant to accept representation by counsel. The *Faretta* Court hinted at a timeliness concern by referring twice to the fact that the defendant's request in that case had been made well before the beginning of the trial. More recently, the Court has observed that "most courts require" a defendant to "elect to conduct his own defense . . . in a timely manner" (Martinez v. Court of Appeal of California, 2000).[65] Although the Court has not yet decided that a denial of self-representation based on a tardy assertion can be constitutional, there is good reason to believe that it would approve of the lower courts' practice, for a timeliness limitation on the *pro se* right furthers "the government's interest in ensuring the integrity and efficiency of the trial" (Martinez v. Court of Appeal of California, 2000).

In sum, the Sixth Amendment includes two fundamental rights—a right to the assistance of counsel and its opposite, a right to dispense with the assistance of defense counsel and conduct one's own defense. In Martinez v. Court of Appeal of California, a recent decision rejecting a claim that convicted defendants have a right to represent themselves on appeal, the Court cast some aspersions on the *Faretta* Court's historical reasoning and the *pro se* right that it recognized. According to Martinez,

> the historical evidence relied upon by Faretta . . . is not always useful because it pertained to times when lawyers were scarce, often mistrusted, and not readily available to the average person accused of a crime. For one who could not obtain a lawyer, self-representation was the only feasible alternative to asserting no defense at all.

Moreover, "[n]o one, including . . . the Faretta majority, attempts to argue that as a rule *pro se* representation is wise, desirable or efficient," and, "it is clear that it is representation by counsel that is the standard, not the exception" (Martinez v. Court of Appeal of California, 2000). Nonetheless, the *Martinez* Court acknowledged that the *Faretta* Court had found self-representation to be a "fundamental" constitutional right, and its opinion cast no doubt on the legitimacy of most of *Faretta*'s underpinnings. It seems highly unlikely that the Court will revisit the issue of the constitutional status of self-representation. Consequently, accused persons will continue to have the choice to be assisted by trained defense lawyers or to serve as their own representatives.

The Allocation of Decision-Making Authority between Counsel and the Accused

An Introduction to the Issues and a General Summary of the Law

This final subsection concerning the nature of the constitutional right to counsel addresses the allocation of decision-making authority between the defendant and his attorney. A threshold choice that certainly belongs to the accused is whether to have the assistance of counsel or to represent himself. If an accused exercises his constitutional entitlement to conduct the defense personally, the authority to make all further decisions regarding the defense is his. Most defendants, however, wisely choose to be represented by trained defense attorneys. The issues considered here are whether the accused who opts for representation by counsel has any decision-making authority, and, if so, how much authority he has.[66] Does the represented defendant have a constitutional right to make whatever decisions he wishes to make? Does the authority to make all decisions instead shift to counsel? Or does the Constitution divide decision-making power, granting some to the accused and some to counsel? While Supreme Court authority concerning these issues is limited, the relevant opinions do provide adequate bases for general conclusions regarding the constitutional allocation of decision-making authority. (If the Constitution included an entitlement to "hybrid" representation—partial representation by counsel and partial self-representation—a defendant would have plenary decision-making authority even when he chose the assistance of counsel. Whenever a defendant wished to dictate a choice, he could elect to act as his own representative. As explained in the preceding subsection, however, the Court has concluded that an accused may be compelled to choose between counsel and self-representation, that is, that there is no right to enjoy both rights simultaneously.[67] As a result, the allocation issues highlighted here arise.)

One view holds that even when a defendant is represented by counsel, he possesses the constitutional authority to make many, if not most, significant defense decisions. This view rests on the notion "that the function of counsel under the Sixth Amendment is to protect the dignity and autonomy of the person on trial by *assisting* him in making choices that are his to make, not to make choices for him" (Jones v. Barnes, 1983 (Brennan, J., dissenting) (italics added). Proponents believe that the "role of the defense lawyer [is] above all to function as the instrument and defender of the client's autonomy and dignity in all phases of the criminal process" (Jones v. Barnes, 1983 (Brennan, J., dissenting)). While they would not require counsel to involve the defendant in making all the routine tactical and strategic choices that arise during the defense of a criminal case, they would require defense attorneys to proffer advice but defer to the defendant's wishes on many, if not all, significant questions.[68]

A majority of the Supreme Court has rejected this position. The prevailing view is that an accused who makes the choice to be represented by a lawyer effectively surrenders most of the decision-making authority that he otherwise would have had and has no constitutional entitlement to make the vast majority of choices involved in conducting the defense.[69] A represented defendant has "the ultimate authority to make" only a small number of "fundamental decisions regarding his case" (Jones v. Barnes, 1983). "Only such basic decisions as whether to plead guilty, waive a jury, . . . testify in one's own behalf," or take an appeal "are ultimately for the accused to make" (Wainwright v. Sykes, 1977). For all of the other "many decisions pertaining to the conduct of the trial, the defendant is 'deemed bound by the acts of his lawyer-agent and is considered to have "notice of all facts, notice of which can be charged upon the attorney" ' " (New York v. Hill, 2000 (quoting Link v. Wabash R. Co., 1962 (quoting Smith v. Ayer, 1879))). Both "law and tradition . . . allocate to . . . counsel the power to make binding decisions" (Faretta v. California, 1975), with regard to all but a select handful of "fundamental" matters. Consequently, when counsel alone decides the array of questions entrusted to her, the accused suffers no constitutional violation.

Fundamental Matters That the Accused Is Entitled to Decide

A defendant who has counsel is constitutionally empowered to make a small number of vitally important decisions. "[T]he accused has the ultimate authority to make certain fundamental decisions regarding the case, [including] whether to plead guilty, waive a jury, testify in his or her own behalf, or take an appeal" (Jones v. Barnes, 1983). An "attorney's usurpation of [these] fundamental decisions can violate the Constitution" (Jones v. Barnes, 1983 (Blackmun, J., concurring)).[70]

The reason that the defendant retains the authority to make this limited number of decisions is that they implicate "fundamental rights" that must be personally waived by an accused. These decisions all involve " 'basic rights that the attorney cannot waive without the fully informed and publicly acknowledged consent of the client' " (New York v. Hill, 2000 (quoting Taylor v. Illinois, 1988)). The decision to be assisted by a lawyer does not alter the fundamental nature of the rights at stake or shift decision-making authority to the lawyer. When the question is whether to exercise or relinquish such "important rights," the Constitution authorizes the accused alone to decide (Wainwright v. Sykes, 1977).

The Supreme Court has specified four decisions that qualify as "fundamental" and, therefore, may be made only by the defendant personally. While there may be others not yet identified, it is unlikely that there are more than a few. The first fundamental decision is whether or not to plead guilty. "The Constitution does not compel an accused who admits his guilt to stand trial against his own wishes" (Adams v. United States *ex rel.* McCann, 1942). If a defendant wishes to, he is entitled to surrender his right to a trial and admit his guilt. He need not have the advice of counsel in order to make a valid choice to plead guilty. On the other hand, counsel may not decide to plead guilty for the accused. The decision to admit one's guilt and accept the consequences is fundamental and must be the personal choice of the defendant.

In Brookhart v. Janis, a defense attorney agreed to a kind of trial that was essentially "the equivalent of a guilty plea." The record demonstrated that the defendant had not "intelligently or knowingly agreed to" have the abbreviated sort of trial that was conducted. The question before the Supreme Court was "whether counsel has the power to enter a plea which is inconsistent with the client's expressed desire and thereby waive his client's constitutional right to plead not guilty and have a trial in which he can confront and cross-examine the witnesses against him." To the Court, the answer was simple. The authority to decide on a plea is the constitutional prerogative of the accused. The constitutional rights relinquished in pleading guilty "cannot be waived by his counsel" (Brookhart v. Janis, 1966). An attorney's failure to respect the accused's entitlement to make this fundamental choice violates the Fourteenth Amendment right to "due process of law" (Brookhart v. Janis, 1966 (Harlan, J., concurring)). Because a guilty plea entered by counsel is invalid, a defendant is entitled to have it vacated and to stand trial.

The Sixth Amendment grants a right to trial by jury for "serious" offenses (Duncan v. Louisiana, 1968). (A "serious" offense is an offense that is punishable by more than six months in jail or by alternative penalties that objectively demonstrate that society deems the offense to be "serious" (Blanton v. City of

Las Vegas, 1989).) However, the Constitution does not mandate trial by jury for all serious offenses. A defendant may be allowed to waive the entitlement to a jury and stand trial before a judge (Adams v. United States *ex rel.* McCann, 1942). The decision to surrender the constitutional entitlement to a jury is a fundamental decision allocated personally to the accused (Jones v. Barnes, 1983). "To deny an accused a choice of procedure in circumstances in which he, though a layman, is as capable as any lawyer of making an intelligent choice, is to impair the worth of great Constitutional safeguards by treating them as empty verbalisms" (Adams v. United States *ex rel.* McCann, 1942). Therefore, counsel does not have the power to decide whether to relinquish or exercise the right to a jury trial. While an attorney is expected to advise her client regarding the relative merits of a jury or a bench trial (a trial in which a judge, not a jury, serves as a trier of fact), the ultimate choice to enjoy or to waive a jury of one's peers is constitutionally entrusted to the accused alone.

Another fundamental decision that the Constitution places in the defendant's hands is whether to take the witness stand and testify at trial (Jones v. Barnes, 1983). An accused has a constitutional right "to testify in his or her own defense," a right that promotes both the detection of the culpable and the protection of the innocent (Rock v. Arkansas, 1987). This basic constitutional entitlement "has sources in several provisions of the Constitution." It is rooted in the Fourteenth Amendment Due Process Clause right to be heard and offer testimony, the Sixth Amendment Compulsory Process Clause right to call favorable witnesses, the implicit, general Sixth Amendment right to make a defense personally, and the Fifth Amendment Self-Incrimination Clause privilege to testify or refuse to testify (Rock v. Arkansas, 1987). The choice to exercise the right to testify belongs to the accused. Counsel should provide expert input but must not override the defendant's wishes by forcing him onto or keeping him from the witness stand. Either action would deprive the defendant of the authority to make a fundamental choice that is entrusted to him by the Constitution.

The final fundamental matter that is entrusted to the defendant is the decision to pursue an appeal of a conviction. While the Supreme Court has declared that the Constitution does not afford a right to appeal a conviction, every jurisdiction grants convicted defendants a right to at least one appeal. "Where appeal is available as a matter of right, a decision to seek or forgo review is for the convict himself, not his lawyer" (Roe v. Flores-Ortega, 2000 (Souter, J., concurring in part and dissenting in part)). Appellate counsel is expected to provide professionally responsible advice, but the choice to pursue or not pursue an appeal, like the choice to stand trial or plead guilty, ultimately belongs to the defendant alone (Jones v. Barnes, 1983). Moreover, because the decision to file an appeal is not a "strategic decision" but "is a purely ministerial task," a lawyer who fails to comply with a client's instruction to file an appeal violates the right to effective assistance of counsel (Roe v. Flores-Ortega, 2000). Such a gross dereliction by an attorney deprives the defendant of both his right to choose and his right to appeal and entitles the defendant to appropriate relief—another opportunity to pursue an appeal.

The Decision-Making Authority Entrusted to Defense Counsel

The overwhelming majority of decisions regarding the conduct of the defense do not implicate fundamental rights of the accused. With respect to each of these decisions, the legal authority to make binding decisions belongs to counsel.[71] Unless a lawyer's decisions are so misguided that they constitute professionally incompetent assistance, "counsel's word on such matters is the last" (New York v. Hill, 2000). The Constitution does not preclude an attorney from permitting the defendant to participate in or make these decisions. Moreover, the duty to render professionally reasonable assistance may well demand that counsel consult with and inform the defendant about matters relevant to the decision-making process. Nonetheless, the Constitution does not require counsel to allow the defendant to choose the course of action to be pursued. No rights of the defendant are violated simply because counsel makes these decisions on her own or contravenes the accused's preferences.

This conclusion follows even when an attorney's decisions effectively waive constitutional or other entitlements that belong to the defendant. "[D]ecision[s] to assert or not to assert constitutional rights or constitutionally based objections at trial [are] necessarily entrusted to the defendant's attorney, who must make on-the-spot decisions at virtually all stages of a criminal trial." With regard to these decisions, the demand for a " 'knowing and intelligent waiver' [by the accused] is simply inapplicable" (Wainwright v. Sykes, 1977 (Burger, C.J., concurring)). Instead, a "waiver may be effected by action of counsel" without a personal choice by the defendant (New York v. Hill, 2000).

Defense counsel has the authority to make "many decisions pertaining to the conduct of the trial" (New York v. Hill, 2000). "[T]he day-to-day conduct of the defense rests with the attorney. [Counsel], not the client has the immediate—and ultimate—responsibility of deciding if and when to object, which witnesses, if any, to call, and what defenses to develop" (Wainwright v. Sykes, 1977 (Burger, C.J., concurring)). A defense attorney ordinarily has the authority to determine "what arguments to pursue, what evidentiary objections to raise, and what agreements to conclude regarding the admission of evidence" (New York v. Hill, 2000). In addition, "scheduling matters are plainly among those for which agreement by counsel generally controls" (New York v. Hill, 2000). In sum, because a "lawyer has—and must have—full authority to manage the conduct of the trial" (Taylor v. Illinois, 1988), counsel is authorized to make binding decisions on an extensive array of matters concerning the conduct of the defense and the progress of the trial process.

The Interstate Agreement on Detainers (IAD) is a "federal law" that "establishes procedures for resolution of one State's outstanding charges against a prisoner of another State." Under the IAD, if a prisoner held in custody by one state makes a request for final disposition of a charge filed by another state, he

" 'shall be brought to trial within one hundred eighty days' " of his request unless a court grants a necessary or reasonable continuance (New York v. Hill, 2000). In New York v. Hill, an attorney agreed to a trial date that fell outside the 180-day period permitted for trial by the IAD. The accused did not take part in or ratify the agreement. Following trial and conviction, the defendant objected, claiming that he was entitled to have the charges dismissed because the trial did not occur within the time period prescribed by the IAD. According to the defendant, it was improper to "allow [a] waiver of any sort" of the time period within which the IAD required trial to be held. Moreover, even if a waiver was possible, it could "be effected only by affirmative conduct not" established in the *Hill* case.

A unanimous Supreme Court disagreed with the defendant's claims. The Court concluded that the right to have trial held by the date specified by statute could be waived and that a waiver of that right could be, and was, "effected by action of counsel." The "scheduling decision"—the decision about when the trial would be held—was one accorded to the defense attorney. The accused had no personal right to control that decision.

In general, anything that can fairly be categorized as a matter of strategy or tactics falls within counsel's domain. "[L]aw and tradition . . . allocate to . . . counsel the power to make binding decisions on trial strategy in many areas" (Faretta v. California, 1975). In Strickland v. Washington, a landmark opinion concerning ineffective assistance of counsel, the Supreme Court concluded that to demonstrate ineffectiveness a defendant "must overcome the presumption that . . . [a] challenged action 'might be considered sound trial strategy' " and declared that counsel's "strategic choices made after thorough investigation of law and facts . . . are *virtually unchallengeable*" (Strickland v. Washington, 1984) (italics added).[72] In Henry v. Mississippi, the Court observed that if an attorney's failure to seek the suppression of illegally acquired evidence was a "deliberate choice of . . . strategy," that choice "would amount to a waiver binding on" the accused (Henry v. Mississippi, 1965). Because a defendant has no constitutional entitlement to make the strategic or tactical choices involved in defending against an accusation, the Constitution is not violated when counsel exerts control over those choices.

While an accused is entitled to decide whether to take an appeal at all, he does not have a constitutional right to dictate the arguments to be made in an appellate brief. Decisions about the content and structure of the brief supporting the appeal of a conviction are entrusted to the appellate lawyer. From among the nonfrivolous claims that might be raised, the attorney is authorized to exercise professional judgment to determine which to include and which to omit (Jones v. Barnes, 1983).

In Jones v. Barnes, a convicted defendant contended that his appointed appellate counsel had an obligation to present all nonfrivolous claims that the client desired to have raised. The Supreme Court held that "[n]othing in the Constitution" required imposition on counsel of "a duty to raise every 'colorable' claim suggested by a client." (As used by the Court, a "colorable" claim is one that appears to or could have some potential merit as opposed to one that is clearly without merit.) It rejected the notion that a "defendant has a constitutional right to compel appointed counsel to press nonfrivolous points requested by the client, if counsel, as a matter of professional judgment, decides not to present those points." In sum, lawyers, not their appellant-clients, have the authority to choose which issues and arguments to present to an appellate court.[73]

On matters within the domain of the defense attorney, an accused cannot establish a constitutional deprivation simply by showing that counsel made a decision on her own or made a decision contrary to the defendant's desires. The lawyer's exercise of her decision-making authority, however, is not wholly beyond constitutional scrutiny. "[C]ounsel's word" on matters over which she has authority is final *unless* the defendant makes "*a demonstration of ineffectiveness*" (New York v. Hill, 2000) (italics added). Thus, an accused can prevail by showing that counsel exercised her prerogatives in a professionally unreasonable manner. Incompetent representation by a defense lawyer—actions, decisions, or judgments that are outside the range of competent performance—can deprive an accused of the Sixth Amendment right to effective assistance of counsel. (The topic of ineffective assistance is discussed in extensive detail in the part of this analysis dealing with the "content" of the right to counsel.)

Counsel has professional obligations to "consult with the defendant on important decisions and to keep the defendant informed of important developments in the course of the prosecution" (Strickland v. Washington, 1984). Decisions made without consulting or informing the accused may be deemed objectively unreasonable and deficient under the Sixth Amendment. Also, if counsel makes professionally unjustifiable choices about what defenses to present, what arguments to make at trial, what objections to raise, or what agreements to reach with the prosecutor, those choices can violate the right to effective assistance. If counsel irresponsibly agrees to disadvantageous scheduling of the trial or, without good reason, fails to include, in an appellate brief, arguments that were suggested by her client and were stronger than those that she did present, her decisions may be deemed constitutionally deficient. In all these instances, constitutional error does not result from the fact that counsel, rather than the accused, made a particular decision. It results from the grossly inadequate way in which counsel exercised her authority to make a binding choice.

The conclusion that the Constitution empowers defense counsel to make all decisions but the few that entail certain fundamental rights rests on two distinct premises. First, pragmatic considerations demand that most decisions be entrusted to counsel. Many decisions "must, as a practical matter, be made without consulting the client. The trial process simply does not permit the type of frequent and protracted interruptions which would be necessary if it were required that clients give knowing and intelligent approval to each of the myriad tactical decisions as a trial proceeds" (Wainwright v. Sykes, 1977 (Burger, C.J., concurring)). A ruling that the defendant is authorized to participate in or control many of the decisions necessary to construct a defense "would make a shambles of orderly procedure" (Wainwright v. Sykes, 1977 (Stevens, J., concurring)).[74]

The rationale for granting a right to the assistance of counsel in our adversary system also supports the conclusion that most decision-making authority should be allocated to counsel, not the accused. A defendant is entitled to legal representation because lawyers have the skills, knowledge, and expertise necessary to cope with professional prosecutors and the complexities of the legal system. The guiding hand of counsel is essential to fair trials because the accused typically does not have the ability to conduct a defense on his own. Authorizing the accused to participate in or dictate choices could "seriously undermine[] the ability of counsel to present the client's case in accord with counsel's professional evaluation" (Jones v. Barnes, 1983). "The very reasons why counsel's participation is of such critical importance in assuring a fair trial for the defendant . . . make it inappropriate to require that his tactical decisions always be personally approved, or even thoroughly understood, by his client" (Wainwright v. Sykes, 1977 (Stevens, J., concurring)). If counsel is to perform her functions in the adversary system—equalizing the imbalance between the accused and the state and championing the defendant's cause to the best of her ability—she must be free to follow the guidance of her education and professional training. Allowing the accused to choose or interfere with counsel's choices could only undermine the effort to conduct fair, balanced adversary contests.[75]

In sum, when a defendant "consent[s], at the outset [of a case], to accept counsel as his representative," he generally relinquishes to the attorney the authority to make most decisions regarding the defense (Faretta v. California, 1975). A defense attorney must exercise reasonable professional judgment in making the array of decisions allocated to her and may well have to consult with her client in order to resolve certain issues. Nonetheless, an attorney does not have to permit the defendant to make any of the numerous decisions that are entrusted to counsel. The accused has the ultimate authority to decide only a very small number of fundamental matters—whether to plead guilty, waive a jury, testify at trial, or take an appeal. With regard to other matters, the Constitution does not grant decision-making authority to the represented defendant. Instead, it permits defense counsel to make final decisions that are binding on the client.

THE SCOPE OF THE RIGHT TO THE ASSISTANCE OF COUNSEL

The first part of this analysis discussed the "nature and character" of the Sixth Amendment guarantee. The object was to explore and explain the essence of the constitutional entitlement—its most basic meaning. The second part of the analysis is concerned with the "scope" of the right to legal representation. The object here is to explore and explain the purview of the right to counsel, that is, the proceedings to which the constitutional entitlement to assistance extends.

The discussion is organized chronologically, focusing initially on the first stages of the criminal process in which defendants have a right to counsel, then continuing through to the final stages in which defendants are entitled to enjoy a lawyer's aid.

The Entitlement to Counsel's Assistance Prior to Trial

The Extension of the Right to Trial Counsel to Critical Pretrial Stages

The historical record suggests that the "core purpose of the counsel guarantee was to assure" that an accused had the assistance of a trained lawyer "at trial" (United States v. Ash, 1973). The Framers of the Bill of Rights provided a right to a trained assistant to assure that the decisive battle with the government in the courtroom would be a fair, balanced fight.[76] Over time, however, Supreme Court interpretations of the right to counsel have expanded its scope. Today the right extends to certain events in the criminal process that occur prior to the actual trial (United States v. Gouveia, 1984). A primary foundation for pretrial expansions of the right to counsel has been the Supreme Court's 1932 landmark opinion in Powell v. Alabama—more specifically, two oft-quoted observations about the defendant's need for, and entitlement to, assistance before a trial begins. According to the Court, an accused individual "requires the guiding hand of counsel *at every step in the proceedings against him*" (Powell v. Alabama, 1932) (italics added). Consequently, he is "as much entitled to aid during" the period from arraignment to trial "as at the trial itself." Based on these premises, the *Powell* Court concluded that the right to retained or appointed assistance must arise sufficiently before the actual commencement of trial to enable adequate preparation of the accused's defense.[77]

In the *Powell* case, the right to the assistance of counsel at stages of the criminal process prior to the trial was not at issue. The precise question before the Court was when the right to counsel *at trial* began. The Court held that a meaningful entitlement to assistance at trial required that defense counsel be able to start working on a case well before the actual start of the trial. Nonetheless, the language in *Powell* has often been invoked to support the conclusion that a defendant has the right to legal representation *at certain pretrial events* in the criminal process. According to the Supreme Court, the right to counsel "is indispensable to the fair administration of our adversary system of criminal justice," and *Powell* made it clear that the "vital need" for assistance extends to the "pretrial stage[s]" of a criminal case (Brewer v. Williams, 1977). Representation by counsel at critical pretrial events—like representation by counsel at trial—is necessary to ensure that the accused's interests will be protected and promoted in the ways contemplated by our adversarial system of criminal justice (United States v. Wade, 1967).

The reasoning underlying the pretrial expansion of the right to assistance at trial merits fuller exploration. It is rooted in a recognition that American criminal justice systems have changed dramatically since the framing of the Bill of Rights and a realization that if the right to counsel were confined exclusively to the trial itself (and adequate preparation time for trial), it would not be able to serve its core purposes. As has been the case with many constitutional rights, substantial changes in the context in which the entitlement to counsel operates—changes unanticipated by the Sixth Amendment's drafters—necessitated changes in the contours of the right itself (United States v. Ash, 1973).

When the Sixth Amendment was adopted, the adversarial contest commenced at trial. The trial was the first and only point of confrontation between the accused and the state. It was the battleground, the time when and the place where a defendant had to face the prosecutor, the government's witnesses, and the evidence of his guilt (United States v. Wade, 1967). There was no need for counsel's help at pretrial events because there were no significant pretrial events.[78]

Over time, the development of organized police forces and "changing patterns of criminal procedure and investigation" led to the addition of significant steps prior to the actual trial (United States v. Ash, 1973). Preliminary events in the courtroom—such as arraignments and preliminary hearings—and preliminary events outside the courtroom—such as law enforcement efforts to secure incriminating evidence from and about an accused—emerged. Recognition of the altered "realities of modern criminal prosecution" and of their impacts on defendants and on their trials prompted the Supreme Court to conclude that the Sixth Amendment guarantee of legal assistance extended to "critical" pretrial stages of criminal proceedings (United States v. Wade, 1967). When new contexts appeared that presented dangers to the accused sufficiently similar to those that justified a right to trial counsel, the Court responded by extending the entitlement to assistance to those contexts (United States v. Ash, 1973).

It was constitutionally justifiable and necessary to recognize a right to counsel at significant pretrial events because what happened at these events could "settle the accused's fate and reduce the trial itself to a mere formality" (United States v. Wade, 1967). If the government could confront unaided laypersons prior to trial, it could gain advantages that would assure convictions and render pointless the assistance of counsel at trial and all the other constitutional fair trial safeguards. Because the adversarial process had grown, the right to counsel had to grow. Otherwise, an inferior, ill-equipped accused could be overpowered or outsmarted by the state and convicted on the basis of imbalanced, unfair pretrial clashes. To ensure the fair and equitable operation of the adversarial system, defendants had to have the equalizing assistance of counsel at pretrial confrontations with the state. A defendant's ability to defend himself against conviction could be damaged in the pretrial process just as much as at the trial itself (Maine v. Moulton, 1985). Consequently, the assistance of counsel "would be less than meaningful," and the fairness of criminal trials would be jeopardized if the right to assistance "were limited to the formal trial itself" (United States v. Ash,

1973). Without an entitlement to pretrial assistance, the right to trial counsel would become "an empty right" (United States v. Wade, 1967).[79]

The Two Prerequisites for an Entitlement to Pretrial Assistance of Counsel

The recognition of a right to pretrial representation by counsel does not mean that defendants have that right at all times prior to the commencement of trial. There are two basic prerequisites for the constitutional entitlement to pretrial assistance. First, the right to counsel must "attach." Second, a post-attachment event must qualify as a "critical stage" of the criminal prosecution. If either of these elements is missing, no Sixth Amendment right can exist.[80]

The Sixth Amendment "right to counsel attaches *only at or after the initiation of adversary judicial proceedings*" (United States v. Gouveia, 1984) (italics added). No individual has a constitutional entitlement to a lawyer's aid at any time or in any setting prior to the commencement of formal charges against him (Moran v. Burbine, 1986). The point of attachment of the right to counsel is rigidly fixed.[81] Only a *formal* accusation will suffice. There is no room for argument that "substance" ought to govern over "form," that is, that a person has effectively been charged with an offense or that the government has made up its mind to pursue charges. Moreover, an individual cannot create or trigger her constitutional right to assistance by retaining a lawyer. In this arena, form governs over substance. The initiation of adversary judicial proceedings is a necessary precondition for the entitlement to legal assistance.[82]

One question is what qualifies as the "initiation of adversarial judicial proceedings." An actual arrest or the issuance of an arrest warrant is not a formal accusation and does not trigger attachment of the right to counsel. On the other hand, an " 'indictment' " by a grand jury—a formal accusation of crime by a body of laypersons—clearly does suffice (Brewer v. Williams, 1977 (quoting Kirby v. Illinois, 1972)). The filing of an " 'information' "—a charging document prepared and filed by a prosecutor—also gives rise to a Sixth Amendment entitlement to assistance. " '[A]rraignment[s]' " and " 'preliminary hearing[s]' "—formal, courtroom stages of the pretrial process at which the individual and the government are present—are "accusations" that trigger attachment of the right to counsel. In addition, any other " 'formal charge' "—that is, any state-initiated step that constitutes a governmental accusation of crime against a particular person—also suffices as a point of attachment.

The right to counsel is "offense specific" (McNeil v. Wisconsin, 1991; Texas v. Cobb, 2001). A formal charge of any sort with respect to one offense does *not* result in attachment of the right to counsel for different, uncharged crimes even if those crimes "are 'factually related' to [the] charged offense" (Texas v. Cobb, 2001). A person is entitled to pretrial assistance for a specific criminal offense *only* if proceedings have been initiated against him for *that* offense (Illinois v. Perkins, 1990; Maine v. Moulton, 1985).[83] It must be noted, however, that for purposes of attachment of the right to counsel, the "definition of an offense is not necessarily limited to the four corners of the charging instrument" (Texas v. Cobb, 2001). Instead, if a defendant, by " 'the same act or transaction,' " violates " 'two distinct statutory provisions' " both violations are the *same offense* unless " 'each provision requires proof of a fact which the other does not' " (Texas v. Cobb, 2001 (quoting Blockburger v. United States, 1932)). In situations where distinct statutory violations do constitute the same offense, if a defendant is formally charged with violating one provision, he is entitled to the assistance of counsel with respect to violation of the other provision as well.

The Supreme Court's fidelity to the requirement that there be a formal "initiation of proceedings" for attachment of the right to counsel is illustrated by the forceful, unhesitating repudiations of Sixth Amendment claims in a number of cases in which defendants who had not been charged contended that they had constitutional entitlements to assistance. In United States v. Gouveia, prisoners claimed that they were entitled to counsel while they were isolated in "administrative detention" during an investigation of the murder of a fellow inmate. Following nineteen months of detention, the prisoners were ultimately indicted for the offense. The Court disagreed with their contention, concluding that because there was no "initiation of adversary judicial proceedings" for any offense prior to the actual indictments, the prisoners' constitutional rights to counsel had not attached during the period of detention (United States v. Gouveia, 1984).

In Moran v. Burbine, officers questioned a suspect after telling the attorney retained by his sister that they would not be doing so and failing to inform the suspect of the attorney's efforts to intercede. Subsequently, the suspect was charged with homicide. The Supreme Court concluded that the officers had not deprived the defendant of a Sixth Amendment entitlement because he had not been formally charged at the time of questioning. Put simply, his right to assistance had not attached (Moran v. Burbine, 1984).

In Kirby v. Illinois, a man was arrested and identified in a police-arranged, face-to-face confrontation with the victim of a robbery. His assertion that he was entitled to counsel at the identification procedure was rejected because the arrest did not constitute an initiation of proceedings, and he had not otherwise been charged with an offense at the time that he was identified (Kirby v. Illinois, 1972).

In Illinois v. Perkins, a man who was in jail, charged with one offense, was questioned about an entirely separate offense by an undercover officer. He maintained that his right to counsel had been violated by the questioning. The Supreme Court ruled against his claim, holding that he had no constitutional guarantee of assistance with regard to the offense that was not yet the subject of a formal accusation (Illinois v. Perkins, 1990).[84]

Finally, in Texas v. Cobb, a man who was indicted for the burglary of a home was questioned about and confessed to killing the woman and child who resided in the home. Even though the burglary and killings were part of the same criminal episode and were closely related, the Court held that the accused was not entitled to the assistance of counsel for a capital murder charge. He had not been formally charged with murder at the time of the questioning, and murder did not constitute the "same offense" as burglary because each offense required proof of a fact which the other did not (Texas v. Cobb, 2001).

A majority of the Supreme Court believes that the formal charge criterion for attachment of the right to counsel is the only defensible interpretation of the Sixth Amendment. This conclusion rests on a number of grounds. First, the Sixth Amendment's language limits its scope to "criminal *prosecutions*" and grants the right to counsel only to "the *accused*" (italics added). The "initiation of proceedings" criterion comports with these two textual limitations, for there can be no "prosecution" until proceedings have formally commenced, and there can be no "accused" without a formal charge (United States v. Gouveia, 1984). Second, the right to a lawyer's assistance historically has been recognized only after a formal prosecution has been commenced.[85] Perhaps most important, the formal charge requirement is thought to be consistent with the substantive rationales for affording a fundamental right to legal representation. The initiation of formal proceedings marks the beginning of an adversarial contest. Only upon actual accusation does the government become a committed opponent. Only then do the two sides solidify their positions and become true adversaries. Only then is the accused brought face-to-face with the "prosecutorial forces of organized society, and immersed in the intricacies of substantive and procedural criminal law" (Kirby v. Illinois, 1972).[86] The right to counsel attaches at this point, and not before, because there is no need for equalization to render the adversarial battle balanced and fair prior to the commencement of hostilities. Moreover, before a "formal accusation" that signifies a decision to seek the conviction of a particular individual, society has powerful interests in a full and unimpeded opportunity to investigate suspects and gather evidence of guilt.[87]

The Court's decision to adhere rigidly to the "initiation of proceedings" standard has been the subject of pointed criticism. (For criticisms by Supreme Court Justices, see Kirby v. Illinois, 1972 (Brennan, J., dissenting); United States v. Gouveia, 1984 (Stevens, J., concurring).)[88] Some consider the criterion excessively rigid, formalistic, and unrealistic.[89] Critics allege that the formal charge requirement fails to account for instances in which government officials have not yet filed a formal accusation, even though they no longer consider an individual to be merely a suspect but, rather, firmly believe him to be the perpetrator of an offense. They maintain that the government can be a committed adversary before it formalizes its commitment.[90] At the point of arrest, the government, in fact, often is sufficiently committed to prosecution of the person apprehended to justify counsel's equalizing assistance.[91] Moreover, the "formal charge" criterion is capable of widespread abuse by government officials who ordinarily have the power to delay the filing of charges and manipulate the scope of the constitutional guarantee. Police and prosecutors who wish to avoid the obstructions that defense counsel might pose can prevent an ill-equipped accused from enjoying the benefits of equalization by postponing the point of formal accusation as long as possible.[92]

The fact that the right to counsel has "attached" does not mean that a defendant has a constitutional right to have a lawyer by his side at all times. It does not even entitle an accused to assistance at every subsequent interaction or contact with government agents. Even after the state has initiated formal judicial proceedings, an accused is not entitled to counsel unless a pretrial event qualifies as a "*critical stage[] of the prosecution*" (United States v. Henry, 1980) (italics added). Because not every encounter with the government or the legal system is a "critical stage," a vitally important question is how to determine whether an event qualifies. The Supreme Court has struggled to find an appropriate way to define those pretrial events that constitute "critical stages." At one time, it espoused the expansive view that counsel was required at any proceeding, formal or informal, where assistance was "necessary to assure a meaningful 'defence' " (United States v. Wade, 1967). If counsel's absence "might derogate from the accused's right to a fair trial," then an event was considered critical. More specifically, a particular stage of the criminal process required counsel if it entailed risks of potential substantial prejudice to the defendant's general entitlement to a fair trial, and if the assistance of a lawyer could prevent and combat that prejudice. In sum, a stage was deemed "critical" if counsel's presence was "necessary 'to protect the fairness of the trial itself' " (United States v. Ash, 1973 (Brennan, J., dissenting) (quoting Schneckloth v. Bustamonte, 1973)).

More recently, the Court has endorsed different, less generous standards for deciding whether a post-accusation event is a critical stage of the prosecution. Under the currently controlling doctrine, an extension of the right to counsel to a pretrial phase of the criminal process is justified only if the event qualifies as a "trial-like confrontation." A stage is critical only if the defendant is physically present and is confronted by the expert prosecutor, the legal system, or both. If an accused is not present or if an accused is present but there is no clash with the adversary or immersion in the legal system of any sort, the stage cannot be critical (United States v. Ash, 1973). Moreover, even if a stage qualifies as a "trial-like confrontation," if later confrontation of the government at trial with counsel's aid can "cure" (i.e., remedy or prevent) any harm that might result from the unaided pretrial clash, the pretrial stage will not be considered critical (United States v. Ash, 1973).

The logic underlying this approach to deciding whether a stage is critical is simple. At trial, a defendant is confronted by a professional prosecutor and the intricacies of the legal system. Equalizing assistance is necessary at trial because an accused needs a "spokesman" and "advisor" either in coping with the expertise of the prosecutor or in comprehending and responding to the complexities of the law (United States v. Ash, 1973). Only those pretrial "confrontations" that are "trial-like" (i.e., those that resemble trials in at least one of these two salient respects) involve the same perils to the untrained layperson that necessitate assistance at trial. Consequently, only at those pretrial events is an extension of the constitutional right to counsel justified.

Those who prefer the previous, broader approach to deciding whether a pretrial event is "critical" believe that the logic underlying the "trial-like confrontation" criterion is excessively simple and fatally flawed. In their view, even if an accused does not need help in dealing with a powerful opponent or legal intricacies *at a particular pretrial event*, counsel's absence from that event might severely hamper her ability to provide adequate assistance *at the trial itself.* When that is the case, counsel's presence is not required at the pretrial event in order to protect the defendant at the time of the pretrial event, but counsel's presence is essential to ensure that counsel will be able to combat the government and cope with legal complexities at the subsequent trial. As will be seen later in this subsection, the "trial-like confrontation" approach that currently controls the inquiry is narrower and more restrictive of the Sixth Amendment entitlement. It leads to recognition of a right to pretrial assistance in fewer situations than the earlier "necessary to a fair trial" approach.

Formal Critical Stages of the Prosecution

A limited number of pretrial events have been deemed "critical stages" of a criminal prosecution. Some are formal steps in the adjudicatory process that occur in the courtroom. Others are informal, out-of-court events. There has been little controversy over decisions to extend the right to counsel to formal, judicial proceedings that precede the trial. In contrast, the Court's decisions to recognize entitlements to legal assistance in informal, extrajudicial stages have been the subject of considerable, often bitter debate and disagreement.

In today's American criminal justice systems, a variety of formal, judicial steps precede the actual trial of a criminal case. Pretrial processes vary to some extent from jurisdiction to jurisdiction. Moreover, the names used in different jurisdictions to describe particular steps in the adjudicatory process are not necessarily the same.[93] What follows is a description of the typical pretrial stages that take place in court.

An individual may make an "initial appearance" in a lower-level magistrate's court. An initial appearance may entail informing the defendant of the charges and of his rights, beginning the process of appointing counsel, and setting the conditions for release on bail. If a defendant desires a preliminary hearing, the magistrate will arrange for one to be held. In a case involving a minor offense, a defendant might plead to a charge.

At a "preliminary hearing," if one is conducted, the magistrate decides whether there is sufficient evidence to require the accused to stand trial. Both sides can present witnesses and evidence, and both can challenge the witnesses and evidence of the opposing side. Typically, the question is whether there is "probable cause" or "reasonable cause" to believe that the defendant committed the offense.

Alternatively, or in addition to, a preliminary hearing, there may be a "grand jury inquiry." A grand jury is a body of laypersons that is authorized to hear evidence and decide whether there is cause to accuse a defendant and require him to stand trial. The presentation of evidence before a grand jury is entirely one-sided. Only the government is present. If the grand jury believes that a charge is warranted, it issues an indictment, charging the defendant with a criminal offense. On the other hand, if the grand jury determines that there is insufficient evidence supporting an accusation, it declines to return an indictment.

If a judge, after a preliminary hearing, or a grand jury, after hearing evidence, decides that there is adequate cause to require the individual to stand trial, the next step is an "arraignment." An arraignment is the accused's first appearance in the trial court—the court with the power to adjudicate the charges against him. At an arraignment, the accused is typically asked to plead to the charges. Unless a guilty plea is entered, the case proceeds to trial.

The Supreme Court has decided three cases involving claims by accused persons that they were entitled to counsel at one of these formal, pretrial stages of the criminal process. In all three, the Court determined that the particular in-court proceeding at issue was "critical" and, therefore, that the defendant had an entitlement to legal assistance.[94] The first case, Hamilton v. Alabama, involved an arraignment. The Court concluded that the accused had a right to counsel at arraignments in Alabama because the particular matters that transpired could "affect the whole trial" (Hamilton v. Alabama, 1961). More specifically, defenses to the charges could be "irretrievably lost" if not asserted at the arraignment, and motions challenging racial exclusion from the grand jury were forfeited if not made at that stage. The aid of counsel was necessary to make the accused aware of all available defenses and to enable him "to plead intelligently." According to *Hamilton*, assistance at trial is needed to make sure that defendants do not make concessions or pay penalties higher than required by the law due to " 'bewilderment or ignorance' " (Hamilton v. Alabama, 1961 (quoting Tomkins v. Missouri, 1945)). Counsel at an Alabama arraignment is essential to guard against similar pitfalls at the arraignment. The *Hamilton* Court carefully confined its holding to the case before it, suggesting that whether arraignments in other states were critical stages would depend upon their particular functions and importance in the adjudication of criminal charges in those states.

In White v. Maryland, a defendant claimed that he had a constitutional right to assistance at a "preliminary hearing." In a very narrow holding, the Court concluded that because the accused had in fact entered a guilty plea at his preliminary hearing, the stage was just as critical as the arraignment in *Hamilton*. The defendant had a constitutional entitlement to counsel because "[o]nly the presence of counsel could have enabled [the] accused to know all the defenses available to him and to plead intelligently" (White v. Maryland, 1963).

Finally, in Coleman v. Alabama, a pre-indictment "preliminary hearing" was deemed a "critical stage" of the prosecution, despite the fact that such a hearing was not a required step in the resolution of charges. The only purposes of the hearing were to determine whether there was sufficient evidence to present the case to a grand jury and, if so, to set bail conditions for the defendant. Moreover, there was no risk that a defendant would lose defenses not proffered at the hearing, and no testimony at the hearing could be admitted against the accused at trial. Consequently, the hearing posed no danger of prejudice to the defendant at trial.

The *Coleman* Court asserted that whether a stage is to be deemed critical for right to counsel purposes depended on " 'whether potential substantial prejudice to defendant's rights inheres in the . . . confrontation and [on] the ability of counsel to help avoid that prejudice' " (Coleman v. Alabama, 1970 (quoting United States v. Wade, 1967)). That standard was satisfied in *Coleman* for a number of reasons. At the preliminary hearing, counsel could protect an accused against an "erroneous or improper prosecution." Through skillful examination of witnesses, a lawyer could expose weaknesses in the state's case and persuade the magistrate not to find adequate cause to support the charges. Additionally, a lawyer's examination of witnesses could develop valuable impeachment evidence for use at trial and could preserve the favorable testimony of a witness who did not appear at the trial. A lawyer also could more effectively discover the content of the state's case against the defendant and could make more effective arguments on matters such as the need for psychiatric examination or the propriety of release on bail. In performing most of these functions, counsel could aid the effort to avoid conviction at trial. Therefore, the "guiding hand of counsel" was as much necessary at an Alabama preliminary hearing "as at the trial itself."[95]

Each of these holdings that classified a formal pretrial phase as a "critical stage" of the prosecution was carefully restricted to the particular proceeding at issue in the case before the Court. Nonetheless, the reasoning of the three opinions suggests that most formal, judicial steps in the processing of criminal cases would also qualify as critical. This would seem to be the case, even though the "critical stage" standard employed in *Coleman* has been supplanted by a stricter criterion. In the first place, each of the formal adjudicatory steps sketched at the outset of this discussion (except a grand jury inquiry that predates a formal accusation) would itself constitute an "initiation of adversary judicial proceedings." Moreover, most of these events would qualify as "trial-like confrontations" with an expert prosecutorial adversary, with the legal system, or with both—confrontations that call for the kinds of legal expertise, strength, and dedication that counsel is expected to provide at trial.

Not every formal judicial step prior to trial, however, qualifies as critical. Even if the right to counsel has attached, there has traditionally been no entitlement to counsel at the secret, one-sided hearings conducted before grand juries (Coleman v. Alabama, 1970 (Burger, C.J., dissenting)). Because the defendant is present only when testifying, the confrontation with the prosecutor and legal system is quite limited in scope. Moreover, even during this courtroom confrontation, the government ordinarily can, and does, deny legal representation.

The grand jury process has a long tradition of secrecy and exclusion. While some states now allow individuals to have a lawyer's assistance when appearing before a grand jury,[96] most jurisdictions still adhere to the view that there are legitimate justifications for excluding everyone except the grand jurors, the prosecutor, and the witnesses called by the prosecutor from the grand jury room.[97]

In addition, "initial appearances" in magistrates' courts might not qualify as "critical" unless they involved more than merely informing an accused of the charges and of his rights, setting initial bail conditions, and scheduling preliminary hearings. Despite the fact that the accused is physically present and confronting the prosecutor and system, initial appearances do not threaten incurable prejudice to the defendant and do not provide meaningful opportunities to promote the accused's chances for a successful defense at trial. What transpires may well be too insignificant to require legal representation.[98]

Informal Critical Stages of the Prosecution

Two kinds of informal, nonjudicial, pretrial events have been deemed critical stages of the prosecution that necessitate the assistance of counsel if they occur after a formal accusation. The first involves certain government efforts to secure incriminating statements from accused persons.[99] The second includes some official methods of obtaining eyewitness identifications of defendants by witnesses to crimes. The holding that the Sixth Amendment guarantee applies when the authorities seek inculpatory admissions from the mouth of the accused—what is known as the "*Massiah* doctrine"—has generated considerable controversy.[100] Moreover, the doctrine that defines the settings in which a defendant is guaranteed counsel is quite complicated—perhaps more complicated than in any other area of right to counsel law.

Before exploring that doctrine, a word of caution is in order. Readers should not confuse the Sixth Amendment guarantee of counsel's assistance in dealing with official efforts to secure admissions of guilt with the much better-known "right to counsel" promised by the "*Miranda* warnings." The two entitlements are "quite distinct" (Rhode Island v. Innis, 1980).[101] *Miranda* grants legal assistance only to suspects who are subjected to "custodial interrogation" by the police (Miranda v. Arizona, 1966). (Briefly, "custodial interrogation" occurs when law enforcement agents subject a person whose liberty is significantly restricted to express questions or equivalent tactics.) Moreover, the lawyer referred to by the *Miranda* warnings is not thought to be a constitutional *right* at all. Instead, the assurance of counsel is a "procedural safeguard[]" designed to protect against violation of a suspect's Fifth Amendment right not to be compelled to be a witness against himself (Michigan v. Tucker, 1974). The right to counsel that is the subject of the instant discussion—the *Massiah* right to counsel—is a pretrial extension of the true, explicit Sixth Amendment entitlement to an equalizer in the adversarial contest with the state.[102] While there is some overlap between these two guarantees of counsel, their different natures and sources lead to very different doctrinal requirements and limitations.

In Massiah v. United States, after the defendant was indicted for narcotics offenses, his codefendant decided to cooperate with the government. While a federal agent listened in by means of a radio transmitter, Massiah and the turncoat codefendant had a conversation in an automobile. The federal agent who had listened testified at trial to inculpatory admissions made by Massiah during the course of the conversation. Based on this testimony and other evidence, Massiah was convicted.

On review, the Supreme Court agreed with the accused's claim that the government's conduct had violated his Sixth Amendment right to counsel. According to the Court, the encounter with the codefendant who had agreed to work with the state constituted a "critical stage" of the prosecution at which the defendant was entitled to a lawyer's help. The government denied the defendant his constitutional entitlement to assistance "when [it] . . . used against him at his trial evidence of his own incriminating words, which *federal agents had deliberately elicited from him after he had been indicted and in the absence of his counsel*" (Massiah v. United States, 1964) (italics added).[103]

While the *Massiah* holding was a major development in right to counsel law, it was not without ambiguity. The precise elements that turned a government effort to secure inculpatory statements into a "critical stage" and triggered the entitlement to counsel were not entirely clear from the exceedingly brief *Massiah* opinion. It was uncertain, for example, whether the codefendant's active participation in the "conversation" was essential to the outcome in *Massiah* (i.e., whether it would have been permissible for him to listen passively to Massiah's admissions). It was unclear whether the outcome would have been different if the federal agent had not listened in and testified to the statements. One could even argue that an essential factor in *Massiah* was the fact that the defendant had already retained a lawyer to represent him in the case. The Supreme Court has revisited the *Massiah* doctrine several times since 1964. The result is a number of refinements and clarifications that have resolved many of the questions surrounding the original ruling but raised others.

The pretrial extension of the right to counsel announced in *Massiah* applies in two different settings. A defendant is entitled to assistance in situations where undercover agents surreptitiously secure admissions. An accused also has a right to representation when known government agents—typically, police officers—openly seek to secure incriminating statements. The *Massiah* Court observed that the Sixth Amendment's protection " 'must apply to indirect and surreptitious interrogations *as well as* those conducted in the jailhouse' " (Massiah v. United States, 1964) (italics added). Subsequently, the Court has rejected the claim that because the *Massiah* case involved "indirect and surreptitious" activity, the right announced there governs *only* undercover contexts and provides no protection against direct, open efforts to secure confessions (Brewer v. Williams, 1977). It has repeatedly reaffirmed the vitality of the entitlement to assistance in both undercover agent settings (Kuhlmann v. Wilson, 1986; Maine v. Moulton, 1985; United States v. Henry, 1980); and face-to-face confrontations with known police officers (Brewer v. Williams, 1977; Michigan v. Jackson, 1986; Patterson v. Illinois, 1988).

In both surreptitious and face-to-face settings, the individual who is in actual contact with the accused—the government informant or the police officer—must engage in "some action, beyond merely listening, that [is] designed deliberately to elicit incriminating remarks" (Kuhlmann v. Wilson, 1986). The stage is not critical, and no right to counsel exists, unless there is *active elicitation*. Passive listening will not suffice.[104] Moreover, the elicitation must be *deliberate*; that is, there must be an intent to evoke statements from the accused. At least in undercover contexts, the active elicitation requirement can be satisfied by merely engaging in conversation with a defendant (United States v. Henry, 1980). There is no need for the informant to question or interrogate the accused about his crimes or anything else.

It is unclear whether mere engagement in conversation by known police officers satisfies the deliberate elicitation criterion. Language in two opinions suggests that a known state agent triggers the protection of counsel only when he actually "interrogates" the accused (Brewer v. Williams, 1980; Kuhlmann v. Wilson, 1986). This suggestion is potentially significant because "interrogation" is a term of art defined by opinions interpreting the Fifth Amendment privilege against compulsory self-incrimination. It occurs only when an officer engages in either "express questioning" or its "functional equivalent," that is, "words or actions on the part of the police . . . that [they] should know are reasonably likely to elicit an incriminating response from the suspect" (Rhode Island v. Innis, 1980). Not all conversations qualify as the functional equivalent of express questioning under this definition. On the other hand, the Court has asserted—albeit in an undercover agent case—that "affirmative interrogation" is sufficient for, but is not required by, the *Massiah* doctrine (United States v. Henry, 1980). The Court's inconsistency and ambiguity have given rise to two possibilities. Officers may be subject to the same Sixth Amendment strictures as undercover operatives. Any intentional and active efforts by officers to secure incriminating statements—including mere conversation—may be enough to trigger an entitlement to counsel's assistance. Alternatively, officers may be less restricted, freer to interact with defendants than their surreptitious counterparts. The right to assistance may exist only if they actually "interrogate" an accused. In that case, only those conversations or actions that put a certain amount of pressure on the defendant to confess would qualify.

The Court has devoted virtually no attention to the demand that the actions of officers or informants be "designed *deliberately* to elicit incriminating remarks" (Kuhlmann v. Wilson, 1986) (italics added). The doctrinal language suggests that the individual who draws the admissions from the accused must subjectively *intend* to do so (United States v. Henry, 1980 (Blackmun, J., dissenting)). If a subjective intent to elicit is required, then either direct proof of the government agent's actual mental disposition or circumstantial evidence of that disposition—the officer's or informant's conduct and incentives, for example—could suffice. However, if there is inadequate proof of an actual intent to elicit—either a purpose to obtain incriminating admissions or knowledge that such admissions would be obtained—the stage would not be "critical" within the meaning of the *Massiah* doctrine. In none of the *Massiah* doctrine cases has the intent of the eliciting agent been at issue. The explanation for that is apparent. When a government operative engages in the active elicitation demanded by the *Massiah* doctrine, there is almost always a solid circumstantial basis for inferring an intent to elicit. Consequently, whether the result would be different in a case where the circumstances did not support an inference of actual intent to elicit remains uncertain.

In face-to-face, known-officer contexts, a "critical stage of the prosecution" exists, and the right to counsel applies, when an officer deliberately and actively elicits information from an individual following formal accusation. In undercover settings involving surreptitious elicitation by informants who are not law enforcement officers, there is an additional requirement before the stage is considered "critical." There must be a basis for "attributing" the active elicitation by the undercover informant to the government, that is, adequate reason to hold the "regular" government employees responsible for the active elicitation of the informant. Because the Sixth Amendment does not regulate the actions of genuinely private parties, it is always necessary to show, at a minimum, that an informant was a "state agent" (i.e., that he or she was acting on behalf of the government). However, state agent status alone is not a sufficient basis for holding the government responsible for an informant's elicitation of disclosures from an accused. Law enforcement officers are chargeable with deliberate elicitation—and, therefore, must respect the entitlement to counsel—only if they either "intentionally creat[e]" (United States v. Henry, 1980) or "knowing[ly] exploit[]" (Maine v. Moulton, 1985) a situation in which they "know" that their undercover operative is likely to act affirmatively to elicit information from the accused. If the facts do not show that the government either intended or knew that its informant would actively prompt admissions by the accused (either by conversation or otherwise), there is no right to assistance even if the informant actively and deliberately elicits such admissions.

This qualification on the definition of a critical stage in undercover settings has never led the Court to reject a right to counsel claim. In both cases that have raised the issue of government responsibility for undercover agents—United States v. Henry and Maine v. Moulton—there were reasons to conclude that government officials intended or knew that their informant would make active efforts to obtain admissions from the accused (Maine v. Moulton, 1985; United States v. Henry, 1980). Factors supporting that conclusion included that the defendant was in custody and, therefore, more likely to need to talk; that the informant was ostensibly a fellow inmate or codefendant whom the accused would trust; that the informant stood to profit if he secured incriminating admissions (either by financial payment or by reduced charges); and that the government's instructions to the informant had not forbidden him from engaging in all active elicitation. By implication, if law enforcement officers structure an encounter in a way that indicates that they do not want and should not expect an undercover informant to actively elicit disclosures, they can prevent the encounter between the informant and accused from becoming a critical stage of the prosecution and avoid the impediments to securing a statement that a defense attorney would undoubtedly pose.

As is always true of the right to a lawyer's assistance, a defendant can waive the right to the assistance of counsel at the critical pretrial stage defined by the *Massiah* doctrine; that is, an accused can forgo representation.[105] "[N]othing in the Sixth Amendment prevents a suspect charged with a crime . . . from voluntarily choosing, on his own, to speak with police in the absence of an attorney" (Michigan v. Harvey, 1990). Waiver questions arise, however, only in direct, known-officer situations. Undercover agents obviously cannot seek waivers from their unwitting targets without destroying the effectiveness of their clandestine operations (United States v. Henry, 1980). Ordinary waiver standards govern the inquiry. To be valid, an accused must intentionally relinquish or abandon a known right (Brewer v. Williams, 1977). Express oral or written waivers are not required, but courts must not presume waivers from silence alone or from confession alone. Instead, there must be at least a circumstantial basis for inferring that the accused has made a decision to surrender the constitutional right to counsel's protection against elicitation by the government (Brewer v. Williams, 1977).

As with all acceptable waivers of the right to counsel, waivers of the *Massiah* entitlement must be both "knowing" and "voluntary." To give a knowing waiver, an accused must have " 'a full awareness of both the nature of the right being abandoned and the consequences of the decision to abandon it' " (Patterson v. Illinois, 1988 (quoting Moran v. Burbine, 1986)). The "key inquiry" is whether the accused was "sufficiently aware of his right to have counsel present during the questioning, and of the possible consequences of a decision to forgo the aid of counsel." As a general rule, the Fifth Amendment-based warnings prescribed by Miranda v. Arizona ("You have the right to remain silent, anything you say can be used against you, and you have the right to have retained or appointed counsel present with you during questioning") contain sufficient information to render an accused's waiver of counsel "knowing." The simple admonishment that one has the right to retained or appointed counsel during questioning provides adequate knowledge of the *nature* of the right being abandoned. Moreover, the warning that anything an accused says can be used against him, the "ultimate adverse consequence" of a choice to make statements to the authorities without legal assistance, informs an accused of what a lawyer can do to assist him (i.e., advise him not to make such statements). An accused who is so informed has adequate "knowledge" of the *consequences* of a decision to surrender the right to counsel. A waiver is not invalid because a defendant lacks a " 'full and complete appreciation of all the consequences flowing' from his waiver" (Patterson v. Illinois, 1988 (quoting Oregon v. Elstad, 1985)). However, if a defendant's lawyer has attempted to contact him during questioning, the defendant is entitled to "know" of that attempt before deciding to abandon his entitlement to assistance. If the authorities do not ensure that he is made aware of the attorney's efforts, a waiver is insufficiently knowing and, therefore, invalid. Moreover, an accused *may* have to know that he has been formally charged with a criminal offense (Patterson v. Illinois, 1988).

Whenever the validity of a waiver of the right to counsel is questioned, a court must always inquire into the accused's knowledge. The inquiry required for a valid waiver of the *Massiah* right to pretrial assistance is less "searching," less "formal" than the inquiry required for a valid waiver of assistance at trial. The reason that less is required is not that the right to assistance against efforts to secure incriminating admissions is less important than the right to assistance at trial. The Sixth Amendment entitlement is vitally important at all stages where it applies. Rather, a lesser inquiry suffices for two reasons. First, counsel's role during questioning is "simple" and "unidimensional" (Patterson v. Illinois, 1988). She merely advises the accused concerning what questions to answer and what questions not to answer. Second, the " 'dangers and disadvantages' " of proceeding without counsel are "less substantial and more obvious to an accused" than the dangers and disadvantages of standing trial without legal aid (Patterson v. Illinois, 1988 (quoting Faretta v. California, 1975)). In essence, a less intensive exploration of the bases for the defendant's waiver is acceptable because there is less that needs to be known and because an accused is more likely to already know it.[106]

The "voluntariness" requirement for a valid waiver of the *Massiah* right to assistance has not been directly addressed in any Supreme Court cases. It seems fair to conclude that the standards regarding the voluntariness of a confession and of a waiver of "*Miranda* rights" also govern the Sixth Amendment inquiry. Under those standards, a waiver is involuntary if the person's will is overborne by government coercion (Colorado v. Connelly, 1986). While personal characteristics that bear upon the strength of the defendant's will are relevant to the determination, unless there is some minimum amount of official coercion that pressures him into surrendering his rights, a waiver is not considered involuntary. Internal, subjective forces that induce an accused to surrender his entitlement to assistance against his "free will" must be factored into the equation but cannot by themselves render a waiver involuntary. Thus, if a mentally ill defendant is "compelled" by his illness to relinquish counsel but is not subjected to official pressures to do so, his waiver is constitutionally voluntary (Colorado v. Connelly, 1986).

A request for counsel is a significant event because it signifies that a defendant is vulnerable and feels incapable of dealing with the authorities without the assistance of a lawyer. If a defendant requests the assistance of counsel, the rules regarding waiver change.[107] The authorities may not approach him and seek a waiver of his right to assistance. If they do, any waiver that they obtain is unacceptable. Even an express, written surrender that is ostensibly knowing and voluntary will not be valid if the defendant previously requested counsel and the police initiated communications with him in the absence of his lawyer (Michigan v. Jackson, 1986). After a defendant has asked for counsel, a waiver of the *Massiah* right is possible *only* if the accused himself "initiates" further communications or exchanges with the authorities. Moreover, not every statement by an accused qualifies as an "initiation" of communications and makes a valid waiver possible. Instead, the accused initiates communications only if his words evince "a willingness and a desire for a generalized discussion about the investigation," that is, only if they demonstrate that he is seeking "to open up a more generalized discussion relating directly or indirectly to the investigation" (Oregon v. Bradshaw, 1983).

This restriction upon the government's ability to obtain a waiver of rights probably applies only if the accused's request for counsel is clear and unequivocal. A request is sufficiently clear only if a reasonable police officer would understand that it was, in fact, a request for counsel's assistance. Words suggesting that the accused "might" have wanted legal assistance are not enough (Davis v. United States, 1994). A clear request made directly to the authorities who intend to elicit admissions is sufficient but is not required. If a defendant, during an appearance in court, makes a general request to a judge for representation by counsel, that request will be treated as a request for assistance during questioning by the authorities. A general request for assistance in coping with the criminal process is presumed to reflect a desire for assistance at "every critical stage of the prosecution" (Michigan v. Jackson, 1986). Moreover, if the accused has made a sufficient request to any state actor, knowledge of that request is imputed to all other state actors. Thus, a waiver would be invalid even if the officer who initiated communications with the defendant and obtained the waiver was truly ignorant of the accused's expressed desire for counsel.

The impact that the *Massiah* right to counsel has on the government's ability to secure statements by surreptitious, undercover methods is different from, and more substantial than, its impact on the efforts of known officers to obtain confessions in face-to-face situations. When a known officer wishes to deliberately elicit disclosures, she can arrange for the presence of counsel or secure a waiver of the right to assistance and can then continue her efforts to elicit disclosures. An undercover operative, however, cannot comply with the constitutional guarantee merely by ensuring that a lawyer is present before she surreptitiously elicits information. In addition, she would have to inform the accused and counsel that she is working for the authorities. The *Massiah* right is an entitlement to have counsel present and to be informed that the informant is a representative of one's adversary, the state. Therefore, when the Sixth Amendment governs undercover encounters, it wholly defeats the government's efforts to operate clandestinely. Both honoring the right to counsel and securing a valid waiver of counsel require divulgence of the fact that the agent is working for the state.

In general, if government agents deliberately elicit admissions from an accused in the absence of counsel or a valid waiver, then the prosecution may not introduce those admissions at trial as evidence of the accused's guilt (Brewer v. Williams, 1977; Massiah v. United States, 1964). There is also a presumption that any "derivative evidence"—evidence that is found as a result of the uncounseled admissions—is inadmissible to establish guilt (Nix v. Williams, 1984). Thus, a defendant's admission that he killed the victim, his revelation of where the murder weapon is located, and the weapon itself are presumptively inadmissible. The basis for the exclusion of this evidence is debatable. According to one view, the sole purpose of exclusion is to deter the authorities from engaging in unconstitutional deliberate elicitation in the future. The prospect of losing the profits of illegal conduct is supposed to discourage similar conduct and induce compliance with the constitutional entitlement to counsel's aid.

An alternative and logically persuasive view is that deterrence is neither the sole nor the primary reason for excluding the evidence. Instead, exclusion is an integral part of the Sixth Amendment entitlement to counsel.[108] Evidence may not be introduced because use of the evidence to convict the defendant would complete the right to counsel violation that began when the information was elicited in the out-of-court, pretrial encounter. According to this position, the role of counsel in our adversary system is to guard the accused against conviction based on unfair advantages gained in an imbalanced clash of adversaries. Counsel plays that role in *Massiah* settings by stopping the defendant from making unwise, incriminating disclosures to the state. If disclosures are not made, the state will not be able to use them to convict the accused. Evidence secured in an imbalanced pretrial confrontation must be barred from the courtroom to preserve the primary benefit of having the assistance of counsel. Use of the evidence at trial would complete the constitutional deprivation by inflicting the harm on the defense that counsel could have prevented.

The language used by the *Massiah* Court provides powerful support for the view that exclusion of illegally obtained evidence is an integral part of the Sixth Amendment right to assistance. The Court specifically held that the defendant "was denied the basic protections of" the Sixth Amendment right to counsel "when there was *used against him at his trial* evidence of his own incriminating words, which federal agents had deliberately elicited . . . in the absence of counsel" (italics added). In subsequent opinions, however, the Court has muddied the waters. Language in some opinions implies that a deprivation of the Sixth Amendment right occurs at the time the government's agent deliberately elicits statements. On the sole occasion that the Court has had to address the rationale for excluding evidence obtained in violation of the *Massiah* doctrine, it began by positing "deterrence" of future uncounseled elicitation as the object of barring evidence (Nix v. Williams, 1984). The Court then explained the defendant's argument that exclusion was an inherent part of his constitutional entitlement to counsel, *assumed* that that argument was valid, but still rejected the claim for exclusion. (The exclusionary claim was rejected on the ground that even if counsel had been present, the same evidence would inevitably have been discovered by lawful means and would have been used at the defendant's trial.)

Consequently, the Court has neither approved nor disapproved of the contention that exclusion under the *Massiah* doctrine is an inseparable part of the Sixth Amendment right.[109]

No matter which reason explains the exclusion of evidence under *Massiah*—and it is possible that both are valid explanations—it is clear that some evidence secured in violation of that doctrine's commands is nonetheless admissible at trial. Evidence derived from statements secured without affording an accused legal assistance may be introduced if that evidence would inevitably have been discovered by lawful means (Nix v. Williams, 1984).[110] In addition, statements obtained in violation of the Michigan v. Jackson branch of *Massiah* doctrine—the branch that holds otherwise valid waivers to be invalid if they are obtained after a suspect clearly requests counsel and the government initiates further communications—may not be used as proof of guilt. They may, however, be introduced to impeach an accused's inconsistent trial testimony, that is, to cast doubt on the truthfulness of that testimony (Michigan v. Harvey, 1990). Whether there are additional instances in which the government may make trial use of statements or other evidence that it has secured by virtue of deprivations of the *Massiah* right to counsel remains to be seen.

As already mentioned, the pretrial extension of the right to trial assistance defined by the *Massiah* doctrine has been exceptionally controversial, perhaps the most stridently debated of all areas of right to counsel law. From the outset, there has been vehement opposition to the decision to extend the right to legal assistance to government efforts to deliberately elicit statements from defendants. Justices of the Supreme Court[111] and legal scholars[112] have raised serious challenges to the constitutional legitimacy of the *Massiah* Court's interpretation of the Sixth Amendment guarantee. They have constructed an array of forceful arguments against the right announced in that case.

The most fundamental contention of *Massiah*'s opponents is that the pretrial extension of counsel defined by the doctrine is "fundamentally inconsistent with traditional notions of the role of the attorney that underlie the Sixth Amendment right to counsel" and "entirely ignores the doctrinal foundation of that right" (United States v. Henry, 1980 (Rehnquist, J., dissenting)). According to this argument, a lawyer's function is to provide legal knowledge and expertise in coping with the system and the trained prosecutor. Because the stage deemed critical by *Massiah* involves no legal questions and no prosecutorial maneuvering, an accused has no need for legal assistance. The right to counsel should not be extended to situations where the reasons for affording the right simply do not exist. In situations where state agents seek to deliberately elicit incriminating admissions before trial—surreptitiously or directly—the government has no "unfair advantage." The accused is perfectly capable of deciding by himself whether to assume the risks of divulging his guilt to another person. Because the defendant is not in a position of inferiority and is equipped to cope with the questions and the persons confronting him, he needs no equalizing assistant.

Opponents also maintain that in the encounters governed by *Massiah* doctrine, the government does not actually "interfere" with the accused's right to counsel, does not disturb or spy on the attorney–client relationship, and does not impede counsel's abilities to investigate and prepare a defense. The government's actions engender no risk of coercion to speak, no risk that admissions of guilt will be unreliable, and, consequently, no risk that innocent persons will be convicted in error (Brewer v. Williams, 1977 (White, J., dissenting); Massiah v. United States, 1964 (White, J. dissenting); United States v. Henry, 1980 (Rehnquist, J., dissenting)).

In sum, critics allege that *Massiah* is a constitutionally unsupportable interpretation of the Sixth Amendment right to counsel that is rooted in an unwarranted "sporting theory of criminal justice" (Brewer v. Williams, 1977 (Burger, C. J., dissenting)). It reflects an illegitimate conception of defense counsel as a "guru who must be present" to protect defendants against their own stupidity (United States v. Henry, 1980 (Rehnquist, J., dissenting)), and constitutes an unnecessary and unjustified impediment to finding the "truth," the central objective of the criminal justice system (Massiah v. United States, 1964 (White, J., dissenting)).[113]

One reason that the *Massiah* extension of counsel is peculiarly vulnerable to such criticisms is the patent inadequacy of the Supreme Court's explanations of the underpinnings of the right. The *Massiah* opinion rested almost entirely on the unembellished assertion that a system that guarantees counsel at trial could not logically grant less to an indicted defendant subjected to police interrogation because a denial of assistance at that point could deprive an accused of effective representation at the " 'only stage' " when it would help (Massiah v. United States, 1964 (quoting Spano v. New York, 1959)). While true, this hardly provides a complete justification for a revolutionary extension of the right to trial counsel to an "informal" pretrial event. Moreover, it did not respond persuasively to the credible attacks of the opponents.

Subsequent explanations of *Massiah*'s foundations have not been more complete or satisfying. The Court has said that *Massiah* "rests squarely on interference with [the] right to counsel" (United States v. Henry, 1980), that counsel's purpose is to combat "the overreaching of the prosecution" (United States v. Ash, 1973), that the *Massiah* doctrine prevents "circumvent[ion]" and "dilut[ion]" of the Sixth Amendment right, that it preserves the accused's entitlement "to rely on counsel as a 'medium' between him and the State," and that it safeguards the defendant's constitutionally guaranteed "opportunity to consult with counsel" (Maine v. Moulton, 1985). These cryptic justifications for the Court's interpretation of the Sixth Amendment are less than convincing.

The best explanation of the constitutional underpinnings of the *Massiah* right to counsel is rooted in the adversarial nature of American criminal justice systems.[114] According to this position, once the government initiates the adversarial contest by accusing a person of crime, it has an obligation not to deal directly with the presumptively vulnerable accused. Counsel is a necessary "medium" in significant interactions between the adversaries to promote rough equality between the state and the accused and to ensure balanced contests. Both surreptitious and direct efforts designed to seal a defendant's fate by securing inculpatory statements are significant dealings or interactions between adversaries. When a known, aboveboard official approaches the defendant, the state may gain advantages from the accused's ignorance of the risks of speaking to his opponent. An attorney can, and is expected to, compensate for such ignorance by advising the defendant of the serious perils of revealing information to the state (Patterson v. Illinois, 1988). If an undercover operative approaches, the state may gain advantages by deceiving the defendant and exploiting his unawareness that he is in the presence of an opponent who is committed to his conviction. Once the government has declared itself an adversary, principles of fair play demand that it not conceal its identity from the accused in an effort to induce him to aid the quest to prove his guilt (Maine v. Moulton, 1985). Instead, it must deal with an equalized defendant as an arm's-length adversary.

Although the assistance provided by a lawyer in such situations does not necessarily entail knowledge of legal complexities, that does not mean that the attorney is not providing "legal assistance" (i.e., the kind of aid that a lawyer is expected to furnish in our adversarial system). Advice not to cooperate with the opponent is surely legal assistance that a lawyer is especially qualified and trained to provide. Moreover, although legally trained prosecutors are not ordinarily present in the encounters governed by *Massiah* doctrine, professional law enforcement officers are intimately involved. They either engage in direct efforts to exploit the unaided accused's vulnerabilities or orchestrate undercover schemes to deceive the accused into disclosing information to the state. It is not illogical to view these settings as instances in which the state is using its superior resources and knowledge to take unfair advantage of a weaker, inherently unequal opponent.

From this perspective, the role and functions contemplated for counsel in *Massiah* contexts are fully consistent with the traditional role and functions of a lawyer at trial. At trial, counsel is expected to provide more than knowledge and advice about legal technicalities. A lawyer has the obligation to furnish needed advice at trial regarding the wisdom of cooperating with the state's efforts to gain a conviction. Surely, the state would not be permitted to approach an unassisted accused in front of jurors and elicit incriminating admissions. Whether done openly, in the person of a prosecutor or police officer, or secretively, by means of an undercover agent, such a confrontation would breach the state's obligation to ensure a fair, balanced adversarial battle. An accused would not be expected to handle such an encounter alone or be faulted for taking a risk and failing to protect himself. Even if the disclosures that resulted from such an imbalanced courtroom confrontation furthered the search for "truth" at trial, the government would be faulted for circumventing the "medium" of counsel and violating adversarial system principles of fair play.

Historically, the resolution of an accusation was confined to trial. When that was the case, defendants had ample protection against government efforts to elicit their incriminating words. The development of full-time, professional police forces and the expansion of the criminal process into the period before trial resulted in official efforts to circumvent the protection that existed when the contest occurred only at trial.[115] If the state could secure statements from an unaided accused before trial, then place those statements before jurors, the disadvantages to the accused and the harm to his defense would be identical to those involved when the state elicits statements from an unaided accused at trial. *Massiah*'s extension of the right to counsel to pretrial encounters prevents the state from making an "end run" around the assistance furnished by trial counsel. Counsel is essential to ensure that the substance of the guarantee of trial assistance is preserved, not nullified. Once the adversarial contest has begun, the state's efforts to exploit the accused's weaknesses or vulnerabilities before trial and then use the fruits of that exploitation to secure a conviction are inconsistent with principles of adversary system fair play. Pretrial confrontations with the defendant without counsel are as unprincipled and unfair as similar confrontations in the courtroom.

Finally, allegations that the entitlement to counsel recognized by the *Massiah* doctrine does not guard against coercion or unreliability and can obstruct the system's ability to ascertain the "truth" in a criminal case, while accurate, are beside the point. Trial counsel often provides protection against perils other than coercion or unreliability. Moreover, measures taken by trial counsel to shield her client—including advice not to take the witness stand and cooperate voluntarily with the state—can certainly impede the search for truth. We do not restrict counsel only to defensive actions that ensure that the truth will be discovered because we believe that unfettered assistance by defense counsel best promotes the search for truth and the other important objectives of the adversarial system of criminal justice.[116]

In sum, the pretrial extension of the right to counsel defined by the *Massiah* doctrine has prompted strenuous criticism. Opponents of *Massiah* offer a number of powerful reasons that a Sixth Amendment right to counsel against official efforts to obtain inculpatory disclosures is without constitutional foundation. The Supreme Court's opinions upholding *Massiah*'s extension of the right to representation have failed to adequately explain the constitutional rationales for that right. Nonetheless, there are logical responses to the criticisms leveled at the doctrine. While the merits of these responses are debatable, they do provide a plausible defense of the *Massiah* Court's holding.

As noted, dissenters from *Massiah* have observed that in the encounters regulated by the doctrine, the government is neither actively interfering with counsel nor disturbing or spying on meetings between the defense attorney and client. The implication is that interference, disturbance, or spying would violate the Sixth Amendment. In Weatherford v. Bursey, the Court addressed the constitutional implications of government intrusions into the attorney–client relationship.

In *Bursey*, the defendant and an undercover agent vandalized offices of the

Selective Service. The agent informed the police. To protect his undercover status from revelation, the authorities arrested and charged their agent along with the defendant. The two retained separate counsel. On two occasions, the accused and his attorney invited the agent to meet with them to discuss the upcoming trial. To maintain his cover, the agent accepted the invitations and met with them. He did not discuss with or pass on to the government any details about the content of the meetings. Although at the time of the meetings the government did not intend to call the undercover agent to testify, ultimately he was called to give an eyewitness account of the crimes. After the defendant was convicted, he brought a civil rights action, alleging that the undercover agent's presence at the meetings had deprived him of his Sixth Amendment entitlement to counsel.

The Supreme Court rejected that claim, holding that under such circumstances a deprivation of counsel could not result from the mere presence of the undercover agent at attorney–client meetings. Unless the agent "communicated the substance of the [attorney–client] conversations [to the government] and thereby created at least a realistic possibility of injury to [the accused] or benefit to the state, there [could] be no Sixth Amendment violation" (Weatherford v. Bursey, 1977). The Court narrowly limited its holding to the specific facts of the *Bursey* case, observing that if the agent had testified at trial as to any conversation between the accused and his lawyer, if any prosecution evidence had originated in those conversations, if any conversations had otherwise been used to defendant's substantial detriment, or even if the prosecution had learned details of the conversations about trial preparations from the agent, there would have been "a much stronger case" for a Sixth Amendment violation. In addition, a constitutionally different outcome might be justified if an actual "member of the prosecuting team" were to attend a lawyer–client meeting, if the authorities, with the purpose of learning what they could about defense plans, instructed an informant to intrude on an attorney–accused relationship, or if an informant himself had decided to intrude and had done so.

In sum, an accused does have a constitutional entitlement to private consultations with his attorney. Government intrusions upon the lawyer–client relationship and overhearing of conversations between counsel and the accused pose a serious threat to significant Sixth Amendment interests. The mere presence of an informant at conversations at the behest of the defendant and his lawyer does not violate the Constitution if the informant is present in order to preserve his undercover status. If the informant shares information about the meetings with the government or uses the information to the accused's disadvantage, if the informant's presence during a lawyer–client discussion comes about under different circumstances, or if a regular member of the prosecution team attends a lawyer–client meeting, a deprivation of the right to counsel may well result.

There is a second type of informal, nonjudicial pretrial event that can qualify as a "critical stage of the prosecution." Certain identification procedures used by the government to secure eyewitness identifications of accused persons by witnesses to crimes are deemed critical and trigger the entitlement to counsel's assistance. The discussion that follows traces the development of the *Wade–Gilbert* doctrine, the doctrine that dictates when counsel is required at government identification processes.

In 1967, in United States v. Wade and Gilbert v. California, the Supreme Court considered, for the first time, whether the Sixth Amendment right to counsel extended to a corporeal "lineup"—an identification process in which an accused and several other individuals are presented to an eyewitness to a crime. Both *Wade* and *Gilbert* involved defendants who had been formally charged with crimes at the time of their lineups. Neither defendant was afforded the assistance of a lawyer. In the Supreme Court, they contended that the Constitution required that the right to counsel be extended to pretrial lineups.

The Court agreed that a lineup was a critical stage of the prosecution because the absence of counsel "might derogate from the accused's right to a fair trial" (United States v. Wade, 1967). According to the majority, the assistance of a lawyer was "necessary to preserve the . . . right to a fair trial as affected by [the] right meaningfully to cross-examine the witnesses against [the accused] and to have the effective assistance of counsel at the trial itself." [117] More specifically, because "potential substantial prejudice" was inherent in a lineup and because counsel could "help avoid that prejudice," an extension of the right to counsel was justified.

The Court attributed the potential for substantial prejudice to four variables—the proverbial untrustworthiness of eyewitness identifications, the many possibilities for intentional and unintentional suggestion in lineup procedures, the fact that witnesses who are misled into erroneous identifications at lineups will not later change their minds, and the inability to reconstruct at trial any infirmities in lineup procedures (United States v. Wade, 1967). These factors make it impossible for trial counsel to effectively cross-examine witnesses who make lineup identifications. If effective cross-examination is impossible, counsel cannot show the fact finder the deficiencies in what are quite likely to be inaccurate identifications. The result is a significant risk that innocent persons will be convicted of crimes that they did not commit.[118]

According to the Court, counsel could help avoid the potential for prejudice by observing the structure and conduct of the lineup and the behavior of the witnesses. Armed with the information gained from these observations, counsel would be able to conduct meaningful cross-examination at trial. Moreover, at the lineup itself counsel might be able to actively prevent some of the prejudicial influences that could lead to untrustworthy identifications. In sum, the Sixth Amendment right to the assistance of counsel is primarily a safeguard of the accused's most basic right to a "fair trial." Counsel's presence at a pretrial lineup is essential to ensure that the entitlement to a fair trial is not fatally undermined before the trial begins.

The reasoning of the Court in *Wade* and *Gilbert* suggested that an accused needs and is entitled to counsel's aid at all kinds of eyewitness identification processes. In United States v. Ash, however, the Court modified its approach to determining whether a pretrial event is a critical stage. Based on that modified approach, a majority concluded that a photographic identification of an accused is not a critical stage of the prosecution.

In *Ash*, witnesses to a bank robbery identified the defendant from an array of photographs shown to them by the authorities. The defendant contended that the exhibition of the photos to the witnesses was a "critical stage" that triggered his right to counsel. The Supreme Court disagreed, reasoning that for an event to qualify as a "critical stage," it must be a "trial-like confrontation" at which the accused needs help in coping with the legal system, the expert prosecutor, or both (United States v. Ash, 1973). Because a defendant is not present at a photograph array, he is not confronted with either legal questions or the expertise of the prosecutor. Because his inferiorities cannot possibly be exploited, there is no need for or reason to extend the right to counsel to a photographic identification process. A lineup qualifies as a critical stage because it is a "trial-like confrontation" at which the accused is present and might be victimized by official "overreaching." Moreover, because the effects of government overreaching at a lineup cannot ordinarily be reconstructed accurately and combated at trial, the pretrial damage to the defense cannot be remedied later at the trial.

Despite its assertions to the contrary, the *Ash* majority clearly departed from the *Wade-Gilbert* approach to deciding when a pretrial event constitutes a critical stage of the prosecution. The effect was to narrow the class of identification processes that trigger an entitlement to legal assistance. Today, an identification process is critical *only* if the accused is physically present at the time of the identification. Both multiperson lineups and single-person "showups" qualify as critical. Other means of securing identifications—the display of single photographs, photographic arrays, photographs of lineups, slide shows, or videotapes of lineups or single-person showups—are not critical stages because they do not involve "trial-like confrontations" between the defendant and the state. Moreover, it is even possible for jurisdictions to modify lineups and other corporeal methods of identification in ways that render them "noncritical." Legislative or other regulations that sufficiently enhance the scientific precision of those identification methods and make accurate reconstruction at trial possible lessen the risks of prejudice and enable counsel to "cure" prejudice at trial. If such regulations were in place, a stage would "cease to be 'critical' " (United States v. Ash, 1973; United States v. Wade, 1967). Counsel would not be needed at the pretrial event because counsel at trial can adequately protect the defendant's interest in a fair adversarial process.[119]

An accused may waive her right to assistance at an identification procedure if the waiver is "intelligent" (United States v. Wade, 1967). There have been no Supreme Court cases discussing the waiver requirements in identification contexts. The general principles governing waivers of constitutional rights—discussed above in connection with the *Massiah* doctrine—would seem to apply. Thus, a surrender of the right to counsel at an identification procedure must be both "knowing" and "voluntary." Because counsel serves a different function at identification sessions than she does when the government seeks inculpatory disclosures, the precise content of what an accused must "know" probably requires some refinement in contexts governed by *Wade*. An awareness that the accused has the right to have retained or appointed counsel present at the lineup, coupled with an awareness that an identification can be used against the defendant at trial and that counsel can safeguard against misidentification, may well be sufficient. On the other hand, it is at least arguable that a more complete, in-depth appreciation of the "dangers and disadvantages" of proceeding without counsel is essential.

The role that counsel is supposed to play at a corporeal identification process has never been definitively explained. The question is an important one, for if an accused is entitled to have counsel represent his interests in particular ways and the government prevents an attorney from doing so, a Sixth Amendment deprivation would occur despite the presence of counsel. According to one view, the role of counsel is essentially that of a passive observer who watches the conduct of the lineup and arms herself to attack a witness' identification at trial (United States v. Ash, 1973 (Brennan, J., dissenting)). The competing view agrees that counsel is expected to observe infirmities in the lineup process but maintains that she is also expected to actively participate in the lineup process. Active representation could include suggestions about how to structure the lineup, objections to features of the process, instructions and advice to the client, and contemporaneous cross-examination of identifying witnesses. The latter view seems more consistent with the reasoning behind the *Ash* Court's narrow definition of a critical stage. Counsel is afforded at trial-like pretrial confrontations in order to play the same active role that she plays at trial. She is the "spokesman for, and advisor to, the accused" (United States v. Ash, 1973). A lawyer at a lineup is expected to protect the accused against efforts by the "prosecuting authorities to take advantage of the accused." She furnishes assistance needed to "counterbalanc[e] any 'overreaching' by the prosecution." The clear implication of this description of counsel's functions is that counsel is expected to actively participate in lineups. The suggestion in a subsequent opinion that defense counsel "can serve . . . his client's . . . interests by objecting to suggestive features of a procedure before they influence a witness' identification" provides additional support for the view that a lawyer's role in pretrial identification sessions does entail active involvement (Moore v. Illinois, 1977).

If counsel is not present and the accused has not waived assistance at a critical identification process, a "*per se* exclusionary rule" applies to an identification made by a witness at the uncounseled session (Gilbert v. California, 1967). This means that the government may *never* make use of such an identification to prove the accused's guilt. A strict, inflexible sanction is considered necessary "to assure that law enforcement authorities will respect the accused's constitutional right to the presence of his counsel." The awareness that potentially probative evidence (i.e., evidence that has value in establishing the guilt of the accused) will be irrevocably lost provides a powerful inducement for officials to make sure that a lawyer is present or that a valid waiver has been obtained before a lineup is held. Subsequent identifications by the same witness, made either at a properly conducted out-of-court identification procedure or in the courtroom, are presumed to be the product of the improper identification session and are presumptively excluded from trial as well. The exclusion of these later identifications, however, is not absolute. If the government shows by "clear and convincing evidence" that a subsequent identification has an "independent origin" (i.e., that it is "based upon observations of the suspect other than the lineup identification"), the identification is admissible (United States v. Wade, 1967). Relevant factors in making this independent origin determination include the extent of the witness' opportunity to observe the crime, the consistency of a pre-lineup description of the suspect by the witness and the actual appearance of the accused, prior identifications of other persons by the witness, prior failures of the witness to identify the accused, the amount of time that elapsed between the crime and the lineup identification, and any relevant facts disclosed about the lineup that suggest either corruption of the process or deficiencies of the witness.

The Entitlement to Counsel's Assistance for and at Trial

Originally, the trial was the sole battleground for the adversarial clash between the government and the individual charged with crime. There were no critical pretrial events that could have significant effects on the outcome of a criminal accusation. Moreover, post-trial efforts to overturn a guilty verdict—direct appeals of and collateral challenges to convictions—were not the norm. It is hardly surprising, therefore, that the Sixth Amendment's "core purpose . . . was to assure 'Assistance' *at trial*" (United States v. Ash, 1973) (italics added). Through the past two centuries, the processes of adjudicating guilt or innocence have undergone significant expansions into both pretrial and post-trial periods. Nonetheless, in modern American systems of criminal justice, the trial remains the focal point and the most critical stage of the adversarial contest.[120] Because the original intent of the Sixth Amendment's Framers was to afford legal representation during the confrontation with the state at trial, and because the trial remains the central event in the resolution of criminal accusations, there is no dispute that the Constitution affords an ample right to assistance of counsel at the trial in the courtroom.[121] The Supreme Court opinions that have addressed questions of entitlement to assistance at pretrial or post-trial events have simply accepted the right to assistance *at trial* as a given.

"The purpose of the trial stage from the State's point of view is to convert a criminal defendant from a person presumed innocent to one found guilty beyond a reasonable doubt" (Ross v. Moffitt, 1974). From the defendant's point of view, the object is to resist all prosecutorial efforts to dispel the presumption of innocence, that is, to prevent the state from satisfying its burden of proof by ensuring that the trier of fact has at least a reasonable doubt about guilt. At trial, both sides present evidence and arguments to the trier of fact in an effort to prevail on the merits. At trial, both society and the defendant have the most at stake. A loss for the state—a verdict of not guilty—will be final. No matter how flawed that decision is, no matter how strong the government's need to vindicate the public interest by trying the case again, the Fifth Amendment guarantee against "double jeopardy" will bar further pursuit of a conviction (Arizona v. Washington, 1978).[122] On the other hand, a loss for the accused—a verdict of guilty—can have devastating impacts on his life and future. While a conviction is not necessarily final—a defendant can seek to overturn the verdict by appeal or collateral attack—the odds of securing a reversal of the finding of guilt are not favorable.[123]

In the adversarial systems that all American jurisdictions adhere to, the government employs a prosecuting attorney to prove the guilt of the defendant. The prosecutor "presents evidence to the court, challenges any witness offered by the defendant, argues rulings of the court, and makes direct arguments to the court and jury seeking to persuade them of the defendant's guilt" (Ross v. Moffitt, 1974). To defend against the state's charges and the prosecutor's efforts to establish their validity, the accused has the Sixth Amendment guarantee of a trained legal assistant. Defense counsel can present exculpatory evidence, challenge the state's case, make arguments, and seek to persuade the court and jury that the defendant is not guilty. The accused's right to the assistance of counsel at trial is unquestionable and unquestioned.[124]

A trial ordinarily begins with jury selection and ends with a verdict. While the entitlement to a lawyer's assistance clearly extends to this entire period, it cannot be limited to that time frame without thwarting counsel's ability to serve her trial functions. Consequently, if a state were to restrict an accused's ability to retain representation to the formal trial itself or were to provide appointed counsel only for the actual trial process, it would undoubtedly violate the defendant's Sixth Amendment right to trial assistance. To be meaningful, the entitlement to assistance *at trial* must instead include the opportunity to have counsel's aid begin *before* the formal commencement of the trial in the courtroom. Counsel must be involved in the case sufficiently in advance to enable her to research the law and investigate the facts fully and to adequately prepare the best defense that she can (Powell v. Alabama, 1932). A lawyer cannot be expected to provide adequate equalization at the trial if she is not involved in a case until the actual beginning of the trial process. If the adversary system is to function fairly and achieve its ostensible ends, counsel must have adequate advance time to get ready to meet the state's evidence and arguments and present the defendant's side of the case.[125] Perhaps it is best to speak of the core Sixth Amendment right as an entitlement to the assistance of counsel *for and at trial.*

In addition, modern American criminal justice systems afford opportunities to seek various sorts of judicial rulings prior to the formal commencement of a trial. A part of counsel's obligation to provide trial assistance is the responsibility to explore and present pretrial motions seeking rulings that promote the defendant's best interests.[126] Pretrial motions can have substantial, sometimes determinative, impacts upon the outcome of the trial. Counsel, for example, might file a motion to suppress (i.e., to exclude from the trial) critical prosecution evidence, alleging that government officials obtained that evidence illegally. She might move to change venue if the atmosphere surrounding the trial suggests a community poisoned by prejudice, or she might seek to have the charges dismissed on constitutional or other grounds. Counsel might attempt to obtain pretrial rulings that defense evidence will be admissible at trial or that government evidence will be inadmissible under the rules of evidence. Appointed counsel might request additional state financial assistance to retain experts who will aid in constructing an adequate defense. For a variety of reasons, including efficiency, these and other pretrial motions are presented to the trial judge and resolved—sometimes after trial-like evidentiary hearings—before the process of selecting a jury and presenting evidence begins. Because of the important role that they play in resolving criminal accusations, pretrial motions should be considered integral parts of the trial itself. Consequently, the right to assistance of trial counsel must include an entitlement to retained or appointed representation sufficiently before trial to enable counsel to research, prepare, and present pretrial motions, to resist prosecution motions contrary to the defendant's interests, and to provide zealous, effective representation at any hearings on these motions.[127] The scope of the right to trial assistance must encompass an opportunity to have counsel involved in the defense well before the formal start of the trial process in the courtroom.

Ordinarily, a trial ends with the return of a verdict and the entry of a judgment by the trial judge. In cases of conviction, defense counsel may attack the verdict by post-trial motion filed in the trial court. Complete legal assistance at trial may well include the preparation and presentation of various kinds of post-trial motions. Counsel, for example, might seek to have the judge enter a judgment of acquittal notwithstanding the jury's verdict, contending that no reasonable juror could have found guilt beyond a reasonable doubt from the evidence presented at trial. Alternatively, a defense attorney might argue that a conviction is unjust and against the weight of the evidence, might claim that critical evidence supporting the conviction was improperly admitted at trial, or might assert that newly discovered, exculpatory evidence casts doubt upon the verdict. On these bases, counsel could request that the judge set aside the finding of guilt and order a new trial.[128] The process of determining guilt or innocence—the trial process—is not completed until the trial judge rules on such post-trial motions. For right to counsel purposes, it seems logical and fair to view such post-trial proceedings as inseparable parts of the trial itself. Full enjoyment of the Sixth Amendment's promise of trial assistance includes a right to representation for purposes of requesting the trial judge to overturn or set aside a verdict.[129]

The preceding discussion rests on the premise that an accused will stand trial before a judge or jury. In reality, many criminal accusations are resolved without trials. After negotiations with prosecutors, a very substantial percentage of those charged with offenses agree to forgo their entitlement to a trial and instead choose to enter a guilty plea.[130] Two cases that predate the modern era of right to counsel jurisprudence provide support for a general right to assistance in guilty plea proceedings. In Townsend v. Burke, a 1948 case in which the accused pleaded guilty and was sentenced in the absence of counsel, the Supreme Court found a deprivation of due process and concluded that the conviction entered upon the plea could not stand. According to the Court, counsel "could have taken steps to see that the conviction . . . [was] not predicated on misinformation or misreading of court records, a requirement of fair play which absence of counsel withheld from this prisoner" (Townsend v. Burke, 1948). In Moore v. Michigan, a 1957 case involving a guilty plea, the Supreme Court acknowledged that the "right to counsel is not a right confined to representation during the trial on the merits." It then held that due process of law afforded an entitlement to representation at the guilty plea proceeding in *Moore* because the defendant's "rights could not have been fairly protected without the assistance of counsel to help him with his defense." Because the accused did not have and did not properly waive counsel, the Court deemed his guilty plea "invalidly accepted" and reversed his conviction (Moore v. Michigan, 1957).

Both of these state court cases were decided at a time when a defendant's constitutional entitlement to appointed counsel in a state *trial* hinged upon a case-specific evaluation of the need for assistance. It is not surprising, therefore, that the findings of due process violations in *Townsend* and *Moore* were explicitly based on the specific facts of each case. Subsequently, however, in the landmark 1963 decision in Gideon v. Wainwright, the Supreme Court abandoned the case-by-case, "special circumstances" approach to deciding whether due process requires states to provide trial counsel for indigents. The *Gideon* Court instead ruled that all defendants charged with felonies are entitled to assistance at trial.[131]

The "guiding hand of counsel is needed at the trial 'lest the unwary concede that which only bewilderment or ignorance could justify or pay a penalty which is greater than the law . . . exacts for the offense which they in fact and in law committed" (Hamilton v. Alabama, 1961). When negotiations and a guilty plea proceeding substitute for and supplant the trial process, an accused has equally powerful interests in avoiding bewildered or ignorant concessions, in not paying penalties greater than the law exacts, and in having a process that comports with adversarial system principles of "fair play."[132] The holding and reasoning of *Gideon*, coupled with the earlier holdings in *Townsend* and *Moore*, provide strong support for a general entitlement to counsel in the guilty plea process. Today, an accused surely has a constitutional right to legal assistance in a guilty plea proceeding whenever the charge is one that would require counsel at a trial.[133]

In sum, in our adversary system the assistance of counsel at trial—the central event in the adjudication of guilt or innocence—is critical to ensure the fairness of the trial process. At no other juncture is the confrontation with "the intricacies of the law and the advocacy of the public prosecutor" more intense (United States v. Ash, 1973). No other phase of the process has a more critical impact upon the accused's fate. An equalizing assistant is essential to ensure a balanced contest, to guarantee a reliable search for truth, and to provide the defendant with a fair opportunity to defend against the charges. Thus, the need for such an assistant is greatest at trial. To fully satisfy this need, the accused must have an entitlement to assistance during the actual trial process, for a period of time prior to the formal start of the trial process, and for a period of time following the rendition of a verdict. An accused must also have an entitlement to assistance when he chooses to relinquish his right to a trial, electing instead to enter a guilty plea.

The Entitlement to Counsel's Assistance after Trial

After a trial is completed and a judgment of conviction is entered, the presiding judge imposes a sentence on the defendant. Following the sentencing, a defendant may seek to overturn his conviction by direct appeal or by a collateral, postconviction challenge. This subsection addresses the constitutional right to the assistance of counsel in the phases of the criminal process following the conclusion of the trial.

The Right to the Assistance of Counsel at Sentencing Proceedings

The Supreme Court has addressed the right to counsel's aid at sentencing on two significant occasions. On both, it concluded that the Constitution granted the defendant an entitlement to a lawyer's assistance. In Townsend v. Burke, the Court considered a combination guilty plea hearing and sentencing at which the defendant was not represented by, not offered appointment of, and not advised of a right to counsel. In imposing sentence, the trial judge "recited against the defendant" several charges for prior offenses. In fact, one of the prior charges had been dismissed, and the defendant had been acquitted of two of the others.

In light of the judge's "emphasis" on the prior charges during the sentencing, the Supreme Court refused to assume that they had not influenced the sentence that he had imposed. It then concluded that the "uncounseled defendant was either overreached by the prosecution's submission of misinformation to the court or was prejudiced by the court's own misreading of the record." "[W]hile [he was] disadvantaged by lack of counsel, . . . [the defendant] was sentenced on the basis of assumptions concerning his criminal record which were materially untrue." If counsel had been available to assist him, she would have been duty-bound either to prevent or to seek a remedy for those false assumptions. A defense lawyer could have afforded the defendant the "opportunity to correct" the "extensively and materially false" foundation on which the trial judge relied.

Even if counsel would "not have changed the sentence, . . . [she] could have taken steps to see that the conviction and sentence were not predicated on misinformation or misreading of court records, a requirement of *fair play* which absence of counsel withheld from" the defendant (Townsend v. Burke, 1948) (italics added). For these reasons, the lack of assistance of counsel at the sentencing proceeding violated the defendant's Fourteenth Amendment right to due process of law.

In Mempa v. Rhay, two Washington cases were consolidated for decision. In both cases, defendants had been convicted of offenses based on guilty pleas (Mempa v. Rhay, 1967). Both defendants were placed on probation, and imposition of sentence was deferred. Subsequently, the prosecutor moved to have each defendant's probation revoked, asserting that each of them had committed another offense. At hearings without defense counsel, trial judges revoked each defendant's probation and sentenced each to a term of imprisonment. Both defendants sought review by the Supreme Court, claiming that they had been deprived of the right to counsel.

The Court agreed that the defendants had been entitled to counsel at the probation revocation and sentencing proceedings. Because the Board of Prison Terms and Paroles (the Board) actually set the length of a prison sentence in Washington, the state's sentencing scheme provided limited opportunities for judicial discretion. A sentencing judge, however, was required to furnish the Board with a recommendation regarding length and to provide information about the "circumstances of the crime and the character of the individual," and the Board placed considerable weight on a judge's recommendations (Mempa v. Rhay, 1967). According to the Supreme Court, "to the extent such recommendations are influential in determining the resulting sentence, the necessity for the aid of counsel in marshaling the facts, introducing evidence of mitigating circumstances and in general aiding and assisting the defendant to present his case as to sentence is apparent." "[M]ore important . . . certain legal rights"—specifically, the right to appeal and the right to withdraw a guilty plea—might well be lost if counsel were not present at the hearing. Consequently, the defendants in *Mempa* had been entitled to legal representation and had suffered constitutional deprivations.[134]

Neither the *Townsend* nor the *Mempa* opinion constituted a blanket holding that defendants are generally entitled to counsel at sentencing proceedings. Both opinions relied heavily on the specific facts of the cases. In *Townsend*, the trial judge's evident reliance on false charges was significant. In *Mempa*, the particular nature of the state's sentencing scheme was integral to the Court's analysis. Still, two statements in the *Mempa* opinion strongly support a general right to assistance at sentencing. The Court asserted that, in light of the landmark holding in *Gideon*, its previous decisions "clearly [stood] for the proposition that . . . counsel . . . is required at every stage of a criminal proceeding where *substantial rights of a criminal accused may be affected*" (italics added). The Court then added that Townsend v. Burke "illustrate[d] the critical nature of sentencing in a criminal case and *might well be considered to support by itself a holding that the right to counsel applies at sentencing*" (italics added). These observations—coupled with the fact that virtually every sentencing proceeding surely involves a need for counsel to marshal the facts, introduce mitigating evidence, and present the defendant's arguments with regard to sentence—provide a firm foundation for the conclusion that a post-trial sentencing proceeding is a "critical stage" of a criminal prosecution, a stage that requires extension of the Sixth Amendment right to trial counsel.[135] Because legal representation is essential to ensure both a justifiable outcome and fair play in the sentencing process, states must permit representation by retained counsel and must offer appointed counsel to indigents. Unless the right to assistance is validly waived, a sentencing in the absence of defense counsel violates the defendant's constitutional entitlement to assistance.[136]

The Right to the Assistance of Counsel on Appeal[137]

Until the late 1800s, a trial was typically the end of the road for a criminal defendant.[138] At common law, "appellate review of any sort was 'limited' and 'rarely used' " (Martinez v. Court of Appeal of California, 2000). In federal courts, the right to appeal a conviction "was nonexistent for the first century of our Nation, and appellate review of any sort was 'rarely allowed' " (Martinez v. Court of Appeal of California, 2000 (quoting Abney v. United States, 1977)). State criminal justice systems "did not generally recognize an appeal as of right until . . . 1889."

Since McKane v. Durston, in 1894, the Supreme Court has held that the "Constitution does not require States to grant appeals as of right to criminal defendants seeking to review alleged trial errors" (Evitts v. Lucey, 1985).[139] Thus, if it is so inclined, a state "need not provide any appeal at all" (Ross v. Moffitt, 1974). Despite the absence of a constitutional mandate, the federal system and every state system of criminal case adjudication grant convicted defendants a statutory right to appeal criminal convictions.[140]

Jurisdictions accord criminal defendants a right to appeal their convictions to higher courts "to assure that only those who are validly convicted have their freedom drastically curtailed." A statutory provision for appeal as a matter of right reflects an implicit determination by the state "that it [is] unwilling to curtail drastically a defendant's liberty unless a second judicial decisionmaker, the appellate court, [is] convinced that the conviction [is] in accord with law" (Evitts v. Lucey, 1985). A defendant's exercise of the right to appeal is an effort to show that the process that led to his conviction was fatally flawed, tainted by a significant error that, at a minimum, justifies a new trial. At trial, the accused attempts to defend against government-initiated efforts to " 'hale [him] into court' . . . and strip [him] of his presumption of innocence" (Ross v. Moffitt, 1974). On appeal, his position is dramatically different. The convicted defendant "initiates the appellate process, seeking not to fend off the efforts of the State's prosecutor but rather to overturn a finding of guilt made by a judge or jury below." His object is to "upset the prior determination of [his] guilt."

Although there is no constitutional right to appeal a criminal conviction, when a defendant exercises a statutory right to appeal, the Constitution does guarantee the assistance of counsel for that appeal. The right to assistance does not spring from the explicit Sixth Amendment promise of counsel. Both in terminology and in intent that provision applies only to the process of adjudicating guilt or innocence in the trial court; it "does not apply to appellate proceedings" (Martinez v. Court of Appeal of California, 2000). Instead, the right to assistance of counsel at the appellate level is rooted in the Fourteenth Amendment. Every defendant has a right to counsel based on that provision's Due Process Clause. In addition, an indigent defendant's right is rooted in the Fourteenth Amendment Equal Protection Clause.

The Court's first foray into the area of assistance on appeal was in Douglas v. California. *Douglas* involved a California statutory scheme that allowed every convicted defendant who could retain counsel to be represented by counsel on appeal. Indigents, however, received appointed assistance only if they requested counsel and the appellate court, after making a preliminary investigation of the record, determined that counsel " 'would be helpful to the defendant or the court.' " If the appellate court concluded that appointed counsel " 'would be of no value to either the defendant or the court,' " the accused did not receive state-provided assistance on appeal. The particular defendants in *Douglas* each had been convicted of thirteen felonies. Both had requested appointed counsel for purposes of assisting the appeals of their convictions, but the appellate court had refused their requests, concluding that " 'no good whatever could be served by appointment of counsel' " (Douglas v. California, 1963).

The Supreme Court held that California's scheme was unconstitutional and that the state had an obligation to appoint representation for *every* indigent in a first appeal taken as a matter of right. The predominant reason for this holding was the discrimination inherent in the state's system and the resulting inequality between those who could afford legal representation on appeal and those who could not. In an earlier case, the Court had held that a state's denial of appellate review to convicted indigents because they were unable to pay for the transcripts required for such review was unconstitutional (Griffin v. Illinois, 1956).[141] According to the *Douglas* majority, the guiding principle in *Griffin* was that states may not "grant appellate review . . . in a way that discriminates against some convicted defendants on account of their poverty." The "evil" involved in a denial of counsel "is the same" as the evil involved in denial of a transcript—"discrimination against the indigent. For there can be no equal justice where the kind of an appeal a man enjoys 'depends on the amount of money he has' " (Douglas v. California, 1963 (quoting Griffin v. Illinois, 1956)).

The Court detailed the discriminatory impact of the California system. Under that scheme, every convicted defendant who could retain counsel received appellate review after full briefing and oral argument by counsel. An indigent defendant received the aid of counsel only if the appellate court could see "injustice" from the "barren record" (Douglas v. California, 1963). If a convicted indigent's trial record did not bespeak potential merit, he was deprived of "[a]ny real chance . . . of showing that his appeal ha[d] hidden merit." In defense of the statutory scheme, California had contended that on its face the statute drew a line only between those with potentially meritorious cases and those whose cases lacked merit. The Court was unpersuaded, responding that in substance the line was between the "rich man" who could present his appeal through counsel in every case and the "poor man" who could not do so in cases prejudged by the appellate court as lacking in merit. According to the majority, "[t]here is lacking that equality demanded by the Fourteenth Amendment where the rich man . . . enjoys the benefit of counsel's examination into the record, research of the law, and marshalling of arguments on his behalf, while the indigent, already burdened by a preliminary determination that his case is without merit, is forced to shift for himself." In reality, those with resources were entitled to a "meaningful appeal," while those who lacked funds had only the right to "a meaningless ritual." The Court agreed that states need not ensure "[a]bsolute equality" between those who have resources and those who do not but concluded that the disparity was too great for constitutional purposes "where the merits of the one and only appeal an indigent ha[d] as of right [was] decided without benefit of counsel."[142]

The breadth and significance of the *Douglas* holding depended, in part, on the exact source of the constitutional right to assistance recognized by the Court. Virtually all of the opinion's reasoning strongly implied that the Equal Protection Clause was the source of the indigent's right to appellate counsel. The majority's opinion, however, never specified that guarantee as the source of its holding. Moreover, in one passage the Court observed that "the right to appeal does not comport with *fair procedure*" when an indigent is forced to make a preliminary showing of merit before counsel is appointed (italics added). That language suggested the possibility that the Due Process Clause also had a role in guaranteeing a lawyer's assistance on appeal.

In 1985, in Evitts v. Lucey, the Court clarified the constitutional basis for and the scope of the right to appellate assistance first recognized in *Douglas*. *Evitts* involved a nonindigent defendant who claimed that his retained lawyer's dereliction in pursuing an appeal had deprived him of the constitutional right to effective appellate assistance. The Court agreed with that contention.

The *Evitts* Court characterized *Douglas* as resting on *both* the Equal Protection and Due Process Clauses of the Fourteenth Amendment. Equal protection was offended by the failure to provide counsel for all indigents because the effect was to make a "vital right" available only to the wealthy (Evitts v. Lucey, 1985). This distinction between the poor and the rich constituted an invidious discrimination. In addition, due process was violated by the refusal to furnish counsel for indigents because the result was to decide "the appeal in a way that was arbitrary with respect to the issues involved" and to deny some defendants "a fair opportunity to obtain an adjudication on the merits of [their] appeal[s]."

Because the defendant in *Evitts* was not indigent and, thus, suffered no discrimination, his claim of deprivation could find no support in equal protection principles. Due process principles alone, however, were adequate to sustain his claim of an entitlement to effective appellate legal assistance. The state argued that because the Constitution did not guarantee any right to an appeal the deprivation of counsel on appeal could not violate due process principles. According to this position, if there was no due process deprivation in the outright denial of an appeal, there could be no due process deprivation in granting an appeal but denying counsel. The Court rejected this argument, explaining that "when a State opts to act in a field where its action has significant discretionary elements, it must nonetheless act in accord with the dictates of the Constitution—and, in particular, in accord with the Due Process Clause." Thus, once a state creates "appellate courts as 'an integral part of the . . . system for finally adjudicating the guilt or innocence of a defendant,' the procedures used in deciding appeals must comport with the demands of" due process (Evitts v. Lucey, 1985 (quoting Griffin v. Illinois, 1956)).

Due process of law demands the assistance of counsel on appeal because it is among the "minimum safeguards necessary to make [an] appeal 'adequate and effective' " (Evitts v. Lucey, 1985 (quoting Griffin v. Illinois, 1956)). In appealing a conviction, the defendant "must face an adversary proceeding that—like a trial—is governed by intricate rules that to a layperson would be hopelessly forbidding. An unrepresented appellant—like an unrepresented defendant at trial—is unable to protect the vital interests at stake." Because "the services of a lawyer will for virtually every layman be necessary to present an appeal in a form suitable for appellate consideration on the merits," counsel's assistance is "the only way to assure an 'adequate and effective' appeal" (Evitts v. Lucey, 1985 (quoting Griffin v. Illinois, 1956)).

Because the Court's opinion in *Douglas* had been so heavily premised on the unequal treatment of indigent defendants, prior to *Evitts* it was at least arguable that a state could deny all criminal defendants counsel on their first appeal as a matter of right. Such a scheme could not possibly violate the Equal Protection Clause for it would involve no invidious discrimination between rich and poor—all would fend for themselves. Moreover, a state might have been able to deny some appellants legal representation as long as it did not treat similarly situated individuals in dramatically disparate ways. After *Evitts*, however, it is clear that the right to counsel on a first appeal as of right extends to *all* convicted defendants (at least all those who would have a right to assistance at trial) because counsel is an essential component of due process in an appellate proceeding. Indigents' right to appointed counsel springs from dual constitutional sources. Others' right to be assisted by counsel is firmly rooted in the guarantee that no state shall "deprive any person of life, liberty, or property without due process of law." By itself, the Due Process Clause furnishes a sufficient constitutional foundation for the right to assistance on appeal.

A first appeal as a matter of right is not the end of the appellate road for a convicted defendant. A limited number of defendants may have a *right* to pursue a second appeal. For most, the recourse remaining is a petition to a higher court for "discretionary review" of the first appellate court's decision. (In states with two-tiered appellate systems, this petition for discretionary review would be addressed to the highest state court. A second petition could then be addressed to the United States Supreme Court. In states with one tier of appellate courts, the only petition for discretionary review would be to the United States Supreme Court.) When a defendant files a second appeal as a matter of right, the appellate court *must* entertain and resolve the appeal. When a defendant petitions for discretionary review, the appellate court decides, according to established criteria, whether the case merits further review. The *Douglas* Court expressly limited its recognition of a right to counsel to *first appeals as of right*. The question of whether there is a constitutional entitlement to assistance upon further appellate review was not addressed.

In Ross v. Moffitt, the Court considered whether there is a right to legal assistance when a convicted defendant petitions either a state Supreme Court or the United States Supreme Court for discretionary review. The two petitioners were indigents who had been refused appointed counsel for purposes of preparing such petitions. The Supreme Court disagreed with their arguments that they had the right to a lawyer's help, holding that the Constitution does not require a state "to provide free counsel for indigent defendants seeking to take discretionary appeals" (Ross v. Moffitt, 1974). Neither the Equal Protection Clause nor the Due Process Clause includes a right to assistance for purposes of seeking discretionary review.

According to the *Moffitt* majority, the determinative constitutional question was whether the state had denied the indigent petitioners "meaningful access" to the appellate systems. If it had done so, both Fourteenth Amendment guarantees would have been offended. On the other hand, if the petitioners were afforded "meaningful access," if they had "an adequate opportunity to present their claims fairly within the adversary system," neither the promise of equal protection nor the guarantee of due process was violated.

Despite the lack of counsel's assistance, those seeking discretionary review are not denied "meaningful access" for the following reasons. Prior to a petition for discretionary review, their claims will already have been presented by a lawyer and ruled upon by an appellate court. On petition for subsequent discretionary review, they will have a transcript or other record of the trial proceedings, an appellate brief from the lower court, possibly an appellate opinion from the lower court, and whatever additional written submissions they are able to make on their own. These documents should supply an "adequate basis for [the court's] decision to grant or deny review." Moreover, the function of discretionary review is quite limited. Its purpose is not to correct every erroneous adjudication by the lower courts. Instead, discretionary review is typically exercised to review cases that have significant legal implications or ramifications. (In North Carolina, for example, even if a lower court decision was not correct, the state Supreme Court could deny review unless the subject of the appeal had significant public interest, the legal principles involved were of major significance, or the decision below was in conflict with a decision of the state Supreme Court.) Based on the wealth of information before it, a court "should be able to ascertain whether . . . the standards . . . for such review" are satisfied.[143]

In sum, despite the lack of counsel's assistance, a convicted defendant has "meaningful access" to the process of discretionary review and "an adequate opportunity to present [his] claims fairly." There is an ample record before the court—based in large part on prior proceedings conducted with a lawyer's assistance—and the particular questions before the court can be resolved adequately and fairly on the basis of this record. Even though a lawyer would be "helpful" and an indigent is "somewhat handicapped" by the lack of assistance, the Constitution is not violated, for precise and absolute equality is not required. As long as the indigent has "meaningful access" and "an adequate opportunity to present his claims fairly," there is no constitutional deprivation.[144] Moreover, although *Moffitt* involved indigent defendants and rested largely on equal protection reasoning, its holding clearly means that states have no obligation to ensure that nonindigent defendants receive adequate assistance in discretionary appeals. As a subsequent opinion observed, Ross v. Moffitt "held that *a criminal defendant does not have a constitutional right to counsel* to pursue discretionary state appeals or applications for review to" the United States Supreme Court (Wainwright v. Torna, 1982) (italics added). That holding applies to rich and poor alike, to retained as well as to appointed counsel.

The Supreme Court has never decided a case involving a claim of entitlement to counsel in a second appeal as a matter of right. (An "appeal as a matter of right" means that the convicted defendant has a statutory entitlement to have the appellate court consider his case. When an appeal is "discretionary," the appellate court is empowered to decide whether the defendant's appeal does or does not merit its attention.) The reasoning of Ross v. Moffitt, however, strongly suggests that the Constitution does not contain a guarantee of assistance for such an appeal. The record provided by the first appeal with counsel's assistance and the fact that the questions in a second appeal are likely to be identical to those raised in the first appeal provide potent support for the conclusion that an appellant without counsel still has meaningful access and a fair opportunity to present his claims. Moreover, the Court's explicit statement in a later opinion that "[o]ur cases establish that the right to appointed counsel extends to the first appeal of right, *and no further*" (Pennsylvania v. Finley, 1987) (italics added) indicates that there is no constitutional entitlement to representation in second appeals taken as a matter of right.

The Right to the Assistance of Counsel in Collateral Attacks upon Convictions[145]

When a defendant fails to seek appellate review within the time allowed or the highest appellate court with jurisdiction over a case either denies a defendant's petition for review or grants review and affirms the lower court, a judgment of conviction becomes "final." Finality, however, does not preclude all further review. Avenues for "postconviction relief"—procedural mechanisms that permit defendants to attack final convictions—remain open. Both state and federal systems statutorily provide and delineate the processes through which convicted defendants may pursue postconviction remedies. State defendants may seek relief in both the state and federal court systems—in the latter by means of a petition for a "writ of habeas corpus" from a federal judge.

A petition seeking postconviction relief is deemed a "collateral attack" upon a conviction because it is outside the chain of direct appellate review. "It is not part of the criminal proceeding itself, and it is in fact considered to be civil in nature" (Pennsylvania v. Finley, 1987). Typically, a collateral challenge is addressed to the authorities who have custody of the petitioner and is framed in terms of a request for release from confinement. Ordinarily, the petition must allege that there was a serious error in the process leading to conviction and imprisonment, an error that renders the confinement of the petitioner "unconstitutional." A collateral attack on a conviction begins with a petition filed at the trial court level. The trial judge's decision is then subject to review by appellate courts in the jurisdiction. As is true of direct appeals, "[s]tates have no [constitutional] obligation to provide this avenue of relief" from convictions (Pennsylvania v. Finley, 1987). For present purposes, the important question is whether prisoners have a constitutional entitlement to the assistance of counsel for purposes of pursuing the statutory postconviction remedies that states do provide.

Pennsylvania v. Finley involved an indigent defendant's claim that he had been denied the assistance of counsel in a state postconviction proceeding. The Supreme Court found no merit in this contention, concluding that the Constitution does not grant a prisoner any right to counsel's assistance in preparing and filing a collateral attack on a conviction. According to the Court, the same "considerations" that support the conclusion that there is no entitlement to assistance upon petition for discretionary appellate review "apply with even more force to postconviction review" (Pennsylvania v. Finley, 1987). Under the "analysis . . . followed in Ross [v. Moffitt]," neither the due process guarantee of "fundamental fairness" nor the equal protection requirement of "meaningful access" for indigents is violated when a petitioner lacks counsel in a postconviction proceeding. Put simply, "since a defendant has no federal constitutional right to counsel when pursuing a discretionary appeal on direct review of his conviction, *a fortiori*, he has no such right when attacking a conviction that has long since become final upon exhaustion of the appellate process."[146]

The clear general rule is that prisoners have no right to legal assistance for collateral attacks on their convictions. Ordinarily, the same rule governs death row inmates—that is, even those condemned to die have no constitutionally guaranteed right to representation when collaterally challenging their convictions or death sentences. It is arguable, however, that some prisoners convicted of capital offenses fall within an exception to the general rule and are constitutionally entitled to a lawyer's aid when seeking collateral relief.

In Murray v. Giarratano, prisoners on death row filed a civil class action suit, claiming that they and other inmates awaiting execution were entitled to government-provided counsel for purposes of pursuing state collateral remedies. The lower courts ruled in their favor, finding Pennsylvania v. Finley distinguishable, in part, because it was not a "capital case" (Murray v. Giarratano, 1989). The Supreme Court held that the lower courts had erred in finding that the inmates had a constitutional entitlement to appointed representation. Four members of the Court believed that "the rule of *Pennsylvania v. Finley* should apply no differently in capital cases than in noncapital cases." They were prepared to "hold that *Finley* applies to those inmates under sentence of death as well as to other inmates" and, consequently, that there was no constitutional right to counsel for death row prisoners seeking postconviction review of their convictions and sentences. The prisoners argued that *Finley* should be distinguished because the Court's precedents indicated a need for more protection in capital cases. The Justices responded that those precedents had "dealt with the trial stage of capital offense adjudication, where the court and jury hear testimony, receive evidence, and decide questions of guilt and punishment." They do not extend to collateral challenges to convictions and death sentences.[147]

Justice Kennedy, who provided the decisive fifth vote for the result in *Giarratano*, refused to join the plurality opinion of Chief Justice Rehnquist. While he agreed that the refusal to appoint counsel in the *Giarratano* case did not violate the Constitution, he carefully confined his opinion to the facts before the Court. According to Justice Kennedy, the requirement of "meaningful access" was satisfied in *Giarratano* because no prisoner on death row had been unable to obtain counsel for post-conviction purposes and because the prison system was staffed with institutional lawyers to assist inmates' preparation of their petitions for relief. He did not endorse the plurality's view that the holding in *Finley* applies equally to capital inmates. Moreover, Justice Kennedy agreed with the four dissenters that "collateral relief proceedings are a central part of the review process for prisoners sentenced to death," that "a substantial proportion of these prisoners succeed in having their death sentences vacated in habeas corpus proceedings," and that the "complexity of [the] jurisprudence in this area . . . makes it unlikely that capital defendants will be able to" succeed "without the assistance of persons learned in the law" (Murray v. Giarratano, 1989) (Kennedy, J., concurring in the judgment). The narrow basis for Justice Kennedy's conclusion and his evident sympathy with the view that capital convicts need representation make it entirely possible that a different set of facts could give rise to a constitutional right to counsel in a capital case collateral proceeding.

In sum, as a general rule, the "cases establish that the right to . . . counsel extends to the first appeal of right, and no further" (Pennsylvania v. Finley, 1987). At the first appeal as of right, indigent and nonindigent defendants are entitled to the assistance of counsel. Beyond that, the Constitution does not guarantee that those challenging their convictions on appeal or those seeking postconviction relief will have the help of a lawyer.

The Right of Self-Representation on Appeal

In Martinez v. Court of Appeal of California, a man who represented himself at trial was convicted of embezzlement and sentenced to twenty-five-years-to-life in prison under a "three strikes" law (Martinez v. Court of Appeal of California, 2000). He filed a motion to represent himself on appeal and a waiver of counsel. The court of appeal denied the motion and required that he be represented by counsel on appeal. Because lower courts had split over the question of whether a convicted defendant has a right of self-representation on appeal, the Supreme Court granted review.

As discussed in an earlier section, the Sixth Amendment does include a fundamental constitutional right of self-representation at trial (Faretta v. California, 1975). A right to represent oneself on appeal, however, can find no support in that provision because the rights granted by the Sixth Amendment are "rights that are available [only] in preparation for trial and at the trial itself" (Martinez v. Court of Appeal of California, 2000). The only plausible foundation for a right of appellate self-representation is the Due Process Clause. For a number of reasons, the *Martinez* Court unanimously held that the guarantee of due process does not include an entitlement to represent oneself on direct appeal of a criminal conviction. Each step in the Court's analysis discerned a critical difference between the constitutional underpinnings for the right of self-representation at trial and the putative underpinnings of a similar right on appeal.

In Faretta v. California, the Court concluded that both British and American history provided a solid foundation for the right to represent oneself at trial. According to the *Martinez* Court there is no similar "historical consensus establishing a right of self-representation on appeal" and "no long-respected right of self-representation on appeal." In part, the absence of historical credentials for self-representation on appeal stemmed from the fact that the right to appeal a conviction did not begin to gain recognition until the late 1800s.

The *Faretta* majority also perceived support for an affirmative right to represent oneself at trial in the structure and language of the Sixth Amendment. The *Martinez* Court concluded that the structure and terms of the Sixth Amendment could furnish no support for a right of self-representation on appeal because "the Sixth Amendment does not apply to appellate proceedings." The rights that it provides are exclusively trial rights.

Finally, *Faretta* rooted the right to present one's own defense at trial "in part in a respect for individual autonomy," which it found to be implicit in the Sixth Amendment (Martinez v. Court of Appeal of California, 2000). At the trial level, the accused's constitutionally protected interest in controlling his own fate outweighs the state's interest in fair and efficient justice. As a general rule, it requires the government to honor a defendant's decision to represent himself. These same Sixth Amendment autonomy principles cannot counterbalance the state's interest at the appellate level, because the Sixth Amendment has no application to the appellate process. Any interests that a convicted defendant has in managing his own appeal and not having a government-selected lawyer forced upon him at the appellate stage must be rooted in the entitlement to due process of law.

For at least two reasons, the *Martinez* Court believed that the due process-based "autonomy interests that survive a felony conviction are less compelling than those" sheltered at trial by the Sixth Amendment. First, the risk of disloyalty by state-appointed counsel and the appellant's suspicions of such disloyalty—weighty considerations at trial—are not substantial concerns at the appellate stage. Second, on appeal, the state has not "hal[ed] a person into its criminal courts." Instead, the defendant has initiated the process himself in an effort to overturn a finding of guilt. On the other hand, at the appellate level "the overriding state interest in the fair and efficient administration of justice remains as strong as at the trial level." In contrast to trial, in "the appellate context, the balance between" the defendant's autonomy interests and the state's fairness and efficiency interests "tips in favor of the State." Consequently, a state acts within its discretion when it denies a convicted defendant's request to represent himself and compels him to "accept against his will a state-appointed attorney." The Constitution does not require states "to recognize a constitutional right to self-representation on direct appeal from a criminal conviction." This holding undoubtedly applies to any subsequent appellate or collateral challenge to a conviction.[148]

The preceding part of this text has discussed the "scope" of the right to counsel's assistance in the criminal process. The Sixth Amendment guarantee of counsel, originally intended as an entitlement at trial, has expanded to the critical pretrial stages of criminal prosecutions in order to counter the threats to the fairness of the adversarial system engendered by expansion of the adjudicatory process into the period preceding the trial. Following a formal accusation, the right to counsel attaches, and an accused is entitled to assistance at both formal, courtroom proceedings and informal, out-of-court events that qualify as "critical stages."

The right to counsel at trial is undisputed and encompasses an entitlement to assistance sufficiently in advance of the formal commencement of trial to allow adequate investigation and preparation and adequate opportunities to explore and pursue pretrial motions. The right to trial counsel also includes a right to aid for purposes of seeking relief in the trial court following a conviction. Moreover, the right to assistance at trial extends to those who choose to plead guilty, guaranteeing that counsel will provide expert aid during negotiations with the government and during guilty plea proceedings in the courtroom. After a verdict has been rendered, the Sixth Amendment guarantees a right to legal assistance for post-trial motion purposes and to prepare for and to represent the defendant during sentencing hearings. When the sentencing phase is over, however, the right to Sixth Amendment assistance comes to an end.

When a defendant takes a first appeal of a conviction as a matter of right, the Due Process Clause guarantee of "fundamental fairness" extends to every defendant an entitlement to the aid of a lawyer for that appeal. Indigent appellants are also protected against discriminatory denials of appellate legal assistance by the Equal Protection Clause. Beyond the first appeal as of right, there is no general constitutional entitlement to a lawyer's help. Thus, in second appeals as of right, in petitions for discretionary appellate review, and in postconviction, collateral attacks on convictions, defendants do not enjoy a right to the assistance of counsel. Finally, the Constitution does not afford convicted defendants any right to represent themselves when appealing or seeking collateral relief from their convictions.

THE CONTENT OF THE RIGHT TO THE ASSISTANCE OF COUNSEL

The first part of this analysis addressed the "nature" of the right to the assistance of counsel. Included were discussions of the fundamental role of lawyers in adversarial systems of criminal justice, the entitlements to retained and appointed counsel, the kinds of prosecutions to which those guarantees extend, waivers of assistance and the constitutional right of self-representation, and the allocation of decision-making authority between counsel and defendant. The second part of this analysis considered the "scope" of the right to counsel. It focused upon entitlements to pretrial assistance, the breadth of the guarantee of representation at trial, and the sources and purview of the right to counsel in post-trial phases of criminal proceedings. This third and final part of the analysis is concerned with the "content" of the right to the assistance of counsel. The topics treated here all involve the substance guaranteed by the Sixth Amendment's promise of "the Assistance of Counsel for [one's] defence" and the other constitutional sources of assistance.

The Sixth Amendment guarantees the assistance of counsel because of the critical roles that a defense lawyer plays in ensuring just results and fair play in adversarial criminal justice systems. "That a person who happens to be a lawyer is present . . . alongside the accused . . . is not enough to satisfy the constitutional command" (Strickland v. Washington, 1984). Mere *formal* compliance with the counsel guarantee cannot fulfill the Sixth Amendment's promise. The right to counsel includes an assurance that the defendant will receive the *substantive* benefits that flow from the equalizing assistance of a trained attorney. To deliver on the Sixth Amendment's pledge, defense counsel must play the roles and serve the functions essential to ensuring that a defendant actually "enjoys" the advantages of having a legal assistant in the battle with the state. The roles and functions required by the constitutional guarantee of counsel—the substantive "content" of the right to counsel—are derived from and rooted in the justifications and rationales for granting a fundamental entitlement to legal representation.

An accused who is not afforded any opportunity for retained or appointed counsel clearly suffers a deprivation of the Sixth Amendment entitlement. An accused who has retained or appointed assistance will also suffer a deprivation of the Sixth Amendment entitlement if counsel fails to provide the substantive legal assistance guaranteed by the Constitution. There are two distinct reasons that a lawyer might not furnish the assistance contemplated by the Sixth Amendment. First, some action by a governmental official might prevent, impede, or restrict counsel's opportunity or ability to perform her constitutional functions. Second, for any of a number of reasons—including lack of experience, time, ability, or commitment—an attorney might simply fail to fulfill the responsibilities that the Constitution imposes upon her. This part of the analysis first deals with official constraints on counsel's efforts to play the roles anticipated by the Sixth Amendment. It then considers inadequacies of performance that result from the lawyer's own deficiencies.

All of the subjects considered in this third and final part of the analysis can be captured by the rubric "ineffective assistance of counsel" in the broadest sense of those terms. Both state hindrances to adequate performance and lawyer incompetence that renders a performance deficient prevent defense counsel from "effectively" playing the roles prescribed by and accomplishing the objectives sought by the Sixth Amendment. As will be seen later in this part, however, the label "ineffective assistance" typically has a more narrow meaning. "Ineffective assistance of counsel" is the doctrinal name given to constitutionally deficient performances that are not caused by the government but, rather, are attributable solely to a lawyer's failures to provide the substantive assistance guaranteed by the Sixth Amendment.[149]

This part of the analysis is divided into several subsections. Each of the first six subsections corresponds to a distinct component of the "content" of the right to counsel. The first subsection discusses the foundational need for adequate investigation and preparation by counsel. The second subsection discusses the entitlement to counsel's active and full participation in the adversary process. The third addresses the accused's entitlement to ample consultation with defense counsel. The fourth considers the right to loyalty from counsel and the problems generated by defense lawyers' conflicts of interest. The fifth subsection treats the basic entitlement to competent performance and the implications of "ineffective assistance" by defense counsel. The sixth focuses upon the right to and content of effective assistance of counsel on appeal. The final subsection discusses the remedies that are provided for deprivations of the constitutional entitlement to counsel's assistance.

As the discussions will make clear, some of the substantive components included within the guarantee of counsel's assistance have not been thoroughly explored or explained by the Supreme Court. The entitlement to partisan advocacy and the right to consult with counsel, for example, have not been extensively developed. Consequently, many of the details concerning these aspects of the right to counsel are sketchy, at best. Other constituents of the guarantee of counsel have been the subject of more comprehensive Supreme Court discussion. The entitlement to competent performance, for example, has been explored in considerable depth in a number of important opinions. As a result, we know quite a bit about the nuances of that facet of the right to counsel.

The Entitlement to Adequate Investigation and Preparation for Trial

In discussing the "scope" of the right to counsel at trial, it was noted that the accused's entitlement to assistance begins sufficiently prior to the trial to ensure adequate investigation and preparation of a defense. This initial subsection regarding the "content" of the right to assistance examines the substance of this entitlement to have counsel investigate and prepare the defendant's case before going to trial. Adequate pretrial investigation and preparation are a necessary foundation for effective assistance at trial.

It is "vitally important" that counsel engage in "thoroughgoing investigation and preparation" before the trial begins. If a defense lawyer does not investigate the case and prepare for trial, a defendant will not "have the aid of counsel in any real sense" (Powell v. Alabama, 1932). Adequate investigation entails looking into all relevant factual aspects of the case—the facts that the prosecution will use to prove guilt and the facts that will assist in refuting the charges. It also involves thorough research of the pertinent legal principles bearing upon resolution of the criminal accusation. Unless counsel has made herself aware of all the apposite facts and law and devoted the time necessary to prepare the witnesses, to formulate arguments and positions, and to plan strategies, defense counsel cannot meaningfully advance the defendant's interests at trial or subject the prosecution's case to the adversarial testing contemplated by the Sixth Amendment. Put simply, solid investigation and preparation are necessary foundations for active and full participation in the adversarial trial process.[150]

A defense lawyer, therefore, must have adequate "opportunities" to investigate and prepare a defense. " 'It is vain to give the accused a day in court, with no opportunity to prepare for it, or to guarantee him counsel without giving the latter any opportunity to acquaint himself with the facts or law of the case' " (Powell v. Alabama, 1932 (quoting Commonwealth v. O'Keefe, 1929)). There are various ways in which a state might obstruct, hinder, or restrict defense counsel's opportunities to investigate and prepare and, thus, deprive the defendant of the substance of counsel's assistance.[151]

First, a state might appoint counsel too late to permit adequate investigation and preparation. "[C]ourts should make every effort to effect early appointments of counsel in all cases" (Chambers v. Maroney, 1970), because tardy appointments can prevent counsel from conducting the legal and factual research and making the preparations needed for effective trial performance. Powell v. Alabama was a capital case in which the trial judge did not appoint counsel to represent the defendants "until the very morning of the trial" (Powell v. Alabama, 1932). The Supreme Court concluded that this tardy provision of assistance failed to satisfy the Constitution because the "defendants were not accorded the right to counsel in any substantial sense." Not to have acknowledged the denial of meaningful assistance that resulted from providing counsel so late in the process would have been "to ignore actualities." The Court did not inquire into counsel's actual performance at the trial but, instead, found that the denial of any real opportunity to investigate and prepare was sufficient to violate the defendants' constitutional right to assistance. The last-minute appointment made more than cursory investigation and preparation virtually impossible, rendering it "unlikely that any lawyer could provide effective assistance" and justifying a "presumption" that the assistance in *Powell* had been inadequate (United States v. Cronic, 1984).

Late appointments of counsel do not always justify a finding that the accused has been deprived of the constitutional entitlement to assistance.[152] The Supreme Court has "refused 'to fashion a per se rule'' of Sixth Amendment violation every time there is a "tardy appointment of counsel." Instead, when counsel is provided at a time that could impair the adequacy of investigation and preparation, but not so late that it is fair to presume that she could not have fulfilled her pretrial responsibilities, a court must examine a lawyer's "actual performance at trial" to determine whether a constitutional deprivation occurred (United States v. Cronic, 1984).

Thus, in Avery v. Alabama, a 1940 case, the trial judge appointed counsel for capital defendants a mere three days before the trial began. The Supreme Court recognized that a late appointment could deny an adequate opportunity to prepare an accused's defense and could constitute a "sham and nothing more than a formal compliance with the Constitution's requirement that an accused be given the assistance of counsel" (Avery v. Alabama, 1940). It concluded, however, that the three days allowed did afford sufficient time to prepare in light of the limited size of the community and the easy access to evidence and witnesses in the case.

In addition, in Chambers v. Maroney, the defendant was represented by appointed counsel from the Legal Aid Society at a trial that ended in a mistrial. A few minutes before his second trial began, a different attorney from the Legal Aid Society appeared to defend him. Apparently, no one had conferred with the defendant in the interim. The accused claimed that appointed counsel's appearance in the second trial "was so belated the he could not have furnished effective legal assistance" (Chambers v. Maroney, 1970). The Court rejected the claim, upholding the Court of Appeals' conclusions, based on the record, that counsel had rendered adequate assistance at trial and that the late arrival of appointed counsel had not caused prejudice to the accused. Again, the circumstances did not justify a presumption that counsel could not have investigated and prepared adequately, and the trial record did not justify a conclusion that the limited time to look into the case and get ready for trial actually impaired the attorney's ability to participate in the adversarial contest.[153]

Deprivation of the opportunity to investigate a case and prepare a defense could also result from a timely appointment of counsel followed by a hasty start of the trial. The actual effects of commencing a trial too soon after appointment are undoubtedly identical to the effects of a late appointment. Moreover, excessively hasty scheduling of a trial could prevent even a retained attorney from having an adequate chance to do the necessary groundwork for trial. While there are no Supreme Court cases that frame the issue in terms of starting trial too soon, the logic of the late appointment cases would suggest that in an extreme case, a presumption of inadequate time would arise. In other cases, the beginning of trial shortly after counsel appeared in a case would generate a cognizable risk that the time was inadequate (i.e., a likelihood that is too high to be ignored and requires an inquiry into the impact on the defense lawyer's performance). Whether counsel's performance was actually impaired would then be determined by an examination of the actual conduct of the defense at trial.

For any number of reasons, a lawyer who is retained or appointed sufficiently before trial to allow adequate investigation and preparation may run into difficulties that prompt a request for a continuance—a postponement of the trial. Such requests are generally entrusted to the sound discretion of trial judges. Because of the burdens and difficulties that trial judges encounter in scheduling proceedings, and because society has an interest in avoiding unnecessary delays and in promoting the "prompt disposition of criminal cases" (Powell v. Alabama, 1932), reviewing courts give great deference to refusals to grant additional time to prepare (United States v. Cronic, 1984). Nevertheless, when there is good reason to delay a criminal proceeding—when counsel has a legitimate need for more time to investigate the facts or law and prepare the accused's defense adequately—the denial of a continuance could deprive an accused of assistance just as surely as a late appointment of counsel or a hasty start of trial.[154] In the interest of ensuring "prompt dispositions," an accused "must not be stripped of his right to have sufficient time to advise with counsel and prepare his defense" (Powell v. Alabama, 1932).

It would be possible, though rare, that the denial of a continuance would be so obviously damaging to the entitlement to adequate investigation and preparation that a court should find a deprivation of assistance without examining the surrounding circumstances (i.e., the actual restrictions on counsel's opportunities and the impacts on her performance at trial). Ordinarily, it would be necessary to inquire into the specific facts of the case to determine whether counsel did not have a sufficient chance to get ready for trial and, consequently, was hampered in her ability to be an effective adversary at trial. Thus, in Avery v. Alabama, the capital case that involved appointment of counsel just three days before trial began, the attorneys "filed a motion for continuance, on the ground that they had not had sufficient time and opportunity since their appointment to investigate and prepare [the defendant's] defense" (Avery v. Alabama, 1940). The motion was supported by affidavits from counsel specifying how little time they actually had to ready themselves to defend the accused. The trial court denied the motion, and the Alabama Supreme Court found that he had not abused his discretion.

The United States Supreme Court concluded that "[u]nder the particular circumstances" the accused was not "denied the benefit of the assistance of counsel." Counsel provided "zealous and earnest" assistance from start to finish. Moreover, counsel's inquiries were facilitated by the fact that in the small, rural community where the events took place people knew each other, and information concerning witnesses and events was "widespread" and "generally known." The attorneys' "examination and preparation of the case, in the time permitted by the trial judge, [were] adequate for counsel to exhaust its every angle." While three days was a brief time to get ready to defend a capital case, in the particular circumstances of *Avery* the lawyers were able to do an able job of investigation and preparation in that time frame. Consequently, the denial of a continuance did not deprive the accused of the substance of his constitutional entitlement to counsel.

In sum, one of the necessary elements of constitutionally adequate assistance is thorough investigation and preparation by counsel. A state might infringe upon a defendant's entitlements by appointing counsel too late, scheduling trial too early, or unjustifiably refusing to postpone a scheduled trial. Any state action that results in too little time for defense counsel to investigate and prepare adequately can deprive the accused of the Sixth Amendment guarantee. In rare, egregious cases where the opportunity to get ready for trial is nonexistent or negligible, a deprivation of counsel must be presumed. In less extreme situations, the accused's right to counsel is violated only if the facts establish that the state's action restricted counsel's investigation or preparation in ways that actually impaired fulfillment of her role in the adversarial trial process.

The Entitlement to Active, Full Participation by Counsel in the Adversarial Process

American systems of criminal justice contemplate adversarial contests. The Sixth Amendment "constitutionalizes" a number of rights that ensure the fair and effective operation of those contests. The rights to speedy and public trials, to impartial juries, to notice of the nature and cause of accusations, to confront unfavorable witnesses, and to compel the presence of helpful witnesses all make significant contributions to the adversarial system's efforts to achieve just results by means of fair processes. None of the Sixth Amendment's guarantees, however, is more essential to the functioning of the adjudicatory process than the right to the assistance of counsel.[155] Without a lawyer's aid, it is quite unlikely that an accused will be able to enjoy the advantages of the other enumerated rights. Without counsel, there is little chance for a fair battle between equally able adversaries. Counsel's most basic role is to ensure that the confrontation between opponents contemplated by our Constitution actually does take place.

At this point, it bears repeating that a lawyer's assistance is essential because the accused has severe deficiencies and disabilities. A defendant who is confronted with the "intricacies of the law and the advocacy of the public prosecutor" (United States v. Ash, 1973) does not possess the "professional legal skill to protect himself" (Johnson v. Zerbst, 1938) and "lacks both the skill and knowledge adequately to prepare [and conduct] his defense" (Powell v. Alabama, 1932). "That which is simple, orderly, and necessary to the lawyer, to the untrained layman may appear intricate, complex, and mysterious" (Johnson v. Zerbst, 1938). The adversarial contest would be grossly imbalanced and thus unfair without the equalizing presence of a legally trained assistant.

In light of counsel's central role in the proper operation of our criminal justice systems, "the right to the assistance of counsel has been understood to mean that there can be no restrictions upon the function of counsel in defending a criminal prosecution in accord with the traditions of the adversary factfinding process . . . constitutionalized in the Sixth . . . Amendment[]." The entitlement to legal representation "ensures to the defense in a criminal trial the opportunity to participate fully and fairly in the adversary factfinding process" (Herring v. New York, 1975). It enables the accused to subject the prosecution's case to "meaningful adversarial testing" and guarantees a fair "process" whose "character [is] a confrontation between adversaries" (United States v. Cronic, 1984). In sum, a core, substantive component of the right to the assistance of counsel is the entitlement to have counsel participate in the adversary process actively and completely. Government actions that meaningfully interfere with a defense attorney's abilities to fulfill this basic function can run afoul of the Sixth Amendment.

This subsection addresses the entitlement to have defense counsel participate fully and actively in the adversarial fact-finding process. There are three components to counsel's participation in that process: partisan advocacy or argument on behalf of the accused, the presentation of the evidence favorable to the defense, and the testing of the prosecution's evidence of guilt.[156]

The Entitlement to Zealous, Partisan Advocacy by Counsel

Originally, criminal trials did not involve the calling of witnesses and the presentation of evidence by the parties. Instead, they consisted exclusively of "argument between the defendant and counsel for the Crown."[157] When the nature of trials changed to focus primarily on testimonial and tangible proof by both sides, "the adversary system's commitment to argument was neither discarded nor diluted." Throughout history and still today, the "very premise of our adversary system of criminal justice [has been] that partisan advocacy on both sides of a case will best promote [its] ultimate objective[s]" (Herring v. New York, 1975). The lawyer's central role in promoting the proper functioning of "the adversarial process protected by the Sixth Amendment requires that the accused have 'counsel acting in the role of an advocate' " (United States v. Cronic, 1984 (quoting Anders v. California, 1967)). Consequently, an essential component of the substance of the constitutional right to legal representation is an entitlement to have counsel serve as a zealous, partisan advocate. Defense counsel must be devoted to and focused upon developing and presenting to the judge and jury the factual and legal arguments that favor the defendant and further his ultimate interest in avoiding conviction. Argument in support of the defendant's cause is necessary to meet and test the case of the prosecution. Active, committed advocacy on the accused's behalf is integral to the adversarial role played by counsel.

Governmental interference with defense counsel's efforts to make arguments on the accused's behalf to the judge or jurors can impair the adversary process and defeat its goals. Without partisan advocacy on both sides, the search for truth is undermined. Moreover, adequate opportunities to present defense arguments are essential to ensure a fair chance to resist society's efforts to deprive the accused of his life or liberty. In short, both the just results and the fair process that are the aims of the adversary system depend on the defense lawyer's active and full participation in the contest. State-created barriers to zealous, partisan advocacy violate the Sixth Amendment when they prevent a defense attorney from participating in the adversary process in the ways contemplated by our constitutional system of criminal justice.

The Supreme Court has dealt with only one case that involved an overt governmental restriction on counsel's ability to argue on behalf of the accused. In Herring v. New York, a state statute permitted a judge, in a bench trial, to deny both the defense and the prosecution any opportunity to make a closing argument (also known as "summation") at the end of the presentation of evidence (Herring v. New York, 1975). After a relatively simple "three-day trial [that] was interrupted by an interval of more than two days," the trial judge in *Herring* exercised this statutory discretion, refusing to hear closing arguments. He then found the defendant guilty.

The accused challenged the constitutionality of the New York statute in the Supreme Court. The Court sustained his claim, concluding that the statutory provision for a complete prohibition of closing argument contravened the Sixth Amendment. According to the Court, a defendant has "a right to be heard in summation of the evidence from the point of view most favorable to him. In denying the [defendant] this right under the authority of its statute, New York denied him the assistance of counsel that the Constitution guarantees." In the

Court's view, an entitlement to make a closing argument is a critical, integral part of the substance of the right to counsel. In every trial, no matter how short or simple it may be, the defense must have an opportunity to present a summation.

In support of its holding, the Court asserted that "closing argument for the defense is a basic element of the adversary factfinding process in a criminal trial," that is, a critical component for the proper operation of that process. "The very premise of our adversary system . . . is that partisan advocacy on both sides of a case will best promote the ultimate objective that the guilty be convicted and the innocent go free." In criminal trials, which are, in essence, fact-finding processes, "no aspect of such advocacy could be more important than the opportunity finally to marshal the evidence for each side before submission of the case to judgment." Closing arguments "sharpen and clarify the issues," for only when all evidence has been presented can counsel

> present their respective versions of the case as a whole. Only then can they argue the inferences to be drawn from all the testimony, and point out the weaknesses of their adversaries' positions. And for the defense, closing argument is *the last clear chance to persuade the trier of fact that there may be reasonable doubt of the defendant's guilt.* (italics added)

Thus, for an accused, an opportunity to present "summation could spell the difference . . . between liberty and unjust imprisonment."

The state's interest in expediting the adjudicatory process cannot justify an absolute ban on summation. The time and resources saved by precluding any closing argument are minimal. They cannot outweigh the accused's weighty interest in having a fair opportunity to forestall an improper conviction. Moreover, while closing argument might have no persuasive effect in some cases, "there is no certain way for a trial judge to identify accurately which cases these will be, until the judge has heard the closing summation of counsel." To guard against an unjustified loss of the chance to persuade a judge that the evidence does not support a criminal conviction, in every bench trial a state must allow counsel to sum up the case from the standpoint and perspective of the accused.

The impact of the holding in *Herring* extends beyond the context in that case. While the *Herring* Court was concerned with the entitlement to present a closing argument to a judge in a bench trial, its reasoning clearly supports the same entitlement in a jury trial. The reasons that closing argument is vital in a bench trial apply with at least equal force to jury trials. Indeed, it is arguable that the opportunity for summation to untrained laypersons entrusted with finding the facts and applying the law to those facts is even more critical for the accused. Consequently, "it has universally been held that counsel for the defense has a right to make a closing summation to the jury" (Herring v. New York, 1975).

On the other hand, the Court carefully limited the scope of its right to counsel holding in two significant respects. First, the Court made it clear that there is no Sixth Amendment right to make "uncontrolled or . . . unrestrained" closing argument. To the contrary, a judge has "great latitude in controlling the duration and limiting the scope of closing summations." The Constitution is not violated when a judge "limit[s] counsel to a reasonable time" or terminates repetitive or redundant argument. The system's interests in the "fair and orderly conduct of the trial" justify such reasonable restrictions on counsel's ability to advocate the accused's cause. The point at which restraints upon closing argument cross the constitutional line and amount to unacceptable infringements upon the right to counsel is uncertain. In every case, a judge should have to permit more than token, *pro forma* summation. Beyond that, however, a judge is authorized to exercise "broad discretion." Only unreasonable limitations on closing argument are forbidden. Whether a judge's restrictions on counsel are unreasonable must depend on the particular circumstances of the case. Thus, the longer and more complex a case, the greater the need for time to sum up. In shorter, less complicated trials, tighter restraints are undoubtedly permissible.

The second clear limit on the *Herring* Court's holding is that it applies *only* to "final argument or summation at the conclusion of the evidence in a criminal trial." The Court pointedly disavowed any implication of "the existence of a constitutional right to oral argument at any other stage of the trial or appellate process." Consequently, it is unclear whether the Sixth Amendment entitlement to have counsel advocate the accused's cause includes an absolute right to offer an argument at any other stage of a criminal case. It is arguable that the adversary system's reliance on partisan advocacy to ensure reliable results and fair process requires that defense counsel be given some opportunity to argue their clients' cases at other significant stages of the proceedings. The Sixth Amendment could be construed to include an entitlement to present oral argument on critical pretrial motions, at the opening of trials, on motions and objections made during trials, or on post-trial motions attacking verdicts. On the other hand, in what some see as overstatement, the *Herring* Court observed that "no aspect of . . . advocacy could be more important than" summation at the end of trial. Because of its unique importance in safeguarding an accused's ultimate interests at trial, closing argument might be the sole constitutional entitlement. At other stages of the criminal process, the government might be able to prohibit all arguments or restrict counsel's advocacy to written submissions without transgressing the Sixth Amendment right to counsel.

In sum, in both jury and bench trials, the right to legal representation includes an entitlement to a reasonable opportunity to present a closing argument at the end of the presentation of evidence. It is uncertain whether the constitutional right to have counsel advocate in favor of the defendant's cause extends beyond closing argument to other phases of the criminal process. Because jurisdictions generally afford counsel at least some opportunity to make arguments at other important points in criminal proceedings, it seems unlikely that the Court will have to decide whether an outright ban on argument at another stage is inconsistent with the Sixth Amendment right to counsel. The ambiguities concerning the reach of the constitutional entitlement to "partisan advocacy" by counsel may well remain unresolved.

The Entitlements to Present and Challenge Evidence

As observed in the preceding section, today trials are no longer simply arguments between the defendant and government. Modern criminal trials include arguments but consist largely of evidentiary presentations by the opposing sides. The adversarial process depends on partisan presentations of the facts. Each side calls witnesses and submits tangible exhibits in an effort to persuade the trier to render a favorable verdict. A premise of our system is that competing evidentiary showings best promote the search for truth.[158] Moreover, the chance to submit evidence is an important part of the right to a fair process and opportunity to contest criminal charges. In addition, the adversarial system contemplates that each side will challenge the evidentiary showings of its opponent by raising objections to evidence, cross-examining and impeaching witnesses, and contesting the reliability and value of exhibits. To ensure both fair results and a fair process, the Sixth Amendment prescribes and expects "meaningful adversarial testing" of each side's evidence (United States v. Cronic, 1984).

Two of defense counsel's primary trial functions are to introduce the evidence that supports the accused's innocence and to challenge the government's evidence of guilt. For the system to operate properly, counsel must be free to perform these functions. The constitutional entitlement to active, full participation in the adversarial process, therefore, must include a right to have counsel present the defense's evidence and challenge the prosecution's evidence. Official restrictions on a defense attorney's abilities to present and contest evidence can deprive the accused of an integral part of the substance of counsel's assistance and violate the Sixth Amendment right to counsel.

In two cases, the Supreme Court has declared state restrictions on counsel's ability to proffer defense evidence to be unconstitutional. Ferguson v. Georgia, a 1961 decision, involved a state that still adhered, by statute, to the common law rule that a defendant was incompetent to testify under oath in his own defense. A second statute gave the accused a right to make an unsworn statement to the judge or jury. Trial judges had discretion to permit counsel to examine their clients on direct examination but could, and ordinarily did, deny the opportunity to do so. At the defendant's trial, the judge did not allow his lawyer to elicit his statement. The defendant was convicted.

Despite the fact that Georgia's prohibition on sworn testimony by the accused was out of step with the modern "consensus . . . that there was no rational justification" for disqualifying the defendant from testifying, the Court did not rule on the propriety of that prohibition (Ferguson v. Georgia, 1961). Instead, it concluded that barring counsel from questioning the accused to elicit his unsworn statement deprived him of his constitutional " 'right to be heard by counsel' " (Ferguson v. Georgia, 1961 (quoting Chandler v. Fretag, 1954)). In a criminal trial, the Constitution requires states to allow counsel to question the accused and assist in presenting his version of the facts to the trier of fact.

The *Ferguson* Court explained why this type of assistance from counsel was of vital interest to an accused. A defendant who must present his statement on his own is "set adrift on an uncharted sea with nothing to guide him." Because he does not have "the 'guiding hand of counsel,' he may fail properly to introduce, or to introduce at all, what may be a perfect defense" (Ferguson v. Georgia, 1961 (quoting Powell v. Alabama, 1932)). Although he is innocent, an accused charged with a serious offense may be "overwhelmed by his situation, and embarrassed, when called upon for explanation." The fact that he is "unlearned, unaccustomed to speak in public assemblies, or to put together his thoughts in consecutive order anywhere" may result in an "incoherent" explanation or one that "overlooks important circumstances." Counsel's aid in presenting the statement may enable the defendant to remedy these deficiencies, present a complete, coherent picture, and prevent an unjust conviction. Because it is counsel's function in the adversary system to assist the untrained, uneducated, legally inferior layman in presenting his evidence—including the critical information that he possesses—and because adequate performance of that responsibility is essential to the proper operation of the system, Georgia's prohibition on counsel's elicitation of the defendant's statement violated the right to counsel.

In Brooks v. Tennessee, a state provision mandated that if an accused was going to testify as part of the defense case, he had to testify first, before any other defense witness. A defense who did not testify first could not testify at all. In *Brooks*, the defendant filed a motion to delay the accused's testimony until other defense witnesses had testified. Despite the fact that the prosecution was willing to "waive the statute," the trial judge, acting under the statutory mandate, denied the motion. The defendant did not take the witness stand and was convicted.

The Supreme Court concluded that the Tennessee provision suffered from the same constitutional infirmity as the statute in Ferguson v. Georgia; that is, it "deprived the accused of [his entitlement to] ' "the guiding hand of counsel at every step in the proceedings against him" ' " (Brooks v. Tennessee, 1972 (quoting Powell v. Alabama, 1932)). According to the Court,

> [w]hether the defendant is to testify is an important tactical decision as well as a matter of constitutional right. By requiring the accused and his lawyer to make that choice without an opportunity to evaluate the actual worth of their evidence, the statute restricts the defense—particularly counsel—in the planning of its case.

Moreover, if the defendant fails to testify first, counsel cannot call him to testify "even though as a matter of professional judgment" she might believe that the defendant's testimony is an important component of an effective defense. Tennessee's restrictions upon counsel's ability to present defense evidence deprived the accused of a lawyer's aid with regard to "the timing of a critical element of his defense." According to the Court, the constitutional right to counsel's assistance forbids such constraints and dictates that "the accused and his counsel may not be restricted in deciding whether, and when in the course of presenting his defense, the accused should take the stand."

Together, *Ferguson* and *Brooks* clearly demonstrate that governmental restrictions on counsel's abilities to decide whether and when to present evidence and on counsel's active involvement in the presentation of evidence can run afoul of the constitutional entitlement to have counsel participate actively and fully in the adversarial fact-finding process. The breadth of the principle that underlies these cases, however, and its significance for other situations are both quite uncertain. Because both cases involved the defendant's "testimony"—a "critical element of his defense"—their impact could be confined to cases in which the government burdens counsel's ability to help the defendant tell the court or jury his side of the story. Moreover, the state interests offered in support of the provisions in *Ferguson* and *Brooks* were not considered sufficiently weighty to support what were undeniably drastic restrictions on counsel's aid in presenting the accused's story. More substantial reasons might justify lesser sorts of restrictions. On the other hand, it is arguable that *any* substantial infringements upon counsel's decisions about how, when, and whether to proffer significant defense evidence deprive the accused of the Sixth Amendment right to the "guiding hand of counsel." Any unjustifiable measure that substantially impedes a lawyer's partisan efforts to present a complete defense version of the facts might violate the right to counsel. (It bears mention that the Sixth Amendment right to counsel is not the only constitutional restraint on state measures that limit defense efforts to present favorable evidence. The Fourteenth Amendment Due Process Clause contains an implicit "right to present a defense" (Montana v. Egelhoff, 1996). Sometimes, though not often, this guarantee prevents states from denying defendants the opportunity to present exculpatory evidence. (See, e.g., Chambers v. Mississippi, 1973; Crane v. Kentucky, 1986).)

The impact of the right to counsel on state power to regulate the admission of evidence should not be overestimated. States have considerable authority to regulate the admissibility of evidence at trial. Many, indeed most, evidentiary and procedural rules that bar or restrict the introduction of various kinds of evidence are constitutionally permissible. Thus, for example, defense counsel ordinarily is not entitled to introduce inadmissible hearsay or improper character evidence, and a state may forbid the introduction of evidence of "voluntary intoxication" without running afoul of the Constitution (Montana v. Egelhoff, 1996). In addition, to promote institutional interests in "truth and fairness," trial judges "must have broad power to cope with the complexities and contingencies inherent in the adversary process" and "must exert substantial control over the proceedings" (Geders v. United States, 1976). Thus, a judge "may determine generally the order in which the parties will adduce proof" and has considerable, though not unlimited, authority to "control the scope of rebuttal testimony," to "refuse to allow cumulative, repetitive, or irrelevant testimony," and to "control the scope of [the] examination of witnesses" (Brooks v. Tennessee, 1972; Geders v. United States, 1976). Evidentiary rules and judicial authority to manage trials are justified by weighty state interests. Moreover, as a general rule they do not severely impair counsel's ability to present a defense. Ordinarily, therefore, the right to the assistance of counsel does not preclude the enforcement of rules limiting the introduction of evidence and does not prevent judges from exercising their authority to control trial proceedings.

In sum, governmental obstructions to questioning the accused and official constraints on deciding whether and when the accused will testify violate the defendant's right to have counsel participate actively and fully in the adversarial fact-finding process. Beyond these extreme cases, a defendant's contention that he was deprived of assistance because the state barred or restricted his lawyer's ability to present evidence is not very likely to succeed today. Rules barring or limiting the admissibility of evidence are likely to be deemed valid.

There are no specific Supreme Court opinions holding that a state's interference with defense counsel's ability to challenge the government's evidence constitutes a violation of the Sixth Amendment right to counsel. Nonetheless, because a primary function of a defense lawyer is to subject the prosecution's case to "meaningful adversarial testing" (United States v Cronic, 1984), it is arguable that a governmental hindrance to counsel's efforts to contest prosecution evidence deprives the accused of the substance of the Sixth Amendment right to assistance. If state action prevented meaningful cross-examination of a government witness, the Sixth Amendment right to be "confronted" with witnesses would be the best foundation for a persuasive constitutional challenge. But if a state were to interfere without good reason with defense counsel's efforts to challenge the prosecution's evidence in some way that did not deprive the accused of his entitlement to confront witnesses, a valid right to counsel claim is conceivable. Thus, for example, a rule that defense counsel could object to only two government documentary exhibits during a trial could be deemed a deprivation of the entitlement to have counsel participate actively and fully in the adversarial fact-finding process.

The Entitlement to Consult with Counsel

Another essential component of the Sixth Amendment guarantee of the assistance of counsel is the defendant's "right to consult with his attorney" (Geders v. United States, 1976). Basically, an accused has a constitutional entitlement to communicate information, concerns, and thoughts to his lawyer, as well as a right to have counsel convey to him information, advice, and assessments of the case. Put simply, as a general rule every "defendant [has] a constitutional right to discuss with his lawyer" the entire range of matters that bear upon the investigation, preparation, and conduct of his defense (Perry v. Leeke, 1989). This

Sixth Amendment entitlement to consultation with counsel necessarily involves two-way communication between the lawyer and client.[159]

A right to consult or discuss matters with counsel is an integral part of the content of the Sixth Amendment promise of assistance because full and free consultation is essential to enable a defense lawyer to perform her constitutionally assigned responsibilities. To be an able equalizer in the contest with the state, counsel must have all the relevant information possessed by the defendant. Adequate investigation and preparation, essentials for effective representation at trial, ordinarily would be impossible without both the defendant's input and the lawyer's expert understanding of the significance of that input.[160] Moreover, the accused is a key witness, as well as a source of other defense witnesses and evidence and of information about potential infirmities and flaws in the government's witnesses and evidence. Counsel has the training necessary to sift through the array of facts conveyed to her and to decide what is and is not relevant and helpful to constructing and conducting an effective legal defense. Two-way exchanges between the accused and defense attorney are critical predicates for counsel's meaningful participation in the adversarial process. Partisan advocacy of the defendant's interests, the presentation of significant exculpatory evidence, and effective confrontation of the governmental adversary depend in substantial measure on what counsel is able to ascertain from and communicate to the accused.[161]

An earlier part of this analysis discussed the Supreme Court's opinion in Faretta v. California. In *Faretta*, the Court pointedly observed that the accused is the one on trial—the individual whose life or liberty is at stake. The Court discerned an implicit right of self-representation in the Sixth Amendment in large part because the "right to make a defense" is a "personal" entitlement granted specifically to "the accused" (Faretta v. California, 1975). When a defendant chooses to be represented by counsel, he surrenders this entitlement to appear as his own representative but does not relinquish the entitlement to participate in constructing a defense. Although most decisions clearly become counsel's prerogative, the defendant is still entitled to make or at least participate in significant decisions about the course of the defense. Meaningful participation in the defense and informed decision making are obviously impossible without opportunities to confer and discuss matters with the expert guide provided by the Constitution. A right to consult, therefore, is critical to preservation of the accused's personal constitutional entitlement to make a defense.

An entitlement to consult with counsel serves additional interests that are less concrete but nonetheless important. "[O]rdinarily a defendant is ill-equipped to understand . . . the trial process without a lawyer's guidance" (Geders v. United States, 1976). The criminal justice system is mysterious, often unfathomable to the lay accused. It is not consonant with adversarial system principles of decent treatment, fair play, and respect for individual dignity to deprive a person of life or liberty by means of a process that he does not, indeed, cannot adequately comprehend. Moreover, society has a distinct interest in ensuring that a defendant does not feel that the criminal justice system "contrives against him" (Faretta v. California, 1975) but, instead, believes that he has been treated fairly.[162] Consultation with defense counsel guarantees that the defendant has a basic understanding of the legal proceedings in which he has become enmeshed. Discussion with one's lawyer can engender a sense that the trial is being conducted fairly and can foster a willingness to accept an unfavorable verdict. Thus, an entitlement to full and free opportunities to confer with counsel is necessary to protect both the defendant's and society's interests in ensuring adequate comprehension of the legal process.

In sum, two-way communication between the accused and his lawyer promotes a number of the objectives of the constitutional right to counsel and of the adversary system of criminal justice. Without discussion between lawyer and client, the lawyer cannot perform the array of responsibilities assigned to her by the adversary system. Without discussion between lawyer and client, a defendant cannot meaningfully participate in making his own defense. Without discussion between lawyer and client, an accused will not have the understanding necessary to ensure the reality and the appearance of fair treatment. For all these reasons, an entitlement to consult with the defense attorney is an indispensable component of the accused's Sixth Amendment entitlement.

"[C]onsultation" with counsel prior to trial is "vitally important" to ensure adequate assistance at trial. Thus, an accused "must not be stripped of his right to have sufficient time [and opportunities] to advise with counsel" before the trial begins (Powell v. Alabama, 1932). Consultation during and at the trial is equally critical. As the trial progresses, "tactical [and other] decisions [need] to be made and strategies [need] to be reviewed. The lawyer may need to obtain from his client information made relevant by [witnesses'] testimony, or he may need to pursue inquiry along lines not fully explored earlier" (Geders v. United States, 1976). Counsel and the accused may need to discuss "the availability of other witnesses, trial tactics, or even the possibility of negotiating a plea bargain" (Perry v. Leeke, 1989). Consequently, the right to consult extends from the time of the first formal accusation—the point at which the right to counsel attaches—through the end of the trial. Logically, the right to discuss matters with one's lawyer must extend as well to the sentencing phase of the proceedings and probably to the process of appealing a conviction. Government obstructions to consultation or restriction of opportunities for consultation at any critical stage of the criminal process may violate the Sixth Amendment right to counsel or the Fourteenth Amendment right to due process of law.

One way that a state might unconstitutionally interfere with the entitlement to consultation is by preventing a defendant from having adequate time to discuss matters with a retained or appointed lawyer. In Powell v. Alabama, the appointment of counsel on the morning that trial commenced was deemed unconstitutional in part because it "stripped" the defendants of their "right to have sufficient time to advise with counsel" (Powell v. Alabama, 1932). Commencement of trial too soon after counsel first appears in a case also can deprive the accused of the constitutionally protected interest in conferring with his lawyer. Moreover, if a state were to erect unreasonable barriers between a defendant who is in custody and his lawyer, restricting access in ways that impeded adequate discussion of the case, it might violate the Sixth Amendment guarantee.

The most obvious form of governmental interference with the right to consult with counsel is a direct, judicial order barring the accused and his attorney from speaking to one another. In two significant cases, the Supreme Court has dealt with trial court prohibitions on attorney–client discussion during the course of trial. The Court's opinions in those cases provide considerable insight into the nature and extent of the Sixth Amendment entitlement to consultation. Nonetheless, because the holding in each case was narrowly framed and limited by the facts of the case, several questions about the entitlement to consultation remain unsettled.

Geders v. United States involved a seventeen-hour overnight recess in a trial called between a testifying defendant's direct examination by his attorney and cross-examination by the prosecutor (Geders v. United States, 1976).[163] At the prosecutor's request, the trial judge ordered the defendant not to talk to anyone—including his attorney—during the recess. Defense counsel objected but ultimately complied with the order not to confer with the accused. Following conviction, the defendant appealed, contending that the prohibition on attorney–client communication during the recess deprived him of the Sixth Amendment right to representation.

The Supreme Court agreed with the defendant's claim, holding that "an order preventing [the accused] from consulting his counsel 'about anything' during a 17-hour overnight recess between his direct- and cross-examination impinged upon his right to the assistance of counsel guaranteed by the Sixth Amendment." Initially, the Court did acknowledge that trial judges have "broad power to sequester witnesses before, during, and after their testimony" (i.e., to order them not to talk to others about their testimony). It also recognized that sequestration ordinarily serves two salutary purposes—it restrains witnesses from tailoring their testimony to that of previous witnesses, and it aids in detecting less than candid testimony. In addition, sequestration during a recess while a witness is still on the stand prevents "improper attempts to influence the testimony in light of the testimony already given."

The Court observed, however, that sequestration has different impacts on defendants and nonparty witnesses. The latter ordinarily have nothing but the ongoing testimony to discuss with counsel, while accused individuals have a number of other reasons to consult and various subjects to discuss with their lawyers. During lengthy overnight recesses, in particular, defendants and their lawyers often discuss the significance of the day's events, working intensively, making tactical decisions, and reviewing strategies. Attorneys may need to seek additional information from defendants in light of the day's evidence or may need to "pursue inquiry along lines not fully explored earlier." Consultation during such periods is critical if counsel is to provide the "guidance" to the "ill-equipped" accused that the Sixth Amendment contemplates. Moreover, sequestration of a defendant at any point in the proceedings "accomplishes less" than sequestration of other witnesses. The defendant is ordinarily present for all testimony and can discuss his own testimony with counsel right up until the point that he takes the stand.

The Court did not deny that the government has interests in preventing improper influence or "coaching" by counsel that will render the prosecutor's cross-examination of the defendant less effective. Those interests can often be protected, however, without infringing on the accused's need to consult with his attorney. The prosecutor, for example, can cross-examine the accused in an effort to expose influences or coaching during a recess, or a judge can schedule testimony in a way that avoids the necessity of calling a recess prior to cross-examination. The Court admitted that available alternatives may not provide complete protection against corruption of the truth-finding process in every case and, thus, may be less effective than a total prohibition on discussion. It concluded, however, that any "conflict" between the state's interest in effective cross-examination and the accused's constitutional interests in consultation "must . . . be resolved in favor of the right to the assistance and guidance of counsel." When a choice must be made, the values promoted by the Sixth Amendment entitlement to consultation prevail over the values promoted by effective cross-examination of an uncounseled defendant.

The Court's holding in *Geders* was exceptionally narrow, limited specifically to judicial orders barring all consultation during seventeen-hour, overnight recesses between direct and cross-examination of the accused. The Court stated explicitly that its opinion was not intended to deal with other sorts of limitations on consultation between attorneys and their clients. Thus, after *Geders* it was uncertain whether a different constitutional result would be justified if a judicial order only partially restricted discussions, barred all consultation during a shorter recess, or impeded communication at a different juncture in the trial.

Thirteen years later, in Perry v. Leeke, the Court resolved some of these ambiguities concerning the right to consult with counsel (Perry v. Leeke, 1989).[164] The majority opinion in *Leeke* implicitly reaffirmed defendants' general entitlement to unrestricted discussions with their lawyers at all times after the right to counsel attaches. It held, however, that the government has the authority to prevent attorney–client consultation during trial in certain, quite limited circumstances. *Leeke* involved a mildly retarded defendant who was instructed by a trial judge not to talk to anyone, including his lawyer, during a fifteen-minute recess called at the end of his direct testimony. Following conviction, the accused sought collateral relief in federal court. The district court declared his conviction invalid. The Court of Appeals reversed, holding that while the prohibition on talking to his attorney did violate the Sixth Amendment, the accused was not entitled to a new trial because the error was "not prejudicial." The evidence of the defendant's guilt was overwhelming, and there was "no basis for believing that [the defendant's] performance on cross-examination would have been different had he been given an opportunity to confer with his lawyer during the brief recess."

The Supreme Court disagreed with both of the appellate court's conclusions. First, the Court held that a showing of prejudice is not necessary when the government unconstitutionally obstructs the accused's entitlement to consult with counsel. More important, the Court held that the prohibition on discussion in *Leeke* did not deprive the defendant of the substance of his Sixth Amendment right to assistance. Acknowledging that "the line between the facts of Geders and the facts of this case is a thin one," the *Leeke* majority nonetheless concluded that it is "a line of constitutional dimension." According to *Leeke*, a prohibition on consultation is constitutionally permissible during "a *short* recess in which it is *appropriate to presume that nothing but the testimony will be discussed*" (italics added). Put otherwise, the Sixth Amendment is not violated by bars on discussion "during a *brief* recess in which there is a *virtual certainty that any conversation between the [accused] and the lawyer would relate to the ongoing testimony*" (italics added). Thus, the "constitutional line" drawn in *Leeke* rests entirely on the length of the trial recess.

In general, judges are authorized to forbid witnesses from discussing their testimony with third parties during trial because the search for truth is enhanced if a witness's testimony is uninfluenced by others' input.[165] Prohibitions on discussion prior to cross-examination are permissible because it is an "empirical predicate of our system of adversary . . . justice that cross examination of a witness who is uncounseled between direct examination and cross-examination is more likely to lead to the discovery of truth than is cross-examination of a witness who is given time to pause and consult with his attorney." According to the *Leeke* majority, these premises apply equally to a defendant once he becomes a witness. The prosecution will be able to elicit the truth more effectively on cross-examination if the accused is unable to obtain advice from counsel concerning the impending cross-examination. Advice from a lawyer at that point in the trial will impede the efficacy of the cross-examination and obstruct the search for truth.

The Court affirmed that a defendant has "an absolute right to . . . consultation" about everything, including his testimony, "before he begins to testify." It concluded, however, that the accused "has no constitutional right to consult with his lawyer while he is testifying." Consultation with counsel while the defendant is on the witness stand undermines the system's overriding interest in discovering the truth without promoting any significant interest of the accused. Thus, a defendant has no entitlement to have testimony interrupted while he is on the stand so that he may obtain counsel's advice about his testimony. Similarly, a "testifying defendant does not have a constitutional right to advice" about his ongoing testimony during a break in that testimony.

According to the Court, during "short" or "brief" recesses at the end of direct testimony when it is "appropriate to presume" and "virtually certain" that the only topic of discussion will be the accused's ongoing testimony, an order prohibiting all discussion with counsel has essentially the same effect as a refusal to grant a recess to permit consultation. It merely prevents a defendant from discussing his in-progress testimony with his lawyer. Such an order is constitutionally valid because it furthers the truth-seeking mission of the trial without depriving the accused of a constitutionally cognizable interest in speaking with and receiving advice from counsel.

During a lengthy recess, such as the one in *Geders*, a prohibition on discussion infringes on the defendant's constitutionally protected interests in conferring with counsel about a wide range of matters that are germane to the conduct of an effective defense. Any harm to the truth-seeking process must be tolerated to preserve the weighty constitutional values that underlie a defendant's "right to unrestricted access to his lawyer for advice on a variety of trial-related matters" (Perry v. Leeke, 1989). The balance of interests weighs in favor of the accused's entitlement to consult. During a sufficiently brief recess, however, the defendant loses merely the opportunity to talk about his ongoing testimony. The Constitution does not protect the accused's interest in having such an opportunity because consultation about ongoing testimony can seriously impede the search for truth without significantly enhancing any important interests of a defendant.[166] During such a recess, the balance tips in favor of the government's interest in effective cross-examination and the system's interest in ascertaining the truth. The governmental and societal interests in preserving the status quo during the break are substantial, while the accused's interest in speaking to counsel is limited, at best.

Three dissenting members of the Court forcefully disagreed with the majority's conclusion in *Leeke*. In their view, the Sixth Amendment entitlement to unrestricted consultation extends even to very brief recesses. According to the dissenters, the defendant's right to legal assistance and guidance at every critical stage of a criminal prosecution precludes the state from barring access to counsel during any recess while the accused is on the witness stand. They discerned serious flaws in the premises that led the majority to the opposite conclusion. The first flaw is the conclusion that the sequestration rules applicable to other witnesses apply equally to defendants. Accused persons have constitutional rights that preclude treating them the same as other witnesses. A second flaw is the assertion that counsel's input between direct and cross-examination will retard the truth-seeking function of the adversary system. According to the *Leeke* dissenters, there is no "empirical" evidence supporting that proposition. To the contrary, a central premise of the Sixth Amendment is that affording the accused an equalizing assistant "enhances the discovery of truth because it better enables the defendant to put the State to its proof." Consequently, access to advice from counsel during a recess prior to the state's cross-examination of the accused "might *increase* the likelihood" that the truth will be discovered (italics added). A third flaw is the "presumption" that only testimony will be discussed during brief recesses. Even during such breaks an accused and his attorney may have occasion to confer about important matters other than his testimony. It is simply not sensible to presume that only testimony will be discussed (Perry v. Leeke, 1989 (Marshall, J., dissenting)).

The dissenters also rejected the majority's assertion that an accused has no constitutional entitlement to discuss his testimony while it is in progress. In their view, the entitlement to consult with counsel does not "turn[] on what the defendant and his attorney discuss or at what point during a trial their discussion takes place." By extending the

> right to have counsel, which includes the concomitant right to communicate with counsel at every critical stage of the proceedings . . . the Constitution seeks "to minimize the imbalance in the adversary system." The [*Leeke*] majority . . . disserve[d] this noble goal by isolating the defendant at a time when counsel's assistance is perhaps most needed. (Perry v. Leeke, 1989 (Marshall, J., dissenting))[167]

The holdings in *Geders* and *Leeke* leave unresolved several important questions about the scope of the right to consult with counsel. One significant question involves the length of recess that can qualify as "brief" or "short." When is a break in the accused's testimony sufficiently brief so that it is appropriate to presume that only ongoing testimony will be discussed and so that it is constitutionally permissible to prohibit any discussion? The *Leeke* majority referred to recesses that were "brief," "short," and "for a few minutes" and upheld a bar order in a case involving a fifteen-minute break. Still, it specified no maximum time limit. Consequently, it is uncertain, for example, whether a one-hour lunch break would be too long to permit a prohibition on consultation.[168]

Another unanswered question is whether a judge may impose a limited prohibition on discussions of ongoing testimony during breaks that are too long to permit total bans on consultation. *Geders* forbade only absolute bars to all discussion. Moreover, *Leeke* declared that there is no constitutional right to advice concerning ongoing testimony. A narrow order not to talk about the accused's testimony might be valid. On the other hand, it is arguable that a limited restriction on communication might impede the ability to consult meaningfully about matters that the accused is entitled to discuss with counsel. Fear of violating a court order restricting discussion could discourage counsel from providing advice about other trial-related matters. Moreover, discussions of legitimate topics might be impossible without consideration of the defendant's ongoing testimony.[169]

Yet another question is whether bars to consultation at other points during a defendant's testimony are ever permissible. The *Leeke* Court concluded that there is no right to advice about ongoing testimony and held that the "Constitution does not compel every trial judge to allow the defendant to consult with his lawyer while his testimony is in progress if the judge decides to interrupt the trial for a few minutes." That language suggests that a judge could prohibit consultation during a sufficiently brief recess called at any point during the accused's testimony. At a minimum, it seems very likely that the holding in

Leeke would be extended to any short recess prior to the conclusion of the government's cross-examination.[170] On the other hand, the facts of *Leeke* did involve a recess at a particular time—between direct and cross-examination. The authority to bar consultation might be confined to breaks occurring at that precise juncture. Whether the logic of *Leeke* would permit any prohibitions on discussion following the government's cross-examination of the defendant—that is, prior to or during redirect or recross-examination—is uncertain.

Together, *Geders* and *Leeke* powerfully support the conclusion that the right to confer with one's attorney during and at trial is broad and generally not subject to limitation by the state. In distinguishing *Geders*, the *Leeke* majority adverted to "the defendant's right to unrestricted access to his lawyer for advice on a variety of trial-related matters." In addition, it characterized the accused's right to advice about his own testimony before taking the stand as "absolute" (Perry v. Leeke, 1989). Governmental interference with communications between lawyer and client while the accused is not on the stand is unlikely to survive constitutional scrutiny. Moreover, when a defendant is on the witness stand, the government may not impede discussions about matters other than the ongoing testimony. Because a defendant does not have a right to advice from counsel about his testimony while he is on the witness stand, a judge may preclude advice by refusing to allow a break in his testimony. A judge may also prohibit the accused from talking to counsel during short recesses called for other purposes when it is virtually certain that only the ongoing testimony will be discussed. Because the Sixth Amendment right to counsel encompasses an entitlement to free and full communication between defendants and their lawyers, state interference with efforts to confer with counsel about other matters at other times deprives the accused of the constitutional entitlement to assistance.

The Entitlement to Loyal Representation by Counsel

The Meaning of Loyalty, Conflicts of Interest, and Multiple Representation of Codefendants

The Sixth Amendment right to the assistance of counsel "contemplates the services of an attorney devoted solely to the interests of his client." Central, essential components of the legal assistance and equalization provided by that guarantee are "[u]ndivided allegiance and faithful, devoted service to" the accused's cause (Von Moltke v. Gillies, 1948). The "duty of loyalty [is] perhaps the most basic of [defense] counsel's duties" (Strickland v. Washington, 1984). Consequently, the constitutional right to counsel includes an entitlement to loyal assistance. Defendants are entitled to receive "unimpaired loyalty" from retained and appointed attorneys (Cuyler v. Sullivan, 1980 (Marshall, J., concurring in part and dissenting in part)). Anything less will not satisfy the substance of the constitutional command.[171]

This facet of the Sixth Amendment's content requires a lawyer's actions, inactions, decisions, tactics, and strategies to be aimed exclusively at promoting the objectives of the defendant. Counsel must actively, zealously seek to further and safeguard the accused's interests. She must not engage in conduct contrary to those interests or refrain from legitimate conduct that will advance those interests. Such disloyalty would be inconsistent with the spirit of the counsel guarantee.

Actions or inactions that betray a lack of undivided allegiance to the defendant's cause can result from a simple lack of commitment and devotion to the accused's objectives. The most typical cause of defense counsel disloyalty, however, is a "conflict of interests." In general, a lawyer has a conflict of interests when she has personal or professional interests that compete with those of the accused. A conflict exists when pursuit of these competing interests calls upon counsel to take steps or make decisions that run contrary to the defendant's best interests.[172] A lawyer might have a financial interest, for example, that would be undermined by zealous, single-minded pursuit of defense strategies. She might have employment opportunities that would be hindered by loyal, unrestrained advocacy on behalf of the accused. She could have personal relationships that would suffer from unimpaired devotion to the defendant's cause.[173] In each of these situations, the lawyer's allegiance is divided, and her loyalty is impaired. In each, her client does not receive unqualified devotion and may not receive faithful, zealous service.

Any "actual conflict of interests [is problematic because it] negates the unimpaired loyalty a defendant is constitutionally entitled to expect and receive from his attorney" (Cuyler v. Sullivan, 1980 (Marshall, J., concurring in part and dissenting in part)). When an attorney finds herself in a conflicted position—a situation where competing interests point in divergent directions—she cannot function as the loyal, dedicated assistant necessary to equalize the accused and ensure that the adversarial system of criminal justice operates properly. Conflicts of interest can "impermissibly imperil [the] right to a fair trial" (Cuyler v. Sullivan, 1980) by preventing counsel from providing the zealous, committed assistance essential to ensure just results by means of fair, balanced contests.

For these reasons, the Sixth Amendment entitlement to the assistance of a lawyer encompasses a "right to conflict-free counsel" (Wheat v. United States, 1988). "Joint representation of conflicting interests is suspect" and inconsistent with the promise of counsel both because of what it tends to induce an attorney to do and "because of what it tends to prevent an attorney from doing" (Holloway v. Arkansas, 1978). "The mere physical presence of an attorney does not fulfill the Sixth Amendment guarantee when the advocate's conflicting obligations have effectively sealed his lips on crucial matters." Consequently, the Supreme Court has recognized that "[d]efense counsel have an ethical obligation to avoid conflicting representations and to advise the court promptly when a conflict of interest arises during the course of trial" (Cuyler v. Sullivan, 1980). The Sixth Amendment promise of undivided loyalty ensures that a defense lawyer will be unimpeded by interests that could constrain her efforts to resist the state's attempts to convict the accused.

The most common situation in which a conflict of interests can arise involves a single attorney who represents multiple criminal defendants charged with the same or related offenses. Joint representation of codefendants "is not *per se* violative of constitutional guarantees of effective assistance of counsel" (Holloway v. Arkansas, 1978).[174] In fact, it might turn out to be advantageous for codefendants to be represented by the same attorney. In some cases, a single attorney is able to present the most unified, coherent, and, thus, persuasive defense for multiple defendants who are jointly charged (Glasser v. United States, 1942 (Frankfurter, J., dissenting)).[175] "[M]ultiple representation" violates the Sixth Amendment only if it "gives rise to a conflict of interest" (Cuyler v. Sullivan, 1980). Nevertheless, it is generally acknowledged that "multiple representation of criminal defendants engenders special dangers" (Wheat v. United States, 1988). Because "a possible conflict of interest inheres in almost every instance of multiple representation" (Cuyler v. Sullivan, 1980), when a defense attorney represents more than one codefendant, there is almost sure to be a cognizable risk that she will be unable to provide the single-minded devotion necessary to combat the prosecution's efforts to secure a conviction.[176]

Three significant Supreme Court decisions regarding the Sixth Amendment entitlement to loyal, conflict-free representation have involved situations in which defense attorneys undertook representation of more than one codefendant. The Court's analyses of these situations have led to the conclusion that deprivations of the constitutional entitlement to loyalty can come about in two distinct ways. First, a judge can insist on or fail to prevent multiple representation that entails an actual conflict or a serious risk of conflict. In that situation, the violation of the Sixth Amendment promise of conflict-free representation is the direct result of governmental action or inaction. Second, due to an extant conflict of interest that is not attributable to state action or inaction, a defense attorney's performance can be less than zealous and loyal. In that situation, the accused suffers a Sixth Amendment deprivation because his lawyer does not provide the dedicated representation essential to a fair adversarial battle.

The previous three subsections of this analysis addressed infringements of the substance of the right to counsel resulting from state impediments of some sort. This subsection considers both state interferences with attorney loyalty and breaches of the duty of loyalty due to lawyers' failures to fulfill their constitutional obligations. For that reason, it foreshadows and provides a suitable transition to the next subsection in the analysis—ineffective assistance of counsel resulting from counsel's deficient performance of one or more of her functions.

Deprivations of the Entitlement to Loyalty Resulting from State Action or Inaction

In Glasser v. United States, two federal prosecutors, Glasser and Kretske, were charged with conspiracy to defraud the United States (Glasser v. United

States, 1942). Each secured separate defense counsel to represent his interests. When Krestke's attorney informed the trial judge that his client no longer wished to be represented by him, the judge requested that Glasser's lawyer also serve as Kretske's counsel. Glasser objected to having his attorney also represent his codefendant. Initially, the attorney expressed concerns about the joint representation. Subsequently, however, the lawyer agreed to represent Kretske if the trial judge wanted him to do so. At trial, the lawyer did represent both Glasser and Kretske. After he was convicted, Glasser appealed, contending that the trial judge's action had violated his Sixth Amendment right to counsel.

The Supreme Court agreed with his claim. The Court began by acknowledging the fundamental importance of the assistance of counsel. It then observed that trial judges have a "duty of seeing that the trial is conducted with solicitude for the essential rights of the accused" and "should protect the right of an accused to have the assistance of counsel." According to the Court, the Sixth Amendment guarantee "contemplates that such assistance be untrammeled and unimpaired by a court order requiring that one lawyer shall simultaneously represent conflicting interests. If the right to the assistance of counsel means less than this, a valued constitutional safeguard is substantially impaired."

The *Glasser* Court found that the trial judge's provision for joint representation breached his duty to the accused. Despite the fact that "[t]he possibility of the inconsistent interests of [the codefendants] was brought home to the" judge, he nonetheless was "responsible for creating a situation which resulted in the impairment of [defendant Glasser's] rights." Defense counsel's joint representation resulted in a "struggle to serve two masters." As a result of this struggle, on at least two occasions the attorney did not do what his duty of loyalty to Glasser would have required because his obligations to Kretske pointed in the opposite direction. He failed to cross-examine a witness when "a thorough cross-examination was indicated in Glasser's interest," and he failed to object to evidence that was arguably inadmissible against Glasser.

In a significant passage, the Court asserted that a trial judge has a "duty to refrain from embarrassing counsel in the defense of the accused by insisting, or indeed, even suggesting that counsel undertake to concurrently represent interests which might diverge from those of his first client, *when the possibility of that divergence is brought home to the court*" (italics added). The trial judge in *Glasser* appointed counsel to represent Kretske, even though he was "advised of the possibility that conflicting interests might arise." Moreover, the record showed that counsel's "representation of Glasser was not as effective as it might have been if the appointment had not been made." Based on these facts, the Supreme Court concluded that the trial judge "denied Glasser his right to have the effective assistance of counsel, guaranteed by the Sixth Amendment."

Thirty-six years later, in Holloway v. Arkansas, the Court reaffirmed and extended the holding in *Glasser*, making it somewhat easier to establish a deprivation of the right to counsel in situations where a trial judge breaches the constitutional duty to prevent a conflict of interest resulting from joint representation (Holloway v. Arkansas, 1978). Holloway involved three defendants jointly charged with robbery and rape. The trial judge appointed a single lawyer to represent all three. Shortly thereafter, appointed counsel made two motions requesting that separate lawyers be appointed for each of the defendants due to the possibilities for conflicts of interests. Specifically, counsel complained that because he had obligations to each defendant, he would not be able to cross-examine any of them in order to protect the interests of the others. The judge denied the requests for separate representation, informing counsel that there was no right to cross-examine the codefendants and that he could simply put any defendant who wanted to testify on the stand to " 'relate what he wants to' " without examination. All three defendants were convicted of all charges.

The Arkansas Supreme Court rejected the contention that the defendants had been denied their constitutional rights to counsel. The defense attorney had not specified the nature of the alleged "conflicting loyalties," and the record did not reveal the existence of any "actual conflict of interests or prejudice to the" defendants. The United States Supreme Court disagreed, holding that the defendants had been deprived of the right to the assistance of counsel. According to the Court, the failure of the trial judge

> either to appoint separate counsel or to take adequate steps to ascertain whether the risk was too remote to warrant separate counsel in the face of the representations made by counsel weeks before trial and again before the jury was empaneled, deprived petitioners of the guarantee of "assistance of counsel."

The Court indicated that if the objections raised had been "dilatory"—that is, if, without justification, they had been raised too late in the proceedings—a court's failure to respond might be constitutional. Barring such circumstances, however, trial judges have an obligation to act to protect the entitlement to loyal, conflict-free representation. When counsel has alerted the judge, the failure to act alone constitutes a violation of the right to counsel and requires a new trial.[177]

Dissenting Justices strenuously objected to the Court's conclusion. In their view, a trial judge's failure to respond to the representations of counsel should lead to a finding of Sixth Amendment deprivation *only* if the record contains "some basis for a reasonable inference that 'conflicting interests' hampered a potentially effective defense" (Holloway v. Arkansas, 1978 (Powell, J., dissenting)). The dissenters believed that, despite a trial judge's inaction, an accused does not suffer cognizable constitutional harm unless a real conflict of interests actually threatens the entitlement to loyal, zealous representation. Without a conflict of interests that actually hinders counsel's performance, the defendant is not denied any substantive component of the right to legal assistance.

In essence, the *Holloway* majority held that the Constitution "requires . . . trial courts to investigate timely objections to multiple representation" (Cuyler v. Sullivan, 1980). This judicial obligation to investigate is rooted, in part, in the fact that a potential for conflict of interest is inherent in every case of multiple representation. The risk that conflicts will arise is always significant. Moreover, an attorney is in the best position to determine whether there is or will be a conflict, has an obligation to advise the judge of conflicts, and makes representations of conflict "virtually under oath" (Holloway v. Arkansas, 1978). Thus, when counsel alerts the judge to the reality of or potential for conflict, the chance that a conflict of interests does exist or will arise is too great to tolerate. Proper regard for the fundamental right to loyalty demands that when a defendant objects to multiple representation, he must be afforded "the opportunity to show that potential conflicts impermissibly imperil his right to a fair trial" (Cuyler v. Sullivan, 1980).

The *Holloway* Court did not require proof that an "alleged conflict actually existed. It simply held that the trial court's error unconstitutionally endangered the right to counsel" (Cuyler v. Sullivan, 1980). The Court's decision not to require a demonstration that counsel had an actual conflict that impaired her performance was due, in part, to the high likelihood of a conflict and, in part, to the difficulty of accurately assessing the impact of a conflict on a lawyer's performance. After the fact, both what counsel did and what she refrained from doing are hard to re-create, and the effects of counsel's actions and failures are hard to ascertain. The Court's decision was also rooted in the belief that an accused should not suffer the risks of impaired performance when he has apprised the trial judge of the potential for conflict. The state should bear the consequences when those risks result from the judge's failure to take the simple steps required to guard against them. In one sense, the holding in *Holloway* is a "prophylactic" rule (Holloway v. Arkansas, 1976 (Powell, J., dissenting)), designed to motivate trial judges to be vigilant in protecting defendants' fundamental right to undivided loyalty from counsel.

A trial judge has a duty to inquire both when specifically alerted by counsel that a conflict of interest exists and when the circumstances otherwise provide actual or constructive notice of a conflict of interest.[178] More specifically, the duty arises whenever the judge "knows or reasonably should know that a particular conflict exists" (Cuyler v. Sullivan, 1980). Awareness "of a vague, unspecified possibility of conflict, such as that which inheres in almost every instance of multiple representation," is insufficient to trigger the duty (Mickens v. Taylor, 2002). Although a duty can arise even when counsel does not raise a specific objection, the "prophylactic" rule of *Holloway*—requiring automatic reversal when a judge fails to investigate without a showing of a conflict, an effect on representation, or prejudice to the outcome—is applicable *only* when defense counsel notifies the Court of the conflict. As is discussed below, in other cases where the judge has an obligation to inquire, reversal is not required unless the defendant shows that an actual conflict adversely affected his attorney's representation of his interests (Mickens v. Taylor, 2002).

When a lawyer informs the judge of a conflict resulting from multiple representation, the safest option is to appoint separate counsel. Dissenters in *Holloway* complained that the Court's holding would result in a rule of separate counsel on demand. The majority, however, asserted that a trial judge has the choice of appointing separate counsel or "exploring the adequacy of the basis of defense counsel's representations regarding a conflict of interests without improperly requiring disclosure of the confidential communications of the client." If a judge is able to ascertain that the risk of conflict is "too remote to warrant separate counsel," there is no constitutional need to ensure separate representation (Holloway v. Arkansas, 1978). In practice, this option has proven to be unrealistic. Courts have generally responded to allegations of conflict by providing separate representation.

Finally, in light of the recent decision in Mickens v. Taylor, it is not entirely clear whether the stringent automatic reversal rule of *Holloway* governs situations in which something other than multiple simultaneous representation of codefendants is the source of an alleged conflict. Thus, if an attorney were to notify a judge that her financial, professional, or personal interest might be in conflict with her client's best interests, it is uncertain whether a judge's failure to take remedial action would by itself constitute a violation of the Sixth Amendment and necessitate reversal of a conviction.[179]

Deprivations of the Entitlement to Loyalty Resulting from a Conflict's Impacts on Counsel's Performance

Unless put on notice by counsel or the circumstances, a judge does not have a duty to investigate the possibility of a conflict of interest in cases of multiple representation. "[N]othing in . . . the Sixth Amendment requires . . . courts themselves to initiate inquiries into the propriety of multiple representation in every case." In all situations where a duty of inquiry does not arise, a judge "may assume either that multiple representation entails no conflict or that the lawyer and his clients knowingly accept such risk of conflict as may exist" (Cuyler v. Sullivan, 1980).[180]

As already noted, automatic reversal based on a judge's failure to act is required only in cases where counsel alerts the judge to the conflict. When a judge is otherwise alerted to a conflict, the judge's failure to act alone does not violate the Sixth Amendment (Mickens v. Taylor, 2002). In that instance, in cases where a judge has inquired and determined that the risk of conflict was too remote to require separate counsel, and in situations where no duty to inquire has arisen, a defendant can still establish a deprivation of the right to loyal representation but must demonstrate that "an actual conflict of interest adversely affected his lawyer's performance" (Cuyler v. Sullivan, 1980; Mickens v. Taylor, 2002). To prove a constitutional violation, he must show "that his counsel actively represented conflicting interests" and either acted or failed to act in some way that was inconsistent with the obligation of loyalty. When the actual conflict has resulted from simultaneous representation of codefendants, the accused "need not demonstrate prejudice"—that is, a negative impact on the outcome of the proceeding (Cuyler v. Sullivan, 1980). When the conflict has a different source, a prejudice showing may, however, be required (Mickens v. Taylor, 2002).

In general, private parties cannot violate the Constitution. Deprivations of constitutional rights require "state action." Nonetheless, when a privately retained lawyer operates under a conflict of interests that adversely affects her representation, an accused is deprived of the Sixth Amendment entitlement to assistance. In that situation, the constitutional violation is attributable to "state action" because "the Sixth Amendment . . . prevents the States from conducting trials at which persons who face incarceration must defend themselves without adequate legal assistance." Whether a lawyer is retained or appointed, if a conflict of interests induces her to act contrary to the defendant's interests or to refrain from acting to further those interests, she renders "inadequate assistance"—assistance that "does not satisfy the Sixth Amendment right to counsel." Because a trial with inadequate legal assistance is lacking a guarantee essential for fairness, it is infected by "a serious risk of injustice." A conviction that results from such a trial "unconstitutionally deprives the defendant of his liberty" (Cuyler v. Sullivan, 1980). The government is responsible for that deprivation because it has conducted the trial and thereby implicated itself in the conviction. In sum, a defendant is constitutionally entitled to loyal, conflict-free representation whether his counsel is appointed or retained. In either case, if conflicting interests adversely affect the lawyer's representation, the right to counsel is violated.

An accused cannot succeed with a claim that he was denied the constitutional entitlement to loyal representation by merely showing the existence of a conflict, that is, that counsel was placed in a position where one interest called upon him to take some step that a conflicting interest militated against. There must also be an "adverse effect" on counsel's performance; that is, a lawyer must do something inconsistent with the accused's interests or refrain from doing something that would further those interests. Thus, if a lawyer consistently acts in a way that favors one client and disadvantages another, only the latter can establish a Sixth Amendment deprivation. The first defendant cannot show that the conflict "adversely affected the adequacy of [the] representation" that he received. Apparently, *minor* actions or omissions by counsel are not sufficient. A constitutional violation occurs "only if the conflict has *significantly affected* counsel's performance thereby rendering the verdict unreliable" (Mickens v. Taylor, 2002) (italics added). In situations involving multiple concurrent representation of defendants, "prejudice" to the outcome of the trial need not be established (Cuyler v. Sullivan, 1980; Mickens v. Taylor, 2002). An accused must demonstrate that a conflict had a negative impact on counsel's assistance, but does not have to show any likelihood that loyal service would have yielded a better outcome.[181] For actual conflicts attributable to other causes, whether prejudice must be proven remains an open question (Mickens v. Taylor, 2002).

Limitations on the Entitlement to Loyal Representation

Although an accused is generally entitled to loyalty from a defense attorney, the Constitution does not require that counsel take every step that would further the best interests of her client and does not bar counsel from doing some things that are contrary to the client's objectives. Important interests can justify an attorney's decision to follow a course of conduct that undermines the defendant's chances to avoid conviction. Put simply, the constitutional entitlement to undivided allegiance is vitally important but is not absolute.

In Nix v. Whiteside, for example, a case that is discussed at greater length in the next section of the analysis, the Supreme Court recognized an important limitation on the Sixth Amendment entitlement to unimpaired loyalty (Nix v. Whiteside, 1986). In that case, a defense attorney was aware that his client intended to tell an embellished, untrue account of the facts in order to bolster his claim of self-defense. The attorney threatened to withdraw or inform the court if the accused took the witness stand and gave the false testimony. In response to the contention that defense counsel's constitutional duty of loyalty to his client precluded him from making such threats, the Supreme Court observed that an attorney's overriding ethical obligation not to present false evidence or perjured testimony permitted—indeed even required—him to take steps that would dissuade his client from testifying falsely. The threats to withdraw or inform the trial court were acceptable means of discouraging falsehood and complying with his professional ethical duties. Thus, an accused's constitutional entitlement to dedicated, faithful service does not require defense counsel to breach important obligations to the criminal justice system. Instead, society's interests in preventing corruption of the truth-finding process outweigh and qualify a defendant's entitlement to loyal representation.[182]

In general, there can be no doubt that "[c]ounsel's duty of loyalty . . . is limited to legitimate, lawful conduct compatible with the very nature of a trial as a search for the truth." In the Court's view, "an attorney's . . . duty to advance the interests of his client is limited by an equally solemn duty to comply with the law and standards of professional conduct" (Nix v. Whiteside, 1986). Whether there are other important interests that restrict the right to devoted, loyal assistance is as yet undetermined.

Waiver of the Right to Loyal, Conflict-Free Representation

As has been discussed in previous sections of this analysis, a defendant ordinarily can waive the right to the assistance of counsel if he relinquishes the right knowingly and voluntarily. In Holloway v. Arkansas, the Supreme Court noted that it had previously concluded that "a defendant may waive his right to the assistance of an attorney unhindered by a conflict of interests" (Holloway v. Arkansas, 1978). Consequently, it seems clear that an accused may be allowed to surrender his entitlement to undivided loyalty and to choose representation by a conflicted lawyer. If the waiver is sufficiently knowing and voluntary, it should be constitutionally acceptable.[183]

Waivers of the right to conflict-free assistance raise particular problems, however, because of the uncertainties that are present in situations where conflict is possible. At the time a waiver is tendered, the nature of a conflict and how it could affect the adequacy of a lawyer's assistance may not be clear enough to enable a "knowing" choice by the accused. The possibilities for conflict and the impacts that a conflict could have on representation may be largely unknowable and speculative until the trial unfolds. Because of these uncertainties, some lower courts have allowed defendants who have waived the right to conflict-free assistance to succeed with later claims that conflicts of interest rendered their lawyers' performances ineffective (Wheat v. United States, 1988). In essence, these courts have decided that a surrender of the right to undivided loyalty can turn out to be insufficiently "knowing" if subsequent events yield conflicts and harmful effects that the accused was unaware of at the time of the putative waiver.[184] The Supreme Court has neither endorsed nor rejected this view. Thus, while a defendant may be allowed to waive the Sixth Amendment entitlement to loyalty, and such a waiver may be constitutionally valid, the uncertainties often present in situations of potential conflict can undermine the validity of such a waiver.[185]

Finally, an earlier section of this analysis discussed the Supreme Court's conclusion in Faretta v. California that an accused has a Sixth Amendment right to waive the assistance of counsel and represent himself at trial (Faretta v. California, 1975). To exercise that right, the defendant need only be competent and willing to furnish a knowing and voluntary waiver of the right to counsel. Arguably, this entitlement to waive the entire right to counsel logically must include a right to waive one component of the right to counsel—in particular, the entitlement to loyalty. However, neither the entitlement to waive assistance entirely nor the right to counsel of choice provides the basis for an unqualified right to waive the right to conflict-free representation. Even if a defendant is able and willing to knowingly and voluntarily relinquish the right to unconflicted assistance, a judge may reject a waiver and insist on representation by a different lawyer if it is shown that the attorney has either an actual conflict of interest or a serious potential for a conflict of interest (Wheat v. United States, 1988). In those circumstances, accused individuals do *not* have a *constitutional* right to surrender their entitlement to loyal, conflict-free assistance and insist on assistance from conflicted counsel. In situations involving an actual conflict or a serious risk of conflict, the state may refuse to allow an attorney to represent a defendant.[186]

The Entitlement to Competent Assistance from Counsel—The "Actual Ineffectiveness" Doctrine

An Introduction to the Relationship between Attorney Incompetence and the Right to Effective Assistance of Counsel

This section discusses the constitutional entitlement to have defense counsel perform her responsibilities competently.[187] This topic is the most intriguing and, arguably, the most important aspect of the content of the Sixth Amendment right to counsel. Of all the components that constitute the substance of the right to legal assistance, the entitlement to competent aid from counsel has by far been the subject of the most opinions from both the Supreme Court and the lower courts.[188] Moreover, no facet of the content of the right to representation provides greater insight into and understanding of the nature of the constitutional promise of counsel than the entitlement to competent assistance. The Supreme Court's discussions of this basic element of the Sixth Amendment right are frequently rooted in detailed explorations of the rationales and justifications for recognizing a fundamental entitlement to legal assistance.

The Supreme Court has long recognized that "the right to counsel is the right to *effective* assistance of counsel" (Kimmelman v. Morrison, 1986; McMann v. Richardson, 1970) (italics added).[189] Each section of this text's analysis of the content of the right to counsel has explored a distinct aspect of the more general entitlement to "effective" assistance. One of the clear messages of these explorations has been that the "[g]overnment violates the right to effective assistance when it interferes in certain ways with the ability of counsel to make independent decisions about how to conduct the defense" (Strickland v. Washington, 1984). Official measures that impede defense counsel's abilities or opportunities to prepare or investigate, to advocate the accused's cause, to participate fully in the adversary process, to consult with the accused, or to render loyal service can deprive the defendant of "effective" legal assistance.

The discussion of conflicts of interest immediately preceding this section of the analysis introduced the idea that the right to effective assistance of counsel can be violated without any governmental interference. If an actual conflict of interest induces an attorney to fail to provide the kind of representation called for by her duty of loyalty, the Sixth Amendment is violated. The discussion in this section confirms that the conflict of interest rule is a specific illustration of a very important general principle. According to that principle, "[c]ounsel . . . can . . . deprive a defendant of the right to effective assistance, simply by failing to render 'adequate legal assistance' " (Strickland v. Washington, 1984 (quoting Cuyler v. Sullivan, 1980)). Whether a defense lawyer's failure to provide able, competent representation results from a conflict of interests, a lack of ability or skill, too little time or resources, benign neglect, or careless oversight, the accused suffers a Sixth Amendment deprivation, for the Constitution guarantees a trial with the "effective assistance of counsel."[190]

The lower courts have acknowledged this constitutional promise of competent legal assistance for many years. Judges have not questioned the proposition that a Sixth Amendment violation does not require governmental obstruction of a lawyer's efforts. They have recognized that an attorney's professional derelictions can deprive the accused of the substance of the right to counsel. Before the Supreme Court weighed in on the subject in 1984, the debate in the lower courts revolved around the proper standards for assessing attorney incompetence. One subject of dispute was how competent a lawyer had to be to satisfy the constitutional mandate of effective assistance, or, looked at from the other direction, how poorly a lawyer had to perform to fail to provide what the Sixth

Amendment promised. Some courts concluded that counsel's service fell short only when it could be characterized as a "farce and mockery." Others were somewhat more demanding, requiring that defense lawyers provide "reasonably effective assistance." None of the standards for judging the adequacy of a lawyer's performance provided a sharp, bright line.[191]

Another question that prompted disagreement in the lower courts was whether an attorney's deficient performance alone was adequate to establish a constitutional deprivation. Some courts concluded that poor-quality representation by itself was a sufficient basis for finding a Sixth Amendment violation. Others maintained that an accused was not deprived of effective assistance unless counsel's defective performance caused "prejudice" to the defense (i.e., adversely affected the accused's chances for success in the proceeding). The standard for assessing prejudice—just how much harm was necessary to sustain a claim—was also a subject of dispute. Some courts required defendants to show that it was "more likely than not" that the deficient performance changed the outcome of the case. Others thought that a lesser likelihood of harm should be sufficient.[192]

For quite some time, the Supreme Court kept its distance from the fray. In 1970, in McMann v. Richardson, the Court did confirm the general principle that "defendants . . . are entitled to the effective assistance of competent counsel" and "cannot be left to the mercies of incompetent counsel" (McMann v. Richardson, 1970). The Court agreed with the lower courts that state interference with counsel's efficacy is not a necessary condition for a violation of the right to counsel. It recognized that incompetent lawyers could deny their clients the constitutional entitlement to effective assistance by failing to furnish adequate professional representation. However, the Court did not address the constitutional standards for determining whether counsel's performance satisfied the Sixth Amendment demand for "effective assistance of competent counsel." In part, the Court's refusal to address the critical issue of standards was probably due to the narrow claim presented by the facts of *McMann*. The defendants in that case claimed that their lawyers' deficient judgments regarding the admissibility of allegedly coerced confessions had rendered their guilty pleas invalid. In part, the Court's refusal probably also reflected a conclusion that the Justices were not yet prepared to confront and resolve the thorny constitutional issues raised by ineffective legal representation resulting from attorney incompetence.

For another fourteen years, the Court allowed the issue of the appropriate criteria for assessing attorney incompetence to percolate in the lower courts. Not until Strickland v. Washington, in 1984—a landmark case in the annals of right to counsel law—did the Court finally begin the process of developing standards for judging the constitutional adequacy of defense attorney performance.[193] Before explaining the *Strickland* standards for assessing "actual ineffectiveness" and their development in a number of subsequent Supreme Court opinions, a general discussion of the reasons that a lawyer's incompetent assistance can deprive a defendant of his Sixth Amendment entitlement is in order.

Why Incompetent Representation by Counsel Violates the Sixth Amendment: The Constitutional Justifications for the "Actual Ineffectiveness" Doctrine

As already mentioned, the Supreme Court has rejected the view that the Sixth Amendment requires the government only to permit defendants to retain counsel, to provide indigent defendants with appointed lawyers, and to refrain from interfering with those lawyers' opportunities and abilities to fulfill their responsibilities. According to the Court, "[t]hat a person who happens to be a lawyer is present at trial alongside the accused . . . is not enough to satisfy the constitutional command" (Strickland v. Washington, 1984). The fundamental guarantee of counsel is a promise of more than the presence of a person with a law degree and bar membership. Rather, the substance of the Sixth Amendment entitlement "to counsel is the right to effective assistance of counsel" (Kimmelman v. Morrison, 1986). Consequently, when a defense lawyer fails to afford adequate representation, the substance of the Sixth Amendment guarantee is lacking.

The Court has found modest support for this interpretation of the constitutional entitlement to counsel in the literal text of the Sixth Amendment. The words of that provision "require[] not merely the provision of counsel to the accused, but 'Assistance,' which is to be 'for his defence.' . . . If no actual 'Assistance' 'for' the accused's 'defence,' is provided, then the constitutional guarantee has been violated" (United States v. Cronic, 1984). The primary basis for holding that "actual ineffectiveness" by counsel violates the constitutional guarantee, however, is that an accused who receives incompetent assistance from his attorney does not in fact receive the protection that the Sixth Amendment contemplates. According to the Court, a holding that the mere presence of a lawyer and an absence of state interference with counsel are sufficient would " 'convert the [right to] . . . counsel into a sham and nothing more than formal compliance with the Constitution's requirement' " (United States v. Cronic, 1984 (quoting Avery v. Alabama, 1940)). The indispensable right to counsel's assistance would be an empty promise, devoid of substantive content if incompetent assistance were acceptable.

The government initiates and conducts criminal trials. The Constitution obligates the government to ensure that those trials are conducted fairly. The state, therefore, must make sure that every critical component of fundamental fairness is present when it seeks to deprive an accused of his life or liberty. One of the most essential elements of fairness in our adversarial system is the assistance of counsel. "[T]he Sixth Amendment right to counsel exists, and is needed, in order to protect the fundamental right to a fair trial." Defense attorneys play "a role that is critical to the ability of the adversarial system to produce just results" (Strickland v. Washington, 1984). Lawyers ensure that the adversarial system functions as a true "confrontation between adversaries." They promote the interests of the defendant and subject the prosecution's case to meaningful "adversarial testing" (United States v. Cronic, 1984). Unless a defense attorney performs her assigned functions and ensures the proper operation of the adversarial system, "a serious risk of injustice infects the trial" (Cuyler v. Sullivan, 1980).

If an accused does not have legal assistance, or if counsel's abilities to perform her responsibilities are significantly impeded by the state, the adversarial testing that guarantees a fair process and a just, accurate result does not occur. The same threats to the fairness of a trial and the accuracy of its result arise if a lawyer is present but performs her job incompetently. If a lawyer does not play the role expected of defense counsel in the adversary system, the meaningful confrontation of the government that is necessary for a fair trial does not take place.[194] Instead, the deficiency of the representation yields an imbalanced contest with a serious risk of an unreliable, unjust outcome. Because the government is obligated to provide fair, balanced adversarial proceedings, "the Sixth Amendment . . . prevents the [government] . . . from conducting trials at which persons who face incarceration must defend themselves without adequate legal assistance" (Cuyler v. Sullivan, 1980) and "mandates that the State bear the risk of constitutionally deficient assistance of counsel" (Kimmelman v. Morrison, 1986). Thus, when the state convicts an accused and deprives him of liberty or life based on a trial in which defense counsel failed to perform competently, the state violates the Constitution.

In sum, "actual ineffectiveness" of counsel violates the Sixth Amendment right to counsel because it jeopardizes the fairness of a proceeding and the integrity of the result just as surely as governmental interference with a defense attorney's performance. Because an "accused is entitled to be assisted by an attorney, whether retained or appointed, who [actually] plays the role necessary to ensure that the trial is fair" (Strickland v. Washington, 1984), an incompetent, inadequate assistant does not fulfill the promise made by our Constitution.[195]

The Doctrinal Standards for Determining "Actual Ineffectiveness" of Counsel: The Landmark Decision in Strickland v. Washington

The Supreme Court's conclusion that incompetent service by a defense attorney violates the Sixth Amendment—the "actual ineffectiveness" doctrine—was a critical step in interpreting the right to the assistance of counsel. Nonetheless, it was merely a first step, a threshold decision that raised an important question: What is the minimum level of competence necessary to satisfy the constitutional command? Put otherwise, how poor must a lawyer's performance be to deprive an accused of the substance of the right to counsel?

In 1984, in Strickland v. Washington, the Supreme Court confronted that question directly. The relatively simple doctrinal standards for judging actual ineffectiveness announced in the Court's lengthy opinion have been explained and refined in a number of significant subsequent opinions. Several important issues have been resolved; others remain unsettled. This section endeavors to explain in some detail what is known and what remains to be learned about the controlling standards for judging "actual ineffectiveness" due to attorney incompetence.

According to the *Strickland* doctrine, an actual ineffectiveness claim "has two components. *First*, the defendant must show that counsel's *performance was deficient*. . . . *Second*, the defendant must show that the deficient performance *prejudiced the defense*" (Strickland v. Washington, 1984) (italics added). Unless a defendant shows both "deficient performance" and "prejudice," he cannot establish a Sixth Amendment deprivation. Moreover, while these dual criteria for assessing counsel's effectiveness "should guide the process of decision," they are not intended to establish "mechanical rules." In every case, "the ultimate focus of inquiry must be on the fundamental fairness of the proceeding." Thus, when an accused contends that defense counsel did not provide adequate assistance, a court "should be concerned with whether . . . the result of the particular proceeding is unreliable because of a breakdown in the adversarial process that our system counts on to produce just results."

To establish that a lawyer rendered a constitutionally "deficient performance," a defendant must show that "counsel made errors so serious that [she] . . . was not functioning as the 'counsel' guaranteed the defendant by the Sixth Amendment." More specifically, "the proper standard for attorney performance is *reasonably effective assistance*" (italics added). A lawyer fails to fulfill the constitutional requirement when her "representation [falls] below an objective standard of reasonableness" or when it is unreasonable when measured by "prevailing professional norms." While it is possible for a "single, serious error [to] support a claim of ineffective assistance of counsel" (Kimmelman v. Morrison, 1986), in judging the adequacy of counsel's performance, the "inquiry must be whether counsel's assistance was reasonable considering all the circumstances" (Strickland v. Washington, 1984).

There is no checklist of "specific guidelines" against which a lawyer's performance can always be evaluated (Strickland v. Washington, 1984).[196] Nonetheless, the "prevailing norms of practice" and the "basic duties" generally entailed in representation of a criminal defendant do provide guides to what is reasonable.[197] A lawyer can fall below the "objective standard of reasonableness" if she inexcusably neglects any of the basic duties that constitute the substance of the right to legal assistance. One duty of every defense lawyer is the duty to furnish the legal expertise, skill, and knowledge called for by the particular case. "[A]ccess to counsel's skill and knowledge is necessary to accord defendants [an] 'ample opportunity to meet the case of the prosecution' " (Strickland v. Washington, 1984 (quoting Adams v. United States *ex. rel.* McCann, 1942)). Counsel can breach this duty if she is ignorant of an important substantive or procedural aspect of the law bearing on the accused's defense or fails to take advantage of the tools that the legal system provides to make a defense and challenge the prosecution.[198] In Kimmelman v. Morrison, a lawyer's failure to seek discovery from the government indicated "a startling ignorance of the law" in the jurisdiction and, thus, constituted a deficient performance (Kimmelman v. Morrison, 1986). In Lockhart v. Fretwell, defense counsel failed to raise a controlling legal precedent that could have prevented a jury from imposing the death penalty on his client. The lawyer's failure to possess and employ the legal knowledge essential for competent representation in that situation was constitutionally unreasonable (Lockhart v. Fretwell, 1993).

Counsel also has duties to investigate the facts and the law and prepare for the particular proceedings facing the accused.[199] Defense lawyers have the duty either "to make reasonable investigations or to make a reasonable decision that makes particular investigations unnecessary" (Strickland v. Washington, 1984). They have a responsibility to devote the time and effort to preparation that are necessary to defend against the accusation. Counsel's failure to make the necessary legal or factual investigations or to prepare to address legal or factual issues can constitute unreasonable, deficient assistance. In Kimmelman v. Morrison, the lawyer's neglect to file a motion to exclude incriminating evidence was attributable to insufficient investigation and a "complete lack of pretrial preparation" (Kimmelman v. Morrison, 1986). The failure amounted to constitutionally deficient performance.

An attorney has an "overarching duty to advocate the defendant's cause" and "a duty to bring to bear such skill and knowledge as will render the trial a reliable adversarial testing process" (Strickland v. Washington, 1984). Both vigorous partisan advocacy on behalf of the accused and active participation in the adversary fact-finding process are essential to confront the case of the prosecution, present the accused's defense, and enable the adversary system to function properly (Herring v. New York, 1975). Representation can fall outside the range of reasonable professional assistance demanded by the Sixth Amendment if an attorney does not engage in zealous, partisan, devoted advocacy of the accused's interests (i.e., if she fails to argue points of fact or law that favor her client). If counsel fails to introduce evidence, call witnesses, examine or cross-examine witnesses adequately, raise objections to government evidence, or perform any of the other functions that are critical to the effective operation of the adversarial fact-finding processes, her performance could be constitutionally deficient.[200]

Defense lawyers are obligated "to consult with the defendant on important decisions and to keep the defendant informed of important developments in the course of the prosecution" (Strickland v. Washington, 1984).[201] An accused has a constitutional entitlement to two-way communication with counsel (Perry v. Leeke, 1989). A defense attorney who fails to fulfill the obligation to confer and consult with her client runs the risk of rendering "objectively unreasonable" assistance that is constitutionally deficient under the *Strickland* doctrine.

Finally, defense counsel has a duty of undivided loyalty to the defendant's interests (Strickland v. Washington, 1984). The Sixth Amendment entitles the accused to an attorney who is devoted solely to the pursuit of his interests (Cuyler v. Sullivan, 1980; Holloway v. Arkansas, 1978). As explained in the preceding section of this analysis, the Constitution is violated if a lawyer's loyalty is impaired by an actual conflict of interest that adversely affects her representation of the defendant's interests (Cuyler v. Sullivan, 1980). When counsel who is engaged in concurrent representation of multiple defendants breaches the duty of loyalty because of an actual conflict of interests, the defendant does not have to show "prejudice" to her defense.[202] However, if a conflict of interests has a source other than multiple concurrent representation, then a demonstration of prejudice may be required (Mickens v. Taylor, 2002). Moreover, if disloyal service is attributable to a source other than a conflict of interests, then the dual *Strickland* standards seem to be controlling. The defendant must show both deficient performance and prejudice. In Nix v. Whiteside, the Court concluded that an attorney did not breach his constitutional duty of loyalty because the actions that he took contrary to the defendant's interests were required by ethical constraints (Nix v. Whiteside, 1986). Nonetheless, the Court analyzed the accused's claim that counsel's disloyalty made him ineffective under *Strickland*'s standards. Consequently, if a lawyer were to decide, for example, that she was morally obligated to help convict her client by producing proof of guilt, or if she were to urge others to come forward with evidence that ensured conviction because she believed that the defendant ought to be punished, her disloyalty could be deemed "unreasonable" and "deficient" under *Strickland.* A Sixth Amendment claim will prevail if that deficiency prejudiced the defense.

The basic duties that counsel might breach on her own correspond to the substantive Sixth Amendment entitlements that can be impaired by active state interference. Discussions in earlier sections of this analysis demonstrated that state impediments to a defense attorney's abilities to investigate and prepare, to advocate the accused's case, to participate fully in the adversarial process, to consult with her client, and to render loyal service all can deny defendants the effective assistance of counsel. The present discussion makes it clear that if an attorney, by action or omission, deprives an accused of any of these basic substantive elements of the guarantee of counsel, the assistance that she provides may be deemed "actually ineffective."

The *Strickland* Court made it clear, however, that it is far from easy for a defendant to establish deficient performance by counsel. The Court pointedly refused to prescribe a checklist of basic responsibilities, asserting that "[p]revailing norms of practice . . . are *only* guides" to what is reasonable and demanding that the "reasonableness" of representation be judged in light of the totality of the circumstances (Strickland v. Washington, 1984) (italics added). The Court also added that "counsel *is strongly presumed* to have rendered adequate assistance and made all significant decisions in the exercise of reasonable professional judgment" (italics added). Any accused who contends that defense counsel rendered a deficient performance has a heavy burden of proof. He must overcome "a *strong presumption* that counsel's conduct falls within the *wide range* of reasonable professional assistance" and that "the challenged action 'might be considered sound trial strategy.' " Moreover, in making the performance evaluation, judges "must be *highly deferential.*" Care must be taken "to eliminate the distorting effects of hindsight" (italics added). Courts must assess a lawyer's performance from counsel's perspective at the time that she made the particular decisions and took the particular actions. The general "reasonably effective assistance" standard, qualified by all of these considerations, amounts to a demand that the accused demonstrate "gross incompetence" in order to establish constitutionally deficient performance (Kimmelman v. Morrison, 1986).[203]

An accused who manages to satisfy the heavy burden of overcoming the presumption of reasonably effective assistance has not yet established a denial of the Sixth Amendment right to counsel. An "actual ineffectiveness" claim has two required elements—deficient performance and prejudice. The Constitution is not violated unless the defendant satisfies both prongs.

To demonstrate prejudice, a "defendant must show that [a lawyer's deficient performance] actually had an adverse effect on the defense" (Strickland v. Washington, 1984). There must be a proven impact on the *result* of the proceeding, not just an effect on the quality of counsel's representation.[204] The defendant must demonstrate more than just "some conceivable effect on the outcome of the proceeding" but does not have to establish "that counsel's deficient conduct more likely than not altered the outcome in the case"; that is, he does not have to show a probability of harm greater than 50 percent. The requisite likelihood of adverse effect falls between these two levels. "The defendant must show that there is a *reasonable probability that*, but for counsel's unprofessional errors, *the result of the proceeding would have been different*" (italics added). While the Court did not quantify the likelihood of harm that qualifies as a "reasonable" probability, it did observe that a "reasonable probability is a probability sufficient to undermine confidence in the outcome." The ultimate question is whether "counsel's errors were so serious as to deprive the defendant of a fair trial, a trial whose result is reliable." The prejudice inquiry is designed to determine whether "the result of the proceeding is unreliable because of a breakdown in the adversarial process that our system counts on to produce just results."

If the defendant claims ineffective assistance *at trial*, to establish prejudice, he must demonstrate "a reasonable probability that, absent the errors, the fact finder would have had a reasonable doubt respecting guilt." If the contention is that counsel was deficient at *a capital sentencing proceeding*, the inquiry is "whether there is a reasonable probability that . . . the sentencer . . . would have concluded that the balance of aggravating and mitigating circumstances did not warrant death." Moreover, in making prejudice determinations, a judge is required to consider the "totality of the evidence" presented to the judge or jury.[205]

The prejudice requirement has been refined in a number of post-*Strickland* decisions. One constant, an essential facet of a prejudice demonstration, is the demand that an accused prove "a reasonable probability" of a different result if defense counsel had not performed deficiently.[206] Later opinions have made it clear, however, that such a showing is not always enough. According to the Court, "an analysis focusing solely on mere outcome determination . . . is defective. To set aside a conviction or sentence solely because the outcome would have been different but for counsel's error may grant a defendant a windfall to which the law does not entitle him" (Lockhart v. Fretwell, 1993). Consequently, prejudice is not established if the outcome that was reached due to counsel's deficient performance was "neither unfair nor unreliable." The concern of the prejudice inquiry is whether an attorney's inadequacy "renders the *result of the trial unreliable or the proceeding fundamentally unfair*. Unreliability or unfairness does not result if the ineffectiveness of counsel does not deprive the defendant of any substantive or procedural right to which the law entitles him" (Lockhart v. Fretwell, 1993).

In so qualifying the prejudice requirement, the Court relied heavily on assertions in *Strickland* that the fairness of the trial and the reliability and justice of the result of the trial are the underlying concerns of the "actual ineffectiveness" doctrine. According to the Court, there are cases in which competent performance by a lawyer would have produced a *less* reliable result and in which the errors of counsel did not render the trial process fundamentally unfair. In such cases, the accused has not suffered prejudice from counsel's deficiency, for neither the reliability of the result nor the fairness of the process has been compromised. In essence, the *Fretwell* Court held that prejudice requires more than a reasonable probability that the result of a proceeding would have been different if counsel had not erred. Prejudice is present only if the different outcome from adequate performance could have been "more reliable" *or* if counsel's deficiencies rendered the proceeding fundamentally unfair.

A reliable or just result is one that accurately reflects both the true facts and the correct law. A different result that would have been a less accurate, less truthful reflection of the actual events that occurred could not be more reliable. In addition, a different result that would have been distorted by "erroneous" legal principles could not be more reliable. In either of these situations, a deficient performance will not be prejudicial and will not support an "actual ineffectiveness" conclusion even if it does produce an outcome different from the outcome that error-free representation would have produced. Moreover, the specific reason that competent performance would have produced a less reliable result than incompetent representation does not matter.

Nix v. Whiteside illustrates this refinement of the prejudice element (Nix v. Whiteside, 1986). All nine members of the Court agreed that "as a matter of law" prejudice cannot be established if a lawyer's inadequate representation in fact prevents an accused from presenting perjurious testimony or precludes the introduction of false evidence. It does not matter that the perjury or falsehood probably would have led the trier of fact to acquit the defendant. Because the different outcome that attorney competence would have attained—an acquittal—would have been based on untruth, it would have been less accurate, less reliable than the conviction that resulted from the lawyer's errors. According to the Court, even grossly incompetent representation cannot undermine "confidence in the result" if that representation keeps the trier of fact from being misled by falsehood and thereby actually *enhances* the reliability of the outcome. Moreover, inadequate representation that excludes perjury or falsehood from a trial does not deprive an accused of any right to which he is entitled—for there is no right to testify falsely. Nor does inadequate representation of this sort compromise the fundamental fairness of the trial in any other way.

The strange facts of Lockhart v. Fretwell also illustrate the narrowing of the prejudice element defined by the majority opinion in that case (Lockhart v. Fretwell, 1993).[207] In *Fretwell*, an attorney unreasonably failed to bring to the court's attention a legal precedent that very likely would have prevented a jury from sentencing his client to death. That precedent would have barred the jury from relying on the sole factor that served as the basis for its decision that the accused should forfeit his life (i.e., a finding that the defendant committed murder for "pecuniary gain"). Several years later, when the defendant's ineffective assistance claim reached the courts, the law had changed. The precedent barring reliance on pecuniary gain in the defendant's capital sentencing proceeding had been overruled. The jury's reliance on the pecuniary gain factor as a basis for sentencing the defendant to death was now considered legally correct.

The Supreme Court held that the defendant had not suffered prejudice because counsel's gross error had in fact prevented the capital sentencing jury from making *a legal error* in his favor. The precedent that would probably have controlled the decision at the time of the sentencing had been an incorrect interpretation of the law. The "life sentence" that the accused would have received if the attorney had raised that erroneous precedent would, therefore, have been less reliable than the death sentence that he did receive. Although the death sentence resulted from deficient legal assistance, it reflected what was now known to be the correct law. Moreover, the attorney's neglect did not make the sentencing proceeding "fundamentally unfair," for the defendant had no legal right to the "windfall" of a legal error in his favor. An incompetent attorney's failure to advocate reliance on a judicial decision that turns out to have been wrong cannot undermine the fairness of a proceeding. In sum, because there was no adverse affect on either the reliability of the result or the fairness of the process, the defendant suffered no prejudice.

The *Fretwell* Court repeatedly indicated that prejudice is shown if *either* unreliability *or unfairness* results from counsel's errors. The "fundamentally unfair proceeding" alternative holds out a possibility for success with an "actual ineffectiveness" claim in some cases where the outcome produced by counsel's poor performance is less reliable than the outcome that competent counsel would have produced. If counsel's actions or omissions somehow rendered the proceeding that yielded the less reliable result "fundamentally unfair," then prejudice should still be found. The Court indicated that proceedings become unfair when a lawyer's errors "deprive the defendant of [a] substantive or procedural right." Thus, if an attorney's neglect deprives an accused of the Sixth Amendment right to be confronted by witnesses, for example, or the Fifth Amendment right not to be compelled to be a witness against himself, a proceeding could be rendered unfair. It is uncertain whether the deprivation of a statutory right could produce fundamental unfairness. Arguably, a process is fundamentally unfair only when the accused suffers the loss of some specific *constitutional* right due to counsel's errors. It is clear, however, that mere gross incompetence or egregiously deficient assistance alone does not make a proceeding fundamentally unfair. The Court requires some additional impact on the fairness of the process.

The facts and reasoning of Kimmelman v. Morrison provide additional insight into the prejudice prong of the *Strickland* standards (Kimmelman v. Morrison, 1986). In *Kimmelman*, an attorney unprofessionally neglected to make a motion to exclude evidence that police arguably obtained as a result of an illegal search and seizure. In Stone v. Powell, a 1976 decision, the Supreme Court had held that a convicted defendant could not raise a Fourth Amendment exclusionary rule claim in a federal habeas corpus proceeding unless he was not afforded a full and fair opportunity to litigate that claim in the state courts (Stone v. Powell, 1976). The central issue in *Kimmelman* was whether a convicted defendant could raise an ineffective assistance of counsel claim in a habeas corpus proceeding if the claim was based on counsel's failure to seek the exclusion of evidence based on a Fourth Amendment violation.

The Court unanimously agreed that there was no bar preventing habeas review of Sixth Amendment ineffective assistance claims, regardless of the nature of the alleged dereliction of counsel (Kimmelman v. Morrison, 1986). The holding of Stone v. Powell governs only Fourth Amendment, not Sixth Amendment claims. In the course of resolving the "reviewability" issue, a majority of the Court indicated that a defendant could establish prejudice under *Strickland* if he demonstrated two things: (1) that the neglected Fourth Amendment claim had merit and (2) that if the evidence had been excluded, there was a reasonable probability that the outcome of the trial would have been different.

Concurring Justices observed that the issue of whether a lawyer's failure to raise a Fourth Amendment objection could constitute prejudice was not actually before the Court. They contended that there was a strong argument that the admission of illegally seized but reliable evidence can never constitute prejudice under *Strickland* (Kimmelman v. Morrison, 1986 (Powell, J., concurring)). The majority's reasoning suggested that it did not agree with that conclusion. In response to the argument that the failure to exclude *reliable* evidence (e.g., narcotics or a murder weapon) could only improve the search for truth and could not undermine the reliability of a trial's result, the majority asserted that the Court had "never intimated that the right to counsel is conditioned upon actual innocence" (Kimmelman v. Morrison, 1986). Because "[t]he constitutional rights of criminal defendants are granted to the innocent and the guilty alike," the *Kimmelman* majority "decline[d] to hold either that the guarantee of effective assistance of counsel belongs solely to the innocent or that it attaches only to matters affecting the determination of actual guilt." It seems clear that the *Kimmelman* majority believed that an incompetent failure to raise a meritorious

Fourth Amendment suppression claim can result in "prejudice" within the meaning of the *Strickland* doctrine.

Lockhart v. Fretwell was decided in 1993, after Kimmelman v. Morrison. There is some disagreement over the significance of the *Fretwell* holding for the issue disputed in *Kimmelman*. Under *Fretwell*, the Court might conclude that an attorney's failure to file a valid motion to suppress reliable evidence is prejudicial because counsel's failure to take advantage of a lawful, legitimate procedural option that would have prevented conviction renders a proceeding "fundamentally unfair." On the other hand, the exclusion of evidence is clearly not a personal constitutional right belonging to the accused who has been the victim of an unlawful search or seizure (United States v. Calandra, 1974). Consequently, the Court might conclude that an incompetent neglect to exclude truthful evidence does not result in an unfair proceeding, does not undermine the reliability of the outcome, and cannot ever support the finding of prejudice essential for a successful "actual ineffectiveness" claim. Which option the Court would choose if it was squarely confronted by that issue today is not at all clear.

As is evident from the preceding discussion, the prejudice component of the *Strickland* doctrine has grown increasingly more complex. The showing of a reasonable probability of a different outcome remains a necessary condition for a successful actual ineffectiveness claim but is not sufficient in all cases. In situations where counsel's deficient representation does not adversely affect the reliability of the outcome and does not render the process unfair in some fundamental respect, prejudice cannot be established even if the competent representation contemplated by the Sixth Amendment would have produced a much more favorable outcome for the defendant.

The Constitutional Justifications for the "Deficient Performance" and "Prejudice" Requirements

A full appreciation of the Court's "actual ineffectiveness" doctrine requires an understanding of the constitutional justifications underlying each of the two *Strickland* requirements. The discussion that follows explains both the rationales for adopting the deficient performance and prejudice demands and the reasons for the particular doctrinal formulations of those demands. To a limited extent, criticisms of the *Strickland* standards are also included.

According to the *Strickland* Court, the criteria that it announced for evaluating "actual ineffectiveness" of counsel were derived from the "purpose" of affording a criminal defendant the right to effective legal assistance—"to ensure a fair trial" (Strickland v. Washington, 1984). To establish that a lawyer's representation failed to fulfill the Sixth Amendment's promise, there must be a sufficient threat to the fairness of the trial. In the Court's view, such a threat is present only when both *Strickland* showings are made, for only then can it "be said that [a] conviction . . . resulted from a breakdown in the adversary process that renders the result unreliable."

The need to show "deficient performance" requires little explanation. The essence of an "actual ineffectiveness" claim is that counsel did not do her job, that she failed for some reason to provide adequate legal representation. Unless an accused can show that some substantive part of the guarantee of counsel's assistance was lacking or that there was some breach of the duties generally owed by a defense attorney, there is clearly no reason to sustain a claim that counsel failed to furnish effective legal assistance.

As already explained, the Court provided an open-ended, unspecific definition of the deficient performance prong. It refused to impose particular obligations, choosing instead to require only that counsel's performance must be "reasonably effective." Moreover, the Court created a strong presumption that any attorney has performed adequately. There are several reasons for this formulation of the deficient performance standard. First, because "[t]here are countless ways to provide effective assistance in any given case," and because "[r]epresentation is an art," the Court believed that it was not possible to prescribe a "particular set of detailed rules for counsel's conduct [that could] satisfactorily take account of the variety of circumstances faced by defense counsel or the range of legitimate decisions regarding how best to represent a criminal defendant." Any attempt to specify particular things that an attorney must or must not do would fail to capture the full range of professionally acceptable and effective assistance. Moreover, detailed constitutional standards of conduct could be counterproductive insofar as they would "interfere with" the "independence" of counsel, "restrict the wide latitude" necessary "in making tactical decisions," and "distract counsel from the overriding mission of vigorous advocacy."

In addition, generalized, undetailed standards for adequate performance and the strong presumption that a lawyer's representation has been adequate guard against "intrusive post-trial inquir[ies] into attorney performance" and a "proliferation of ineffectiveness challenges." Awareness by counsel that her conduct would later be subjected to "[i]ntensive scrutiny" to determine if it satisfied "rigid requirements . . . could dampen the ardor and impair the independence of defense counsel, discourage the acceptance of assigned cases, and undermine the trust between attorney and client." Moreover, any criteria that invited excessive challenges to counsel's representation could cause serious damage to our system's interest in finality. The *Strickland* standards for judging the constitutional adequacy of a lawyer's performance reflect a concern with preventing all such harms.

Justice Marshall was the sole dissenter in *Strickland.* While he agreed with the need for a "deficient performance" requirement, he vehemently opposed the majority's formulation of that element. In his view, the "reasonably effective" assistance standard "is so malleable that . . . it will either have no grip at all or will yield excessive variation" (Strickland v. Washington, 1984 (Marshall, J., dissenting)). "To tell lawyers and the lower courts that they must behave 'reasonably' . . . is to tell them almost nothing." Because the Court's formulation suffers from "debilitating ambiguity," it cannot provide meaningful protection for the constitutional right to effective assistance. Lawyers instructed that they must be "reasonable" will have no guidance as to what constitutes adequate representation, and lower courts reviewing attorney performances will not be able to identify and will not be required to disapprove of lawyers' incompetence. According to Marshall, because "many aspects of the job of a criminal defense attorney are more amenable to judicial oversight," it is possible to prescribe more "particularized standards designed to ensure that all defendants receive effective legal assistance."

Justice Marshall also objected to the "strong presumption" that counsel's performance is within the range of reasonable assistance and to the mandate that courts show deference to a lawyer's judgments. In his view, a presumption of competence and deferential review can only result in "covert[]" validation of "convictions and sentences obtained on the basis of incompetent conduct by defense counsel." Defendants are entitled to more protection against ineffective assistance than the Court's formulation of the performance prong affords.[208]

The prejudice element of the *Strickland* test requires, at a minimum, a showing of a reasonable probability that competent performance would have produced a different result. Moreover, unless the lawyer's deficiencies rendered the trial "fundamentally unfair" in some respect, prejudice does not exist if the result of attorney incompetence is "more reliable" than the result that reasonably effective assistance would have produced. Unlike the "deficient performance" requirement, the need to prove prejudice is not self-evident or inherent in the notion of "actual ineffectiveness." In fact, no other kind of right to counsel violation claim requires an accused to demonstrate an adverse effect on the outcome of his trial. Insofar as they demand a showing of prejudice, "actual ineffectiveness" claims are unique and considerably more difficult to establish.

The Supreme Court went to great pains to justify the conclusion that a defendant does not suffer a Sixth Amendment loss when his attorney provides grossly incompetent assistance unless there is also an unfavorable effect on the outcome. The Court began with the critical premise that the purpose of "counsel is to ensure that a defendant has the assistance necessary to justify reliance on the outcome of the proceeding" (Strickland v. Washington, 1984). The right to counsel exists "to ensure a fair trial," that is, a trial with a reliable, "just result." Unless an accused demonstrates an adverse impact on the outcome, he has not shown that his lawyer's errors defeated the purpose for granting legal assistance. Unless he establishes that an attorney's missteps had a negative effect on the outcome of his case, he has not shown that the interest protected by the entitlement to counsel was jeopardized. Thus, while adequate performance by all defense attorneys is a desirable objective, an accused suffers a deprivation of the substantive benefits of counsel's assistance only when mistakes by his attorney alter the outcome of a proceeding.[209]

The decision to set the level of likelihood that a result was changed by counsel's misperformance at a "reasonable probability" reflects an accommodation of both the accused's and the criminal justice system's interests. If any probability of harm to the defendant's opportunity for a favorable result sufficed, the institutional interest in the finality of verdicts would be overridden in many cases where defense counsel's poor performance did not harm the defendant. The small chance that the defendant actually suffered an injury of the sort that the right to counsel protects against does not outweigh the clear, substantial, systemic cost of granting a new trial. On the other hand, if a defendant had to show that it was more likely than not that he would have prevailed if counsel had not erred, many instances in which a lawyer's deficiencies did change the outcome for the worse would go unremedied. The countervailing systemic interest in finality cannot justify the significant number of constitutional deprivations that would result from so burdensome a prejudice requirement. The *Strickland* majority believed that the "reasonable probability" standard strikes just the right balance between the accused's interests in effective assistance and a fair trial and the state's interest in finality. Under that standard, a constitutional violation is found when, but only when, the likelihood that a defendant did not enjoy the substantive protection guaranteed by the Sixth Amendment is too high to be ignored.[210]

The refinement of the definition of prejudice explained in Lockhart v. Fretwell is also justified by the "purposes" for granting a constitutional right to counsel. In the Court's view, the right to counsel is afforded to defendants to protect their interests in reliable outcomes and fundamentally fair processes. If the result of a lawyer's gross incompetence turns out to be *more* reliable and if that incompetence did not render the trial process fundamentally unfair, an accused does not suffer the loss of any interest protected by the right to counsel. Recognizing a right to counsel violation in such cases would be a "windfall," for it would grant relief to those who have sustained no constitutional harm.

As noted earlier, when a defendant alleges ineffective assistance for any reason other than counsel's incompetence, that is, because he lacked a lawyer's aid, because the state impeded counsel's representation, or because counsel operated under an actual conflict of interest resulting from multiple concurrent representation, prejudice is not required. The *Strickland* Court offered a number of justifications for treating "actual ineffectiveness" cases differently. The Court did not deny that prejudice is relevant in all cases where an accused contends that he was denied counsel's assistance. Indeed, in light of its assertions that the purpose of the right to assistance is to ensure a fair trial with a reliable result, such a denial would have been indefensible. In cases of outright denial of legal assistance, state interference with counsel's representation, or proven conflicts of interest, the demand for adverse effect on the outcome is satisfied by a "presumption" of prejudice. These kinds of impediments to effective assistance are "legally presumed to result in prejudice" because "[p]rejudice is so likely that case-by-case inquiry into prejudice is not worth the cost" (Strickland v. Washington, 1984). An accused will receive a windfall in very few cases, and the instances of unjustified relief are offset by the savings in judicial time and effort. Moreover, in cases where counsel is absent or obstructed by the government, the "circumstances" that impair the efficacy of counsel are "easy to identify." Because the government is "directly responsible" for the "impairments," it can easily prevent them. For these reasons, the state ordinarily can guard against costly retrials, and it would be unfair to saddle the defendant with the risks of deficient assistance.

The logic underlying the presumption of prejudice in conflict of interest situations is different. First, when an attorney operates under a conflict that impairs her representation, she "breaches the duty of loyalty, perhaps the most basic of counsel's duties." In addition, "it is difficult to measure the precise effect on the defense of representation corrupted by conflicting interests." Finally, defense counsel has an obligation to "avoid conflicts of interest," and courts have an obligation to inquire into situations where conflicts are likely. For these reasons, "it is reasonable for the criminal justice system to maintain a fairly rigid rule of presumed prejudice" in conflict of interest cases. (It merits mention that the Court more recently has observed that the presumption of prejudice in conflict of interest cases might arise *only* in cases where the conflict has been generated by multiple concurrent representation (Mickens v. Taylor, 2002).)

When an accused has received ineffective assistance due to an incompetent performance by his attorney, the "government is not responsible for, and hence [was] not able to prevent" the impaired representation. Moreover, "errors come in an infinite variety and are as likely to be utterly harmless . . . as they are to be prejudicial." Defense counsel cannot be accurately instructed about "what conduct to avoid" because the kinds of missteps that constitute deficient performance cannot "be defined with sufficient precision." In these cases, it is much less probable that Sixth Amendment harm has occurred, and the state cannot be blamed for the risk that does exist.[211] Thus, a presumption of prejudice is unjustifiable. An appropriate balancing of the interests involved supports a requirement that the defendant must demonstrate prejudice.

Justice Marshall stridently disagreed with the *Strickland* majority's analysis and with their adoption and formulation of the prejudice element. In his view, grossly incompetent assistance alone violates the Sixth Amendment. A defendant should not have to show any effect on the outcome of the trial. It "is often very difficult to tell whether a defendant . . . would have fared better if his lawyer had been competent" (Strickland v. Washington, 1984 (Marshall, J., dissenting)). It is "senseless" and unfair to require a defendant to prove that harm occurred, when, as a practical matter, such harm is often unprovable. The accused should not bear the risks of counsel's gross incompetence. "[M]ore fundamentally," the prejudice demand is unjustifiable because the right to counsel does not exist only "to reduce the chance that innocent persons will be convicted." The entitlement to legal assistance is granted both to promote reliable, accurate results and "to ensure that convictions are obtained only through fundamentally fair procedures." Counsel is a process right, a part of the larger adversary system entitlement to fair play. According to Justice Marshall, when an accused receives unreasonable, deficient assistance, he is deprived of the "meaningful assistance in meeting the forces of the state" that is guaranteed by the Sixth Amendment. Whether or not the result of the proceeding is affected, the accused suffers constitutional harm in the denial of a balanced contest. The resulting deprivation of fundamental fairness is a kind of "prejudice" that should be constitutionally cognizable.[212]

The Scope of the Strickland "Actual Ineffectiveness" Doctrine

The deficient performance and prejudice standards that currently control "actual ineffectiveness" inquiries govern claims that counsel performed incompetently during the *trial* phase of a case. In Nix v. Whiteside, a case that involved alleged incompetence during a trial, the Court analyzed the defendant's claim according to the *Strickland* standards (Nix v. Whiteside, 1986). Presumably, the trial phase includes both formal and informal "critical" pretrial stages, the period needed for investigation and preparation before a trial actually begins, and the time during which defense counsel formulates, files, and responds to pretrial motions and requests. Errors made at any of these stages must be evaluated under the two *Strickland* prongs.

The *Strickland* standards also pertain to allegations of "actual ineffectiveness" in capital sentencing proceedings. Both Strickland v. Washington and Lockhart v. Fretwell involved claims that counsel's performance was deficient in the sentencing phase of a capital case. The similarities of those proceedings to trials on guilt or innocence led the Court to conclude that the deficient performance and prejudice demands should be used to judge counsel's efficacy (Strickland v. Washington, 1984).[213]

The same standards also apply to a contention that a guilty plea is invalid because of counsel's incompetent assistance during the plea process.[214] In Hill v. Lockhart, the Court observed that when a defendant is represented during a plea process and pleads guilty upon the advice of an attorney, the only way to attack the voluntariness of that plea is to establish that counsel's advice was incompetent (Hill v. Lockhart, 1985). The "two-part standard" announced in *Strickland* is "applicable to ineffective assistance claims arising out of the plea process" because the reasons that underlie the two requirements are equally relevant in the guilty plea context. Moreover, the demand that prejudice be shown "serve[s] the fundamental interest in the finality of guilty pleas."[215]

In the guilty plea context, the deficient performance test is identical. Because the prejudice requirement "focuses on whether counsel's constitutionally ineffective performance affected the outcome of the plea process," its verbal formulation requires some modification (Hill v. Lockhart, 1985). To establish prejudice, an accused must show "a *reasonable probability* that, but for counsel's errors, *he would not have pleaded guilty and would have insisted on going to trial*" (italics added). A defendant must demonstrate a cognizable likelihood that he would have chosen to stand trial but apparently does not have to establish a reasonable probability that the result of the trial would have been different from the result of the guilty plea.[216]

The *Strickland* Court reserved the question of whether the same standards govern claims that defense counsel rendered inadequate assistance during "ordinary," noncapital sentencing proceedings. Ordinary sentencing hearings typically "involve informal proceedings and standardless discretion in the sentencer" (Strickland v. Washington, 1984). For these reasons, they "may require a different approach to the definition of constitutionally effective assistance." Thus, it is not yet settled whether the *Strickland* tests apply to all sentencing processes, apply only to those that are relatively formal and governed by discretion-limiting standards, or apply only to capital sentencing proceedings.[217]

As discussed in an earlier section, the defendant's entitlement to effective assistance of counsel on appeal is rooted in the Due Process and Equal Protection Clauses of the Fifth and Fourteenth Amendments, not in the right to counsel guarantee of the Sixth Amendment. Because of the different textual sources of the right and because the body of law governing effective appellate assistance has developed separately from the *Strickland* line of authority, the appropriate constitutional standards for evaluating a claim that counsel failed to provide competent assistance on appeal are discussed in a separate section that immediately follows this section of the analysis.

A Summary of and Reflections upon the Meaning of the "Actual Ineffectiveness" Doctrine

Incompetent representation by a retained or appointed defense lawyer that is not attributable to governmental action or inaction can deprive a criminal defendant of the Sixth Amendment right to "effective assistance" of counsel. "Actual ineffectiveness" is established if an accused proves that "deficient performance" by his attorney caused "prejudice" to his defense. The standards for ascertaining whether a performance was deficient are general, somewhat vague, and open-ended. Lawyers must render "reasonably effective assistance" under prevailing professional norms. Moreover, there is a strong presumption that counsel's representation was reasonable, a presumption that the accused must overcome with evidence. Prejudice occurs only if there is a "reasonable probability" that the deficiency in the performance produced a different outcome from the one that would have resulted from adequate representation. In addition, counsel's errors must undermine the fundamental fairness of the process or diminish the reliability of the outcome. Without both deficient performance and prejudice, there is no deprivation of the Sixth Amendment entitlement to effective legal assistance.

According to the Supreme Court, the core purpose of granting a constitutional right to counsel is to guarantee that criminal defendants receive "fair trials." The dual doctrinal requirements for assessing "actual ineffectiveness" claims are derived from and dictated by that purpose. The Court's decision to construe the Sixth Amendment guarantee in light of the values and interests that it serves is eminently sensible. Moreover, it seems appropriate to conclude that "fair trials" are the objective of the right to counsel. The questionable aspect of the Court's reasoning is its narrow understanding and depiction of the nature and meaning of a "fair trial."

In the *Strickland* majority's view, a "just result" is the sole objective, and a result is "just" when there is no substantial risk that it is "incorrect." These premises are in tension with the alternative understanding of adversary system fairness discussed in the very first section of this text's analysis. According to that view, fairness depends on more than just the accuracy of a proceeding's result. A fair trial is one that reaches substantively correct results by means of processes that accord with adversary system notions of fair play. The *Strickland* Court's reasoning does not acknowledge that the right to counsel furthers the independent and distinct goal of a balanced adversarial contest between equals. Implicitly, it seems to reject the view that legal assistance is provided to ensure that defendants have fair opportunities to confront prosecutors and contest charges.

In subsequent opinions exploring the prejudice element—most notably, Lockhart v. Fretwell and Nix v. Whiteside—the Court continued to emphasize the vital importance of reliability in evaluating the effectiveness of counsel. In *Fretwell,* however, the Court did acknowledge that the right to counsel serves to ensure a fundamentally fair criminal process. According to the *Fretwell* Court, the prejudice inquiry is concerned with "whether counsel's deficient performance renders the result of the trial unreliable *or the proceeding fundamentally unfair*" (Lockhart v. Fretwell, 1993) (italics added). A defendant needs to demonstrate "[u]nreliability *or unfairness*," and the deprivation of either a "substantive *or procedural right*" will suffice (italics added). This seemingly broader conception of what a "fair trial" entails and of the purposes served by the assistance of counsel undercuts the suggestion in *Strickland* that the Sixth Amendment right exists solely to ensure factually and legally correct results.

The particular kinds of deficient performance that render trials "fundamentally unfair" are not at all clear. *Fretwell* indicates that a deprivation of fundamental fairness occurs only when counsel's conduct infringes on some independent right or entitlement of the accused. According to the Court, a trial can be fair even though a lawyer's performance was abominable, falling woefully short of the norms of reasonable professional assistance. The right to a minimally adequate performance by one's "adversary system equalizer" is not a component of procedural fairness. This restricted view of the entitlement to counsel and of the concept of "fair process" is certainly debatable.

The Entitlement to Competent Representation by Counsel on Appeal

The Right to Effective Assistance of Appellate Counsel

An earlier section of this text explained the scope of a convicted defendant's constitutional right to the assistance of counsel in the appellate process and in collateral attacks on convictions. Both indigent and nonindigent defendants have the right to a lawyer's assistance in a first appeal taken as a matter of right (Douglas v. California, 1963; Evitts v. Lucey, 1985). Convicted defendants, however, do not have a constitutional right to counsel for purposes of pursuing discretionary appeals (Ross v. Moffitt, 1974) or to assist their efforts to obtain collateral relief (Pennsylvania v. Finley, 1987). The right to legal assistance in a first appeal is grounded in both the Due Process and Equal Protection Clauses of the Fifth and Fourteenth Amendments (Evitts v. Lucey, 1985), not in the Sixth Amendment right to counsel.[218] The latter provision has no application after the trial and sentencing processes are completed (Martinez v. Court of Appeal of California, 2000).

Like the right to counsel at trial, the right to counsel on appeal includes an entitlement to "have the *effective* assistance of an attorney" (Evitts v. Lucey, 1985) (italics added). A convicted defendant's entitlement to due process of law is violated if his lawyer renders incompetent assistance on appeal. This due process right to effective assistance extends only as far as the right to appellate counsel itself, that is, only to the first appeal taken as a matter of right. Ineffective assistance by a lawyer on a discretionary appeal is not constitutionally objectionable, for an accused does not have a constitutional entitlement to legal assistance at that stage of the adjudicatory process (Wainwright v. Torna, 1982).

The Supreme Court's recognition of a right to effective representation by counsel on appeal is based on the same reasoning as the right to effective assistance at trial. Both at trial and on appeal, the adversarial system "is premised on the well-tested principle that truth—as well as fairness—is 'best discovered by powerful statements on both sides' " (Penson v. Ohio, 1988, quoting Kaufman, "Does the Judge Have a Right to Qualified Counsel?," 61 *A.B.A. L.J.* 569, 569 (1975))). The objective of a convicted defendant on appeal is "to demonstrate that the conviction, with its consequent loss of liberty, is unlawful" (Evitts v. Lucey, 1985). Like a trial, an appellate proceeding is adversarial in nature and is "governed by intricate rules that to a layperson would be hopelessly forbidding" (Evitts v. Lucey, 1985). A trained legal expert is necessary to enable the defendant to cope with the superior resources of his government adversary and with the complexities of the legal system. Without legal assistance, the appellate process will not be a balanced confrontation between roughly equal adversaries. Consequently, meritorious appeals will go unrecognized and unvindicated. In sum, counsel's aid is vital to ensure that the appellate process reaches just results by fair methods.

The mere presence of a retained or appointed lawyer does not satisfy the substance of the due process guarantee of appellate counsel. "[N]ominal representation on appeal as of right—like nominal representation at trial—does not suffice to render the proceedings constitutionally adequate" (Evitts v. Lucey, 1985). An appellant "whose counsel is unable to provide effective representation is in no better position than one who has no counsel at all." The Constitution grants a right to the effective assistance of counsel on appeal because incompetent, ineffective representation would convert the "right to counsel on appeal . . . [into] a futile gesture." The appellate process and the results of that process are fair and just only if an attorney " 'plays the role necessary to ensure that the [appeal] is fair' " (Evitts v. Lucey, 1985 (quoting Strickland v. Washington, 1984)). A lawyer who performs incompetently does not play that role. Only effective assistance protects the defendant's fundamental interests and furthers the vital objectives that underlie the constitutional right to counsel on appeal.

Counsel at trial is a shield that protects the accused against the government's efforts to strip him of the presumption of innocence. Counsel on appeal is a sword that assists the convicted defendant's efforts to overturn a finding of guilt (Ross v. Moffitt, 1976). The object of an appeal is to show an error at trial that justifies a reversal of the guilty verdict. Counsel must "examine[] the trial record with an advocate's eye, identifying and weighing potential issues for appeal" (Smith v. Robbins, 2000 (Souter, J., dissenting)). A lawyer is expected to provide "partisan scrutiny of the record and assessment of potential issues." If she discovers potential error, counsel "prepares and submits a brief on the merits and argues the appeal." Thus, counsel's role in the appellate process is somewhat different in nature from her role at trial. Nevertheless, the entitlement to effective appellate assistance includes the same basic components as the entitlement to effective trial assistance. The fundamental duties and responsibilities of counsel on appeal bear a striking resemblance to those imposed upon trial counsel.[219]

An accused has an entitlement to " 'conscientious investigation' " from appellate counsel (Anders v. California, 1967 (quoting Ellis v. United States, 1958)). An appellate lawyer has a duty to "diligently investigate[]" both the record and the governing legal principles in search of "possible grounds of appeal" (Anders v. California, 1967). Thorough preparation is also essential. Appellate counsel "must master the trial record, thoroughly research the law, and exercise judgment in identifying the arguments that may be advanced on appeal" (McCoy v. Court of Appeals of Wisconsin, 1988). At every step along the appellate road, counsel also must bring to bear the legal expertise, knowledge, talents, and skills necessary to ensure a meaningful confrontation with the government and the legal system. The accused has an entitlement to counsel on appeal because the appellate process is adversarial and because an unaided layman cannot comprehend or cope with the intricacies of the law (Evitts v. Lucey, 1985). An effective lawyer is obligated to know or learn the applicable law, to appreciate the legal significance of particular facts and events, and to exercise the legal skills vital to effective written and oral argument.

Perhaps the most critical aspect of the right to counsel on appeal is the entitlement to active, partisan advocacy. The constitutional promise of effective assistance on appeal entitles the appellant to "the benefit of adversary examination and presentation of the issues" (Penson v. Ohio, 1988). An attorney must not function as a "friend of the court assisting in a detached evaluation of the appellant's claim" but must be "an active advocate" on behalf of the appellant's cause (Evitts v. Lucey, 1985). Counsel must " 'support [her] client's appeal to the best of [her] ability' " by providing "vigorous and effective advocacy" of the defendant's objective—a reversal of the conviction (Jones v. Barnes, 1983 (quoting Anders v. California, 1967)). The "need for forceful advocacy does not come to an abrupt halt as the legal proceeding moves from the trial to the appellate stage." To the contrary, a "fair [appellate] process can only be attained" if counsel functions as "an active advocate in behalf of his client" (Penson v. Ohio, 1988).

Although there is typically a greater need for counsel to communicate with an accused at the trial stage, an appellate lawyer also has a responsibility to consult with her client. In the "vast majority" of cases, counsel has an obligation to inquire specifically whether the defendant wishes to take an appeal of a conviction (Roe v. Flores-Ortega, 2000). A failure to consult with the client regarding his desires will breach this duty and impair counsel's effectiveness. Moreover, whenever vigorous partisan advocacy of the appellant's interests requires an attorney to go beyond the trial record and convey information to or secure information from her client, she surely has an obligation to do so.

Finally, like trial counsel, an appellant is entitled to have counsel render loyal service. The " 'right to counsel guaranteed by the Constitution contemplates the services of an attorney devoted *solely* to the interests of [her] client.' A criminal appellant is entitled to a single-minded advocacy" (Penson v. Ohio, 1988 (quoting Glasser v. United States, 1942)) (italics added). An attorney, therefore, must not have or pursue interests that conflict with the appellant's interests. Professional ethical obligations and the duty not to burden the judicial system with frivolous claims do place some limits on an attorney's zealous pursuit of the appellant's cause (Smith v. Robbins, 2000). Nevertheless, in the absence of sufficiently weighty countervailing interests, undivided loyalty is required. If counsel is not devoted to the appellant's objectives, if she does not play her parts in the appellate process with unfettered allegiance to her client, she deprives the appellant of the substance of the right to legal representation.

Standards for Evaluating Ineffective Assistance of Appellate Counsel

Initially, the Supreme Court recognized a basic entitlement to effective appellate assistance without prescribing the standards for judging ineffectiveness (Evitts v. Lucey, 1985). Recently, it has become clear that the doctrinal standards that govern ineffectiveness inquiries at trial—the two-pronged test of Strickland v. Washington—also apply to claims of ineffective assistance by appellate counsel (Roe v. Flores-Ortega, 2000; Smith v. Robbins, 2000).[220] Ordinarily, a defendant must demonstrate both that his attorney rendered a "deficient performance" and that he suffered "prejudice" as a result of counsel's errors. These standards were explored in considerable detail in the discussion of ineffective assistance at trial that immediately precedes this section of the analysis. The primary focus here will be on their particular meaning and significance at the appellate level.[221]

To show deficient performance, an appellant must establish that counsel's representation on appeal was "objectively unreasonable" (Smith v. Robbins, 2000). As at trial, there are no detailed rules or guidelines by which to determine whether appellate assistance is professionally unreasonable (Roe v. Flores-Ortega, 2000).[222] Nonetheless, the basic responsibilities of appellate counsel discussed above can certainly serve as "guides" to what is reasonable. Serious breaches of these duties may well render a performance deficient. Thus, for example, failures to investigate or prepare a potential claim, failures to advocate the appellant's cause competently, or disloyalty to the appellant's objectives could be bases for finding counsel's appellate representation deficient. As a general rule, a court must take into account all the surrounding circumstances and all of the factors that bear upon whether challenged conduct was reasonable under the prevailing norms of professional appellate assistance. Moreover, a judge must evaluate the reasonableness of counsel's actions or omissions from the vantage point of the attorney at the time of the challenged conduct, and " 'judicial scrutiny' " must be " 'highly deferential' " (Roe v. Flores-Ortega, 2000 (quoting Strickland v. Washington, 1984)).

In some cases, the manner in which a lawyer handles an appeal will clearly fall short of the representation demanded by *Strickland*'s deficient performance standard. If a convicted defendant instructs his lawyer to appeal and the lawyer fails to file a notice of appeal, thereby forfeiting the defendant's right to appeal, she "acts in a manner that is professionally unreasonable" (Roe v. Flores-Ortega, 2000).[223] The failure to file a requested appeal is deficient performance because the defendant reasonably relies on counsel to carry out his wishes, and counsel's failure to file "reflects inattention to . . . [those] wishes." The filing of a notice of appeal "is a purely ministerial task," and the neglect to file "cannot be considered a strategic decision." For the same reasons, if a jurisdiction's appellate process requires that a statement containing specified factual information be filed along with an appellate brief, and if a lawyer fails to file such a statement and the appeal is dismissed for noncompliance with this formality, then counsel's performance is objectively unreasonable and constitutionally deficient (Evitts v. Lucey, 1985). Finally, if an appointed lawyer who believes that an appeal would be "frivolous" does not comply with the steps that are constitutionally necessary for proper withdrawal from representation (steps that are discussed later in this section), the lawyer's dereliction will satisfy the *Strickland* standard for deficient performance (Penson v. Ohio, 1988).

In most situations, however, the unreasonableness of an attorney's appellate assistance will not be as clear. A careful assessment of the actions and omissions of counsel based on the totality of relevant circumstances will be necessary. Thus, if an attorney does not file a notice of appeal in a case in which the defendant does not clearly tell counsel whether he wishes to take an appeal, the failure to file is not "per se deficient" (Roe v. Flores-Ortega, 2000). To decide whether the attorney's performance was deficient, a court must determine whether the attorney consulted with the defendant about a potential appeal and, if not, whether the failure to consult was unreasonable in light of what the attorney "knew or should have known" (Roe v. Flores-Ortega, 2000). In certain circumstances, a failure to talk to a defendant about his desires regarding an appeal could be quite reasonable.

An appointed lawyer might conclude that an appeal would be frivolous and might comply with the procedural steps that are constitutionally necessary to withdraw from representation. If a defendant contends that in so doing the attorney rendered ineffective assistance, the question is whether "counsel was objectively unreasonable in failing to find arguable issues" and to file a merits brief raising those issues. The defendant must show that "a reasonably competent attorney would have found [at least] one nonfrivolous issue warranting a merits brief" (Smith v. Robbins, 2000).

An attorney does not have a constitutional obligation to raise every nonfrivolous issue that a convicted defendant wishes to raise on appeal (Jones v. Barnes, 1983).[224] In deciding what arguments to make, a lawyer is expected to exercise reasonable professional judgment. Such judgment often militates in favor of choosing among potentially meritorious arguments. It is ordinarily wise strategy for an attorney to exclude weaker appellate arguments so they do not distract from the stronger arguments that support a reversal. The mere failure to make arguments that the client wants to include is not deficient performance. Instead, an attorney's omission of a particular issue qualifies as deficient only if it was professionally unreasonable not to include that issue. To establish counsel's deficiency, the defendant must show that the particular issue that was not raised "was clearly stronger than issues that counsel did present" (Smith v. Robbins, 2000). Only then is the *Strickland* standard satisfied.[225]

Strickland's two-pronged ineffectiveness doctrine demands a showing that a lawyer's deficient performance caused "prejudice" to the appellant.[226] As a general rule, courts must "presume that the result of the proceedings on appeal is reliable, [and must] require [the appellant] to prove the presumption incorrect in his particular case" (Smith v. Robbins, 2000). The convicted defendant ordinarily must overcome the presumption of reliability by demonstrating that appellate counsel's mistakes adversely affected the outcome of the appeal. More specifically, to establish that counsel's misperformance caused prejudice, the appellant "must show a reasonable probability that, but for his counsel's [errors] . . . he would have prevailed on his appeal" (Smith v. Robbins, 2000). Thus, even if an appellant demonstrates that his attorney unprofessionally "fail[ed] to press a particular argument on appeal" or unreasonably "fail[ed] to argue an issue as effectively as he or she might" (Penson v. Ohio, 1988), he can succeed with an ineffective appellate assistance contention only if he also demonstrates a "reasonable probability" that the appellate court would have ruled in his favor if counsel had pressed the omitted argument or argued the issue more effectively. In essence, a court should validate a claim of ineffective appellate assistance only if it discerns a cognizable likelihood that competent performance by counsel would have demonstrated that the appeal had merit.

There are some instances in which appellate assistance is so deficient that prejudice will be presumed. In those situations, the general demand for a showing of prejudice is suspended. The appellant can prevail with an ineffective assistance of counsel claim merely by demonstrating the seriousness of the errors committed by appellate counsel. Specifically, a lawyer's incompetent performance is sufficiently egregious to give rise to a presumption of prejudice if it actually or effectively deprives a convicted defendant of the opportunity for appellate review (Evitts v. Lucey, 1985; Roe v. Flores-Ortega, 2000)[227] or if it leaves the appellant "completely without representation during the appellate court's actual decisional process" (Penson v. Ohio, 1988). When the consequence of unprofessional representation is either no appellate process at all or essentially no legal assistance during the appellate process, there is no reason to presume a "reliable" outcome. Just as when an accused is actually denied legal assistance for all or part of a trial, a presumption of prejudice on appeal arises (Penson v. Ohio, 1988; Roe v. Flores-Ortega, 2000).

In Evitts v. Lucey, a lawyer neglected to file a "statement of appeal" at the time that he filed his client's merits brief. State law required the dismissal of a defendant's appeal when a statement of appeal did not accompany the brief. The "particularly egregious" failure by counsel "essentially waived [the defendant's] opportunity to make a case on the merits." The Supreme Court found that the appellant's situation was "difficult to distinguish . . . from that . . . of someone who had no counsel at all" (Evitts v. Lucey, 1985). Consequently, prejudice was presumed, and a new appeal was granted.

In Roe v. Flores-Ortega, the Supreme Court stated that if an attorney unreasonably fails to file a notice of appeal, a resulting "forfeiture of [the] proceeding itself"—that is, the deprivation of "an appeal altogether"—also gives rise to a presumption of prejudice. To trigger that presumption, the appellant does have to demonstrate that counsel's neglect "caused" the loss of his opportunity to appeal. To do so, he must establish a "reasonable probability" that "but for counsel's deficient performance, he would have appealed" (Roe v. Flores-Ortega, 2000). However, there is no need to demonstrate any likelihood that an appeal would have been successful or even to specify the particular arguments that would have been raised if the appellant had the opportunity to appeal (Roe v. Flores-Ortega, 2000).

Finally, in Penson v. Ohio, appellate counsel sought to withdraw from representation after concluding that an appeal would have been "frivolous." He did not file a brief calling attention to matters in the record that might arguably support an appeal. Moreover, the appellate court allowed the attorney to withdraw without finding the appeal to be frivolous and neglected to appoint counsel after it found that there were nonfrivolous issues to be raised. Because "the denial of counsel in [*Penson*] left [the appellant] completely without representation during the appellate court's actual decisional process," a "presumption of prejudice" was justified (Penson v. Ohio, 1988). The defendant did not have to show a "reasonable probability" of success on appeal.[228]

In sum, most allegations of incompetent assistance in the appellate process require showings of both deficient performance by counsel and resulting prejudice. An appellant must show a sufficient likelihood—a reasonable probability—that competent assistance would have yielded a successful appeal. In limited instances, however, when grossly deficient performance deprives the client of an appellate decision or of any meaningful assistance during the appeal, there is no need to show any likelihood that an appeal would have been successful. Prejudice will be presumed, a deprivation of the right to effective appellate assistance will be found, and a new appeal will be granted.

The Right to Appellate Counsel and the Special Problem of "Frivolous" Appeals

Constitutional principles of equality and fair process found in the Fourteenth Amendment Equal Protection and Due Process Clauses require that appointed appellate counsel provide "the same diligent and thorough evaluation of" a convicted indigent defendant's case that a privately retained lawyer ordinarily will provide (McCoy v. Court of Appeals of Wisconsin, 1988). A particularly difficult problem arises when appointed counsel suspects that an appeal could be frivolous, that is, that there might be no arguable legal bases for challenging a conviction. Those situations engender tension between the lawyer's constitutional obligations to her client and her responsibilities to the legal system.[229] The instant discussion explains how the Supreme Court has resolved that tension.

If there are nonfrivolous issues to be raised on appeal, a defendant is entitled to have counsel actively and vigorously advocate his cause (Jones v. Barnes, 1983). Whether or not success is likely, if an appeal has possible merit, "[t]he constitutional requirement of substantial equality and fair process can only be attained where counsel acts in the role of an active advocate in behalf of [her] client" (Anders v. California, 1967). However, counsel may not "consume the time and the energies of the court or the opposing party by advancing frivolous arguments. An attorney . . . is . . . under an ethical obligation to refuse to prosecute a frivolous appeal" (McCoy v. Court of Appeals of Wisconsin, 1988). A convicted defendant is not entitled to have his lawyer pursue frivolous issues on appeal, for "the canons of professional ethics impose limits on permissible advocacy" and impose on counsel the "obligation . . . not to clog the courts with frivolous . . . appeals" (Polk County v. Dodson, 1981).

Cases involving this tension between counsel's obligation to advocate her client's cause and her duty not to pursue frivolous claims have prompted spirited disagreements among the members of the Supreme Court. All Justices have agreed, however, that a convicted defendant does not have the constitutional entitlement to have counsel advocate a frivolous cause. In such cases, there is

in essence, . . . a limited exception to the requirement . . . that indigent defendants receive legal representation on their first appeal as of right. The exception is predicated on the premise that while the Fourteenth Amendment demands active and vigorous appellate

> assistance for indigent criminal defendants, it does not demand that . . . appointed counsel [pursue] . . . wholly frivolous arguments. (Penson v. Ohio, 1988)

Thus, when an attorney concludes that an appeal has no potential merit, she should inform the court of this conclusion and seek to withdraw from the case (McCoy v. Court of Appeals of Wisconsin, 1988). If the appeal is in fact frivolous, withdrawal does not deny the appellant the "fair representation" demanded by the Constitution (Penson v. Ohio, 1988).

It merits mention that both retained and appointed counsel are obligated not to pursue frivolous appeals. Upon concluding that an appeal would have no merit, a privately retained lawyer "has a duty to advise the client that it would be a waste of money to prosecute the appeal and that it would be unethical for the lawyer to go forward with it" (McCoy v. Court of Appeals of Wisconsin, 1988). While an appointed attorney has the same obligation, she faces a "dilemma" that a retained lawyer does not. For state-provided counsel, "withdrawal is not possible without leave of court, and advising the court of counsel's opinion that the appeal is frivolous would appear to conflict with the advocate's duty to the client" (McCoy v. Court of Appeals of Wisconsin, 1988). That explains why the cases decided by the Supreme Court have all involved lawyers appointed to represent indigent defendants and why the doctrine discussed in this section refers specifically to the duties imposed on and the procedures to be followed by appointed appellate attorneys.

An attorney should not seek permission to withdraw on grounds of "frivolity" until she has thoroughly considered the merits of a case. Because every appellant is constitutionally entitled to active advocacy on his behalf, there are certain things that an appellate attorney must do before she seeks to terminate her role in a case. A lawyer is obligated to support her client's cause "to the best of [her] ability" by conducting "a conscientious examination of" the case before concluding that an appeal would be "wholly frivolous" (Anders v. California, 1967). Counsel must conduct a "diligent and thorough evaluation of the case" before arriving at the conclusion that there is no potential merit in an appeal and asking a court for permission to withdraw (McCoy v. Court of Appeals of Wisconsin, 1988). A convicted defendant has "the right to have an attorney, zealous for [his] interests, evaluate his case and attempt to discern nonfrivolous arguments" that might be raised on appeal (Smith v. Robbins, 2000).

A court simply may not permit counsel to withdraw from representation on the basis of an unembellished conclusion that an appeal would be frivolous (Anders v. California, 1967). A "criminal appellant may not be denied representation on appeal based on appointed counsel's bare assertion that he or she is of the opinion that there is no merit to the appeal" (Penson v. Ohio, 1988). To allow withdrawal based on such a "bare assertion" would create intolerable risks that convicted defendants would be effectively deprived of the assistance on appeal to which they are entitled. First, a lawyer's mere conclusion that an appeal has no potential merit does not provide an assurance that counsel conducted the "conscientious review" and "diligent and thorough evaluation" required in all cases. Moreover, a mere assertion does not furnish a sufficient basis for a court to determine whether the "frivolity" exception to the right to effective appellate assistance really does apply. Something more is required "to provide the appellate courts with a basis for determining whether appointed counsel have fully performed their duty to support their clients' appeals to the best of their ability" and to "assist[] the court in making the critical determination whether the appeal is indeed so frivolous that counsel should be permitted to withdraw" (McCoy v. Court of Appeals of Wisconsin, 1988). Something more is required "to ensure that those indigents whose appeals are not frivolous receive the counsel and merits brief" to which they are entitled on appeal. Something more is required to prevent the narrow exception to the right to effective appellate assistance from "swallowing the right itself" (Smith v. Robbins, 2000).

As a safeguard against unwarranted withdrawals by appellate counsel and unjustified deprivations of the fundamental right to effective assistance on appeal, the Constitution requires states to follow "prophylactic" procedures whenever an attorney seeks to end her participation (Smith v. Robbins, 2000). A state may not allow counsel to refuse to pursue an appeal unless it adheres to some "device for assuring that the constitutional rights of indigent defendants are scrupulously honored" (McCoy v. Court of Appeals of Wisconsin, 1988). States are not bound to any one particular procedural mechanism for safeguarding the right to appellate assistance; they have the discretion to choose any approach that adequately protects the constitutional rights at stake. In general, a procedure will satisfy the Equal Protection and Due Process Clauses if it " 'afford[s] adequate and effective appellate review to indigent defendants' " (Smith v Robbins, 2000). A review of four significant Supreme Court opinions provides helpful illustrations of valid and invalid procedures for deciding whether counsel may refuse to represent an appellant on the ground that there are no arguable bases for an appeal.

Anders v. California was the first Supreme Court case to address the issues raised by an appointed lawyer's effort to withdraw from representation based on his conclusion that an appeal was completely lacking in merit (Anders v. California, 1967). A California appellate court had allowed counsel to refuse to represent the indigent appellant based on counsel's "bare conclusion" that " 'there [was] no merit to the appeal.' " The court had denied the appellant's request for appointment of another lawyer, had allowed the appellant to file his own brief, and had unanimously upheld his conviction. The Supreme Court found that California's procedure did not adequately safeguard the right to counsel on appeal. Twenty-one years later, in Penson v. Ohio, an attorney was permitted to withdraw based on his certification that he had carefully reviewed the record, had found no errors, and would not file a "meritless appeal." For three reasons, the Supreme Court held that the Ohio court had committed error and had deprived the appellant of his constitutional right to counsel. First, counsel's adorned conclusion statement was not an adequate basis on which to permit withdrawal. Second, the Ohio court should not have permitted withdrawal *before* it determined that an appeal in fact would have been frivolous. Finally, the Court should have afforded representation by counsel once it determined, as it did, that there were nonfrivolous issues in the case (Penson v. Ohio, 1988).

In Anders v. California, after the Court rejected California's procedure, it proceeded to specify a procedure that would be constitutionally valid. According to that procedure, if counsel's conscientious review leads to the belief that an appeal would be frivolous, she should request permission to withdraw. This request is to be "accompanied by a brief referring to anything in the record that might arguably support the appeal"—what has come to be known as an "*Anders* brief" (Anders v. California, 1967). The appellant should be given a copy of this brief and should be afforded time to raise any additional points that he wishes to raise. At that point, "after a full examination of all the proceedings," the appellate court "decide[s] whether the case is wholly frivolous." If the court finds that an appeal would be frivolous, it "may grant counsel's request to withdraw and dismiss the appeal." However, "if it finds any of the legal points arguable on their merits (and therefore not frivolous) it must, prior to decision, afford the indigent the assistance of counsel to argue the appeal."[230] At one time, the *Anders* procedure was thought to be a constitutionally mandated minimum. Today, it is clear that *Anders* simply prescribes one method of complying with the dictates of the Fourteenth Amendment.

McCoy v. Court of Appeals of Wisconsin involved a procedure that "supplemented" the steps prescribed by *Anders*. Wisconsin required counsel not only to call the court's attention to matters in the record that could arguably support an appeal but also to "cite the principal cases and statutes and the facts in the record that support the conclusion that the appeal is meritless." Furthermore, counsel had to provide "a brief statement of why these citations [led her] to believe that the appeal lacks merit" (McCoy v. Court of Appeals of Wisconsin, 1988).

The Supreme Court deemed this procedure constitutionally legitimate.[231] In the majority's view, the Wisconsin rule required a brief that provided an ample basis for the review demanded by the Constitution. It furnished the appellate court with a foundation for determining whether an attorney had diligently searched the record and for deciding whether counsel had correctly concluded that an appeal would be frivolous. The Court rejected the contention that the Wisconsin procedure burdened the right to effective assistance on appeal by requiring counsel to discuss the reasons that she found that there was no merit in the issues that she mentioned as possible bases for appeal. According to the Court, the requirement that counsel discuss why she thought the appeal lacked merit serves to provide further evidence that an attorney has conducted a thorough review and furnishes an "additional safeguard against mistaken conclusions by counsel." As long as counsel conducts the kind of conscientious review that is constitutionally required, she "does not violate . . . her duty to the client by supporting a motion to withdraw with a brief that" explains why the appeal lacks merit (McCoy v. Court of Appeals of Wisconsin, 1988).

In Smith v. Robbins, a recent and quite controversial case, the Supreme Court approved a revised California procedure that varied quite dramatically from the procedure outlined in the *Anders* opinion (Smith v. Robbins, 2000). Under the new California procedure,

> counsel, upon concluding that an appeal would be frivolous, files a brief with the appellate court that summarizes the procedural and factual history of the case, with citations of the record. He also attests that he has reviewed the record, explained his evaluation of the case to his client, provided the client with a copy of the brief, and informed the client of his right to file a *pro se* supplemental brief. He further requests that the court independently examine the record for arguable issues.

Counsel does not explicitly state that an appeal would be frivolous or request leave to withdraw. "Instead, he is silent on the merits of the case and expresses his availability to brief any issues on which the court might desire briefing." The appellate court conducts a review of the entire record. If it "finds the appeal to be frivolous, it may affirm. If, however, it finds an arguable (i.e., nonfrivolous) issue, it orders briefing on that issue." The most noteworthy difference from an *Anders* brief is the absence of a requirement that counsel call attention to matters in the record that might arguably support the appeal.

A bare five-member majority of the Supreme Court concluded that the revised California procedure was far superior to the procedures that it disapproved of in *Anders* and *Penson* and that the new procedure was "at least comparable" to the procedures that it had endorsed in *Anders* and *McCoy*. According to the majority, California's approach is adequate to ensure that those whose appeals are not frivolous do receive the assistance of counsel to which they are entitled. It is constitutionally valid because, like the *Anders* and *McCoy* procedures, it "afford[s] indigents the adequate and effective appellate review that the Fourteenth Amendment requires."

Four dissenters strongly disagreed with the standards used by the majority to evaluate the adequacy of procedures for appointed counsel's withdrawal on appeal. They also rejected the conclusion that the new California procedure was sufficiently protective of the right to assistance of appellate counsel. In their opinion, the "adequate and effective appellate review" standard and the revised California procedure do not provide adequate assurances that an attorney for an indigent appellant "has done his best as a partisan" (Smith v. Robbins, 2000 (Souter, J., dissenting)). Nor do they provide an appellate court with an adequate basis for deciding whether counsel's conclusion that an appeal would be frivolous is correct. The dissenters asserted that the Constitution demands more substantial evidence that counsel has played the role that she is expected to play in the appellate process. In their view, the majority's vague standard for judging states' procedures does not safeguard the adversary system entitlement to partisan advocacy from appellate counsel. Unlike the procedure prescribed by the *Anders* Court, the revised California procedure does not provide an "affirmative and express indicator that an advocate has been at work." It "does not assure even the most minimal assistance of counsel in an adversarial role."

Relief for Deprivations of the Right to the Assistance of Counsel: Automatic Reversal and Harmless Error

Remedies for Violations of the Right to Counsel and the Harmless Error Doctrine

The previous sections of this analysis of the constitutional right to the assistance of counsel have dealt with the nature, scope, and content of the right to a lawyer's aid. This final discussion is concerned with the consequences of violations of the right to counsel. Denial of the constitutional entitlement to legal representation does not result in the dismissal of criminal charges or in setting the defendant free. Instead, the remedy for most deprivations of trial assistance is simply a new trial at which the accused has adequate assistance. Moreover, denials of a lawyer's aid at a sentencing proceeding will result only in a new sentencing proceeding, and violations of the Fourteenth Amendment right to counsel on appeal entitle the defendant to nothing more than a new appeal. In addition, infringements upon the Sixth Amendment right to representation in a formal pretrial proceeding such as an arraignment, a preliminary hearing, or a hearing on a pretrial motion may justify only a new pretrial proceeding with effective assistance. If the denial of aid at the pretrial stage had no cognizable effect on the outcome of the trial itself, a new trial is probably unwarranted.

In general, when deciding whether to grant relief for an error at the trial court level, appellate courts adhere to the "harmless error" doctrine.[232] If a court agrees with an appellant that a mistake was made but concludes that the error did not have a sufficient effect on the outcome of the lower court proceeding, the error will be deemed harmless, and the result below—the conviction or sentence—will be affirmed. Harmless error rules "serve a very useful purpose insofar as they block setting aside convictions for small errors or defects that have little, if any, likelihood of having changed the result of the trial" (Chapman v. California, 1967). Underlying the doctrine are a pragmatic recognition that few trials can be perfect and a realization that it would be extremely costly to conduct a new proceeding every time an appellate court discerned error.[233] In cases where the impact of an error was minor, at best, a new trial would be an undeserved windfall for the accused.[234] According to the Supreme Court,

> the harmless error doctrine is essential to preserve the "principle that the central purpose of a criminal trial is to decide the factual question of the defendant's guilt or innocence, and promotes public respect for the criminal process by focusing on the underlying

fairness of the trial rather than on the virtually inevitable presence of immaterial error." (Arizona v. Fulminante, 1991 (quoting Delaware v. Van Arsdall, 1986))

Harmless error rules are enormously beneficial to our criminal justice systems. Nonetheless, they are not risk-free. If applied too liberally in close cases, "harmless-error rules can work very unfair and mischievous results" (Chapman v. California, 1967). The objective, therefore, is to strike an appropriate balance by devising appellate standards "that will save the good in harmless-error practices while avoiding the bad, so far as possible" (Chapman v. California, 1967).[235]

The most significant question in this subsection is whether violations of the Sixth Amendment right to the assistance of counsel can ever be "harmless error." Put otherwise, the inquiry is whether an accused who has suffered a denial of the Sixth Amendment right to counsel is always entitled to relief of some sort.

Harmless Error Standards and Violations of Constitutional Rights[236]

Trial errors that do not constitute *constitutional* violations can be deemed harmless on appeal. The jurisdiction in which the particular appeal is taken sets the legal standards for deciding whether such a nonconstitutional error is harmless. In the federal system, for example, a nonconstitutional error is considered harmless and will not lead to the reversal of a conviction if a court "is sure that the error did not influence the jury, or had but very slight effect" (Kotteakos v. United States, 1946). On the other hand, an error is not harmless if it "had substantial and injurious effect or influence in determining the jury's verdict" (Kotteakos v. United States, 1946).[237] Each state is free to formulate its own harmless error standards for errors that do not implicate constitutional rights.

"[S]ome constitutional rights [are] so basic to a fair trial that their infraction" is not subject to harmless error analysis (Chapman v. California, 1967). Violations of these rights "by their very nature cast so much doubt on the fairness of the trial process that, as a matter of law, they can *never* be considered harmless" (Satterwhite v. Texas, 1988) (italics added). When an appellate court discovers such a violation, "prejudice is presumed" (Strickland v. Washington, 1984). Only one response is constitutionally acceptable—automatic reversal of the defendant's conviction or sentence. On the other hand, not "all federal constitutional errors, regardless of the facts and circumstances, must always be deemed harmful" (Chapman v. California, 1967). There are "some constitutional errors which in the setting of a particular case are so unimportant and insignificant that they may, consistent with the Federal Constitution, be deemed harmless, not requiring the automatic reversal of the conviction" (Chapman v. California, 1967).[238]

Federal law dictates the standard by which to assess harmlessness for those constitutional violations that can be considered harmless.[239] On direct appeal of a conviction or sentence, the standard adopted is very demanding. A constitutional error can be deemed harmless only if a court is "able to declare that it was *harmless beyond a reasonable doubt*" (Chapman v. California, 1967) (italics added). Moreover, the "beneficiary of the error"—the prosecution—has the "burden to show that [the violation] was harmless" under this "beyond a reasonable doubt" standard (Chapman v. California, 1967). When a court finds constitutional error in a "collateral" challenge to a conviction—a petition for a writ of habeas corpus, for example—the standard of harmlessness is considerably less stringent. At that stage of the adjudicatory process, the federal standard for nonconstitutional errors on direct appeal applies to constitutional errors. Consequently, an error is harmless unless it had "substantial and injurious effect or influence in determining the jury's verdict" (Kotteakos v. United States, 1946). Put otherwise, there must be " 'actual prejudice' " to the defendant (Brecht v. Abrahamson, 1993 (quoting United States v. Lane, 1986)).

The Supreme "Court has applied harmless error analysis to a wide range of errors and has recognized that most constitutional errors can be harmless" (Arizona v. Fulminante, 1991).[240] The Court "generally [has] held that if the prosecution can prove beyond a reasonable doubt that a constitutional error did not contribute to the verdict, the error is harmless and the verdict may stand" (Satterwhite v. Texas, 1988). Constitutional violations that can qualify as harmless are " 'trial error[s]'—errors which occur[] during the presentation of the case to the jury, and which may therefore be quantitatively assessed in the context of other evidence presented" (Fulminante v. Arizona, 1991).[241] It is fair to treat "trial errors" as potentially harmless because the likelihood that they have had a deleterious impact on the verdict is not exceptionally high and because the degree of impact they have had can be accurately measured.[242] Nevertheless, because these errors do involve deprivations of fundamental rights, the government can avoid a new trial only if it establishes "beyond a reasonable doubt" that the error did not affect the outcome of the trial.

Only a limited number of constitutional errors can never be harmless and will always result in automatic reversal on appeal or in a collateral challenge. A violation falls into this category if it amounts to a "structural defect[] in the constitution of the trial mechanism" (Arizona v. Fulminante, 1991). The denial of a constitutional right qualifies as such a "structural defect" *only* if it affects the "entire conduct of the trial from the beginning to end" or if it "affect[s] the framework within which the trial proceeds" and is not "simply an error in the trial process itself." A structural defect involves the denial of a " 'basic protection[],' " such as the guarantee of the assistance of counsel at trial, the entitlement to jury instructions regarding the reasonable doubt standard, the promise of an impartial judge, or the right to a public trial. When such a defect is present, "a criminal trial cannot reliably serve its function as a vehicle for determination of guilt or innocence, and no criminal punishment may be regarded as fundamentally fair' " (Arizona v. Fulminante, 1991 (quoting Rose v. Clark, 1986)).[243]

When an appellate court discovers a structural defect, it must presume that prejudice resulted, and, consequently, it cannot employ harmless error analysis.

The presumption arises for two reasons. First, when a structural defect occurs, it is highly likely that prejudice to the defendant did in fact result. Harmless error review would ordinarily be a waste of judicial time and effort. Second, in some instances the impacts of a structural defect cannot be measured accurately. In those cases, fairness to the defendant requires a presumption of prejudice and a new proceeding. Thus, the only legitimate response to a structural defect is automatic reversal of a conviction or sentence.

Sixth Amendment right to counsel violations fall into both categories of constitutional error. Most deprivations of assistance are "structural defects" that cannot be harmless and lead to "automatic reversal" of convictions. Some, however, are subject to harmless error review under the federal constitutional standards described above.

Violations of the Right to Counsel Not Subject to Harmless Error Review

When an accused who is entitled to retained or appointed assistance at trial does not have, and has not validly waived, a lawyer, the resulting violation of the right to counsel "can never be harmless error" (Arizona v. Fulminante, 1991).[244] "Actual or constructive *denial of the assistance of counsel altogether* is legally presumed to result in prejudice" (Strickland v. Washington, 1984) (italics added). Gideon v. Wainwright provides a clear illustration of this principle. In that landmark case, a trial judge refused to appoint counsel for an indigent defendant accused of a felony. The Supreme Court reversed his conviction without evaluating whether there was any chance that legal assistance would have changed the outcome of the trial. Relief for such a deprivation was *automatic*.

In some cases, a complete deprivation of legal assistance at a formal, "critical," pretrial stage of the criminal process will yield a presumption of prejudice and automatic reversal. Thus, if an accused is denied counsel at a critical "arraignment" in a capital case and pleads guilty, reversal of the resulting conviction is automatic without inquiry into the effects of counsel's absence on the outcome of the proceeding. "When one pleads to a capital charge without benefit of counsel, [courts] do not stop to determine whether prejudice resulted" (Hamilton v. Alabama, 1961). If an accused is deprived of legal representation at a preliminary hearing and pleads guilty to a capital charge, and that plea is later introduced against him at trial, the constitutional violation is not subject to harmless error analysis—prejudice is presumed, and the conviction must be reversed (White v. Maryland, 1963). As will be seen later, not all deprivations of assistance at critical, formal, pretrial proceedings lead to a presumption of prejudice. Some are subject to harmless error analysis. The line between those that are automatically reversible and those that can be harmless has not been clearly delineated.

Partial deprivations of counsel's assistance at trial are also considered "structural defects" for harmless error purposes. Meaningful governmental interferences with or obstructions of a lawyer's opportunities or abilities to fulfill her constitutional functions cannot be harmless but, instead, are presumed to be prejudicial (Strickland v. Washington, 1984). Thus, if counsel is barred from making a closing argument in a bench trial, a resulting conviction will be reversed without examination of the impact of the lack of argument on the verdict. The government has no opportunity to demonstrate harmlessness (Herring v. New York, 1975). In addition, if a judge prohibits discussion between a defense lawyer and the accused during trial at a time when the accused is entitled to consult with his attorney, there is no assessment of whether the lack of consultation affected the outcome. The violation of the entitlement to counsel is presumptively prejudicial and automatically reversible (Geders v. United States, 1976; Perry v. Leeke, 1989).

At least some violations of the Sixth Amendment due to "conflict of interest" problems are not subject to harmless error analysis. Prejudice is presumed when the deprivation of counsel is directly attributable to the government. Thus, if a judge fails to inquire into the potential for conflict or to appoint separate representation in a case where she has been actually notified by counsel of the risk of conflict, the Sixth Amendment violation cannot be harmless. Instead, "whenever a trial court improperly requires joint representation over timely objection reversal is automatic" (Holloway v. Arkansas, 1978). In addition, if counsel who is representing codefendants is in a position of conflict that adversely affects her representation of an accused's interests, there is no need for the accused to demonstrate "prejudice" to the opportunity for a favorable verdict. Moreover, the government cannot avoid retrial by demonstrating that the disloyal service from counsel had no impact on the outcome of the trial. Once the denial of counsel is shown, relief must be granted (Cuyler v. Sullivan, 1980).

A variety of justifications has been offered to support the presumption that these sorts of right to counsel violations are always prejudicial and the conclusion that they should be excluded from harmless error review. Because of the "fundamental importance of the assistance of counsel" to the proper operation of the adversarial system, "a pervasive denial of counsel casts [substantial] doubt on the fairness of the trial process" (Penson v. Ohio, 1988). Both outright denial of counsel and meaningful official impediments to counsel's functioning impair the adversarial process that the criminal justice system relies on to produce just results by means of fair contests. The resulting impairments of the process "are so likely to prejudice the accused that the cost of litigating their effect in a particular case is unjustified" (United States v. Cronic, 1984). Moreover, the circumstances that violate "the Sixth Amendment right . . . are easy to identify and, for that reason and because the [government] is directly responsible, easy for the government to prevent" (Strickland v. Washington, 1984). The high likelihood of prejudice means that a rule of automatic reversal will rarely provide relief for uninjured defendants. The government's ability to identify and prevent violations means that automatic reversal need not be inordinately costly to the criminal justice system and that it is fair to impose any costs that do result on the government.

In actual conflict of interest situations, the rule of automatic reversal is based on the fact that counsel has breached "the duty of loyalty, perhaps the most basic of counsel's duties. Moreover, it is difficult to measure the precise effect on the defense of representation corrupted by conflicting interests" (Strickland v. Washington, 1984). In conflict of interest situations, "an inquiry into a claim of harmless error would require . . . unguided speculation" (Holloway v. Arkansas, 1978). If the government could preserve a conviction and avoid a new trial by demonstrating a lack of harm, an accused might well be denied relief despite a high likelihood that he was prejudiced by his lawyer's breach of a fundamental obligation. Consequently, "it is reasonable for the criminal justice system to maintain a fairly rigid rule of presumed prejudice for conflicts of interest" (Strickland v. Washington, 1984). (This reasoning is tempered, however, to a certain extent by the recent suggestion that defendants may have to demonstrate prejudice in actual conflict cases not involving multiple concurrent representation (Mickens v. Taylor, 2002).)

Denials of the Sixth Amendment right of self-representation are also "structural defects" that are not subject to harmless error review (Arizona v. Fulminante, 1991). If a judge improperly refuses to grant a defendant's request to waive counsel and represent himself, a conviction will be reversed without inquiry into whether the constitutional error was prejudicial. "The right [to represent oneself] is either respected or denied; its deprivation cannot be harmless" (McKaskle v. Wiggins, 1984). The reasons for treating denials of self-representation as automatically reversible are different from the reasons for so treating deprivations of counsel's aid. First, "the right of self-representation is a right that when exercised usually increases the likelihood of a trial outcome unfavorable to the defendant" (McKaskle v. Wiggins, 1984). Consequently, in virtually every case the government would be able to establish that a refusal to allow an accused to serve as his own representative was "harmless beyond a reasonable doubt." If denials of the Sixth Amendment entitlement to self-representation could be considered harmless, violations of that right would be encouraged and would almost always go unremedied. In addition, the values promoted by the right of self-representation—the individual dignity and autonomy of the accused—are in fact infringed upon every time a judge unjustifiably denies a defendant's request. The government can never prove that a deprivation of the right to be one's own representative was "harmless" to the constitutional interests that underlie that fundamental Sixth Amendment right. Consequently, violations of the right to represent oneself are "not amenable to 'harmless error' analysis" (McKaskle v. Wiggins, 1984).

Violations of the Right to Counsel Subject to Harmless Error Review

In the situations discussed in the preceding paragraphs, the question of whether a deprivation of counsel had an effect on the result of the proceeding is irrelevant to the decision to grant relief. In other situations, however, the impact of inadequate representation by counsel on the outcome of a proceeding is a critical determinant of whether relief will be granted. In some of these situations, the effect of counsel's deficiencies on the outcome is measured by means of traditional harmless error analysis. In others, the harmless error doctrine is ostensibly inapplicable, but the impact of a lawyer's poor performance on the result determines whether a constitutional violation occurred.

Claims that the right to counsel was denied by a lawyer's incompetent assistance—"actual ineffectiveness" claims—fall into the latter category. The doctrine of Strickland v. Washington holds that a violation of the Sixth Amendment is not established unless the defendant proves both a deficient performance by his lawyer and resulting prejudice. Technically, when such a deprivation is proven, it cannot be "harmless." In reality, however, the inquiry involved in harmless error analysis—whether the result of the proceeding was adversely affected by the impairment of counsel's performance—is incorporated into the definition of the constitutional right to effective assistance. To demonstrate a Sixth Amendment violation, an accused must show "prejudice" to the result of his trial or sentencing. He must show "a reasonable probability" that if counsel had not performed poorly, the result would have been different.[245]

In substance, this is "harmless error" analysis with a vengeance.[246] It poses a greater obstacle to relief than the formal harmless error doctrine. Constitutional harmless error review ordinarily requires the *government* to shoulder the burden of showing an absence of harm. It denies relief only if the government shows that an error either was "harmless beyond a reasonable doubt" or did not have "substantial and injurious effect or influence on the jury." The "actual ineffectiveness" of counsel doctrine requires the *defendant* to carry the burden. It denies relief unless the accused shows that a deficient performance by counsel created a "reasonable probability" of harm to the result of his trial. Thus, while harmless error analysis is technically not applicable, it makes no sense to classify incompetent assistance claims as Sixth Amendment violations that yield "automatic reversal." There is no remedy for even egregiously deficient assistance from a lawyer unless there is a demonstrated significant likelihood that the inadequacy of counsel's representation in fact adversely affected the outcome of the trial.[247]

The requirement that an accused show "prejudice" to the outcome in order to gain a new trial or sentencing rests on justifications that distinguish incompetent assistance situations from the types of counsel deprivations that are presumed to be prejudicial. First, deficient performances by counsel are just as likely to be harmless as harmful. In addition, inadequate representation is neither easy to identify nor easy to prevent. Counsel cannot be informed with sufficient precision of the steps to be taken or the actions to be avoided, and the government is not responsible for and cannot avoid the lawyer's deficiencies.[248] In sum, even though an attorney has done her job incompetently, there is not a high likelihood that harm has occurred, and the state cannot be blamed for any risk of injury to the accused. Without an inquiry into the effect of counsel's representation on the outcome, an intolerable number of defendants would receive undeserved relief. Automatic reversal would result in numerous windfalls—new trials for criminal defendants whose first trials were sufficiently fair—and would impose unnecessary costs on criminal justice systems. For these reasons, a presumption of prejudice is thought to be unjustified; relief is granted only if harm is shown (Strickland v. Washington, 1984).

Some total denials of legal assistance at *formal*, pretrial, critical stages are subject to harmless error review. In Coleman v. Alabama, indigent defendants did not receive appointed counsel at a preliminary hearing. For a number of reasons, the Supreme Court concluded that they were entitled to assistance at that hearing and, therefore, had suffered constitutional violations. Turning to the question of whether the defendants were entitled to new trials, the Court observed that no evidence from the preliminary hearing had been admitted into the defendants' trials. (This stood in contrast to the situation in White v. Maryland, in which a guilty plea at a preliminary hearing conducted without counsel was introduced at a subsequent trial.) The *Coleman* Court remanded the cases to the lower courts for a determination of "whether or not [the defendants] were . . . prejudiced [in some other way] by the absence of counsel at the preliminary hearing" and specified that the "test to be applied" was the harmless beyond a reasonable doubt standard prescribed in Chapman v. California (Coleman v. Alabama, 1970). Thus, if the government could demonstrate that the denial of aid at the preliminary hearing did not prejudice the defendants at trial, no relief was warranted.

A defendant who is deprived of counsel at an *informal*, critical, pretrial stage of the proceedings is generally entitled to have any evidence obtained at that stage excluded from his trial. When a court fails to prevent the introduction of such evidence, it commits constitutional error. The erroneous introduction of evidence from a critical pretrial encounter with the government, however, does not "affect[]—and contaminate[]—the entire proceeding" (Satterwhite v. Texas, 1988). Instead, "the effect of the Sixth Amendment violation is" confined to a narrow part of the process. "[T]he evil caused by [the] Sixth Amendment violation is limited to the erroneous admission of particular evidence at trial" (Satterwhite v. Texas, 1988). Consequently, a right to counsel violation of this sort is classified as a "trial error." It does not yield automatic reversal but, instead, is subject to harmless error analysis.

A handful of cases provides helpful illustrations of this sort of right to counsel deprivation and the governing harmless error doctrine. In Milton v. Wainwright, the Court concluded that if statements were deliberately elicited from an accused individual in violation of the right to counsel recognized in Massiah v. United States, the erroneous admission of those statements at trial is subject to harmless error analysis. On appeal, if the government shows that the introduction of the statements was "harmless beyond a reasonable doubt"—that is, if the appellate court concludes, beyond a reasonable doubt, that the jury would have arrived at the same verdict without the statements—a conviction will stand (Milton v. Wainwright, 1972). In United States v. Wade, the Court recognized a Sixth Amendment right to counsel's assistance at a pretrial lineup and held that eyewitness identifications made at a lineup are inadmissible if the accused has been deprived of counsel (United States v. Wade, 1967). The erroneous admission of such an identification, however, is subject to harmless error analysis under the governing constitutional standards (Moore v. Illinois, 1977). Finally, in Estelle v. Smith, the Supreme Court held that a defendant in a capital case is entitled to counsel when deciding whether to submit to a psychiatric examination designed to determine whether he would be dangerous in the future. Defense counsel has to be given notice of such a psychiatric examination. If the accused does not receive his constitutional due, a psychiatrist who has examined him may not testify (Estelle v. Smith, 1981). Nevertheless, if a judge mistakenly allows the government to introduce psychiatric testimony secured in violation of the defendant's Sixth Amendment right, a conviction does not necessarily have to be reversed. If the error is shown to have been harmless, the defendant will receive no relief (Satterwhite v. Texas, 1988).

Relief for Violations of the Right to the Assistance of Counsel on Appeal

Denials of the right to the assistance of appellate counsel typically result in a new appeal. Thus, if an indigent accused is completely deprived of the assistance of an appointed lawyer, a court must grant a new appeal with legal assistance (Douglas v. California, 1963). If an accused has retained or appointed assistance, but counsel performs so inadequately that she either deprives the accused of the appellate process entirely or provides no real representation, a new appeal is also warranted. Consequently, if counsel neglects to file a notice of appeal that a defendant wishes to have filed (Smith v. Robbins, 2000) or causes the dismissal of an appeal by failing to file a necessary paper with an appellate court (Evitts v. Lucey, 1985), an accused is entitled to a new appeal. Similarly, if an attorney fails to comply with the steps necessary to withdraw from an appeal thought to be "frivolous," an accused is entitled to a new proceeding at which counsel provides the requisite representation (Penson v. Ohio, 1988). In all these situations, because the damage to the appellant's interest in having an appeal with effective legal assistance is apparent, there is no need to ask whether the accused was harmed before granting a new appellate process with counsel. "Because the fundamental importance of the assistance of counsel does not decrease as the prosecutorial process moves from the trial to the appellate stage, the presumption of prejudice must extend as well to the denial of counsel on appeal," and it is "inappropriate to apply . . . harmless error analysis" before granting relief (Penson v. Ohio, 1988).

Cases where an appellant receives a lawyer's aid and the lawyer's deficiency is less extreme are treated differently. If a lawyer's performance does not deprive the accused of an appeal or if counsel does furnish some assistance, relief is warranted only if the appellant demonstrates that counsel's deficient performance caused "prejudice" to the outcome of his appeal (Smith v. Robbins, 2000). Thus, for example, if an attorney fails to raise issues that would have been stronger than those raised in the brief that she filed, if she incompetently formulates or presents the arguments in support of reversal, or if she complies with a constitutionally adequate process for withdrawal from a frivolous appeal but unprofessionally misjudges the merits of that appeal, a new appeal is warranted only if there is a "reasonable probability that, but for his counsel's" deficient assistance the appellant "would have prevailed on his appeal" (Smith v. Robbins, 2000). In these situations, "harm" is highly relevant to the decision to grant relief, and the burden of establishing harm is on the defendant. Poor performances by counsel that do not significantly damage the chances for obtaining appellate relief from convictions do not justify further appellate review.[249]

NOTES

1. For discussions of the historical origins of the adversary system, see generally Stephan Landsman, "The Rise of the Contentious Spirit: Adversary Procedure in Eighteenth Century England," 75 *Cornell L. Rev.* (1990) 497; Stephan Landsman, "A Brief Survey of the Development of the Adversary System," 44 *Ohio St. L.J.* (1983) 713.

2. For more extensive discussions of the adversary system, see Stephan Landsman, *Readings on Adversarial Justice: The American Approach to Adjudication* (St. Paul, MN: West Publishing Co., 1988); Stephan Landsman, *The Adversary System: A Description and Defense* (Washington, DC: American Enterprise Institute, 1984); David Luban, "The Adversary System Excuse," in *The Good Lawyer: Lawyers' Roles and Lawyers' Ethics*, David Luban ed. (Totowa, NJ: Rowman & Allenheld, 1983); Lloyd Weinreb, "The Adversary Process Is Not an End in Itself," 2 *J. Legal Ethics* (1998) 59. For additional sources regarding the adversary system, see Franklin D. Strier and Edith Greene, *The Adversary System: An Annotated Bibliography* (Littleton, CO: Fred B. Rothman, 1990).

3. Bruce A. Green, "Why Should Prosecutors 'Seek Justice'?" 26 *Fordham Urb. L.J.* (1999) 607, 612 (discussing the prosecutor's duty to seek justice and its sources).

4. Martin Marcus, "Above the Fray or Into the Breach: The Judge's Role in New York's Adversarial System of Criminal Justice," 57 *Brook. L. Rev.* (1992) 1193 (judge is neutral and detached magistrate who resolves conflicts); Landsman, *Readings on Adversarial Justice* 77–169 (discussing role of judges and juries in adversarial system).

5. Catherine L. Carpenter, "The All or Nothing Doctrine in Criminal Cases: Independent Trial Strategy or Gamesmanship Gone Awry?" 26 *Am. J. Crim. L.* (1999) 257 (discussing the tension between the truth-seeking functions of the jury and the deference given to parties to fashion their own trial strategies).

6. Monroe Freedman, "Our Constitutionalized Adversary System," 1 *Chap. L. Rev.* (1998) 57 (maintaining that adversary system is not only a process but also a substantive core of rights).

7. James J. Tomkovicz, "An Adversary System Defense of the Right to Counsel Against Informants: Truth, Fair Play, and the *Massiah* Doctrine," 22 *U.C. Davis L. Rev.* (1988) 44–45.

8. For contrary views, see Marvin E. Frankel, *Partisan Justice* (New York: Hill and Wang, 1980) 37 (arguing that the role of lawyers in the adversarial system is to subvert the truth); Franklin Strier, "Making Jury Trials More Truthful," 30 *U.C. Davis L. Rev.* (1996) 95–98 (arguing that the combination of jury trials and adversarial justice impedes

truth seeking); Gary Goodpaster, "On the Theory of American Adversary Criminal Trial," 78 *J. Crim. L. & Criminology* (1987) 121–23 (arguing that the truth-seeking function is not an adequate justification of the system).

9. Landsman, *The Adversary System* 37.

10. Tomkovicz, "An Adversary System Defense of the Right to Counsel Against Informants," 47–49.

11. See generally Elizabeth Thornburg, "Metaphors Matter: How Images of Battle, Sports, and Sex Shape the Adversary System," 10 *Wis. Women's L.J.* (1995) 237–40 (discussing how the sporting metaphor impacts the administration of justice).

12. The description of the inquisitorial alternative and the quotations in this paragraph are taken from Landsman, *The Adversary System* 48–50.

13. Tomkovicz, "An Adversary System Defense of the Right to Counsel Against Informants," 40; Joseph Grano, "*Rhode Island v. Innis*: A Need to Reconsider the Constitutional Premises Underlying the Law of Confessions," 17 *Am. Crim. L. Rev.* (1979) 27.

14. Tomkovicz, "An Adversary System Defense of the Right to Counsel Against Informants," 51.

15. Francis Heller, *The Sixth Amendment to the Constitution of the United States* (Lawrence: University of Kansas Press, 1951) 27, 120; Jay Sterling Silver, "Equality of Arms and the Adversarial Process: A New Constitutional Right," 1990 *Wis. L. Rev.* 1037–38; H. Richard Uviller, "Evidence from the Mind of the Criminal Suspect: A Reconsideration of the Current Rules of Access and Restraint," 87 *Colum. L. Rev.* (1987) 1169.

16. William Beaney, *The Right to Counsel in American Courts* (Ann Arbor: University of Michigan Press, 1955) 1.

17. Bruce A. Green, "Lethal Fiction: The Meaning of 'Counsel' in the Sixth Amendment," 78 *Iowa L. Rev.* (1993) 433 (thoroughly discussing what the Sixth Amendment entitlement to "counsel" does and should mean).

18. Green, "Lethal Fiction," 434, 459–65, 470–73.

19. Alfredo Garcia, "The Right to Counsel Under Siege: Requiem for an Endangered Right?" 29 *Am. Crim. L. Rev.* (1991) 41–42, 59 (describing the purpose of Sixth Amendment rights, including the right to counsel, as to establish an "equilibrium of forces between the prosecution and the accused"); Tomkovicz, "An Adversary System Defense of the Right to Counsel Against Informants," 40 (stating that counsel is essential as an "equalizer" for the accused in the battle with the state).

20. Beaney, *The Right to Counsel in American Courts* 27–30.

21. For scholarly discussions of the reasons for recognition of a constitutional right to counsel of choice, see Wayne D. Holly, "Rethinking the Sixth Amendment for the Indigent Criminal Defendant: Do Reimbursement Statutes Support Recognition of a Right to Counsel of Choice for the Indigent?" 64 *Brook. L. Rev.* (1998) 187–89; Green, "Lethal Fiction," 441–42; Eugene L. Shapiro, "The Sixth Amendment Right to Counsel of Choice: An Exercise in the Weighing of Unarticulated Values," 43 *S.C. L. Rev.* (1992) 350–56, 381–82; Garcia, "The Right to Counsel under Siege," 85–86.

22. Garcia, "The Right to Counsel Under Siege," 86–92 (agreeing that right to counsel of choice "is not absolute" but criticizing the Supreme Court's narrow interpretation of that constitutional right).

23. Shapiro, "The Sixth Amendment Right to Counsel of Choice," 350, 354 (sug-

gesting that the Court's failure to specify the strength of the "presumption" in favor of counsel of choice makes its "meaningful implementation" difficult).

24. Holly, "Rethinking the Sixth Amendment for the Indigent Criminal Defendant," 191–93.

25. For discussions and criticisms of the *Wheat* decision, see Holly, "Rethinking the Sixth Amendment for the Indigent Criminal Defendant," 194–96; Pamela S. Karlan, "Discrete and Relational Criminal Representation: The Changing Vision of the Right to Counsel," 105 *Harv. L. Rev.* (1992) 687–97; Garcia, "The Right to Counsel Under Siege," 100–104; Bruce A. Green, " 'Through a Glass, Darkly': How the Court Sees Motions to Disqualify Criminal Defense Lawyers," 89 *Colum. L. Rev.* (1989) 1201; William J. Stuntz, "Waiving Rights in Criminal Procedure," 75 *Va. L. Rev.* (1989) 797–801.

26. Holly, "Rethinking the Sixth Amendment for the Indigent Criminal Defendant," 197–98.

27. For discussions and criticisms of the Court's decisions in *Caplin & Drysdale* and *Monsanto*, see Karlan, "Discrete and Relational Criminal Representation," 705–13; Shapiro, "The Sixth Amendment Right to Counsel of Choice," 356–66; Stacy Caplon, "Under Advisement: Attorney Fee Forfeiture and the Supreme Court," 55 *Brook. L. Rev.* (1989) 111–63.

28. For a detailed empirical study of whether indigents receive a quality of legal assistance comparable to that rendered to accused individuals who retain representation, see Robert Hermann, Eric Single, and John Boston, *Counsel for the Poor: Criminal Defense in Urban America* (Lexington, MA: Lexington Books, 1977).

29. Hermann, Single, and Boston, *Counsel for the Poor*, 20.

30. See Stephen J. Schulhofer and David D. Friedman, "Rethinking Indigent Defense: Promoting Effective Representation through Consumer Sovereignty and Freedom of Choice for All Criminal Defendants," 31 *Am. Crim. L. Rev.* (1993) 73, for a discussion of the problems caused by state funding of defense counsel, descriptions of the existing systems for affording counsel to indigents, and proposals for reform.

31. Beaney, *The Right to Counsel in American Courts* 27–33; David Fellman, *The Defendant's Rights Today* (Madison: University of Wisconsin Press, 1976) 211; Hermann, Single, and Boston, *Counsel for the Poor* 11.

32. For a thorough account of the details of the *Powell* case, see James Goodman, *Stories of Scottsboro* (New York: Pantheon Books, 1994).

33. John C. Klotter and Jacqueline R. Kanovitz, *Constitutional Law for Police* (Cincinnati, OH: W.H. Anderson Co., 1968) 220.

34. See Beaney, *The Right to Counsel in American Courts* 33–44, for a discussion of the precedents for *Zerbst* and the Court's decision in *Zerbst.*

35. For a discussion of the application of the Betts v. Brady holding in the Supreme Court and the lower courts, see Beaney, *The Right to Counsel in American Courts*, 160–98; for criticism of the *Betts* rule, see Yale Kamisar, "The Right to Counsel and the Fourteenth Amendment: A Dialogue on 'The Most Pervasive Right' of an Accused," 30 *U. Chi. L. Rev.* (1962) 1.

36. For general discussions of the *Gideon* case, see Anthony Lewis, *Gideon's Trumpet* (New York: Random House, 1964); Jerold H. Israel, "*Gideon v. Wainwright*: The 'Art' of Overruling," 1963 *Sup. C. Rev.* 211.

37. See Laurence A. Benner, "Tokenism and the American Indigent: Some Perspectives on Defense Services," 12 *Am. Crim. L. Rev.* (1975) 667; C. Anthony Friloux Jr.,

"Equal Justice Under the Law: A Myth, Not a Reality," 12 *Am. Crim. L. Rev.* (1975) 691; David Bazelon, "The Defective Assistance of Counsel," 42 *U. Cin. L. Rev.* (1973) 1, for suggestions that the noble ideal sought by *Zerbst* and *Gideon* has not been achieved in practice.

38. Fellman, *The Defendant's Rights Today*, 211.

39. Steven Duke, "The Right to Appointed Counsel: *Argersinger* and Beyond," 12 *Am. Crim. L. Rev.* (1975) 610–12.

40. Duke, "The Right to Appointed Counsel," 613.

41. Francis H. Heller, *The Sixth Amendment to the Constitution of the United States* (Lawrence: University of Kansas Press, 1951) 9–10.

42. William M. Beaney, "The Right to Counsel" 150–51, in *The Rights of the Accused in Law and Action*, Stuart S. Nagel ed. (Beverly Hills, CA: Sage Publications, 1972); Paul B. Weston and Kenneth M. Wells, *Law Enforcement and Criminal Justice: An Introduction* (Pacific Palisades, CA: Goodyear Publishing Co. 1972) 145–46.

43. Duke, "The Right to Appointed Counsel," 615–16.

44. See John M. Junker, "The Right to Counsel in Misdemeanor Cases," 43 *Wash. L. Rev.* (1968) 685, for a general discussion of the precedential and policy bases for a right to counsel in misdemeanor cases and the extent of that right. For a suggestion that if states can afford to hire prosecutors, they should sustain the costs of providing counsel for indigent defendants, see Weston and Wells, *Law Enforcement and Criminal Justice*, 146.

45. Barbara Bison Ford, Note, "*Argersinger v. Hamlin* and the Collateral Use of Prior Misdemeanor Convictions of Indigents Unrepresented by Counsel at Trial," 35 *Ohio St. L.J.* (1974) 173–74.

46. Fellman, *The Defendant's Rights Today*, 217–18.

47. Joel W.L. Millar, Comment, "*Nichols v. United States*, the Right to Counsel and Collateral Sentence Enhancement: In Search of a Rationale," 144 *U. Pa. L. Rev.* (1996) 1189; Ford, "*Argersinger v. Hamlin* and the Collateral Use of Prior Misdemeanor Convictions," 176–79.

48. Alfredo Garcia, *The Sixth Amendment in Modern American Jurisprudence: A Critical Perspective* (Westport, CT: Greenwood Press, 1992) 36; Peter W. Tague, "An Indigent's Right to the Attorney of His Choice," 27 *Stan. L. Rev.* (1974) 73; Ronald A. Case, Annotation, "Indigent's Right to Choose Particular Counsel Appointed to Assist Him," 66 *A.L.R.3d* (1975) 996.

49. For discussion and criticism of the failure to give an indigent a choice, see Stephen J. Schulhofer and David D. Friedman, "Rethinking Indigent Defense: Promoting Effective Representation Through Consumer Sovereignty and Freedom of Choice for All Criminal Defendants," 31 *Am. Crim. L. Rev.* (1993) 102–12.

50. Joseph G. Cook, *Constitutional Rights of the Accused: Trial Rights* (Rochester, NY: Lawyers Co-operative Publishing Co., 1974) 97–100; Wade R. Habeeb, Annotation, "Determination of Indigency of Accused Entitling Him to Appointment of Counsel," 51 *A.L.R.3d* (1973) 1108.

51. Duke, "The Right to Appointed Counsel," 625–31.

52. Francis M. Dougherty, "Validity, Construction, and Application of State Recoupment Statutes Permitting State to Recover Counsel Fees Expended for Benefit of Indigent Criminal Defendants," 39 *A.L.R. 4th* (1985) 597.

53. James J. Tomkovicz, "Standards for Invocation and Waiver of Counsel in Confession Contexts," 71 *Iowa L. Rev.* (1986) 1045.

54. John F. Decker, "The Sixth Amendment Right to Shoot Oneself in the Foot: An Assessment of the Guarantee of Self-Representation Twenty Years After *Faretta*," 6 *Seton Hall Const. L.J.* (1996) 517–23 (discussing the standards for competency to waive counsel and opt for self-representation).

55. Tomkovicz, "Standards for Invocation and Waiver of Counsel in Confession Contexts," 1055–56 (concluding that for waivers of Sixth Amendment right to assistance of counsel in pretrial confession settings defendant must truly choose to forgo equalizing assistance and must understand consequences of that choice).

56. See Decker, "The Sixth Amendment Right to Shoot Oneself in the Foot," 510–17, for a discussion of lower court variations over the process required for a valid waiver.

57. William J. Stuntz, "Waiving Rights in Criminal Procedure," 75 *Va. L. Rev.* (1989) 795–96 (arguing that although the *Faretta* Court framed the right to self-representation as an affirmative Sixth Amendment right, that right is not distinct from a waiver of the right to counsel).

58. See Decker, "The Sixth Amendment Right to Shoot Oneself in the Foot," 490–98; Paul Marcus, "The *Faretta* Principle: Self-Representation Versus the Right to Counsel," 30 *Am. J. Comp. L.* (supplement) (1982) 551, for concise discussions of the *Faretta* decision.

59. Randolph N. Jonakait, "Foreword: Notes for a Consistent and Meaningful Sixth Amendment," 84 *J. Crim. L. & Criminology* (1992) 730–34 (maintaining that unlike most other Bill of Rights provisions, the Sixth Amendment provides positive and personal rights, not mere negative restraints on the government).

60. Tomkovicz, "Standards for Invocation and Waiver of Counsel in Confession Contexts," 1055 (suggesting that failure to have assistance of counsel "engenders undeniable risks of an unfair trial").

61. Tomkovicz, "Standards for Invocation and Waiver of Counsel in Confession Contexts," 1055; see also Robert M. Cover and T. Alexander Aleinikoff, "Dialectical Federalism: Habeas Corpus and the Court," 86 *Yale L.J.* (1977) 1079 (discussing the tension in a system of justice that both protects autonomy and also insists on representation by counsel).

62. Decker, "The Sixth Amendment Right to Shoot Oneself in the Foot," 523–33 (discussing standby counsel, the *McKaskle* decision, and lower courts' efforts to discern the acceptable role for standby counsel).

63. Decker, "The Sixth Amendment Right to Shoot Oneself in the Foot," 537–44.

64. Susan Bandes, "Taking Some Rights Too Seriously: The State's Right to a Fair Trial," 60 *S. Cal. L. Rev.* (1987) 1030–31 (criticizing the courts' failures to identify the state's interests in denying hybrid representation and assess whether those interests actually justify denial of hybrid representation).

65. For a discussion of lower court decisions regarding timely assertion of the *Faretta* right, see Decker, "The Sixth Amendment Right to Shoot Oneself in the Foot," 544–50.

66. For general discussions of the allocation of decision-making authority in cases where an accused is represented by counsel, see Rodney J. Uphoff and Peter B. Wood, "The Allocation of Decisionmaking Between Defense Counsel and Criminal Defendant: An Empirical Study of Attorney-Client Decisionmaking," 47 *U. Kan. L. Rev.* (1998) 1; Richard H. Chused, "*Faretta* and the Personal Defense: The Role of a Represented Defendant in Trial Tactics," 65 *Cal. L. Rev.* (1977) 636.

67. For arguments in favor of according defendants the right to "hybrid" represen-

tation, see Chused, "*Faretta* and the Personal Defense," 651–55. For arguments against "hybrid" representation, see Vivian O. Berger, "The Supreme Court and Defense Counsel: Old Roads, New Paths—A Dead End?," 86 *Colum. L. Rev.* (1986) 41–44.

68. Chused, "*Faretta* and the Personal Defense," 651–56, 663–85 (advocating a more expansive decision-making role for the represented defendant and offering suggestions for implementing that role).

69. Berger, "The Supreme Court and Defense Counsel," 9, 11–12, 26, 33.

70. Uphoff and Wood, "The Allocation of Decisionmaking Between Defense Counsel and Criminal Defendant," 17–18.

71. Uphoff and Wood, "The Allocation of Decisionmaking Between Defense Counsel and Criminal Defendant," 18; see also Berger, "The Supreme Court and Defense Counsel," 33 (acknowledging the courts' "generally authoritarian view of counsel's proper relationship to the accused"); Chused, "*Faretta* and the Personal Defense," 636–38 (observing that tradition generally gives the lawyer, not the defendant, control over defense decisions, particularly those involving tactics).

72. Uphoff and Wood, "The Allocation of Decisionmaking Between Defense Counsel and the Criminal Defendant," 20; Chused, "*Faretta* and the Personal Defense," 638; Berger, "The Supreme Court and Defense Counsel," 33.

73. For a discussion of *Barnes*, see Berger, "The Supreme Court and Defense Counsel," 46–49.

74. For a different view, see Chused, "*Faretta* and the Personal Defense," 652–654 (suggesting that "efficiency concerns have been overstated" and that there are pragmatic reasons to allow the accused greater involvement in decision making).

75. For a different view, see Chused, "*Faretta* and the Personal Defense," 655 (arguing that the "superior ability of counsel" does not justify depriving the accused of authority to decide many matters).

76. Tomkovicz, "An Adversary System Defense of the Right to Counsel Against Informants," 10–11, 39–40, 55; Tomkovicz, "Standards for Invocation and Waiver of Counsel in Confession Contexts," 980–82.

77. For a thorough discussion of the facts underlying Powell v. Alabama, see James Goodman, *Stories of Scottsboro* (New York: Vintage Books, 1994) 1–23.

78. Tomkovicz, "Standards for Invocation and Waiver of Counsel in Confession Contexts," 982.

79. For discussions of extensions of the right to trial counsel to pretrial contexts in response to the evolution of American criminal justice systems and of the justifications for those extensions of the trial right, see Tomkovicz, "An Adversary System Defense of the Right to Counsel Against Informants," 10–11, 23–24, 55–59; Tomkovicz, "Standards for Invocation and Waiver of Counsel in Confession Contexts," 982; Wayne S. Moss and James T. Kilbreth III, "*Maine v. Moulton*: The Plain Meaning of 'Deliberate Elicitation': The State's Position," 23 *Am. Crim. L. Rev.* (1985) 64.

80. H. Richard Uviller, "Evidence from the Mind of the Criminal Suspect: A Reconsideration of the Current Rules of Access and Restraint," 87 *Colum. L. Rev.* (1987) 1158; Joseph D. Grano, "*Rhode Island v. Innis*: A Need to Reconsider the Constitutional Premises Underlying the Law of Confessions," 17 *Am. Crim. L. Rev.* (1979) 5–7.

81. Uviller, "Evidence from the Mind of the Criminal Suspect," 1164 (noting that "the offer of the sixth amendment remains dormant until the actual commencement of legal proceedings against" an individual and that "the constitutional guarantee of counsel accrues only to the charged defendant").

82. Grano, "*Rhode Island v. Innis*: A Need to Reconsider the Constitutional Premises Underlying the Law of Confessions," 11–18, 25–31 (contending that initiation of formal proceedings criterion is the only workable line for attachment of the right to counsel). For a different view, see Tomkovicz, "An Adversary System Defense of the Right to Counsel Against Informants," 63–71 (discussing the initiation of formal proceedings standard and suggesting that the right to counsel should attach at the time of arrest); "The Supreme Court—1971 Term," 86 *Harv. L. Rev.* (1972) 159–62 (criticizing limitation of the right to counsel to post-accusation lineups).

83. For discussions of the "offense-specific" nature of the right to counsel, see Pamela S. Karlan, "Discrete and Relational Criminal Representation: The Changing Vision of the Right to Counsel," 105 *Harv. L. Rev.* (1992) 678–79; Tomkovicz, "An Adversary System Defense of the Right to Counsel Against Informants," 84–85. See also John C. Klotter and Jacqueline R. Kanovitz, *Constitutional Law*, 8th ed. (Cincinnati, OH: Anderson Publishing, 1999), 306–7; Joshua Dressler, *Understanding Criminal Procedure*, 2nd ed. (New York: Matthew Bender, 1997) 439.

84. For a critical discussion of Illinois v. Perkins, see Honorable Charles E. Glennon and Tayebe Shah-Mirani, "*Illinois v. Perkins*: Approving the Use of Police Trickery in Prison to Circumvent *Miranda*," 21 *Loy. U. Chi. L.J.* (1990) 811.

85. Grano, "*Rhode Island v. Innis*: A Need to Reconsider the Constitutional Premises Underlying the Law of Confessions," 26 (maintaining that "[h]istory . . . reinforces what the sixth amendment's language makes plain"—that the right to counsel is a "trial guarantee[]" that does not apply "outside the judicial context").

86. For a contrary view, see Grano, "*Rhode Island v. Innis*: A Need to Reconsider the Constitutional Premises Underlying the Law of Confessions," 26 (suggesting that this premise is somewhat weak, for "legal issues may affect an accused's extrajudicial decisions before the judicial process begins").

87. For discussions of the rationales for the "initiation of proceedings" prerequisite for attachment of the right to counsel, see Tomkovicz, "An Adversary System Defense of the Right to Counsel Against Informants," 63–65; Tomkovicz, "Standards for Invocation and Waiver of Counsel in Confession Contexts," 983–85; Wayne R. LaFave, Jerold H. Israel, and Nancy J. King, *Criminal Procedure*, 3rd ed. (St. Paul, MN: West Publishing, 2000) 325–27.

88. For scholarly criticisms of the "initiation of proceedings" standard, see Karlan, "Discrete and Relational Criminal Representation," 674–75; Uviller, "Evidence From the Mind of the Criminal Suspect," 1167, 1212; Yale Kamisar, "*Brewer v. Williams*, *Massiah*, and *Miranda*: What Is 'Interrogation'? When Does It Matter?," 67 *Geo. L.J.* (1978) 81–83.

89. Uviller, "Evidence from the Mind of the Criminal Suspect," 1167 (calling the formal accusation point of attachment "awkward," "indefensible," "logically vulnerable," and "without a principled basis"); Grano, "*Rhode Island v. Innis*," 9 (noting that "many observers" find "merit [in] the claim that" the initiation of judicial proceedings line "exalts form over substance"); Kamisar, "*Brewer v. Williams, Massiah, and Miranda*," 81 (suggesting that the formal accusation criterion for attachment of the right to counsel is arbitrary and formalistic and asserting that "a suspect's need for 'a lawyer's help' . . . may be as great, or greater, before the commencement of judicial proceedings as afterwards").

90. Welsh S. White, "*Rhode Island v. Innis*: The Significance of a Suspect's Assertion of His Right to Counsel," 17 *Am. Crim. L. Rev.* (1979) 58 (suggesting that the

"*actual* beginning of the adversary process" occurs before a formal accusation and asserting that the "formal commencement of proceedings" is not "likely to signal a change in the suspect's position vis-a-vis the police").

91. For suggestions that arrest should trigger the right to counsel, see Tomkovicz, "An Adversary System Defense of the Right to Counsel Against Informants," 69–71; Welsh S. White, "Police Trickery in Inducing Confessions," 127 *U. Pa. L. Rev.* (1979) 591–92; White, "*Rhode Island v. Innis*," 58–59.

92. White, "*Rhode Island v. Innis*," 58 (voicing the concern with police manipulation of the "formal commencement of proceedings" criterion for attachment of the right to counsel); Kamisar, "*Brewer v. Williams, Massiah*, and *Miranda*," 81 (maintaining that the "initiation of proceedings" point of attachment "can often be manipulated by law enforcement authorities"); but see Grano, "*Rhode Island v. Innis*," 16–17 (conceding that "the opportunity for police manipulation may be somewhat greater when the sixth amendment line is drawn at the start of judicial proceedings rather than at some point of custody" but arguing that "[s]ome police manipulation is possible . . . under any sixth amendment" criterion).

93. For a summary of the typical steps in the processing of a criminal case, see National Advisory Commission on Criminal Justice Standards and Goals, *Courts* (1973) 11–15.

94. John C. Klotter and Jacqueline R. Kanovitz, *Constitutional Law for Police* (Cincinnati, OH: W.H. Anderson Co., 1968) 221–27 (discussing the three Supreme Court cases that have recognized a right to counsel at formal, pretrial proceedings in the courtroom).

95. Douglas L. Colbert, "Thirty-Five Years After *Gideon*: The Illusory Right to Counsel at Bail Proceedings," 1998 *U. Ill. L. Rev.* 32 (stating that "many states reacted to Coleman [v. Alabama] by eliminating the preliminary hearing, thereby" delaying defendants' enjoyment of the right to counsel).

96. Kathryn E. White, Comment, "What Have You Done with My Lawyer?: The Grand Jury Witness's Right to Consult with Counsel," 32 *Loy. L.A. L. Rev.* (1999) 935 (citing states that have begun to allow witnesses to consult with an attorney); Wayne F. Foster, Annotation, "Validity and Construction of Statutes Permitting Grand Jury Witnesses to Be Accompanied by Counsel," 90 A.L.R.3d (1980) 1340 (documenting state cases that have upheld statutes authorizing lawyers to consult with witnesses in the grand jury room).

97. For discussions of the justifications for maintaining secrecy and privacy in the grand jury process, see the following: Yale Kamisar, Wayne R. LaFave, and Jerold H. Israel, *Modern Criminal Procedure*, 9th ed. (St. Paul, MN: West Publishing, 1999), 680–82; N. Gary Holten and Lawson L. Lamar, *The Criminal Courts: Structures, Personnel, and Processes* (New York: McGraw-Hill, 1991) 197–98; Marc L. Miller and Ronald F. Wright, *Criminal Procedures—The Police* (New York: Aspen Law & Business, 1999), 788–89; Jonathan D. Schiffman, *Fundamentals of the Criminal Justice Process* (San Francisco: Lawyers Cooperative Publishing Co., 1986), 47–48. See also Daniel C. Richman, "Grand Jury Secrecy: Plugging the Leaks in an Empty Bucket," 36 *Am. Crim. L. Rev.* (1999) 339 (observing that a judge does not preside over grand jury proceedings and that a witness is subject to questioning by the prosecutor " 'without counsel present' "); William B. Lytton, "Grand Jury Secrecy—Time for a Reevaluation," 75 *J. Crim. L. & Criminology* (1984) 1102–3 (noting that a witness may not have an attorney present in a grand jury room); Mary Emma Hixon, "Bringing Down the Curtain on the

Absurd Drama of Entrances and Exits—Witness Representation in the Grand Jury Room," 15 *Am. Crim. L. Rev.* (1978) 307 (noting that although a witness has a right to counsel outside the grand jury room, the protection provided is not "adequate" and has proven to be a charade); White, "What Have You Done with My Lawyer?" 907 (suggesting that a witness's rights are jeopardized even when an attorney is present outside the grand jury room).

98. For a contrary view, see Colbert, "Thirty-Five Years After *Gideon*," 21–37 (arguing that pretrial bail hearings are analogous to other proceedings in which the Court has recognized a right to counsel and that extending the right to counsel to those hearings "would be in harmony with the Supreme Court's critical stage . . . analysis").

99. Tomkovicz, "An Adversary System Defense of the Right to Counsel Against Informants," 63–71 (arguing that the right to counsel at this "critical stage" should attach at the time of arrest).

100. See Tomkovicz, "An Adversary System Defense of the Right to Counsel Against Informants," 22–35, for a discussion of the controversy surrounding the *Massiah* doctrine.

101. Tomkovicz, "Standards for Invocation and Waiver of Counsel in Confession Contexts," 976–93 (explaining the distinctions between the *Miranda* and *Massiah* doctrines).

102. Tomkovicz, "An Adversary System Defense of the Right to Counsel Against Informants," 40–62 (suggesting that principles of adversary system equalization and fair play underlie the *Massiah* right).

103. For a discussion of the history of developments leading up to and following the announcement of the *Massiah* doctrine, see Tomkovicz, "An Adversary System Defense of the Right to Counsel Against Informants," 9–22.

104. For a dissenting view, see Tomkovicz, "An Adversary System Defense of the Right to Counsel Against Informants," 77–83 (suggesting reasons why *Massiah*'s branch of the right to counsel should regulate passive reception of disclosures).

105. Tomkovicz, "Standards for Invocation and Waiver of Counsel in Confession Contexts," 1044–47 (discussing proper standards for waiver of the Sixth Amendment right to counsel).

106. George E. Dix, "Federal Constitutional Confession Law: The 1986 and 1987 Supreme Court Terms," 67 *Texas L. Rev.* (1988) 316–18 (explaining that the level of knowledge required for a valid waiver should increase as a case progresses from the less to the more formal stages of prosecution).

107. Tomkovicz, "Standards for Invocation and Waiver of Counsel in Confession Contexts," 1037–43 (discussing the constitutional standards that ought to govern invocations of the Sixth Amendment right to counsel).

108. James J. Tomkovicz, "The *Massiah* Right to Exclusion: Constitutional Premises and Doctrinal Implications," 67 *N.C. L. Rev.* (1989) 751 (concluding that exclusion by virtue of *Massiah* right to counsel deprivation is part of the constitutional right and must be treated differently from exclusion resulting from violation of other constitutional safeguards).

109. For criticism of the *Massiah* doctrine exclusionary rule, see generally Office of Legal Policy, U.S. Dep't of Justice, Truth in Criminal Justice Series, Report No. 3, "Report to the Attorney General on the Sixth Amendment Right to Counsel under the *Massiah* Line of Cases" (1986), 22 *U. Mich. J. L. Reform* (1989) 661.

110. Silas Wasserstrom and William J. Mertens, "The Exclusionary Rule on the Scaf-

fold: But Was It a Fair Trial?," 22 *Am. Crim. L. Rev.* (1984) 156–79 (criticizing the rationale of Nix v. Williams).

111. Tomkovicz, "An Adversary System Defense of the Right to Counsel Against Informants," 25–27 (summarizing the arguments of Supreme Court Justices opposed to the *Massiah* right to counsel).

112. Uviller, "Evidence from the Mind of the Criminal Suspect," 1137; Grano, "*Rhode Island v. Innis*," 1; George E. Dix, "Undercover Investigations and Police Rulemaking," 53 *Tex. L. Rev.* (1975) 203. See also Office of Legal Policy, U.S. Dep't of Justice, Truth in Criminal Justice Series, Report No. 3, "Report to the Attorney General on the Sixth Amendment Right to Counsel under the *Massiah* Line of Cases" (1986), 22 *U. Mich. J.L. Reform* (1989) 661.

113. James J. Tomkovicz, "The Truth About *Massiah*," 23 *U. Mich. J.L. Reform* (1990) 641 (summarizing arguments leveled against the *Massiah* doctrine).

114. Tomkovicz, "An Adversary System Defense of the Right to Counsel Against Informants," 39–62 (discussing adversary system premises for *Massiah* right to counsel); see also Uviller, "Evidence from the Mind of the Criminal Suspect," 1173–83 (discussing counsel's role according to "preventive assistance" and "adversarial assistance" theories).

115. Tomkovicz, "An Adversary System Defense of the Right to Counsel against Informants," 55–62 (observing that extension of Sixth Amendment protection to pretrial stage is justified by the fact that adversarial conflicts now occur before trial).

116. Tomkovicz, "An Adversary System Defense of the Right to Counsel Against Informants," 49–51 (discussing fair play values promoted by right to counsel); Dix, "Federal Constitutional Confession Law," 270 (suggesting that *Massiah* holding is "consistent with . . . the protection of human dignity interests").

117. Joseph D. Grano, "Prophylactic Rules in Criminal Procedure: A Question of Article III Legitimacy," 80 *Nw. U. L. Rev.* (1985) 119–23 (opining that although the Court has explained the *Wade-Gilbert* entitlement to counsel as necessary to preserve other rights, that entitlement is part of the Sixth Amendment right to counsel, not a mere prophylactic protection for other rights).

118. For general discussions of the problems generated by and the risks inherent in eyewitness identifications and methods used to obtain them, see Elizabeth F. Loftus, *Eyewitness Testimony* (Cambridge, MA: Harvard University Press, 1996); Brian L. Cutler and Steven D. Penrod, *Mistaken Identification* (New York: Cambridge University Press, 1995); Lawrence Taylor, *Eyewitness Identification* (Charlottesville, VA: Michie Co., 1982); Gary L. Wells and Eric P. Seelau, "Eyewitness Identification: Psychological Research and Legal Policy on Lineups," 1 *Psychol., Pub. Pol'y, & L.* (1995) 765; Neil Colman McCabe, "The Right to a Lawyer at a Lineup: Support From State Courts and Experimental Psychology," 22 *Ind. L. Rev.* (1989) 905.

119. William Pena Wells and Brian L. Cutler, "The Right to Counsel at Videotaped Lineups: An Emerging Dilemma," 22 *Conn. L. Rev.* (1990) 387–95 (summarizing lower court opinions and concluding the Supreme Court would probably hold that counsel is not required at a lineup that is videotaped, a result that allows police to circumvent the Sixth Amendment right to counsel).

120. David J. Bodenhamer and James W. Ely Jr., *The Bill of Rights in Modern America after 200 Years* (Bloomington: Indiana University Press, 1993) 107 (referring to "the trial as the centerpiece of American justice").

121. Joseph G. Cook, *Constitutional Rights of the Accused*, 3rd ed. (Deerfield, IL: Clark Boardman Callaghan, 1996) 8–21; David Fellman, *The Defendant's Rights Today*

(Madison: University of Wisconsin Press, 1976) 223; William M. Beaney, "The Right to Counsel," in *The Rights of the Accused in Law and Action*, Stuart S. Nagel ed. (Beverly Hills, CA: Sage Publications, 1972) 154.

122. John C. Klotter and Jacqueline R. Kanovitz, *Constitutional Law*, 7th ed. (Cincinnati, OH: Anderson Publishing Co., 1995) 462; for a recent, thorough discussion of double jeopardy law, see George C. Thomas, *Double Jeopardy: The History, the Law* (New York: New York University, 1998).

123. Statistics Division, Admin. Office of the U.S. Courts, "1999 Report of the Director," (1999) 11, Table B-5 (demonstrating that in 1999 the average rate of reversal for criminal appeals in the federal circuit courts was 5.7 percent); Office of Justice Programs, U.S. Dep't. of Justice, "Compendium of Federal Justice Statistics, 1998" (1998) 76 (stating that in criminal appeals in 1998 "district court decisions were reversed or remanded back to the court in 8% of the cases"); see also "Courting Reversal: The Supervisory Role of State Supreme Courts," 87 *Yale L.J.* (1978) 1197–1200 and Appendix 8 (concluding, based on a study of sixteen sample states from 1870 to 1970, that the reversal rate for criminal appeals in state supreme courts was 35.6 percent); Honorable Vito J. Titone, "The Judiciary as Political Stepping-Stone: The Case for More Temperate Debate," 12 *St. John's J. Legal Comment.* (1996) 36 (noting that in criminal appeals brought before the New York Court of Appeals, "less than one quarter [of appellants] . . . obtain reversal").

124. Klotter and Kanovitz, *Constitutional Law* 418 (observing that the assistance of counsel "at" and "during" the criminal trial is "fundamental").

125. Cook, *Constitutional Rights of the Accused* 8–67 to 8–71; Paul B. Weston and Kenneth M. Wells, *Law Enforcement and Criminal Justice: An Introduction* (Pacific Palisades, CA: Goodyear Publishing Co., 1972), 144; Chester J. Antieau, *Modern Constitutional Law* (Rochester, NY: Lawyers Co-operative Publishing Co., 1969) 326–27.

126. Lee Epstein and Thomas G. Walker, *Constitutional Law for a Changing America: Rights, Liberties, and Justice*, 3rd ed. (Washington, DC: CQ Press, 1998) 574; Robert Hermann, Eric Single, and John Boston, *Counsel for the Poor: Criminal Defense in Urban America* (Lexington, MA: Lexington Books, 1977) 16.

127. Stephen Gillers, *Getting Justice: The Rights of People* (New York: Basic Books, 1971) 125.

128. Cook, *Constitutional Rights of the Accused* 8–100; Hermann, Single, and Boston, *Counsel for the Poor* 16.

129. Wayne R. LaFave, Jerold H. Israel, and Nancy J. King, *Criminal Procedure*, 3rd ed. (St. Paul, MN: West Publishing Co., 2000) 570 (suggesting that a "proceeding [that] involves no more than an extension of a trial ruling, and occurs shortly after trial, as in a post-verdict motion for judgment of acquittal, . . . should be treated as subject to the Sixth Amendment").

130. Weston and Wells, *Law Enforcement and Criminal Justice* 185 (noting that "[a]t least 90 percent of all persons convicted of crime in the United Sates are convicted by their plea of guilty"); see also Bodenhamer and Ely, *The Bill of Rights in Modern America* 103–4 (observing that early in the twentieth century plea bargaining led to a high percentage of cases being resolved by guilty pleas and that the expansion of access to counsel in the 1960s "did not lessen the percentage of cases resolved by plea bargains").

131. For general discussions of the *Gideon* case, see Anthony Lewis, *Gideon's Trumpet* (New York: Random House, 1964); Jerold H. Israel, "*Gideon v. Wainwright*: The 'Art' of Overruling," 1963 *Sup. Ct. Rev.* 211.

132. For discussion of the importance of the assistance of counsel during the process of plea bargaining and in guilty plea proceedings, see Beaney, "The Right to Counsel," in *The Rights of the Accused in Law and Action* 165–66; Weston and Wells, *Law Enforcement and Criminal Justice* 186–88; Dominick R. Vetri, Note, "Guilty Plea Bargaining: Compromises by Prosecutors to Secure Guilty Pleas," 112 *U. Pa. L. Rev.* (1964) 887–89.

133. For a thorough documentation of the problems and abuses generated by defense attorney involvement in the plea negotiation process and a conclusion that "the difficulty of providing effective representation within the guilty-plea system may reflect the intolerable nature of the system itself," see Albert W. Alschuler, "The Defense Attorney's Role in Plea Bargaining," 84 *Yale L.J.* (1975) 1313.

134. For discussions of Mempa v. Rhay and its implications, see Cook, *Constitutional Rights of the Accused* 8–23 to 8–28; Beaney, "The Right to Counsel," in *The Rights of the Accused in Law and Action* 157–61; George W. Pugh and M. Hampton Carver, "Due Process and Sentencing: From *Mapp* to *Mempa* to *McGautha*," 49 *Tex. L. Rev.* (1970) 27–30.

135. Cook, *Constitutional Rights of the Accused* 8–24 to 8–26 ("*Mempa* would appear to leave no doubt that counsel is at least required at actual sentencing"); Beaney, "The Right to Counsel," in *The Rights of the Accused in Law and Action* 161 ("Mempa v. Rhay holds that there is an absolute right to counsel at sentencing"); Pugh and Carver, "Due Process and Sentencing," 30 ("[I]t is clear from *Mempa* that the sentencing stage of criminal proceedings is a 'critical stage' and accordingly that the sixth amendment right to counsel . . . requires" counsel at that stage.). For a thoughtful pre-*Mempa* discussion of the roles of and need for counsel at sentencing proceedings, see Sanford H. Kadish, "The Advocate and the Expert-Counsel in the Peno-Correctional Process," 45 *Minn. L. Rev.* (1961) 806–12, 825–32.

136. Pugh and Carver, "Due Process and Sentencing," 25–40 (discussing the precedents supporting the right to counsel at sentencing and "what the right to counsel [at sentencing] implies" with respect to defendants' procedural entitlements in sentencing proceedings).

137. For brief discussions of the case law concerning the right to counsel on appeal, see Epstein and Walker, *Constitutional Law for a Changing America* 573–74; Klotter and Kanovitz, *Constitutional Law* 443; Cook, *Constitutional Rights of the Accused* 8–29 to 8–34.

138. James Fitzjames Stephen, *A History of the Criminal Law of England* (London: Macmillan and Co., 1883) 308–10.

139. Marc M. Arkin, "Rethinking the Constitutional Right to a Criminal Appeal," 39 *UCLA L. Rev.* (1992) 503 (discussing and challenging the accepted law and conventional wisdom regarding the lack of a constitutional right to an appeal in criminal cases); Alex S. Ellerson, "The Right to an Appeal and Appellate Procedural Reform," 91 *Colum. L. Rev.* (1991) 375–86 (arguing that a due process right to an appeal should be recognized in criminal cases); James E. Lobsenz, "A Constitutional Right to an Appeal: Guarding Against Unacceptable Risks of Erroneous Conviction," 8 *U. Puget Sound L. Rev.* (1985) 375–84 (same).

140. 28 U.S.C. §1291 (1994) (statutory basis for a criminal defendant's right to appeal in federal criminal cases). For examples of state statutory provisions that afford criminal defendants rights to appeal, see Cal. Penal Code § 1237 (Deering 2000) (California); Fla. Stat. Ann. § 924.06 (West 1999) (Florida); Iowa Code § 814.6 (1999) (Iowa); N.Y.

C.P.L.R. §§ 450.10–450.55 (Consol. 1999) (New York); Texas Crim. Proc. Code Ann. 44.02 (Vernon 2000) (Texas).

141. Francis A. Allen, Comment, "*Griffin v. Illinois*: Antecedents and Aftermath," 25 *U. Chi. L. Rev.* (1957) 151 (discussing the significance of Griffin v. Illinois).

142. Garcia, *The Sixth Amendment in Modern American Jurisprudence* 10–11 (discussing the Court's opinion in Douglas v. California).

143. Beaney, "The Right to Counsel," in *The Rights of the Accused in Law and Action* 157 (suggesting that there may well be a greater need for counsel in discretionary appeals than in appeals as of right).

144. Garcia, *The Sixth Amendment in Modern American Jurisprudence* 13–15 (criticizing the decision in Ross v. Moffitt).

145. For brief discussions of the law concerning the right to assistance in collateral attacks on criminal convictions, see Cook, *Constitutional Rights of the Accused* 8–34 to 8–37; LaFave, Israel, and King, *Criminal Procedure* 559–62.

146. LaFave, Israel, and King, *Criminal Procedure* 560 (suggesting a "stronger case could be made" for the right to counsel in collateral challenges to convictions than in discretionary appeals of convictions).

147. For commentary critical of the Court's opinion in Murray v. Giarratano and supportive of a right to counsel in collateral challenges by capital convicts, see Clive A. Stafford Smith and Remy Voisin Starns, "Folly by Fiat: Pretending that Death Row Inmates Can Represent Themselves in State Capital Post-Conviction Proceedings," 45 *Loy. L. Rev.* (1999) 55; Brad Snyder, Note, "Disparate Impact on Death Row: *M.L.B.* and the Indigent's Right to Counsel at Capital State Postconviction Proceedings," 107 *Yale L.J.* (1998) 2211; Alice McGill, Comment, "*Murray v. Giarratano*: The Right to Counsel in Postconviction Proceedings in Death Penalty Cases," 18 *Hastings Const. L.Q.* (1990) 211; Michael A. Mello, "Is There a Federal Constitutional Right to Counsel in Capital Post-Conviction Proceedings?" 79 *J. Crim. L. & Criminology* (1989) 1065.

148. For pre-*Martinez* discussions of the constitutional right to represent oneself on appeal, see John F. Decker, "The Sixth Amendment Right to Shoot Oneself in the Foot: An Assessment of the Guarantee of Self-Representation Twenty Years After *Faretta*," 6 *Seton Hall Const. L.J.* (1996) 590–95; Michael C. Krikava and Charlann E. Winking, "Right of an Indigent Criminal Defendant to Proceed *Pro Se* on Appeal: By Statute or Constitution, a Necessary Evil," 15 *Wm. Mitchell L. Rev.* (1989) 103.

149. For general discussions of the right to effective assistance and the ineffective assistance of counsel doctrine, see John M. Burkoff and Hope L. Hudson, *Ineffective Assistance of Counsel* (New York: Clark Boardman Callaghan, 1993); Garcia, *The Sixth Amendment in Modern American Jurisprudence* 30–40.

150. Richard Klein, "The Emperor *Gideon* Has No Clothes: The Empty Promise of the Constitutional Right to Effective Assistance of Counsel," 13 *Hastings Const. L.Q.* (1986) 663–66 (discussing the vital importance of counsel's preparation and investigation); Joshua Dressler, *Understanding Criminal Procedure*, 2nd ed. (New York: Matthew Bender, 1997) 531 (asserting that counsel has a basic duty to investigate thoroughly); David Fellman, *The Defendant's Rights Today* (Madison: University of Wisconsin Press, 1976) 218 (noting that for accused to enjoy "effective assistance," defense counsel "should have adequate time to prepare a defense properly").

151. Charles H. Whitebread and Christopher Slobogin, *Criminal Procedure: An Analysis of Cases and Concepts*, 4th ed. (New York: Foundation Press, 2000) (discussing the various categories of impermissible state interference with defense counsel's perform-

ance); Gary Goodpaster, "The Adversary System, Advocacy, and Effective Assistance of Counsel in Criminal Cases," 14 *N.Y.U. Rev. L. & Soc. Change* (1986) 64 (stating that "counsel might be ineffective because she was operating under some state imposed disability such as a short time to prepare"); Klein, "The Emperor *Gideon* Has No Clothes," 638 (discussing various types of trial court interference that inhibit counsel from rendering effective assistance).

152. Burkoff and Hudson, *Ineffective Assistance of Counsel* 5–8 (noting that lower "[c]ourts have generally been unsympathetic to th[e] argument" that "counsel was appointed so late in the process that adequate preparation was impossible").

153. Whitebread and Slobogin, *Criminal Procedure* 942–43 (discussing *Powell, Avery*, and *Chambers* and asserting that "tardy appointment of counsel is not always a violation of the Sixth Amendment"); Wayne R. LaFave, Jerold H. Israel, and Nancy J. King, *Criminal Procedure*, 3rd ed. (St. Paul, MN: West Publishing, 2000) 610–11 (concluding that late appointment of counsel establishes a *per se* violation of the Sixth Amendment only in a rare, extreme case and that otherwise a limitation on counsel's preparation time is a factor that bears upon the issue of counsel's effectiveness); Joseph G. Cook, *Constitutional Rights of the Accused: Trial Rights* (Rochester, NY: Lawyers' Cooperative Publishing Co., 1974) 122–25 (discussing the issue of inadequate preparation time for counsel and noting that "a limitation on the amount of time available for preparation does not per se establish a denial of the assistance of counsel").

154. Fellman, *The Defendant's Rights Today* 219 (asserting that "an attorney . . . is entitled to a continuance if the circumstances warrant" and that "it is error for a judge to deny a motion for a continuance where he has allowed no time at all for counsel to prepare or only a very small amount of time").

155. Jerold H. Israel, Yale Kamisar, and Wayne R. LaFave, *Criminal Procedure and the Constitution: Leading Supreme Court Cases and Introductory Text* (St. Paul, MN: West Publishing, 2000) 274 (noting that "the right to counsel" is "sometimes called 'the most pervasive right' of the accused or 'the master key' to all rights"); Charles J. Ogletree Jr., "An Essay on the New Public Defender for the 21st Century," 58 *Law & Contemp. Probs.* (1995) 82. ("Providing competent counsel is the best means of ensuring the proper operation of the constitutional safeguards designed to protect the innocent and less culpable from unfair punishment.")

156. For a concise, insightful discussion of the Supreme Court's precedents involving state interference with counsel's full participation in the adversary process, see LaFave, Israel, and King, *Criminal Procedure* 606–8.

157. James Fitzjames Stephen, *A History of the Criminal Law of England* (London: Macmillian, 1883) 326.

158. Goodpaster, "The Adversary System, Advocacy, and Effective Assistance of Counsel in Criminal Cases," 87 (discussing the important role that counsel plays in shaping the meaning of evidence for the fact-finder and asserting that a "[t]rial is a contest over the meaning of evidence").

159. Klein, "The Emperor *Gideon* Has No Clothes," 667–68 (discussing the importance of two-way communication between defense counsel and the accused); see also Sheldon Krantz, Charles Smith, et al., *Right to Counsel in Criminal Cases: The Mandate of Argersinger v. Hamlin* (Cambridge, MA: Ballinger Publishing Co., 1976) 179–82 (discussing the need and reasons for consultation between defense attorney and defendant).

160. Klein, "The Emperor *Gideon* Has No Clothes," 667 (recognizing the relationship between communication and adequate investigation by counsel).

161. Jay Sterling Silver, "Equality of Arms and the Adversarial Process: A New Constitutional Right," 1990 *Wis. L. Rev.* 1025–41 (thoroughly addressing the relationship between consultation and the proper operation of the adversarial system of justice).

162. Silver, "Equality of Arms and the Adversarial Process," 1027, 1029 (mentioning the significance of the defendant's feelings that the process has been "just").

163. Joseph G. Cook, *Constitutional Rights of the Accused*, 3rd ed. (Rochester, NY: Lawyers' Co-operative Publishing Co., 1996) 8–84 to 8–85 (summarizing the *Geders* case).

164. See Silver, "Equality of Arms and the Adversarial Process," 1007 et seq., for a thorough examination and discussion of the Court's opinion in Perry v. Leeke.

165. Silver, "Equality of Arms and the Adversarial Process," 1013–16 (discussing the practice of witness sequestration and its purposes).

166. Silver, "Equality of Arms and the Adversarial Process," 1030 (contending that a brief recess between direct examination and cross-examination of the accused is a "critical stage" during which he is entitled to consultation with counsel).

167. Silver, "Equality of Arms and the Adversarial Process," 1017, 1022, 1025 (asserting that the Perry v. Leeke Court "draws ill-reasoned conclusions, fabricates facts, makes unfounded presumptions, cites cases with respect to propositions for which they do not stand or which they actually reject and fails to cite case law unfavorable to its position" and maintaining that the "majority opinion reveals a distrust of criminal defense attorneys and a lack of insight into cross-examination" that "have ominous implications for the adversarial process").

168. Silver, "Equality of Arms and the Adversarial Process," 1022 (suggesting that the Perry v. Leeke opinion "breeds uncertainty").

169. Silver, "Equality of Arms and the Adversarial Process," 1022 (suggesting that it is not easy to distinguish between discussion of the accused's testimony and other "trial-related matters").

170. Silver, "Equality of Arms and the Adversarial Process," 1024–25 (asserting that "it is likely that cross-examination would be ineffective if a defendant were permitted to consult with counsel at the very moment the cross-examiner had him on the ropes or was about to spring a carefully laid trap").

171. Kevin McMunigal, "Rethinking Attorney Conflict of Interest Doctrine," *5 Geo. J. Legal Ethics* (1992) 856–59 (suggesting that meaning of attorney "loyalty" is unclear and that concept should either be more clearly defined or "jettison[ed]").

172. McMunigal, "Rethinking Attorney Conflict of Interest Doctrine," 843–47 (describing and critiquing various definitions of the terms "conflict of interest").

173. For a variety of illustrative situations giving rise to conflicts of interest, see Jeffrey Kirchmeier, "Drink, Drugs, and Drowsiness: The Constitutional Right to Effective Assistance of Counsel and the *Strickland* Prejudice Requirement," *75 Neb. L. Rev.* (1996) 453 n.133; Jeff Brown, "Disqualification of the Public Defender: Toward a New Protocol for Resolving Conflicts of Interest," 31 *U.S.F.L. Rev.* (1996) 15–16; McMunigal, "Rethinking Attorney Conflict of Interest Doctrine, 829–30; Bruce A. Green, "Her Brother's Keeper: The Prosecutor's Responsibility When Defense Counsel Has a Potential Conflict of Interest," 16 *Am. J. Crim. L.* (1989) 328–29; Gary T. Lowenthal, "Successive Representation by Criminal Lawyers," 93 *Yale L.J.* (1983) 18–28, 35–64.

174. Gary T. Lowenthal, "Why Representing Multiple Defendants Is a Bad Idea Al-

most Always," 3 *Crim. Just.* (1988) 6 (noting that "neither the courts nor the bar have prohibited multiple representation of criminal defendants").

175. For discussions of reasons that might militate in favor of joint representation, see Brown, "Disqualification of the Public Defender," 11; Lowenthal, "Why Representing Multiple Defendants Is a Bad Idea," 6; "Developments in the Law—Conflicts of Interest in the Legal Profession. IV. Conflicts of Interest and the Criminal Lawyer," 94 *Harv. L. Rev.* (1981) 1373, 1380–81; see also Nancy J. Moore, "Conflicts of Interest in the Simultaneous Representation of Multiple Clients: A Proposed Solution to the Current Confusion and Controversy," 61 *Tex. L. Rev.* (1983) 275–77 (concluding that the benefits of multiple representation tend to be overestimated and that "it benefits criminal codefendants only infrequently").

176. For consideration of the nature and extent of the risks engendered by joint representation of codefendants, see Brown, "Disqualification of the Public Defender," 11–13; Moore, "Conflicts of Interest in the Simultaneous Representation of Multiple Clients," 273–75; "Conflicts of Interest and the Criminal Lawyer," 1381–83.

177. Kirchmeier, "Drink, Drugs, and Drowsiness," 450; Lowenthal, "Successive Representation by Criminal Lawyers," 40–41; "Developments in the Law—Conflicts of Interest in the Legal Profession," 1388–89.

178. Joshua Dressler, *Understanding Criminal Procedure*, 2nd ed. (New York: Matthew Bender, 1997) 540–41; Green, "Her Brother's Keeper," 331; Richard Klein, "The Relationship of the Court and Defense Counsel: The Impact on Competent Representation and Proposals for Reform," 29 *B.C.L. Rev.* (1988) 573–75.

179. Lowenthal, "Successive Representation by Criminal Lawyers," 40–42 (advocating application of *Holloway* to a conflict of interest arising from a different source); see also Klein, "The Relationship of the Court and Defense Counsel," 573–76 (suggesting that duty of inquiry imposed by *Holloway* should be extended beyond the conflict of interest contexts to situations where defense attorneys are not adequately performing their functions).

180. Bruce A. Green, " 'Through A Glass, Darkly': How the Court Sees Motions to Disqualify Criminal Defense Lawyers," 89 *Colum. L. Rev.* (1989) 1201 (decision in Cuyler v. Sullivan not to impose general obligation on judges to inquire into potential conflicts rested on assumption that attorneys will behave ethically in determining whether joint representation will give rise to a conflict of interest).

181. For discussions of the Court's opinion in Cuyler v. Sullivan, see Green, " 'Through a Glass Darkly,' " 1206–8, 1224–25; Lowenthal, "Successive Representation by Criminal Lawyers," 26–28; "Developments in the Law—Conflicts of Interest in the Legal Profession," 1390.

182. Garcia, *The Sixth Amendment in Modern American Jurisprudence* 45–48 (discussing *Nix* and accusing the *Nix* majority of "issuing [a] skewed perspective on the problem of client perjury").

183. Green, "Her Brother's Keeper," 331 (discussing possibility of waiver of "right to an independent attorney"); Lowenthal, "Why Representing Multiple Defendants Is a Bad Idea," 6 (considering issues raised by waivers of right to separate representation).

184. Lowenthal, "Why Representing Multiple Defendants Is a Bad Idea," 6 (asserting that the "preferable" approach is to examine record for actual conflict despite purported waiver).

185. "Developments in the Law—Conflicts of Interest in the Legal Profession," 1393–95 (outlining arguments against allowing waivers of loyal representation in cases of conflict and in situations involving multiple representation).

186. For discussions and criticism of the *Wheat* opinion and of its implications, see Garcia, *The Sixth Amendment in Modern American Jurisprudence* 38–40; Eugene L. Shapiro, "The Sixth Amendment Right to Counsel of Choice: An Exercise in the Weighing of Unarticulated Values," 43 *S.C. L. Rev.* (1992) 345–56; William J. Stuntz, "Waiving Rights in Criminal Procedure," 75 *Va. L. Rev.* (1989) 797–801.

187. For discussions of the topic of attorney incompetence and the constitutional law in this area, see John M. Burkoff and Hope L. Hudson, *Ineffective Assistance of Counsel* (New York: Clark Boardman Callaghan, 1993); Donald A. Dripps, "Ineffective Assistance of Counsel: The Case for an *Ex Ante* Parity Standard," 88 *J. Crim. L. & Criminology* (1997) 242; Kirchmeier, "Drink, Drugs, and Drowsiness," 425; William S. Geimer, "A Decade of *Strickland*'s Tin Horn: Doctrinal and Practical Undermining of the Right to Counsel," 4 *Wm. & Mary Bill of Rts. J.* (1995) 91; Klein, "The Emperor *Gideon* Has No Clothes," 625.

188. Burkoff and Hudson, *Ineffective Assistance of Counsel* 1–3 ("Ineffective assistance of counsel is one of the most—if not the most—common appeal grounds asserted by convicted criminal defendants as appellants."); *Id.* at v ("The number of reported state and federal cases in which ineffective assistance was raised . . . jumped from about 700 in 1985 to 1,700 in 1992, a 250 percent increase in less than a decade!").

189. Klein, "The Emperor *Gideon* Has No Clothes," 629 (noting that "the Supreme Court [has] clearly stated that 'defendants . . . are entitled to the *effective* assistance of *competent* counsel' "); Martin C. Calhoun, Note, "How to Thread the Needle: Toward a Checklist-Based Standard for Evaluating Ineffective Assistance of Counsel Claims," 77 *Geo. L.J.* (1988) 418 (observing that "the Supreme Court [has] . . . recognized effective assistance of counsel as a separate right rooted in the sixth amendment").

190. For discussions of the considerable magnitude of and reasons for the problem of defense counsel incompetence, see Klein, "The Emperor *Gideon* Has No Clothes," 657–63; Vivian O. Berger, "The Supreme Court and Defense Counsel: Old Roads, New Paths—A Dead End?" 86 *Colum. L. Rev.* (1986) 60–64; Barbara R. Levine, "Preventing Defense Counsel Error—An Analysis of Some Ineffective Assistance of Counsel Claims and Their Implications for Professional Regulation," 15 *U. Tol. L. Rev.* (1984) 1295–1300; William W. Schwarzer, "Dealing with Incompetent Counsel—The Trial Judge's Role," 93 *Harv. L. Rev.* (1980) 634.

191. For discussions of the various standards adopted by the lower courts in the years prior to the Supreme Court's intervention, see Kirchmeier, "Drink, Drugs, and Drowsiness," 431–34; Geimer, "A Decade of *Strickland*'s Tin Horn," 164–68; Berger, "The Supreme Court and Defense Counsel," 65–74; Joel Jay Finer, "Ineffective Assistance of Counsel," 58 *Cornell L. Rev.* (1973) 1078–81; see also Annotation, "Modern Status of Rule as to Test in Federal Court of Effective Representation by Counsel," 26 A.L.R. Fed. 218; Gregory G. Sarno, Annotation, "Modern Status of Rules and Standards in State Courts as to the Adequacy of Defense Counsel's Representation of Criminal Client," 2 A.L.R.4th 27.

192. Berger, "The Supreme Court and Defense Counsel," 71–73 (documenting various formulations of the prejudice demand and noting that most courts did require a showing of prejudice).

193. Kirchmeier, "Drink, Drugs, and Drowsiness," 434–40 (discussing *Strickland* standards); Calhoun, Note, "How to Thread the Needle," 422–37 (discussing *Strickland*); Berger, "The Supreme Court and Defense Counsel," 74–100 (thoroughly examining the *Strickland* decision); see also Geimer, "A Decade of *Strickland*'s Tin Horn," 91–95

(suggesting that *Strickland* was detrimental to defendants' right to effective assistance of counsel).

194. Martin Marcus, "Above the Fray or Into the Breach: The Judge's Role in New York's Adversarial System of Criminal Justice," 57 *Brook. L. Rev.* (1992) 1200 ("Ineffective assistance of counsel disturbs the assumptions of the adversarial model, since neither truth nor justice may result if the prosecution fights hard for its position but the defendant's advocate is not equally rigorous.").

195. Richard L. Gabriel, "The *Strickland* Standard for Claims of Ineffective Assistance of Counsel: Emasculating the Sixth Amendment in the Guise of Due Process," 134 *U. Pa. L. Rev.* (1986) 1269–71 (explaining Sixth Amendment and adversarial system rationales for requirement of "effective" assistance).

196. Calhoun, "How to Thread the Needle," 425, 434–36 (discussing and criticizing the Court's rejection of a checklist approach to counsel's responsibilities); Berger, "The Supreme Court and Defense Counsel," 81–87 (discussing the Court's refusal to adopt a checklist of specific duties for defense attorneys); Klein, "The Emperor *Gideon* Has No Clothes," 654–55 (asserting there is a need for more particularized standards of attorney performance).

197. Klein, "The Emperor *Gideon* Has No Clothes," 650–54 (summarizing the professional standards pertaining to competent representation by defense counsel).

198. Finer, "Ineffective Assistance of Counsel," 1085–86 (discussing counsel's duty to know the law).

199. Gary Goodpaster, "The Adversary System, Advocacy, and Effective Assistance of Counsel in Criminal Cases," 14 *N.Y.U. Rev. L. & Soc. Change* (1986) 90–91 (citing the failure to investigate as one of the common "deficiencies of criminal defense attorneys"); Levine, "Preventing Defense Counsel Error," 1374 (noting that the failure to "investigate a defense or seek the suppression of evidence" is a frequent source of ineffective assistance claims); Dorothy Linder Maddi, "Trial Advocacy Competence: The Judicial Perspective," 1978 *Am. B. Found. Res. J.* (1978) 144 (observing that in a survey of trial judges "[i]nadequate preparation was identified as the most prevalent form of incompetence"); Finer, "Ineffective Assistance of Counsel," 1086–87 (addressing the duty to investigate facts and prepare the case).

200. Levine, "Preventing Defense Counsel Error," 1357–62 (discussing common defense counsel errors at trial such as "failures to object to inadmissible evidence, improper prosecutorial arguments or erroneous jury instructions"); Finer, "Ineffective Assistance of Counsel," 1092–1108 (exploring various kinds of failures by counsel to participate in the adversary process).

201. Klein, "The Emperor *Gideon* Has No Clothes," 667–69 (discussing the duty to communicate and consult with the defendant); see also Steven Zeidman, "To Plead or Not to Plead: Effective Assistance and Client-Centered Counseling," 39 *B.C. L. Rev.* (1998) 841 (asserting that defense counsel's obligation to consult with the defendant even extends to the pleading stage).

202. Kirchmeier, "Drink, Drugs, and Drowsiness," 450–55 (discussing conflict of interest cases and absence of prejudice demand when attorney ineffectiveness is due to conflict).

203. Geimer, "A Decade of *Strickland*'s Tin Horn," 155–60 (contending that *Strickland* standard for deficient performance readily permits "denial of claims," fails "to provide reviewing courts with even a semblance of a bright line to minimize inconsistent application," and "permits the worst lawyering"); Calhoun, "How to Thread the

Needle," 431 (referring to "*Strickland*'s excessively deferential performance prong"); Klein, "The Emperor *Gideon* Has No Clothes," 640 (noting that the *Strickland* Court, "in discussing the [deficient performance] prong . . . , sent a clear message to lower courts that there is a strong presumption that counsel's conduct was constitutionally adequate").

204. Kirchmeier, "Drink, Drugs, and Drowsiness," 465–74 (maintaining that there should be a presumption of prejudice for cases where a lawyer has been sleeping, intoxicated, or mentally impaired).

205. Geimer, "A Decade of *Strickland*'s Tin Horn," 131–38 (contending that *Strickland*'s prejudice demand "involves 'unarticulated harmless error' " analysis that has been turned on its head and has made it more difficult for defendants who are denied competent assistance to get relief); Calhoun, Note, "How to Thread the Needle," 433, 455 (referring to the prejudice requirement as "a big mistake" by the Court and asserting that it turns the "basic constitutional right to effective assistance of counsel into the proverbial 'eye of the needle' "); Gabriel, "The *Strickland* Standard for Claims of Ineffective Assistance of Counsel," 1276–79 (claiming that *Strickland* prejudice requirement effectively shifts burden of proving harmless error from the state to the defendant).

206. Gabriel, "The *Strickland* Standard for Claims of Ineffective Assistance of Counsel," 1279–81 (arguing that the "reasonable probability" of a different result standard is "unworkable on a practical level" and that satisfaction of that standard is "virtually impossible").

207. For a thorough summary and discussion of Lockhart v. Fretwell, see Jennifer N. Foster, Note, "*Lockhart v. Fretwell*: Using Hindsight to Evaluate Prejudice in Claims of Ineffective Assistance of Counsel," 72 *N.C. L. Rev.* (1994) 1369.

208. Vivian Berger, "The Chiropractor as Brain Surgeon: Defense Lawyering in Capital Cases," 18 *N.Y.U. Rev. L. & Soc. Change* (1990–1991) 251 (maintaining that "*Strickland*'s strong presumption of reasonable performance, coupled with its tough prejudice test, make most sixth amendment challenges hopeless").

209. Berger, "The Supreme Court and Defense Counsel," 89–96 (discussing and criticizing the Court's rationales for the prejudice requirement); Gabriel, "The *Strickland* Standard for Claims of Ineffective Assistance of Counsel," 1266–69 (criticizing the *Strickland* opinion for focusing on the correctness of the result and neglecting the "legitimacy of the means" by which the result is reached).

210. For a critical perspective on the "reasonable probability" standard, see Gabriel, "The *Strickland* Standard for Claims of Ineffective Assistance of Counsel," 1281 (maintaining that *Strickland*'s reasonable probability of a different result standard demands that the accused prove something that is "virtually impossible" to prove).

211. For a different perspective on this question, see Dripps, "Ineffective Assistance of Counsel: The Case for an *Ex Ante* Parity Standard," 286–306 (proposing a standard for "assessing the adequacy of defense counsel prior to the trial" in order to prevent incompetent representation); Marcus, "Above the Fray or into the Breach," 1193 (contending that not only are there appropriate ways for judges to intervene at trial to assure competent representation, but there are also measures that a judge may take in the pleading and sentencing phases to protect the defendant's right to effective assistance of counsel); William W. Schwarzer, "Dealing with Incompetent Counsel—The Trial Judge's Role," 93 *Harv. L. Rev.* (1980) 649–65 (proposing guidelines for judicial monitoring of defense counsel's performance and for intervention to prevent inadequate representation).

212. Gabriel, "The *Strickland* Standard for Claims of Ineffective Assistance of Coun-

sel," 1269–72 (asserting that counsel is one of the "procedural rights [that] must be protected in their own right").

213. For the view that the *Strickland* doctrine has not provided adequate protection in capital cases, see Ellen Kreitzberg, "Death Without Justice," 35 *Santa Clara L. Rev.* (1995) 485 (arguing that the *Strickland* standard "fails to ensure effective representations in capital cases" and that the *Strickland* decision deserves "much of the blame" for the courts' failures to "impose the death penalty in a manner that is consistent with the constitutional requirements"); Ira Robbins, 1990 A.B.A. Crim. Just. Sec.—Task Force on Death Penalty Habeas Corpus, *Toward a More Just and Effective System of Reviewing State Death Penalty Cases*, 53 (observing that "[e]ven in [death penalty] cases in which the performances of counsel have passed constitutional muster under *Strickland v. Washington* . . . , the representation provided has nevertheless been of very poor quality"); Berger, "The Chiropractor as Brain Surgeon," 245 (asserting that in capital cases "defense counsel too often deliver—and courts at all levels too often tolerate, when indeed they do not encourage—performance so shoddy as to render the law in its application a mockery of the sixth *and* eighth amendments").

214. Zeidman, "To Plead or Not to Plead," 849 (discussing the constitutional obligations of criminal defense attorneys during the pleading stage and arguing that lawyers have the obligation to inform their clients "on the wisdom of accepting or rejecting a plea"); Marcus, "Above the Fray or Into the Breach," 1210 ("Just as a defendant may have ineffective assistance of counsel at trial, so defense counsel may inadequately serve the defendant in negotiating and entering into a plea"); but see Goodpaster, "The Adversary System, Advocacy, and Effective Assistance of Counsel in Criminal Cases," 81 ("The ineffective assistance problem is much harder to reach in guilty plea cases because there is no evidentiary record from which to assess counsel's alleged failings."); Albert W. Alschuler, "Personal Failure, Institutional Failure, and the Sixth Amendment," 14 *N.Y.U. Rev. L. & Soc. Change* (1986) 149 (arguing that, unlike the trial setting, our "plea negotiation system insulates attorneys from review and often makes it impossible to determine whether inadequate representation has occurred").

215. Berger, "The Supreme Court and Defense Counsel," 109–12 (discussing the application of *Strickland* to "claims of inadequate assistance rendered in connection with guilty pleas"); Klein, "The Emperor *Gideon* Has No Clothes," 669–72 (discussing inadequate representation during the plea bargaining process); see also Emily Rubin, Note, "Ineffective Assistance of Counsel and Guilty Pleas: Toward a Paradigm of Informed Consent," 80 *U. Va. L. Rev.* (1994) 1699 (discussing ineffective assistance in the context of plea bargaining and proposing a model test).

216. For critical assessments of Hill v. Lockhart, see Richard Klein, "The Relationship of the Court and Defense Counsel: The Impact on Competent Representation and Proposals for Reform," 29 *B.C. L. Rev.* (1988) 549–52 (disapproving of the *Lockhart* standard for ineffective assistance as "extraordinarily harsh," asserting that proof of "prejudice to courts that desire finality will be most difficult," and contending that the formulation of the prejudice element "overlooks the many serious ways a defendant suffers from inadequate counsel"); Rubin, "Ineffective Assistance of Counsel and Guilty Pleas," 1703–6 (criticizing the Hill v. Lockhart decision and arguing that the prejudice standard demands too much proof from defendants and is underinclusive, excluding some defendants who are significantly harmed by counsel's incompetent assistance in guilty plea situations).

217. Klein, "The Emperor *Gideon* Has No Clothes," 673–75 (discussing the need for effective assistance of counsel in the sentencing phase of a criminal proceeding).

218. Lissa Griffin, "The Right to Effective Assistance of Appellate Counsel," 97 *W. Va. L. Rev.* (1994) 15–19 (discussing the constitutional foundations for the right to assistance of counsel on appeal of criminal convictions); Eduardo I. Sanchez, Note, "The Right to Counsel and Frivolous Appeals: Assistance to the Court or Advocacy for the Indigent Client—Which is the Real *McCoy*?" 43 *U. Miami L. Rev.* (1989) 931–33 (discussing the due process and equal protection sources for the right to appellate assistance).

219. Griffin, "The Right to Effective Assistance," 36–37 (listing the duties of appellate counsel).

220. Griffin, "The Right to Effective Assistance," 4 (concluding that the Strickland v. Washington standard for ineffectiveness of counsel should apply at the appellate level and discussing how the application of that standard should differ on appeal).

221. Griffin, "The Right to Effective Assistance," 37–41 (asserting that the differences between the trial forum and the appellate forum require differences in the standards used to judge ineffective assistance of counsel).

222. Griffin, "The Right to Effective Assistance," 42–44 (maintaining that the differences between the trial and appellate courts and the functions of counsel at each level make it possible to detail specific duties and rules for effective assistance of counsel at the appellate level).

223. Griffin, "The Right to Effective Assistance," 22–23, 41–42 (concluding that an attorney's failure to secure access to an appeal is *per se* deficient and prejudicial).

224. Griffin, "The Right to Effective Assistance," 26–31 (discussing Jones v. Barnes and ineffective assistance claims based on failures to raise issues on appeal); Vivian O. Berger, "The Supreme Court and Defense Counsel: Old Roads, New Paths—A Dead End?" 86 *Colum. L. Rev.* (1986) 29–48 (discussing and critiquing Jones v. Barnes); Karen Krisher, "*Jones v. Barnes*, the Sixth, and the Fourteenth Amendments: Whose Appeal Is It Anyway?" 47 *Ohio St. L.J.* (1986) 179 (analyzing Jones v. Barnes).

225. Griffin, "The Right to Effective Assistance," 44–47 (concluding that the standard for judging whether appellate counsel was ineffective regarding the selection of issues should be whether "the omitted issue or issues are of sufficient merit that a reasonably competent lawyer would have raised them on appeal").

226. For an argument to the contrary, see Griffin, "The Right to Effective Assistance," 47 (asserting that there is "no justification for a separate prejudice requirement in evaluating ineffectiveness of appellate counsel claims").

227. Griffin, "The Right to Effective Assistance," 22–23, 41–42 (concluding that an attorney's failure to secure access to an appeal is *per se* deficient and prejudicial).

228. Frederick D. Junkin, Note, "The Right to Counsel in 'Frivolous' Criminal Appeals: A Reevaluation of the Guarantees of *Anders v. California*," 67 *Tex. L. Rev.* (1988) 205–10 (contending that if "counsel violates *Anders*' requirements, an appellate court should apply a per se rule and grant a defendant a new appeal" without further inquiry and offering two justifications for that approach).

229. Junkin, "The Right to Counsel in 'Frivolous' Criminal Appeals," 182–83 (noting that the situation where a lawyer concludes that an appeal has no merit "is particularly troublesome, because it forces counsel to balance conflicting ethical obligations").

230. Junkin, "The Right to Counsel in 'Frivolous' Criminal Appeals," 181–95 (discussing and defending the *Anders* opinion).

231. For criticism of the Court's conclusion, see Sanchez, "The Right to Counsel and

Frivolous Appeals," 935–43 (arguing that *McCoy* is inconsistent with the spirit of *Anders* and with the due process and equal protection principles that underlie the entitlement to the assistance of counsel in the appellate process).

232. For general accounts of the history and evolution of the harmless error doctrine, see David McCord, "The 'Trial'/'Structural' Error Dichotomy: Erroneous and Not Harmless," 45 *U. Kan. L. Rev.* (1997) 1403–7; James Edward Wicht III, "There Is No Such Thing as a Harmless Constitutional Error: Returning to a Rule of Automatic Reversal," 12 *BYU J. Pub. L.* (1997) 75–84; Harry T. Edwards, "To Err Is Human But Not Always Harmless: When Should Legal Error Be Tolerated?" 70 *N.Y.U. L. Rev.* (1995) 1173–80.

233. For a critical view, see Wicht, "There Is No Such Thing as a Harmless Constitutional Error," 100–107 (contending that the costs of applying the harmless error rule to "constitutional errors" are substantial and advocating a return to the automatic reversal rule for all constitutional errors).

234. Wicht, "There Is No Such Thing as a Harmless Constitutional Error," 75–76 (providing a graphic illustration of an unwarranted reversal for an insignificant error in the era "[p]rior to the advent of the harmless error rule" and concluding that at that time "the threat of convictions being reversed on such minor technicalities was great").

235. Wicht, "There Is No Such Thing as a Harmless Constitutional Error," 97–99 (arguing that with regard to violation of a constitutional right the balance always tips in favor of vindication of the right and justifies abandonment of the harmless error rule).

236. For discussions of the application of the harmless error rule to constitutional violations, see McCord, "The 'Trial'/'Structural' Error Dichotomy," 1401; Wicht, "There Is No Such Thing as a Harmless Constitutional Error," 73; Daniel J. Meltzer, "Harmless Error and Constitutional Remedies," 61 *U. Chi. L. Rev.* (1994) 1; Craig Goldblatt, Comment, "Harmless Error as Constitutional Common Law: Congress's Power to Reverse *Arizona v. Fulminante*," 60 *U. Chi. L. Rev.* (1993) 985; Tom Stacy and Kim Dayton, "Rethinking Harmless Constitutional Error," 88 *Colum. L. Rev.* (1988) 79.

237. Edwards, "To Err Is Human But Not Always Harmless," 1174–75, 1178–80, 1191–93, 1199–1202 (discussing the *Kotteakos* standard and its focus on the effect of an error on the jury's decision rather than on the guilt of the defendant).

238. For criticisms of the application of harmless error analysis to constitutional errors, see Wicht, "There Is No Such Thing as a Harmless Constitutional Error," 78–79, 86–93, 97–99 (noting that the doctrine of harmless constitutional error is a relatively modern development, criticizing the decision to apply harmless error analysis to constitutional violations, and maintaining that no constitutional errors should be harmless); Stacy and Dayton, "Rethinking Harmless Constitutional Error," 81–82 (criticizing the modern harmless error doctrine applied to constitutional errors).

239. Meltzer, "Harmless Error and Constitutional Remedies," 26–28 (asserting that the best explanation for the constitutional harmless error doctrine is that it is "constitutional common law"); Goldblatt, "Harmless Error as Constitutional Common Law," 986, 105–12 (arguing that harmless error rules are constitutional common law that can be changed by Congress).

240. Wicht, "There Is No Such Thing as a Harmless Constitutional Error," 80–82 (stating that the Supreme Court "currently holds that most constitutional errors can be harmless" and providing examples that illustrate the dramatic expansion of the constitutional harmless error doctrine).

241. McCord, "The 'Trial'/'Structural' Error Dichotomy," 1412–16 (noting that the Court "actually proposed three definitions of trial error" which "in fact . . . are different

and largely inconsistent" and have "significant ambiguities" and discussing those three definitions).

242. For a contrary view, see Wicht, "There Is No Such Thing as a Harmless Constitutional Error," 93–97 (arguing that the standards are unworkable and that courts cannot accurately measure the impact of constitutional errors).

243. For a thorough consideration and criticism of the Court's trial error–structural error dichotomy, see McCord, "The 'Trial'/'Structural' Error Dichotomy," 1401; see also, Wicht, "There Is No Such Thing as a Harmless Constitutional Error," 84–86 (criticizing the distinction between trial and structural errors).

244. Bruce A McGovern, Note, "Invalid Waivers of Counsel as Harmless Errors: Judicial Economy or a Return to *Betts v. Brady*," 56 *Fordham L. Rev.* (1987) 431 (concluding that if the error that a court finds is an invalid waiver of the right to counsel, harmless error analysis should not apply).

245. Richard L. Gabriel, Comment, "The *Strickland* Standard for Claims of Ineffective Assistance of Counsel: Emasculating the Sixth Amendment in the Guise of Due Process," 134 *U. Pa. L. Rev.* (1986) 1279–81 (arguing that the "reasonable probability" of a different result standard is "unworkable" because of the "virtual impossibility of proving that a jury would have reached a different result").

246. William Geimer, "A Decade of *Strickland*'s Tin Horn: Doctrinal and Practical Undermining of the Right to Counsel," 4 *Wm. & Mary Bill of Rts. J.* (1995) 131 (observing that the *Strickland* prejudice requirement is harmless error analysis"; Gabriel, "The *Strickland* Standard for Claims of Ineffective Assistance of Counsel," 1278 (same).

247. Geimer, "A Decade of *Strickland*'s Tin Horn," 131–33 (contending that the *Strickland* prejudice requirement "turn[s] harmless error on its head"); Gabriel, "The *Strickland* Standard for Claims of Ineffective Assistance of Counsel," 1278–79 (asserting that the *Strickland* prejudice requirement "effectively shifts the burden of proving harmless error from the state to the defendant" and concluding that "the Court in *Strickland* erred" in doing so).

248. For an argument that this factor should not matter, see Gabriel, "The *Strickland* Standard for Claims of Ineffective Assistance of Counsel," 1278–79 (arguing that the fact the state did not cause the deprivation when counsel's ineffectiveness is due to incompetence is "irrelevant" to the determination of who should have the burden of proving harm).

249. Harvey E. Bines, "Remedying Ineffective Representation in Criminal Cases: Departures From Habeas Corpus," 59 *Va. L. Rev.* (1973) 960 (noting that the remedy for ineffective assistance should be proportional to the harm and, therefore, that "the remedy for ineffective assistance in prosecuting an appeal is only a delayed appeal").

Bibliographical Essay

CHAPTER 1: A HISTORY OF THE RIGHT TO COUNSEL

An Introduction

The resources reviewed in the bibliographical essay for the history of the right to counsel are grouped into sections that correspond to the four historical periods described in the text—from the early English common law through the end of the eighteenth century in Britain; the American colonial and Revolutionary periods; the years surrounding the development of the Constitution and the Bill of Rights—1787–1791; and from the adoption of the Sixth Amendment through the landmark 1963 Supreme Court decision in Gideon v. Wainwright. Two noteworthy resources pertinent to all four periods are addressed first.

In the 1950s, two general treatments of the constitutional right to counsel were published. Although somewhat dated, these two texts make valuable contributions to our understanding of the historical and doctrinal evolution of the constitutional entitlement to a lawyer's assistance. Francis Heller provides a succinct summary of the common law criminal procedure in England, a survey of the history of the Sixth Amendment, which includes a discussion of colonial developments concerning the rights ultimately included in that guarantee, and thorough analyses of the important Supreme Court right to counsel cases through Betts v. Brady. William Beaney details the history of the right to assistance in both England and America. He also devotes attention to the right to counsel doctrine that unfolded prior to the mid-1950s. These two significant and well-written texts, both of which predate the Supreme Court's revolutionary decision in Gideon v. Wainwright, are: Francis H. Heller, *The Sixth Amendment to the Constitution of the United States: A Study in Constitutional Development* (Lawrence: University of Kansas Press, 1951); and William M. Beaney, *The Right to Counsel in American Courts* (Ann Arbor: University of Michigan Press, 1955).

Humble Beginnings: The English Common Law Right to the Assistance of Counsel

The following sources offer a wealth of useful information about the English common law system of criminal law and procedure: J.S. Cockburn, *Crime in England, 1550–1800* (Princeton, NJ: Princeton University Press, 1977); Theodore F. Plucknett, *A Concise History of the Common Law* (London: Butterworth & Co., 4th ed. 1948); and James Fitzjames Stephen, *A History of the Criminal Law of England* (London: Macmillan and Co., 1883). Cockburn's work is a collection of edited essays that provide excellent insights into British criminal procedure prior to and for a brief period after the framing of the United States Constitution. Plucknett's text sketches the history of the criminal law and its enforcement. It considers how the change from private prosecution to state prosecution of crime precipitated changes in trial procedures. Stephen's comprehensive work is widely considered to be the most thorough, detailed treatment of the evolution of the English criminal law. It addresses both substantive and procedural aspects of the criminal law, beginning with the Roman era and continuing through nineteenth-century England. Although Stephen only briefly considers the historical and contemporary role of counsel in the British criminal process, his text is an essential resource for those who wish to understand the forces that were involved in the evolution of the entitlement to the assistance of counsel in England. William Holdsworth's multivolume treatment of the substantive and procedural developments of the English law also merits mention. This exhaustive series, which is considerably longer than Stephen's work, is: William S. Holdsworth, *A History of English Law* (London: Methuen & Co., 7th ed. 1956).

Additional historical details about and perspectives on British criminal procedure can be found in John H. Langbein, "The Criminal Trial Before the Lawyers," 45 *University of Chicago Law Review* (1978) 263. Langbein concludes that the traditional source of insight into British criminal procedure—the State Trials Law Reports—does not furnish reliable evidence of the character of criminal trials. He cites two reasons for this unreliability. First, the reports were compiled in hindsight from questionable secondary sources. In addition, the reported cases are limited to trials involving high-profile political charges or crimes of a "sensational nature" (e.g., witchcraft, bigamy, and homicide). Thus, they do not fully represent the array of criminal cases that were prosecuted. From his analysis of the Old Bailey Session Papers, Langbein concludes that criminal trials at common law were more like the inquisitorial proceedings in contemporary continental Europe than the adversarial trials in modern common law jurisdictions.

J.M. Beattie's thorough examination of the British criminal law and procedure from the mid-seventeenth century through the end of the eighteenth century provides a very useful context that can enhance understanding of the common law attitude toward the assistance of counsel. His work is particularly pertinent to this text because he focuses specific attention on the use of defense counsel at common law, exploring the origins of the rule prohibiting counsel in felony cases and the possible explanations for the eventual judicial relaxation of that rule. The text is: J.M. Beattie, *Crime and the Courts in England, 1660–1800* (Princeton, NJ: Princeton University Press, 1986).

J.B. Post provides an in-depth treatment of the history of and rationale for the common law rule forbidding counsel in felony cases and allowing assistance for lesser offenses. While Post acknowledges that the paucity of case reporters at the relevant time precludes certainty about the rationale for the common law approach, he proffers several compelling explanations. One possibility that he suggests is a general sentiment that it was not proper for a subject to have counsel against the king when the king was a party to a case, suing *ex officio*. He also considers the traditional explanations that truly innocent persons could demonstrate their innocence without lawyers' assistance and that the introduction of counsel would prolong trials and result in judicial backlogs. Post notes that judges did not apply the common law rule uniformly and that their inconsistency contributed to its eventual demise. His article is: J.B. Post, "The Admissibility of Defence Counsel in English Criminal Procedure," 5 *Journal of Legal History* (December 1984) 23.

Stephen Landsman, one of the foremost analysts of the adversary system, documents and explains the evolution of the role of counsel in British criminal trials based on an examination of the Old Bailey Session Papers. He concludes that the legal reform movements of the mid-eighteenth century and the reconceptualization of trials as adversarial proceedings account for changes in counsel's roles. J.M. Beattie undertakes a detailed exploration of the history and development of defense lawyers' roles in the English criminal courts and of their impacts on trial procedures. His well-written and concise article is replete with endnotes containing a wealth of details about the British history of defense counsel. These articles are: Stephen Landsman, "The Rise of the Contentious Spirit: Adversary Procedure in Eighteenth Century England," 75 *Cornell Law Review* (1990) 497; and J.M. Beattie, "Scales of Justice: Defense Counsel and the English Criminal Trial in the Eighteenth and Nineteenth Centuries," 9 *Law & History Review* (1991) 221.

A Departure from the British Common Law Rule: The Right to Counsel in America Prior to the Adoption of the Sixth Amendment

Two collections of legal materials from the pre-constitutional period in America are exceedingly helpful. Francis Thorpe's collection, which was authorized by an Act of Congress, is the definitive collection of state constitutional documents. It includes not only constitutions but also colonial charters and other organic laws of each state. The text is: Francis N. Thorpe, *The Federal and State Constitutions, Colonial Charters, and Other Organic Laws of the States, Territories, and Colonies Now or Heretofore Forming the United States of America* (photo. reprint, New York: William S. Hein & Co., 1993) (Washington, DC: Government Printing Office, 1909). In addition, John Cushing has produced a series of compilations of photo reprints of the earliest laws of the original thirteen states. Cushing's works provide additional source materials that shed light on the history of the right to counsel in America prior to the adoption of the Constitution. Illustrative texts are: *The First Laws of the State of North Carolina*, John D. Cushing, editor (photo. reprint, Wilmington, DE: Michael Glazier, 1984) (1791); and *Earliest Printed Laws of Pennsylvania*, John D. Cushing, editor (photo. reprint, Wilmington, DE: Michael Glazier, 1978) (1714).

The Formulation of a National Constitution and the Adoption of the Sixth Amendment Right to the Assistance of Counsel

Several resources provide detailed information concerning the history of the United States Constitution and the Bill of Rights. All but one of the works reviewed here are collections of primary documents from the relevant period.

Jonathan Elliot is responsible for the most valuable collection of primary documents pertaining to the history of the United States Constitution. About Elliot's work, Joseph Story stated: "I can scarcely imagine a more acceptable present to the public; and to statesmen it must be invaluable, as a repository of facts, as well as of the arguments, respecting the great points of constitutional law." Elliot's five volumes document the Revolutionary history of the United States. They contain: the Journal of the Federal Convention, the ratification letters, letters from prominent political figures of the time that illuminate the original meaning of the Constitution, important documents and materials from the state ratifying conventions, and James Madison's notes of the debates at the 1787 Convention. The work is: Jonathan Elliot, *The Debates in the Several State Conventions, on the Adoption of the Federal Constitution, as Recommended by the General Convention at Philadelphia in 1787* (photo. reprint, Buffalo, NY: William S. Hein & Co., 1996) (Philadelphia: J.B. Lippincott & Co., 2nd ed. 1881).

Max Farrand's collection of documents is also indispensable. His four-volume set and subsequent supplement contain a wide array of sources that document the proceedings at the Constitutional Convention, including: the Secretary's Journal; Madison's Debates; the notes of Robert Yates, Rufus King, James McHenry, William Pierce, William Paterson, Alexander Hamilton, and George Mason; and notes from the Committee of Detail. Farrand's collection is extremely useful because the records are assembled by date, enabling the reader to follow the chronological progression of the convention and survey the notes from various sources for each day. The text is: *The Records of the Federal Constitution of 1787*, Max Farrand, editor (New Haven, CT: Yale University Press, 1966).

Another excellent, multivolume work that compiles a rich array of reprinted primary source materials pertaining to the adoption of the Constitution and Bill of Rights is Bernard Schwartz, *The Roots of the Bill of Rights* (New York: Chelsea House Publishers, 1980). The Schwartz set includes: the Declaration of Independence; contemporaneous state constitutions and declarations; federalist and anti-federalist writings regarding the merits of adopting the Constitution; primary documents from the state ratifying conventions; the "legislative history" of the Bill of Rights; and state materials relating to the adoption of the Bill of Rights.

A handful of works documents the debate between the federalists and the anti-federalists over the adoption of the Constitution. The Federalist Papers are the collected essays of Alexander Hamilton, John Jay, and James Madison that were written under the pseudonym "Publius" during the ratification period. The essays—which were propaganda intended to inform and influence the public in favor of the proposed Constitution—contain excellent explanations and discussions of the merits of constitutional governance. Herbert Storing's seven-volume set was the first, and is still the most comprehensive, collection of the writings of the anti-federalist thinkers. Storing's series begins with an excellent introductory volume discussing the political climate at the time that the Constitution was framed. His second volume contains the writings of delegates to the Federal Convention who refused to sign the proposed Constitution, including: Elbridge Gerry, George Mason, Robert Yates, John Lansing, Luther Martin, and Edmund Randolph. The subsequent volumes organize anti-federalist writings by state. Storing's work includes an exceptionally helpful author/subject index that enables readers to find particular paragraphs addressing subjects of interest. The set is: *The Complete Anti-Federalist*, Herbert J. Storing, editor (Chicago: University of Chicago Press, 1981). For a shorter collection of both federalist and anti-federalist writings, see *The American Constitution: For and*

Against, the Federalist and Anti-Federalist Papers, J.R. Pole, editor (New York: Hill and Wang, 1987).

The History of the Right to Counsel after Ratification of the Sixth Amendment

The relationship between the Bill of Rights and the Fourteenth Amendment is the subject of a pair of articles in the *Stanford Law Review*. While the two articles analyze the question from different perspectives, their conclusions are similar. Charles Fairman sifts the historical record surrounding the drafting and subsequent adoption of the Fourteenth Amendment, focusing particularly on the words and opinions of the Framers and defenders of that provision in the Thirty-ninth Congress. Fairman asserts that "the record of history is overwhelmingly against" the conclusion that section 1 of the Fourteenth Amendment was intended to impose the restrictions of the first eight amendments upon the states. Stanley Morrison undertakes an exhaustive review of the Supreme Court's treatment of the issue of incorporation. He devotes specific attention to Justice Hugo Black's position that the intent of the Fourteenth Amendment was to apply the Bill of Rights to the states, making them subject to the identical constraints that bind the federal government. Morrison concludes that Black's thesis does not find support in the historical record. The two pieces are: Charles Fairman, "Does the Fourteenth Amendment Incorporate the Bill of Rights? The Original Understanding," 2 *Stanford Law Review* (1949) 5; and Stanley Morrison, "Does the Fourteenth Amendment Incorporate the Bill of Rights? The Judicial Interpretation," 2 *Stanford Law Review* (1949) 140.

James Goodman furnishes a context for Powell v. Alabama—the Supreme Court's first significant opinion concerning defendants' constitutional entitlement to the assistance of counsel in state proceedings. He relates the facts surrounding the alleged rape with which the defendants were charged, the circumstances of their arrests, and the details of their trials. Goodman's work makes a very significant contribution, providing background information that helps place the *Powell* case in both social and historical contexts. His book is: James Goodman, *Stories of Scottsboro* (New York: Pantheon Books, 1994).

Anthony Lewis provides an excellent narrative of the facts behind the Warren Court's landmark holding regarding indigent defendants' constitutional entitlement to appointed representation—Gideon v. Wainwright. Lewis' renowned account of the story of Clarence Earl Gideon and the revolutionary decision that his case precipitated makes a most valuable contribution to the historical record. Anyone interested in a full appreciation of the *Gideon* case and its significance should review the text: Anthony Lewis, *Gideon's Trumpet* (New York: Random House, 1964).

CHAPTER 2: ANALYSIS

The Nature and Character of the Right to the Assistance of Counsel

The Reasons for and Roles of Counsel in the Adversary System

Many commentators have undertaken the task of explaining the general theory and operation of the adversary system. One of the foremost analysts and proponents of the adversary system is Stephan Landsman. In an article in the *Ohio State Law Journal*, Landsman proffers a brief, insightful history of the origins and development of the adversary system and concludes that history furnishes a "lesson concerning the value of preserving traditional legal methods." In addition, Landsman has authored a brief, quite well written text that can serve as an excellent primer for any serious student of the adversary system. In the book, he concisely captures and describes the adversarial approach, its history, and certain nonadversarial aspects of the American system. He also presents criticisms of and offers defenses of the adversarial method of adjudication. While Landsman's focus on the history of the adversary system—and particularly his considerable reliance on the historical resistance to change—may cause him to slight some of the potential infirmities in the operation of that system today, on the whole his text provides a solid foundational treatment of the topic. These two sources are: Stephan Landsman, *The Adversary System: A Description and Defense* (Washington, DC: American Enterprise Institute, 1984) and Stephan Landsman, "A Brief Survey of the Development of the Adversary System," 44 *Ohio State Law Journal* (1983) 713.

The adversary system is not without its detractors. In "Making Jury Trials More Truthful," 30 *U.C. Davis Law Review* (1996) 95, Franklin Strier takes a rather pessimistic view of the system's operation and results, contending that the system does not accomplish its primary goal—ascertainment of the truth—because it contains "impediments" to the truth-seeking process and "devices" that corrupt the search for truth. According to Strier, the combination of an adversarial approach and trial by jury "deliver[s] a witch's brew of injustices" that are particularly harmful to the truth-seeking process. He provocatively proposes the adoption of a number of systemic reforms that are "inquisitorial" in nature. Whether the flaws and deficiencies in the current system are as serious as Strier would have it is a debatable question.

Marvin Frankel is also highly critical of the adversary system, particularly in the criminal justice arena. In his view, "the worship of the adversary struggle in the criminal law leads to extensive paralysis of the process" and to a system that in actual operation "makes a mockery of the adversary values everyone professes." He suggests that we "try to make the processes of truth finding and sanctioning less insistently combative" and calls for "more effective ideas for breaking the adversary mold and seeking criminal procedures that are both fairer and more effective." Frankel's scathing indictments and descriptions of the harmful effects of our devotion to adversarial ideals can be found in: Marvin E. Frankel, *Partisan Justice* (New York: Hill and Wang, 1980). The text is an excellent piece of scholarship concerning the adversary system.

David Luban also thoroughly explores and criticizes the premises offered as justifications for our adversary system. Ultimately, however, he concludes that the system should survive because it finds the truth and preserves legal rights as well as any alternative approach, because "*some* adjudicatory system is necessary," and because we have always adhered to the adversarial method. For those concerned with moral, ethical, and professional aspects of the adversary system, Luban's work is an excellent resource. His interesting, if somewhat unsettling, views are set forth in: David Luban, "The Adversary System Excuse," in *The Good Lawyer: Lawyers' Roles and Lawyers' Ethics*, David Luban, editor (Totowa, N.J.: Rowman & Allenheld, 1983).

The author of the instant text has addressed the roles played by lawyers in ensuring the effective functioning of the adversary system. In an article with the ultimate goal of assessing the justifiability of extending the right to counsel to pretrial settings in which government agents attempt to secure inculpatory admissions from those accused of crimes, James Tomkovicz explores the nature of the adversary system, the parts played by lawyers in that system, and the ways in which the guarantee of counsel's assistance enhances the search for truth and promotes "fair play" values. Tomkovicz suggests that the accused's entitlement to counsel can be seen as a promise of "full equalization" in the clash with the state, a promise that is essential to American notions of "fair play." He concludes that the adversarial premises on which our criminal justice system rest provide an ample justification for granting criminal defendants assistance against pretrial investigative efforts by police officers and undercover operatives. The article is: James J. Tomkovicz, "An Adversary System Defense of the Right to Counsel against Informants: Truth, Fair Play, and the *Massiah* Doctrine," 22 *U.C. Davis Law Review* (1988) 1.

Jay Sterling Silver is among the commentators who contend that the Supreme Court's lack of faith in the adversarial process has tilted "the delicate balance" in favor of the prosecution. In his view, the integrity of the criminal justice system has been compromised by the Court's interpretations of the right to the assistance of counsel. The remedy is to acknowledge that the criminal justice system can achieve its fundamental goals only by adherence to "the principle of *equality of arms*." Silver reflects upon the meaning and significance of an "implied constitutional right to an *equality of arms*" and declares that right to be necessary to the balance of forces that is an essential predicate for the pursuit of truth and fairness in the adversarial process. Silver analogizes to trial by battle in which each combatant was assured equal weaponry and armaments and concludes that while courtroom opponents need not have "equal skill or resources," they must be "equally armed for combat" when it comes to "the procedural rights" that enable them "to formulate and present" their positions. His incisive analysis is contained in: Jay Sterling Silver, "Equality of Arms and the Adversarial Process: A New Constitutional Right," 1990 *Wisconsin Law Review* 1007.

There are far too many scholarly discussions of the adversary system and of counsel's place in that system to describe in this bibliographical essay. For those interested in pursuing additional sources pertaining to the nature and character of the adversary system, there is an excellent, relatively recent, and extensive bibliographical resource: Franklin D. Strier and Edith Greene, *The Adversary System: An Annotated Bibliography* (Littleton, CO: Fred B. Rothman, 1990). This text categorizes sources under a variety of subtopics and pointedly summarizes the content of those sources. Anyone researching or writing about the adversary system will find it to be a most useful point of departure.

The Right to Retained Counsel of Choice

The nature of the legal assistance guaranteed by the Constitution is the focus of an article by Bruce Green. Green is highly critical of the current definition of "counsel" employed by the Supreme Court and lower courts in the criminal context. He challenges the assumption that every attorney who passes the bar examination and is licensed to practice is qualified to try criminal cases. Because the stakes are so high in criminal cases—particularly, in capital cases—Green believes that the constitutional entitlement to counsel was understood by the Framers and should be understood to encompass only those lawyers who are adequately trained in criminal law. He makes a credible case for ensuring that the constitutional guarantee has real substance by limiting the class of attorneys who can satisfy the Sixth Amendment's promise of legal representation, but is realistic in acknowledging that his proposal "is unlikely to win favor soon in the Supreme Court or in any other court." His thorough arguments in favor of a redefinition of "counsel" are presented in: Bruce A. Green, "Lethal Fiction: The Meaning of 'Counsel' in the Sixth Amendment," 78 *Iowa Law Review* (1993) 433.

The right to counsel of choice is the focus of an article by Eugene Shapiro. Shapiro analyzes the modern Supreme Court opinions that recognize the existence of such a Sixth Amendment right—*Wheat, Caplin & Drysdale*, and *Monsanto*. He asserts that the opinion in *Wheat* created an "analytical vacuum" and perceptively points out that although the Court recognized a presumption in favor of a Sixth Amendment right to counsel of choice, it provided no guidance regarding the strength of that presumption. According to Shapiro, that deficiency, coupled with "the failure to discuss the source of the right in depth" or to explain the "values underlying the right to counsel of choice," undercut the validity of the balancing analysis adopted for determining whether the right to choose has been infringed. Shapiro asserts that in *Caplin & Drysdale* and *Monsanto*, the Court failed to "express a clear view of the interests served by" the right to choose. In his opinion, this failure impeded a meaningful assessment of whether the government's interests really did justify infringement upon the accuseds' presumptive entitlements to choose their own representatives. Shapiro's criticisms are well warranted, and his contention that genuine adherence to the entitlement to choose requires an "articulation of the values underlying the right to counsel of choice" seems amply justified. For those interested in exploring the potential justifications for an accused's right to choose counsel, Shapiro's article is one of the better resources. His views can be found in: Eugene L. Shapiro, "The Sixth Amendment Right to Counsel of Choice: An Exercise in the Weighing of Unarticulated Values," 43 *South Carolina Law Review* (1992) 345.

Alfredo Garcia, in an article concerned with aspects of the right to counsel other than just the right to choose, is also highly critical of the Supreme Court's right to counsel of choice jurisprudence, calling it "seriously flawed." Garcia's concerns are different from Shapiro's. In his view, the *Wheat* and *Caplin & Drysdale* opinions reflect a devotion to "crime control" and "efficiency" that led to a "depreciation of the critical role of the defense attorney in the criminal process." There is considerable merit to Garcia's conclusions that the Court's rulings have rendered the right to retained counsel of choice "revocable at the whim of the government" and that the results are "inimical to the basic thrust and ideal of the adversary system of adjudication: an even 'fight' between two skillful opponents." The article is: Alfredo Garcia, "The Right to Counsel under Siege: Requiem for an Endangered Right?" 29 *American Criminal Law Review* (1991) 35.

Pamela Karlan has proffered an interesting theoretical perspective on the reasons for the Supreme Court's hostility toward and narrowing interpretations of criminal defendants' right to retained counsel of choice. In her view, criminal defense attorneys once filled only fleeting, temporary needs for assistance, whereas today defense counsel might well engage in ongoing associations with clients—what she terms "relational criminal representation." According to Karlan, the decisions that have restricted the entitlement to counsel of choice—*Wheat* and *Caplin & Drysdale*—are explicable as reactions to a perception that relational representation provides unacceptable opportunities for the guilty to engage in criminal activity and avoid conviction. Karlan's probing explanation of the Supreme Court's stingy approach to the right to retained counsel of choice is intriguing and worthy of consideration. The article is: Pamela S. Karlan, "Discrete and Relational Criminal Representation: The Changing Vision of the Right to Counsel," 105 *Harvard Law Review* (1992) 670.

The indigent criminal defendant's lack of a constitutional entitlement to choose counsel is the subject of Wayne Holly's article, "Rethinking the Sixth Amendment for the Indigent Criminal Defendant: Do Reimbursement Statutes Support Recognition of a Right to Counsel of Choice for the Indigent?" 64 *Brooklyn Law Review* (1998) 181. Holly provides a useful review of the rationales offered for denying indigents a right to choose their own legal assistants and concludes that those rationales "are either outmoded or illusory." Holly furnishes two reasons for his conclusion that those who do not have the means to secure counsel should have an entitlement to choose their appointed representatives. First, indigent defendants, like those with the means to retain counsel, have vital interests in selecting their representatives. Second, recoupment statutes enable the government to recover the costs of appointing counsel for indigents. Holly proposes an "analytical framework" for analyzing indigents' claims that they have been deprived of that entitlement. Some will find Holly's logic to be persuasive, while others will conclude that his conclusions are impracticable.

The Indigent's Right to Appointed Counsel

As noted in the analysis, Gideon v. Wainwright is among the most noteworthy landmarks in the development of American right to counsel law. The importance of the Court's conclusion that states have a general constitutional obligation to furnish indigents with legal assistance endures today. Anthony Lewis' engaging, well-known account of the circumstances and events that surrounded and precipitated the decision in *Gideon* can provide those interested in the right to counsel with a useful context for and a different perspective on the Court's landmark ruling. The text is: Anthony Lewis, *Gideon's Trumpet* (New York: Random House, 1964).

In addition, Jerold H. Israel's classic article on *Gideon* is essential reading for anyone interested in understanding the Court's decision to reject the "special circumstances" approach of Betts v. Brady. In "*Gideon v. Wainwright*: The 'Art' of Overruling," 1963 *Supreme Court Review* 211, Israel furnishes a lucid synopsis of the *Gideon* opinions and the Court's holding. He emphasizes the importance of *Gideon* as one of a relatively limited number of cases in which the Supreme Court had directly overruled a prior constitutional holding. Because most states had already recognized an entitlement to assistance, Israel considers it "hardly startling" for the Court to have extended a general right to appointed assistance to criminal defendants in state courts. The more interesting aspect of the decision was the untraditional manner in which the Court overruled Betts v. Brady. Deeming Justice Black's approach unpersuasive, Israel describes alternative methods of overturning *Betts* that would have been preferable. Of the six criminal procedure decisions handed down on the same day, Israel deems *Gideon* "probably not the most important in terms of legal theory or practical effect"—an assessment of the decision's stature that seems questionable today. Nonetheless, his recognition that, to maintain credibility, the Supreme Court must not only provide legitimate bases for its rulings but also overrule precedents in ways that preserve respect for the Court and for its prior decisions makes an important and still timely contribution. Israel's article is probably the most significant contemporaneous scholarly reflection on the Court's landmark ruling.

The issue pertaining to indigents' entitlement to assistance that is a frequent subject of scholarly attention is the quality of the representation provided by appointed counsel. A couple of empirical studies published in the 1970s reach somewhat different conclusions about the quality of appointed assistance. Laurence A. Benner, in "Tokenism and the American Indigent: Some Perspectives on Defense Services," 12 *American Criminal Law Review* (1975) 667, concludes that in many states indigent defendants were not receiving adequate legal representation. Based on statistical information from the 1960s and 1970s, Benner maintains that the deficiencies were the product of inexperienced counsel, excessive restrictions of the scope of counsel's representation, a lack of thorough investigation, and a lack of access to the aid of experts. Robert Hermann, Eric Single, and John Boston conducted an empirical study of the quality of appointed assistance in New York, Los Angeles, and Washington, D.C., in the early 1970s. They posed the following bottom-line question: "All other things being equal, can a person accused of crime who has a free, state-paid lawyer expect an outcome different from that of an accused person who hires a lawyer?" Based on statistical data and interviews with defendants, judges, prosecutors, and defense attorneys, they concluded that the conviction and imprisonment rates for defendants with appointed counsel are substantially similar to those for defendants with retained lawyers. In their view, the widely shared assumption that appointed counsel's aid was substandard was unfounded. In comparing the results achieved by appointed counsel and retained counsel, the authors eliminated "rich" defendants with "famous attorneys," deeming them statistically insignificant. The defendants with retained counsel taken into account were those with "moderate incomes" and those who could "scrape together enough" to hire less than the best assistance. The text is: Robert Hermann, Eric Single, and John Boston, *Counsel for the Poor: Criminal Defense in Urban America* (Lexington, MA: Lexington Books, 1977).

Because these two studies were published approximately twenty-five years ago, they do not capture the current state of legal representation for the criminally accused. Nonetheless, they address an exceedingly significant question—the actual quality of the legal representation afforded indigents. Benner's article pinpoints variables that may still impede the provision of adequate legal aid. The Hermann, Single, and Boston text suggests that common assumptions about the inadequacies of appointed legal representation should not go unquestioned and highlights the need for a thorough, modern study to evaluate the actual health of the fundamental right recognized in *Gideon*.

Several scholars have concluded that the theoretical promises and aspirations of *Zerbst* and *Gideon* have not been realized in practice. Stephen Schulhofer and David Friedman have investigated the relationship between financial considerations and the quality of appointed representation. They conclude that there is an "acute" need for "effective reform" of a system in which state funding of criminal defense attorneys gives rise to inherent conflicts of interest. Highlighting several of the more severe defects, they propose a privatized, "free market for defense services." Upon reviewing an array of proposals for privatizing indigent representation, they conclude that a voucher system would be the best remedy for the current ills. The Schulhofer and Friedman article provides a valuable service by identifying the problems with the extant system of government-funded representation for indigent defendants and proposing an innovative solution that promotes choice by indigents. They acknowledge that "there are legitimate concerns that without large increases in the resources devoted to indigent defense, the reforms [they] propose may make little difference," but they contend that even with the present inadequate levels of funding, a voucher system will have some positive impacts. The article is: Stephen J. Schulhofer and David D. Friedman, "Rethinking Indigent Defense: Promoting Effective Representation through Consumer Sovereignty and Freedom of Choice for All Criminal Defendants," 31 *American Criminal Law Review* (1993) 73.

Ten years after *Gideon*, Judge David Bazelon put forth a candid and persuasive, if somewhat pessimistic and discouraging, critique of the quality of appointed assistance in a noteworthy article, "The Defective Assistance of Counsel," 42 *University of Cincin-*

nati Law Review (1973) 1. He concludes that "a great many—if not most—indigent defendants do not receive the effective assistance of counsel guaranteed by the 6th Amendment." Judge Bazelon discusses deficiencies in the system that allow and even tacitly approve of ineffective representation by appointed lawyers, identifies a variety of systemic disadvantages for indigent defendants, and reviews a number of reform proposals—including competency standards, certification, closer appellate scrutiny, and changes in pretrial and post-trial procedures. His intimate familiarity with the system and its defects is evident. His proposals seem practical, potentially effective, and less controversial than some. His call for a "radical rethinking of [the] role" of defense counsel not because it is "constitutionally mandated" but because it "may well be a moral imperative" and "is the humane thing to do" merits serious attention from all who value the adversary system and the essential role that counsel plays.

Another topic that has drawn the attention of commentators is the *scope* of the entitlement to appointed assistance, that is, whether indigents ought to have a right to state-provided assistance in *all* criminal prosecutions. Prior to the Supreme Court's first decision regarding the right to appointed counsel for misdemeanor charges, John Junker documented the status of misdemeanants' right to counsel in state courts and discussed the policies, constitutional concerns, and precedents bearing upon that issue. He concluded that the relevant considerations militated in favor of a right to state-provided assistance for those accused of misdemeanors. Following the Supreme Court's decision in Argersinger v. Hamlin, Steven Duke opined that courts were construing that decision too narrowly. In his view, *Argersinger* did not hold that the right to appointed assistance did not extend beyond misdemeanor prosecutions involving incarceration. Instead, *Argersinger*, properly understood, required counsel if a defendant receives a sentence of actual imprisonment *or* if the potential consequences of conviction for an offense are otherwise "significant," that is, if they involve "deprivations equivalent to a loss of liberty." Duke also discussed at length the standards that should be used to determine which accused misdemeanants receive appointed counsel. Those interested in exploring arguments against the Supreme Court's decision to restrict the right to appointed counsel to misdemeanors leading to actual jail time should consult these two articles: John M. Junker, "The Right to Counsel in Misdemeanor Cases," 43 *Washington Law Review* (1968) 685; and Steven Duke, "The Right to Appointed Counsel: *Argersinger* and Beyond," 12 *American Criminal Law Review* (1975) 601.

Yet another concern addressed by scholars is the failure to accord indigent defendants a *choice* of counsel. One significant article advocating recognition of a right to choose for indigents is discussed in the preceding subsection of these bibliographical essays. That article is: Wayne D. Holly, "Rethinking the Sixth Amendment for the Indigent Criminal Defendant: Do Reimbursement Statutes Support Recognition of a Right to Counsel of Choice for the Indigent?" 64 *Brooklyn Law Review* (1998) 181. In another piece adopting the same stance, Peter Tague thoroughly canvasses reasons that support according indigents a say in the selection of counsel. Those reasons include improving the relationship between lawyer and client, ensuring competent and vigorous advocacy, and increasing the level of participation by an accused in his defense. Tague honestly acknowledges the contrary government interests but believes that those interests can be accommodated within a system that affords indigents a choice. While this article was written before many of the relevant modern right to choose decisions, it provides a thorough and illuminating examination of the competing interests involved in deciding whether to recognize a right to counsel of choice for indigent defendants. The article is:

Peter W. Tague, "An Indigent's Right to the Attorney of His Choice," 27 *Stanford Law Review* (1974) 73.

Waiver of the Right to Counsel and the Constitutional Right of Self-Representation

Two articles address issues pertaining to waiver of the Sixth Amendment right to counsel in some depth. In a piece in the *Iowa Law Review*, the author of the instant text, James Tomkovicz, thoroughly discusses Supreme Court doctrine regarding valid waivers of both the Sixth Amendment right to counsel and the Fifth Amendment entitlement to assistance in "confession contexts." Tomkovicz is critical of the Court's failure "to provide sufficient guidance" and of its neglect "to refer to the meanings and purposes of the . . . sixth amendment[] to justify the standards it has prescribed." He explores the purposes of the two constitutional guarantees of counsel and proposes meaningful, detailed standards for evaluating whether an individual has asserted or waived those guarantees—standards that are logically tied to the rationales for promises of counsel's assistance. Tomkovicz furnishes useful explanations of the governing Sixth Amendment waiver standards and of their deficiencies and proffers refinements of the law that are constitutionally defensible. The article is: James J. Tomkovicz, "Standards for Invocation and Waiver of Counsel in Confession Contexts," 71 *Iowa Law Review* (1986) 975.

William J. Stuntz tackles the general subject of waivers of Fourth, Fifth, and Sixth Amendment rights by criminal defendants in "Waiving Rights in Criminal Procedure," 75 *Virginia Law Review* (1989) 761. According to Stuntz, "[o]ne of the major problems of American criminal procedure is the seeming tension between the breadth of the constitutional rights that protect defendants and the ease with which those rights may be waived." He rejects the simplistic and "cynical" view that the explanation for that tension is the Justices' aversion to guilty defendants' use of constitutional rights as shields. Instead, Stuntz believes in a "more attractive explanation for the current waiver doctrines. [T]hose doctrines make sense," he claims, "on the assumption that the rights being waived often aim to protect persons other than those who assert them or interests other than those upon which the police have infringed." The presence or absence of a need to safeguard third-party interests can furnish a plausible explanation for the Court's differential treatment of the "intentional relinquishment of a known right" standard for waiver. Defendants are more likely to be protected by stringent waiver standards when that protection also serves to shield the intended third-party beneficiaries. When third parties do not stand to benefit, the Court is more likely to relax waiver standards, thereby diluting the protection afforded criminal defendants. Stuntz's perception that constitutional waiver standards are variable is on target. His theoretical explanation for that variation is intriguing and certainly unconventional. The accuracy of his assessment of the underlying reasons for variable constitutional waiver standards, however, is debatable. At the very least, Stuntz's view that the substance of waiver standards is influenced by the need to protect defendants' rights, the need to ensure ample room for effective law enforcement, *and* the need to guard against future infringements of third-party interests provides a fresh perspective on waiver questions.

The right of self-representation recognized by the Supreme Court in Faretta v. California has been the subject of remarkably scant commentary. John Decker has produced by far the most substantial reflection upon *Faretta*. He maintains that the *Faretta* decision has created "chaos" and has led to trials "that make a mockery of justice and disrupt courtroom procedure." In his view, it is likely that "criminal defendants have lost more

than they have gained when they elect to proceed pro se." Although they may "knowingly" waive the assistance of counsel, accused individuals may not—indeed, in reality many do not—understand that they are relinquishing a source of knowledge and expertise concerning trial complexities, courtroom procedures, and evidentiary rules. In addition, *pro se* representation inflicts damage on the decorum of court proceedings. Decker's thoughtful article explores the atypical consequences of *Faretta*. Ordinarily, the recognition of new constitutional rights will increase defendants' protection against government overreaching. The right of self-representation, however, disadvantages those who exercise it and affords the government an additional edge in the adversarial battle. Decker's article is essential reading for those fascinated by the unique constitutional right to forgo counsel and defend oneself. His review of the multifarious issues raised by *Faretta* is painstaking. Moreover, his exploration of the inherent conflict between an entitlement to autonomy and the Sixth Amendment goal of trial fairness hones in on the central quandary of the *Faretta* decision. The article is: John F. Decker, "The Sixth Amendment Right to Shoot Oneself in the Foot: An Assessment of the Guarantee of Self-Representation Twenty Years After *Faretta*," 6 *Seton Hall Constitutional Law Journal* (1996) 483.

Paul Marcus is notably more sanguine about the *Faretta* right. In his brief article, "The *Faretta* Principle: Self-Representation versus the Right to Counsel," 30 *American Journal of Comparative Law* (supplement) (1982) 551, Marcus provides a helpful depiction of the relationship between the Sixth Amendment rights to counsel and to self-representation. He examines the tension between these rights and the confusion and dilemmas resulting from that tension. He agrees that the entitlement to go *pro se* can lead to incompetent defenses, disruptive behavior, and an array of other problems for judges and lawyers. Nonetheless, in his view, the right is infrequently invoked, and, when it is exercised, significant problems rarely do arise. Moreover, Marcus suggests that the problems that do crop up "may be . . . a small price to pay to insure that the defendant who so desires, can exercise his right of self-representation." Marcus' perspectives on self-representation provide an interesting counterpoint to Decker's perhaps too negative assessment of the impacts of the *Faretta* right. However, Decker's piece includes a much more thorough treatment of *Faretta* and provides considerably more support for his unfavorable evaluation of self-representation.

The Allocation of Decision-Making Authority between Counsel and the Accused

Uphoff and Wood observe that both legal scholars and judges "are sharply divided" about "the proper division of decisionmaking power or responsibility between counsel and client" and that in general "lawyers are relatively free to decide for themselves whether they will share decisionmaking power with their clients." They provide a useful description of the two primary approaches to decision making—the "lawyer-centered model" and the "participatory, client-centered model." They assert that neither the legal profession's ethical rules nor judicial precedents offer "a definitive answer to the proper allocation of decisionmaking power." On the basis of an "exploratory" empirical study that they conducted, Uphoff and Wood conclude that most defense lawyers "adopt a more lawyer-centered approach to decisionmaking." Most do not, in fact, share the authority with their clients, though a significant minority are willing to do so. Noting that theirs is "the first systematic look at both the ideological commitment to, and the actual practice of, client-centered decisionmaking among criminal defense lawyers," they suggest that there is a need to assess whether lawyers with a "client-centered approach" provide better representation than those adhering to the "traditional approach." Their piece, which makes vital contributions to this significant right to counsel issue, is: Rodney J. Uphoff and Peter B. Wood, "The Allocation of Decisionmaking Between Defense Counsel and Criminal Defendant: An Empirical Study of Attorney-Client Decisionmaking," 47 *University of Kansas Law Review* (1998) 1.

The state of the law regarding the accused's authority to make defense decisions is the subject of two significant articles. Richard Chused believes that the Supreme Court's opinion in Faretta v. California has important bearing on the question of defendants' authority to make tactical decisions. In "*Faretta* and the Personal Defense: The Role of a Represented Defendant in Trial Tactics," 65 *California Law Review* (1977) 636, he argues that *Faretta* not only gives defendants a right to conduct their own defenses but also grants "represented defendants . . . a constitutional right to control trial tactics." In his view, the impact of *Faretta* "is much more dramatic than the courts have yet recognized. It provides a constitutional basis for overruling the illogical and inconsistent doctrine that counsel must control tactics." Chused proceeds to propose an interesting framework for implementing the constitutional right to "mixed" or "hybrid" representation that he believes to be the logical consequence of *Faretta*.

Vivian Berger disagrees with Chused's "radical thesis." She observes that some have argued that ineffective assistance of counsel claims could be averted if criminal defendants were given at least partial control of decisions affecting their fate. Berger correctly asserts that precedents like Jones v. Barnes reflect "the concept of lawyer preeminence" when it comes to the allocation of decision-making authority. Her claim that Supreme Court "dictum" has rejected Chused's view that *Faretta* supports a constitutional right to hybrid representation is on target. Highlighting the flaws in Chused's logic, Berger sets forth reasons that militate strongly against recognition of an entitlement to mixed or joint representation. Moreover, she believes "that the advocates of a fluid, 'contractual' hybrid defense greatly underestimate the negative consequences likely to follow from changing what is now a privilege . . . into a right." Her article, which is both ambitious and well conceived, is: Vivian O. Berger, "The Supreme Court and Defense Counsel: Old Roads, New Paths—A Dead End?," 86 *Columbia Law Review* (1986) 9.

While Chused's position has much to commend it, it is not consonant with the spirit of the most relevant decisions. Although his discovery of a basis for a right to joint decision-making authority in the language and logic of *Faretta* is not patently implausible, it surely stretches *Faretta* beyond its intended reach. Moreover, it is arguable that Chused gives insufficient weight to the adverse practical consequences resulting from a right to hybrid representation. Berger's views accurately reflect the state of the law regarding decision-making authority. Her analysis and critique are well reasoned and rooted in a realistic assessment of the perils posed by an entitlement to mixed representation.

The Scope of the Right to the Assistance of Counsel

There are relatively few scholarly treatments of the scope of the right to counsel. None of the sources that are the subjects of the essays that follow contain a comprehensive discussion of the topic. Many, if not most, of them focus primarily on relatively narrow aspects of the scope of the Sixth Amendment entitlement to assistance.

The Entitlement to Counsel's Assistance Prior to Trial

The Extension of the Right to Trial Counsel to Critical Pretrial Stages

The author of this text has written two pieces that include relatively concise explanations of the expansion of the Sixth Amendment entitlement to assistance into the period prior to the trial itself and of the rationales for that expansion. Those interested in the process and logic of extending the right to counsel to pretrial clashes between the prosecution and the defendant should consult: James J. Tomkovicz, "An Adversary System Defense of the Right to Counsel Against Informants: Truth, Fair Play, and the *Massiah* Doctrine," 22 *U.C. Davis Law Review* (1988) 1 and James J. Tomkovicz, "Standards for Invocation and Waiver of Counsel in Confession Contexts," 71 *Iowa Law Review* (1986) 975.

The Two Prerequisites for an Entitlement to Pretrial Assistance of Counsel

One of the Tomkovicz articles also devotes a considerable amount of attention to the topic of "attachment" of the right to counsel. Tomkovicz explains the currently controlling criterion for attachment of the entitlement to assistance—a formal initiation of adversarial judicial proceedings—and the reasons offered by the Court to support that doctrinal limitation. He discusses the arguments in favor of and against eliminating the attachment requirement and granting a right to assistance to all individuals engaged in certain encounters with the government prior to trial. After concluding that a temporal limit on the scope of pretrial assistance can be logically defended, Tomkovicz asserts that the right "must begin no later than upon the initiation of formal proceedings" and concludes that it would be preferable to accord a right to counsel immediately after arrest because the current criterion risks the elevation of form over substance and creates risks of "bad faith manipulation" of the entitlement to counsel by "deliberate delay" of the formal charging process. According to Tomkovicz, "rigid adherence to initiation betrays a weakness in the commitment to fair play values." The pertinent analyses can be found in: James J. Tomkovicz, "An Adversary System Defense of the Right to Counsel Against Informants: Truth, Fair Play, and the *Massiah* Doctrine," 22 *U.C. Davis Law Review* (1988) 1.

Other scholars have offered harshly critical assessments of the restriction of the vital Sixth Amendment guarantee of counsel to the period following a formal initiation of charges. Although H. Richard Uviller believes that the *Massiah* right to counsel itself is illegitimate, he has declared that "the asserted reasons for" concluding that the right to assistance attaches only "at formal accusation are unpersuasive" when applied to the situations governed by the *Massiah* rule. According to Uviller, the ability of counsel to furnish aid "surely does not depend on whether the conversation with the police or their spy occurs before or after arraignment." Moreover, "[n]either semantics nor reason" precludes the conclusion that an accusation occurs upon "arrest." In his view, the decision to fix the point of attachment at formal accusation is an "awkward . . . , indefensible position" that is "logically vulnerable" and "without a principled basis." Welsh White has cogently argued that the Sixth Amendment entitlement to counsel should be triggered at "the *actual* beginning of the adversary process, that is to say, the point at which officers are trying to obtain evidence to convict a suspect and the suspect views the officers as agents of the prosecution." He finds the formal initiation of proceedings line to be flawed because it is subject to official manipulation and because "it is not . . . likely to signal a change in the suspect's position vis-a-vis the police." Because the police are often convinced of guilt when they arrest a suspect, a formal charge "will not necessarily alter either their perception of their relationship to the suspect or the tactics they will be likely to employ." Yale Kamisar has stated that the "right to counsel should not 'turn on a moment arbitrarily fixed as the beginning of judicial proceedings,' a point that can often be manipulated by law enforcement authorities." According to Professor Kamisar, a "suspect's need for 'a lawyer's help,' . . . may be as great, or greater, before the commencement of judicial proceedings."

These indictments of the Supreme Court's criterion for attachment of the right to counsel can be found in: H. Richard Uviller, "Evidence from the Mind of the Criminal Suspect: A Reconsideration of the Current Rules of Access and Restraint," 87 *Columbia Law Review* (1987) 1137; Welsh S. White, "*Rhode Island v. Innis*: The Significance of a Suspect's Assertion of His Right to Counsel," 17 *American Criminal Law Review* (1979) 53; and Yale Kamisar, "*Brewer v. Williams*, *Massiah*, and *Miranda*: What Is 'Interrogation'? When Does it Matter?," 67 *Georgetown Law Journal* (1978) 1.

A contrasting and challenging perspective on the constitutional validity of the initiation of proceedings standard can be found in Joseph D. Grano, "*Rhode Island v. Innis*: A Need to Reconsider the Constitutional Premises Underlying the Law of Confessions," 17 *American Criminal Law Review* (1979) 1. Professor Grano reviews the two prominent alternatives to the "initiation of proceedings" criterion, the "focus" line and the "custody" line, and documents the "shortcomings" of each of these options. Grano responds to the various concerns of the Court's critics and suggests that governmental manipulation is a possibility no matter where the attachment line is drawn. In light of the defects in the alternative points of attachment, he asserts that the "initiation of proceedings" standard is "[b]y default, the only point left for attachment of sixth amendment rights." Moreover, in Grano's estimation, there are ample substantive reasons that support that point of attachment. In the first place, "Sixth amendment guarantees *are* trial guarantees." In addition, history supports the recognition of a right to assistance only within the judicial context. Finally, "police investigation of an unsolved crime cannot be analogized to a judicial trial," and such an analogy would "threaten society's vital interest in successful law enforcement." Restricting counsel to the period after formal accusation and permitting law enforcement to operate before that point without counsel's interference is defensible as the "product . . . of historical compromise." Grano's direct responses to opponents of the "initiation of proceedings" criterion and his thoughtful, well-reasoned explanation of the bases for limiting the right to counsel to the period after formal charges merit serious consideration.

Informal Critical Stages of the Prosecution

Of the two "informal" stages that have been deemed "critical stages" by the Supreme Court, the critical stage defined by the *Massiah* doctrine is clearly the most controversial. It has been the subject of considerable scholarly attention. The author of this text, James Tomkovicz, has written a series of four articles addressing the Court's decisions extending the right to counsel to the government's deliberate elicitation of incriminating statements. Together, the pieces constitute an exhaustive treatment of the *Massiah* doctrine. Those interested in pursuing the underpinnings and nuances of that doctrine will find them helpful. The most significant of these articles explains the evolution of the *Massiah* doctrine from the precursor decisions through the more recent refinements of doctrinal details. It explores the relatively thin justifications offered by the Supreme Court for *Massiah*, the more substantial arguments offered by dissenting opponents of *Massiah*, and the split among scholars who have evaluated the decision. The article highlights the dispute over *Massiah*, assessing the arguments for and against that doctrine, questioning whether it is truly rooted in the Sixth Amendment, and proffering a defense that is based on the nature of our adversary system and the roles played by counsel in that system. Ultimately, Professor Tomkovicz concludes that adversarial principles of "fair play" can provide a solid justification for an entitlement to counsel's aid against direct and surreptitious government efforts to secure incriminating admissions from those accused of crimes. He devotes particular attention to situations involving undercover informants. Tomkovicz concludes by addressing a number of specific issues pertaining to *Massiah*—the formal charge requirement for attachment of the right, the requisite bases for attributing informant conduct to the government, the need for "active" elicitation, and the rejected good faith independent investigation exception to *Massiah*. The pertinent article is: James J. Tomkovicz, "An Adversary System Defense of the Right to Counsel Against Informants: Truth, Fair Play, and the *Massiah* Doctrine," 22 *U.C. Davis Law Review* (1988) 1.

Tomkovicz's three other pieces address narrower aspects of the *Massiah* right to counsel. One article, in the *Iowa Law Review*, James J. Tomkovicz, "Standards for Invocation and Waiver of Counsel in Confession Contexts," 71 *Iowa Law Review* (1986) 975, contrasts the *Massiah* right with the entitlement to assistance guaranteed by *Miranda*, distinguishing the origins, objectives, and criteria for those two guarantees of a lawyer's help. The article then thoroughly examines and critiques the extant standards for waiving the *Massiah* and *Miranda* guarantees, ultimately proposing standards that the author finds most defensible.

In another piece, James J. Tomkovicz, "The *Massiah* Right to Exclusion: Constitutional Premises and Doctrinal Implications," 67 *North Carolina Law Review* (1989) 751, Tomkovicz focuses his attention on the result of a *Massiah* violation—the exclusion of an incriminating admission from trial. He asserts that the nature of the *Massiah* right to counsel militates convincingly in favor of the conclusion that evidentiary exclusion is a part of the entitlement to counsel, not simply a deterrent remedy. In that regard, it is different from Fourth Amendment and *Miranda* exclusion, which rest primarily on deterrent rationales, and should not be subject to all of the same qualifications. According to the article, *Massiah* exclusion must be broader if the essence of the right to counsel is to be preserved.

Finally, in James J. Tomkovicz, "The Truth About *Massiah*," 23 *Michigan Journal of Law Reform* (1990) 641, the author reiterates his previously expressed views concerning the bases for *Massiah*. He also responds to the arguments in a Department of Justice report that scathingly criticizes the *Massiah* guarantee of assistance as constitutionally unjustified and contrary to the search for truth and justice. Tomkovicz is highly critical of the "rhetorical approach" taken by the Justice Department's report, deeming it "a skillful advocate's indictment." While he maintains that *Massiah* is constitutionally defensible, Tomkovicz concedes that the substance of the arguments presented by the Department of Justice "reflects different value preferences that pose a serious challenge to *Massiah*." Those seeking a concise summary of the debate over *Massiah* should review this piece.

As has been noted, the *Massiah* doctrine has many critics. H. Richard Uviller is prominent among those who find reasons to question the legitimacy of the pretrial right to counsel discerned by the *Massiah* Court. As part of an ambitious effort "to describe the many manifestations of cognitive evidence" from suspects, "the diverse techniques for its capture, and the varied and intricate doctrines developed for control of law enforcement's notorious appetite for such evidence," he focuses intense attention on the *Massiah* doctrine, declaring it to be "the villain of [his] piece." In Uviller's view, "[n]one of the apologia" for extending the right to assistance to the contexts governed by *Massiah* "survives close scrutiny . . . , compelling the conclusion that the sixth amendment provision has been misapplied as an artificial device of cloture on government efforts to obtain cognitive evidence." Uviller accurately describes the development of the *Massiah* doctrine from 1964 through 1986, perceptively explaining that the real significance and effect of the rule is to preclude both covert and direct post-accusation efforts to obtain admissions. He isolates core questions concerning the justifiability of the doctrine, pointing out the "frailty of the Court's own explanation" for *Massiah.* Uviller then engages in a careful search for a rational foundation for the Court's extension of the Sixth Amendment right. He first describes the view that our adversary system requires counsel to serve "as an all-purpose partisan, a champion awarded to the citizen from the moment of his accusation." From this "heroic conception of the lawyer's role," a conception that Uviller does not endorse, he proceeds to consider and reject the arguments in favor of three potential roles for defense counsel that might undergird the *Massiah* doctrine—lawyer as provider of "preparatory assistance," lawyer as provider of "preventive assistance," and lawyer as provider of "adversarial assistance."

Uviller concludes that *Massiah*'s pretrial extension of the Sixth Amendment right to counsel is entirely unjustified. In his view,

> those seeking to narrow access to a suspect have failed to sustain the burden of demonstrating that such access to cognitive evidence is inconsistent with the fundamental tenets of the adversary system. Consequently, the true basis for *Massiah* and its brood probably [must be] judicial discomfort with the anomalous inquisitorial component of the adversarial design, [which] engendered the desire to limit such inquisition by any restriction, however arbitrary.

With regard to the use of "covert agents," he contends that the Court should have found appropriate regulation in the Fourth Amendment guarantee against unreasonable searches and seizures.

These views are set forth in: H. Richard Uviller, "Evidence from the Mind of the Criminal Suspect: A Reconsideration of the Current Rules of Access and Restraint," 87 *Columbia Law Review* (1987) 1137. While Uviller's reasoning and conclusions regarding *Massiah* are far from indisputable, his articulate and temperate critique of the doctrine is highly theoretical, creative, logical, and thorough. Uviller treads ground unexplored by others and provides credible ammunition for those opposed to the Court's decision to extend the right to counsel to government efforts to secure incriminating statements from accused individuals. His work deserves serious attention.

George Dix is also critical of the *Massiah* doctrine. In a small subsection of a far-reaching piece devoted to the general topic of regulating undercover activities by governmental operatives, he asserts that "*Massiah* . . . leaves the law with a blanket prohibition against the use of some self-incriminating statements obtained by undercover investigators, a prohibition supported by a rationale grossly inappropriate to the task." In Dix's view, the *Massiah* doctrine is simply not an appropriate limitation on the conduct of undercover surveillance by the authorities. His positions are explained in: George E. Dix, "Undercover Investigations and Police Rulemaking," 53 *Texas Law Review* (1975) 203.

Readers interested in the fullest exposure to the voices of those opposed to *Massiah* should also review the array of arguments mustered by federal prosecutors in: Office of Legal Policy, U.S. Dep't of Justice, Truth in Criminal Justice Series, Report No. 3, "Report to the Attorney General on the Sixth Amendment Right to Counsel Under the *Massiah* Line of Cases" (1986). This report has been reprinted in 22 *Michigan Journal of Law Reform* (1989) 661.

The other informal pretrial event that triggers a right to counsel is an identification process at which an accused is physically present—a lineup, for example. The general subject of the deficiencies in eyewitness identifications and in the processes used to secure them has been the topic of a number of scholarly treatments. Readers who wish to acquire a solid foundational understanding of the underlying problems that have given rise to the need for legal protection might wish to consult: Elizabeth F. Loftus, *Eyewitness Testimony* (Cambridge, MA: Harvard University Press, 1996). Loftus' objective is "to draw together into one coherent framework the empirical work on eyewitness testimony, and to examine the role that this testimony has played in the American legal system." She discusses a variety of scientific findings regarding the "acquisition, retention, and retrieval" of information by human beings and relates these findings to the subject of eyewitness identification. She also addresses "the impact of eyewitness testimony . . . on the legal system." More specifically, she documents the "enormous credibility" that it "is likely to have with juries," exposes a number of "common but mistaken beliefs about eyewitness testimony," and explains "the legal status of eyewitness testimony." She criticizes the Supreme Court for dismantling the safeguards "against faulty convictions" that it initially constructed. According to Loftus, her

> book faces in two directions[,] . . . inward to the field of experimental psychology with the purpose of providing a theoretical framework . . . [and] . . . outward toward the rest of the world in an attempt to say how this body of research should be fitted into society as a whole, and into the legal system in particular.

This groundbreaking and highly readable work makes distinctive contributions to our understanding of the infirmities of eyewitness identifications and the sources of those infirmities. It also raises important questions about the validity of the premises upon which the Supreme Court has relied in discerning and developing constitutional doctrines that regulate the admissibility of eyewitness identifications.

Brian Cutler and Steven Penrod have also documented the problems with eyewitness testimony and have undertaken an assessment of whether legal safeguards afford effective protection against the serious risks of misidentification inherent in eyewitness identification evidence. Cutler and Penrod ask whether counsel, juries, expert testimony, or judges can effectively counteract the potential for serious error engendered by eyewitness identifications. Their significant, detailed analyses and conclusions can be found in: Brian L. Cutler and Steven D. Penrod, *Mistaken Identification* (New York: Cambridge University Press, 1995).

According to Joseph Grano, the entitlement to counsel at lineups and other corporeal identification processes "is sometimes viewed as prophylactic," that is, as a protective device for " 'the underlying constitutional right to a fair trial.' " However, Grano believes that the entitlement to counsel in identification contexts "is rooted squarely in the sixth amendment's right to counsel provision." In his view, "a violation of the right to counsel at lineups is a violation of the Constitution itself." The persuasive reasoning in support of his sensible conclusions can be found in: Joseph D. Grano, "Prophylactic Rules in

Criminal Procedure: A Question of Article III Legitimacy," 80 *Northwestern University Law Review* (1985) 100.

A most useful discussion of how the current doctrine defining the entitlement to assistance at identification processes allows the authorities to "circumvent an accused's sixth amendment right to counsel" can be found in William Pena Wells and Brian L. Cutler, "The Right to Counsel at Videotaped Lineups: An Emerging Dilemma," 22 *Connecticut Law Review* (1990) 373. Wells and Cutler review Supreme Court doctrine pertaining to the right to counsel at identification processes. They describe a number of lower court opinions that hold, in light of the Supreme Court's decision in United States v. Ash, that there is no right to counsel when a witness is shown a videotaped lineup of an accused. In their view, the *Ash* Court "retreated from recognizing the right to counsel by denying its existence in circumstances where the accused is physically absent and the lineup is in any way 'preserved' for future scrutiny." They contend that "[o]nce video technology becomes prevalent, the Court must reverse its decision in *Ash*" to prevent resurrection of "all the dangers" that originally prompted the Supreme Court to extend the right to counsel to lineups. While Wells and Cutler call upon the Court to "recognize the right to counsel at videotaped lineups as constitutionally mandated," they realistically acknowledge the likelihood "that the Court will decline to extend" the right to counsel to that context. Their prediction that the Court will reject an entitlement to counsel at videotaped lineups is on target. Their criticisms of the logic that dictates that holding are well warranted. Their contention that the refusal to afford assistance when videotaped lineups are used cannot be reconciled with the actual reasons for granting an entitlement to assistance at live lineups is difficult to refute and exposes the logical weaknesses in the reasoning and doctrine developed by the Supreme Court.

The Entitlement to Counsel's Assistance for and at Trial

This subsection of the analysis focuses upon both the undisputed Sixth Amendment promise of assistance of counsel at trial and the limited guarantee of counsel in post-trial proceedings. Most of the scholarship discussed in the following essays pertains to issues raised by claims of entitlements to assistance in the plea bargaining process, in appellate proceedings, and in collateral attacks upon convictions.

Because the Supreme Court's landmark decision in Gideon v. Wainwright regarding the entitlement to assistance at trial was also discussed in the third subsection of the first part of the analysis, the bibliographical essays corresponding to that subsection contain discussions of two significant works pertaining to the *Gideon* case. Those works are: Anthony Lewis, *Gideon's Trumpet* (New York: Random House, 1964); and Jerold H. Israel, "*Gideon v. Wainwright*: The 'Art' of Overruling," 1963 *Supreme Court Review* 211.

It is widely accepted that the right to trial assistance extends to plea proceedings. Albert Alschuler has written a monumental article concerning the actual effects of defense counsel representation during the guilty plea process. Alschuler notes that it is generally accepted that the right to legal assistance is "a primary safeguard of fairness in plea bargaining" and observes that this view seems to be shared by the Supreme Court. He then sets out to determine whether lawyers really do significantly enhance the fairness of guilty plea negotiations and concludes that "current conceptions of the defense attorney's role are often more romanticized than real."

Alschuler evaluates the role played by counsel based on interviews of participants in the plea process conducted in ten urban jurisdictions. His disturbing and unsettling, although well-supported, conclusions are that the plea bargaining system is "necessarily destructive of sound attorney–client relationships," that it "subjects defense attorneys to serious temptations to disregard clients' interests," and that only the outright abolition of plea bargaining could remedy the "problems and incongruities" created by the system. In Alschuler's considered opinion, as a result of unavoidable "bureaucratic pressures and conflicts of interest," defense attorneys fail to "safeguard[] the fairness of the plea-negotiation process" and "invariably [have] personal interests that depart from those of [the] client." Professor Alschuler's realistic and insightful assessment of the role of counsel in the day-to-day operation of the guilty plea process can be found in: Albert W. Alschuler, "The Defense Attorney's Role in Plea Bargaining," 84 *Yale Law Journal* (1975) 1179.

The Entitlement to Counsel's Assistance after Trial

The Right to the Assistance of Counsel at Sentencing Proceedings

Pugh and Carver thoroughly analyze the significance of the right to assistance at post-trial sentencing proceedings. Their work carefully examines the history of the recognition of that right and calls for sentencing standards to assist lawyers' efforts to provide assistance at the sentencing stage. They also discuss the procedural advantages that defendants enjoy as a result of the entitlement to representation at the sentencing stage of the criminal process. Pugh and Carver assert that sentencing must be considered a "critical stage" of the adversary process, a stage that triggers a need for and a right to the Sixth Amendment guarantee of counsel's aid and expertise. The article is: George W. Pugh and M. Hampton Carver, "Due Process and Sentencing: From *Mapp* to *Mempa* to *McGautha*," 49 *Texas Law Review* (1970) 25.

Another exceptionally perceptive treatment of the right to counsel for sentencing purposes, written before the Supreme Court's decision in Mempa v. Rhay, can be found in: Sanford H. Kadish, "The Advocate and the Expert—Counsel in the Peno-Correctional Process," 45 *Minnesota Law Review* (1961) 803. Professor Kadish's concerns extend beyond postconviction sentencing by judges and include both "administrative sentencing" (i.e, release decisions by parole boards) and "commitment redeterminations" (i.e., decisions to revoke probation or parole). Based on the important contributions that trained counsel can make to the fair administration of all dispositional proceedings, he builds a weighty case for granting convicted defendants the right to a lawyer's assistance in these phases of the criminal process. Kadish acknowledges that there are countervailing practical concerns but does not believe that they outweigh the advantages of ensuring legal representation in "crucial stages of the criminal process in which decisions of the greatest impact upon the life of the offender are made." For those concerned with the limited scope of the defendant's constitutional entitlement to counsel's assistance once an initial sentencing decision is completed, Kadish's piece is essential reading.

The Right to the Assistance of Counsel on Appeal

As noted in the analysis, the Supreme Court adheres to the view that there is no constitutional right to appeal a conviction. That view appears in the Court's opinions pertaining to the right to counsel during the appellate process. The Court has not furnished a convincing rationale for the conclusion that the Constitution does not contain a right to appeal. In an article in the *UCLA Law Review*, Marc Arkin examines the Court's position and builds an impressive case for the opposite conclusion. After reviewing the current doctrine, he examines the significance of a right to appeal and the role of appellate review in the criminal process. He then endeavors to demonstrate that the conventional wisdom that a criminal appeal is not a "part of the historic tradition of due process" is of questionable validity. To the contrary, Arkin contends that at the time our nation was founded, "there were significant avenues for review of criminal cases, . . . [that] persisted throughout the nineteenth century, and . . . [that] the rhetoric of review was closely associated with contemporary understanding of fair adjudication."

After casting doubt on the historical foundation upon which the denial of a constitutional entitlement to appeal has been premised, Arkin engages in a lengthy analysis of due process constructs. Ultimately, he concludes that "the integral constitutional role played by the criminal appeal" can find support in the "fairness model" of due process, which "stresses the evolving nature of constitutional standards and requires all government procedures, whether historic or modern, to satisfy an independent inquiry based on current notions of fairness." Moreover, recognition of a constitutional foundation for the right to appeal would be neither superfluous nor overly burdensome on courts. It would "insulate[] basic procedural requirements from the winds of legislative change and invest[] them with a dignity that otherwise may be lacking." In addition, the conclusion that the right to appeal a criminal conviction has constitutional roots "would lend a greater seriousness to the debate regarding the nature of post-trial . . . process and would shift the debate away from concerns of calendar control toward issues of rights and accuracy." The theoretically important and thought-provoking piece in which these views are set forth is: Marc M. Arkin, "Rethinking the Constitutional Right to a Criminal Appeal," 39 *UCLA Law Review* (1992) 503.

The Right to the Assistance of Counsel in Collateral Attacks upon Convictions

The right to counsel for purposes of collaterally attacking criminal convictions has not been the subject of a great deal of scholarly attention. One noteworthy, recent article posits the thesis that the Eighth Amendment guarantee against cruel and unusual punishment is violated when those convicted of capital offenses are denied the "fundamental right" to counsel in state postconviction proceedings. Clive Smith and Remy Starns review the pertinent decisions, focusing particular attention on Murray v. Giarratano. They explain in considerable detail why capital inmates are simply incapable of representing themselves effectively in collateral challenges to their convictions and death sentences. Smith and Starns point out that others have generally assumed that any right to counsel in postconviction challenges stems from either the Due Process or Equal Protection Clause. Their reliance, instead, on an Eighth Amendment argument that rests heavily on the evidence of contemporary values provided by the large majority of states that do guarantee counsel in capital cases is interesting. The article is: Clive A. Stafford Smith and Remy Voisin Starns, "Folly by Fiat: Pretending That Death Row Inmates Can Represent Themselves in State Capital Post-Conviction Proceedings," 45 *Loyola Law Review* (1999) 55. In a brief analysis that predates the Smith and Starns article, Alice McGill asserts that the "reliability" demanded by the Eighth Amendment in capital cases necessitates appointed counsel for indigents in postconviction proceedings. Her views are presented in: Alice McGill, Comment, "*Murray v. Giarratano*: The Right to Counsel in Postconviction Proceedings in Death Penalty Cases," 18 *Hastings Constitutional Law Quarterly* (1990) 211.

Prior to the Supreme Court's decision in Murray v. Giarratano, Michael Mello constructed an impressive and creative case in favor of recognizing a general right to counsel for indigents in capital postconviction proceedings. While Mello is not averse to a holding that one particular constitutional provision mandates a right to assistance, his article draws upon several "elements" derived from a number of constitutional guarantees and various lines of authority. According to Mello, when combined, strains of Sixth Amendment, due process, equal protection, and Eighth Amendment doctrine require the "recognition of a right to counsel in capital post-conviction proceedings." Mello's skillful interweaving of diverse constitutional themes is intriguing and ultimately rests heavily upon the well-recognized principle that death is different and requires heightened legal protection. The article is: Michael A. Mello, "Is There a Federal Constitutional Right to Counsel in Capital Post-Conviction Proceedings?" 79 *Journal of Criminal Law and Criminology* (1989) 1065.

The Right of Self-Representation on Appeal

Prior to the Court's decision in Martinez v. Court of Appeal of California, a couple of articles discussed the question of self-representation on appeal. John Decker's noteworthy reflection upon *Faretta* is discussed in the section of these bibliographical essays corresponding to the fifth subsection of the first part of the analysis chapter. In that lengthy piece, Decker briefly considers the issue of self-representation in postconviction phases of the criminal process. He reviews the splits and confusion in the lower courts, noting that most had taken a quite restrictive view toward defendant's claims of a right to act *pro se* on appeal and in collateral proceedings. While Decker does not expressly predict how the Supreme Court would resolve the issue of *pro se* representation in a first appeal, he suggests that the relevant precedents militate against any substantial entitlement to represent oneself. The article is: John F. Decker, "The Sixth Amendment Right to Shoot Oneself in the Foot: An Assessment of the Guarantee of Self-Representation Twenty Years After *Faretta*," 6 *Seton Hall Constitutional Law Journal* (1996) 483.

In a narrow article focused on the right to *pro se* representation on appeal, Krikava and Winking contend that a denial of self-representation on a first appeal violates the indigent defendant's entitlement to equal protection. Their assertion that forcing a lawyer upon an indigent results in unconstitutional discrimination seems unpersuasive in light of the differences between the entitlement to counsel and the entitlement to self-representation. Their reasoning is set forth in: Michael C. Krikava and Charlann E. Winking, "The Right of an Indigent Criminal Defendant to Proceed *Pro Se* on Appeal: By Statute or Constitution, a Necessary Evil," 15 *William Mitchell Law Review* (1989) 103.

The Content of the Right to the Assistance of Counsel

This part of the analysis in the text is concerned with the "content" of the right to counsel (i.e., the substantive entitlements that constitute the guarantee of legal assistance). Most of the subtopics addressed in this part have been the subject of limited, if any, scholarly commentary. Only two have attracted substantial attention: the right to loyalty and threats posed by conflicts of interest and the entitlement to competent performance by defense counsel.

The Entitlement to Adequate Investigation and Preparation for Trial

Richard Klein has written a significant article exploring the devastating impacts of the underfunding of criminal defense agencies on indigent defendants' right to the effective assistance of counsel. Klein observes that the failure to fund defenders adequately has resulted in excessive caseloads that prevent adequate preparation and investigation of cases. "[C]aseload pressures and insufficient funding have led to widespread failings by defenders of their duty to investigate." In his view, "[t]horough preparation of a case is perhaps *the most important aspect of effective advocacy*" (italics added), for even the most capable counsel cannot fulfill his constitutional roles if his investigation and preparation have been deficient. Klein's conclusions are supported by surveys of trial attorneys and judges in which significant percentages—over half of each group—expressed the view that inadequate preparation was the predominant cause of defense counsel incompetence. Because he does not believe that public funding is likely to increase, Klein suggests that lawyers' registration fees and the interest on lawyer trust accounts be diverted to remedy the problems that he has identified.

Although Klein's discussion of the duties to investigate and prepare constitutes a very brief portion of his analysis, his treatment highlights the vital significance of criminal defendants' entitlements to adequate investigation and preparation by counsel. His exposure of the unfortunate realities that impede investigation and preparation is both enlightening and sobering, and his proposals for alternative sources of funding are thought-provoking. The article is: Richard Klein, "The Emperor *Gideon* Has No Clothes: The Empty Promise of the Constitutional Right to Effective Assistance of Counsel," 13 *Hastings Constitutional Law Quarterly* (1986) 625.

The Entitlement to Active, Full Participation by Counsel in the Adversarial Process

No significant resources directly pertinent to the right to have counsel fully participate in the adversarial process were discovered in researching this text.

The Entitlement to Consult with Counsel

One article that devotes substantial attention to the defendant's constitutional entitlement to consult with counsel is: Jay Sterling Silver, "Equality of Arms and the Adversarial Process: A New Constitutional Right," 1990 *Wisconsin Law Review* 1007. The broad thesis of Silver's work (which is discussed more throughly in the bibliographical essays corresponding to the first subsection of the first part of the analysis) is that "a lack of faith in" the adjudicatory process has prompted the Supreme Court to tilt the "delicate balance between the prosecution and defense . . . in favor of the state." Believing that the Court's decision in Perry v. Leeke provides a graphic illustration of the detrimental effects of the Court's lack of faith, Silver engages in a thorough analysis and critical assessment of the majority opinion. He maintains that one of the premises for the Court's holding that limited bans on attorney–client consultation are permissible, "a distrust of criminal defense attorneys," has "ominous implications for the adversarial process." He maintains that a "brief but nonreciprocal ban on communication between the defendant and his attorney impinges on the right to counsel . . . and is inconsistent with due process." Silver would remedy these constitutional problems by "accord[ing] formal recognition to the principle of equality of arms, a principle essential to fairness and effectiveness in our adversarial search for truth." Although his focal concern is considerably broader, Silver's article provides unique insights into the critical importance of unfettered communication between the accused and his lawyer.

The Entitlement to Loyal Representation by Counsel

As explained in the text, conflicts of interest pose the primary threat to defendants' Sixth Amendment entitlement to loyalty from counsel. Scholars have shown considerable interest in the issues surrounding and generated by conflicts of interests. Kevin McMunigal, in an article that does not focus narrowly on criminal contexts, addresses the general topic of conflicts from an ethical perspective. According to McMunigal, while lawyers' conflicts of interest yield " 'the most litigated questions of professional responsibility,' " the governing doctrine suffers from serious "confusion" that is the consequence of a "failure to clearly articulate and answer the central questions which lie at the heart of the subject." McMunigal opines that "the primary task of conflict of interest doctrine is to formulate an appropriate response to situations which threaten impairment of an attorney's functioning." He believes that competition among three different approaches to conflict questions has produced "conceptual dissonance" that is a "primary source of confusion." McMunigal exhaustively examines and critiques the "risk avoidance approach," highlighting the appropriate questions to be asked from that perspective. He does not endeavor to provide answers to those questions, however, acknowledging that his analysis is "only a beginning" of the process of remedying the unclarities and ambiguities that plague conflict of interest law.

McMunigal admirably accomplishes his simple, though ambitious, goals—"to demonstrate the need for rethinking attorney conflict of interest doctrine" and "to provide the first steps toward a clearer, more sophisticated treatment of attorney conflict of interest doctrine." He insightfully identifies the "hard questions," that is, "how to respond to threats" to an attorney's performance generated by conflicts and "how to distinguish risks which are acceptable from those which are unacceptable." McMunigal's piece is an excellent, informative resource for those interested in exploring the complexities of conflict of interest determinations. The article is: Kevin McMunigal, "Rethinking Attorney Conflict of Interest Doctrine," 5 *Georgetown Journal of Legal Ethics* (1992) 823.

Bruce Green focuses on a vitally important issue of legal ethics that has significant implications for the fairness of criminal trials: What are the obligations of prosecutors who are aware of defense attorney conflicts of interest? According to Green, the codes of professional responsibility treat that question "superficially," yet the "need for . . . guidance is ever increasing" due to concern that "motions to disqualify opposing counsel based on conflicts of interest may be used to obtain an unfair tactical advantage." Green asserts that prosecutors who are aware of potential defense counsel conflicts should disclose them to defense counsel and then, if no remedial action is taken, should inform trial judges of those conflicts. Moreover, prosecutors also have the duty to seek judicial hearings at which accused persons may either waive their rights to conflict-free assistance or seek representation by unconflicted attorneys. Green also maintains that in certain cases, prosecutors have obligations to help eliminate conflicts of interest that would otherwise lead to defense counsel disqualification. He cogently argues that government attorneys should move to disqualify defense attorneys only if: (1) an accused cannot provide a valid waiver; (2) a serious conflict is likely to undermine the appearance of a fair and ethical trial; or (3) legitimate government interests could be impaired by defense counsel's conflict.

The article—Bruce A. Green, "Her Brother's Keeper: The Prosecutor's Responsibility When Defense Counsel Has a Potential Conflict of Interest," 16 *American Journal of Criminal Law* (1989) 323—is an interesting and analytically coherent discourse on the questions that arise and the options that are available when government attorneys learn that defense lawyers may have conflicting interests and divided loyalties. The answers proposed seem to be the result of a genuine effort to balance the competing concerns of the defendant, the government, and society.

In Gary T. Lowenthal, "Successive Representation by Criminal Lawyers," 93 *Yale Law Journal* (1983) 1, the author focuses on conflicts of interest that arise when criminal defense attorneys encounter former clients who are government witnesses in cases against current clients. A quandary results because the former client has divulged information to the lawyer on the understanding that it would be used exclusively for her benefit while ethical duties weigh in favor of using that information to zealously promote the current client's interests. Based on his empirical study, Lowenthal concludes that this sort of "divided loyalty" is "commonplace" for active criminal defense attorneys. Based on a nationwide survey, he asserts that public defenders hold diverse views concerning the appropriate response when placed in such a position. In Lowenthal's opinion, this attorney confusion is a reflection of the ambiguities in the codes of professional responsibility. Moreover, the courts have a "tendency to overlook the complexities of successive representation," and their resolutions of the issues betray a "lack of coherence."

Lowenthal argues that efforts to provide "more direction" and to alert trial courts in advance to instances of successive representation will enhance "the fairness and reliability of the criminal justice system." He proposes a framework that would impose an ethical obligation on defense counsel and on prosecutors to notify the court of prior representation. Judges would then conduct "pre-trial . . . judicial inquir[ies] to determine the existence and potential effects of successive representation." Lowenthal is realistic, acknowledging that his proposals would not eliminate either the problems of divided loyalty or the adversarial abuses of ill-motivated government disqualification motions. He is optimistic, however, that the steps that he suggests would ensure that all players in the process are aware of potential risks and would minimize the risk of disqualification motions based on questionable motives. This article contains a superior analysis of the conflict of interest problem in criminal cases. The author's efforts to illuminate a neglected, though frequent, source of conflicts of interest for defense lawyers, his emphasis on before-the-fact efforts to prevent the damage inflicted by these conflicts, and his constructive, feasible suggestions for prophylactic steps deserve serious consideration.

Jeff Brown shares Lowenthal's concern with successive representation. His point of departure is the California provision for the appointment of public defenders to represent indigent defendants—more specifically, an exception to that provision that precludes appointment of a public defender when a conflict of interest would result. Brown believes that the criminal justice system is plagued by serious, unremedied conflicts. He claims that in California "[t]en to thirty percent of all indigent criminal defendants are involved in conflict of interest cases." He discusses four situations that engender conflicts but focuses particular attention on the conflicts that are the most difficult to remedy—those that arise when victims or witnesses are either past or present clients of the same public defender office that is presently representing an accused defendant. Brown concludes that in such cases there is a need for a "new protocol" that should involve "a rigorous review of cases for potential conflicts of interest, and more definitive and accepted standards, in order to resolve conflict of interest problems facing public defender offices across the country today." Brown believes that the problems that currently exist can be remedied "[o]nly by taking client privacy seriously, by making a scrupulous assessment of cases for potential conflicts of interest, and by clarifying standards for disqualification."

Brown's portrayal of the frequency with which conflicts arise seems realistic. He helpfully identifies the unique threats posed by prior or current representation of a victim or witness. His calls for reform, like those of Lowenthal, are motivated by a sincere perception of an acute need for meaningful preventive measures. His article is: Jeff Brown, "Disqualification of the Public Defender: Toward a New Protocol for Resolving Conflicts of Interest," 31 *University of San Francisco Law Review* (1996) 1.

Nancy J. Moore claims that the ethical rules regarding "multiple representation of clients with conflicting interests" are "[o]ne of the most fertile sources of confusion." In a significant article in the *Texas Law Review*, she explores the multiple representation dilemma, identifying inadequacies in the standards for determining the ethical propriety of representing multiple clients and proposing "a new general standard based upon client capacity for informed and voluntary consent." Moore applies that standard to three common multiple representation situations, concluding that while multiple representation can satisfy ethical concerns in the two civil contexts, it cannot be consistent with ethical constraints in situations involving multiple representation of criminal codefendants. In her view, "there is so little likelihood that criminal codefendants have the capacity for informed and voluntary consent that the profession ought, as a prophylactic rule, to prohibit multiple representation in all cases." Moore maintains that a requirement of separate counsel "is constitutionally permissible." She examines the relevant precedents and sets out the reasoning that supports her conclusion that a ban on multiple representation of codefendants does not violate a constitutional "right to waive effective assistance" or the Sixth Amendment right to counsel of choice. Moore's concern with criminal defendants' capacity for giving sufficiently knowing and voluntary waivers of the entitlement to conflict-free assistance is understandable and may well reflect the realities of multiple representation contexts. Nevertheless, her conclusion that the Sixth Amendment right to counsel of choice is not violated by a prophylactic rule mandating separate representation seems out of line with Supreme Court precedent, particularly the *Wheat* decision. Consequently, it is doubtful that her preventive scheme would survive constitutional scrutiny. The article is: Nancy J. Moore, "Conflicts of Interest in the Simultaneous Representation of Multiple Clients: A Proposed Solution to the Current Confusion and Controversy," 61 *Texas Law Review* (1982) 211.

A good general source for pursuing the wealth of legal and ethical issues and details surrounding the topic of conflicts of interest is: "Developments in the Law—Conflicts of Interest in the Legal Profession," 94 *Harvard Law Review* (1981) 1244. This 250-page piece opens with the observation that "[f]rom 1908 to the present, the lawyer with conflicting interests has provided bench and bar with one of the toughest problems in legal ethics." It then painstakingly describes and analyzes the law concerning conflicts of interest. The topics include: models of ethical regulation, conflicts in private practice, conflicts and the criminal lawyer, conflicts in representation of the poor, conflicts and government attorneys, conflicts with the public interest, and sanctions for conflicts. Readers who desire further insights into a broad array of issues, rules, and judicial decisions concerning conflicts of interest will wish to consult this resource.

The Entitlement to Competent Representation by Counsel—The "Actual Ineffectiveness" Doctrine

Since the Supreme Court's landmark 1984 decision in Strickland v. Washington, there have been a number of very good scholarly treatments of the Sixth Amendment right to competent representation by defense counsel. Many of the discussions are highly critical of the *Strickland* Court's formulation of the doctrinal requirements for establishing "actual ineffectiveness."

William Geimer is among the most vocal and strident critics of Strickland. In William S. Geimer, "A Decade of *Strickland*'s Tin Horn: Doctrinal and Practical Undermining of the Right to Counsel," 4 *William & Mary Bill of Rights Journal* (1995) 91, he accuses the *Strickland* Court of "ensur[ing] that *Gideon* guarantees little more than the presence of a person with a law license alongside the accused during trial" and of "fostering tolerance of abysmal lawyering." His object is "to illuminate the pernicious effects of *Strickland* on . . . doctrines . . . essential to fairness in criminal cases, and on the legal profession itself." According to Geimer, as a doctrinal matter, *Strickland* turns the harmless error doctrine on its head (by putting the burden of showing harm on the defendant) and deincorporates the fundamental right to counsel. As a practical matter, it permits lawyers to abandon their clients and to perform their duties incompetently.

Geimer calls for a revival of the right to effective legal representation. He contends that the organized bar ought to recognize that incompetence is unethical and ought to help refashion a realistic, minimum constitutional standard. He also maintains that individual lawyers should report incompetence, litigate competence prior to trial, and consider refusing to participate in a system that is not fulfilling the constitutional promise of effective representation. Finally, Geimer advocates a campaign by academics to bring down *Strickland.* Perhaps Geimer's indictments of the *Strickland* doctrine are warranted. His conclusions and his call to arms would be more persuasive, however, if he had at least entertained—and rebutted—the countervailing considerations that might be offered to support *Strickland.* Nonetheless, for those interested in a full understanding of the case against *Strickland,* Geimer's piece is important reading.

Richard Klein's approach to the issue of ineffective assistance is distinctly realistic and pragmatic. He focuses on the damage to the guarantee of effective assistance and the resulting threats to the adversary system that are the consequence of the severe underfunding of the agencies that provide representation for indigent criminal defendants. He reviews the genesis of indigents' right to "effective assistance," details the growth of appellate claims of ineffective assistance and the systemic impediments to proving those claims, distinguishes between ineffectiveness due to trial court interference and ineffectiveness due to counsel's incompetence, and analyzes *Strickland* and other relevant Supreme Court decisions. In light of his conclusion that there are serious obstacles to appellate relief, Klein contends that "it is crucial that substantial efforts be made to insure that counsel act effectively and competently at the trial level." He calls upon the legal profession to prescribe clear guidance regarding what lawyers must do "to provide competent representation," concluding that past attempts "are too general to be of much practical assistance." According to Klein, "particularized standards" of competent representation are both necessary and feasible.

Klein documents the seriousness of the "underfunding" problem for criminal defense agencies and highlights the variety of specific ways in which inadequate resources result in deficient assistance and undermine the foundational premises of the adversary system. He argues that the "legal profession has an obligation to insure that the system providing representation for indigent defendants complies with professional standards of competency, and with the constitutional requirements of effective assistance of counsel and equal justice under law." Finally, he suggests that the bar could fulfill its obligation by dedicating professional registration fees to subsidize effective assistance for indigents, or, alternatively, by ensuring that interest on lawyers' trust fund accounts is used for that purpose. Klein provides a convincing, if sobering, portrait of the realities of ineffective assistance for indigents that result from deficient funding and judicial impediments to appellate relief. He does not seek a solution in the usual places—the reform of the "ineffective assistance" doctrine or increased government funding. Instead, Klein creatively and constructively looks to the legal profession as a source of the funds necessary to combat ineffective representation. His call upon the legal profession to intervene and rescue the Sixth Amendment guarantee has considerable merit but seems unlikely to be heeded. The article is: Richard Klein, "The Emperor *Gideon* Has No Clothes: The Empty Promise of the Constitutional Right to Effective Assistance of Counsel," 13 *Hastings Constitutional Law Quarterly* (1986) 625.

Donald Dripps lends his voice to the chorus, observing that "*Strickland*'s critics rightly claim that the current right-to-counsel doctrine is dysfunctional." In his opinion, "[t]he root of the problem . . . lies in *Gideon*'s focus on the *right to counsel* to the neglect of the *right to a fair trial*." He documents the evidence that the assistance actually furnished to indigent defendants is woefully deficient and explores the origins of the deficiencies. He believes that it is possible for courts to "design a constitutional doctrine" that will induce "legislatures to provide a minima of support for indigent defense." After examining the development of the controlling doctrine from *Gideon* through *Strickland*, Dripps arrives at the radical conclusion that after-the-fact review of counsel's effectiveness is inherently flawed. In his view, the alternative that can produce results is an "*ex ante* parity standard" that evaluates the adequacy of counsel before the fact and seeks to determine whether there is "rough equality" between defense counsel and prosecutors "in litigation effectiveness." Dripps discusses the remedial steps that could be employed at the pretrial stage to ensure the necessary equality and explains why an *ex ante* approach is likely to promote a solution to the current crisis in criminal defense. He acknowledges that his approach "is novel" but persuasively argues that an after-the-fact approach to the problem of incompetent representation offers little hope for remedying the extant crisis. His case for a revolutionary before-the-fact approach based on "parity" is inviting, challenging, and definitely worthy of serious attention from those who value the fundamental right to counsel. The article is: Donald A. Dripps, "Ineffective Assistance of Counsel: The Case for an *Ex Ante* Parity Standard," 88 *Journal of Criminal Law & Criminology* (1997) 242.

Jeffrey Kirchmeier focuses more narrowly on *Strickland*'s controversial "prejudice" demand. After exploring the development of the right to competent assistance, he discusses the cases in which prejudice is not a necessary component for an ineffective assistance of counsel finding. He then explains why sleeping, intoxicated, or otherwise substantially mentally impaired defense counsel should not be judged under the dual *Strickland* standards. According to Kirchmeier, the reasons for presuming competence and requiring prejudice to be shown are simply inapplicable in these situations. The premises underlying the conclusion that prejudice need not be shown when counsel is absent or has a conflict of interests support the same conclusion when counsel sleeps or is substantially mentally impaired. Kirchmeier's focus on the somewhat limited—though significant—problems of sleeping and impaired defense attorneys yields a most useful exposition of the logical underpinnings of *Strickland* and suggests that there are discrete situations where incompetent counsel claims should not be governed by *Strickland*'s demanding "actual ineffectiveness" doctrine. The article is: Jeffrey L. Kirchmeier, "Drink, Drugs, and Drowsiness: The Constitutional Right to Assistance of Counsel and the *Strickland* Prejudice Requirement," 75 *Nebraska Law Review* (1996) 425.

Vivian Berger has addressed the subject of ineffective assistance in a couple of articles. In Vivian O. Berger, "The Supreme Court and Defense Counsel: Old Roads, New Paths—A Dead End?" 86 *Columbia Law Review* (1986) 9, an ambitious piece that is broadly concerned with trends in the development of the Sixth Amendment right to assistance, she opines that the extent to which defense attorneys actually render incompetent representation is actually unknown and that estimates of its widespread nature typically are the product of "guesswork" and "anecdotal" evidence. Nonetheless, it "seems likely that counsel inadequacy poses a very severe, if difficult to measure, problem." Berger summarizes the law prior to *Strickland* and the doctrine promulgated in *Strickland.* She is unpersuaded by the reasons offered by the majority to support the deficient performance standard but nonetheless finds that there were alternative justifications for refusing "to constitutionalize specific directives to counsel." Berger expresses genuine concern over the "deleterious aspects" of the prejudice demand imposed by the *Strickland* Court. She carefully analyzes both the Court's "negative case" and its "affirmative case" for requiring a showing of prejudice, ultimately concluding that neither is persuasive. In her view, to show a Sixth Amendment deprivation, a defendant should not have "to show that he would have fared better in some respect, had his lawyer been competent . . . [b]oth because the right to effective assistance rests on concern with process as much as results and because injury is difficult to prove in many cases where it doubtless exists." Berger provides a helpful summary of the underpinnings of the *Strickland* doctrine. Her temperate approach to *Strickland* and willingness to entertain possible rationales for the two *Strickland* criteria lend credibility to her argument against the Court's adoption of the prejudice demand.

In a brief contribution to a death penalty colloquium, Vivian O. Berger, "The Chiropractor as Brain Surgeon: Defense Lawyering in Capital Cases," 18 *New York University Review of Law & Social Change* (1990–1991) 245, Professor Berger focuses on the reality of ineffective assistance in capital cases. She asserts that "in the capital defense setting defense counsel too often deliver—and courts at all levels too often tolerate, when indeed they do not encourage—performance so shoddy as to render the law in its application a mockery of the sixth and eighth amendments." In her view, there are a number of reasons that capital defense lawyers are so often deficient. Those reasons include: incompetence, meager compensation, fear of social reprisal, a lack of specialized capital defense expertise, the emotional strains of the role, and socioeconomic and racial differences between the lawyers and the defendants, their families, and their friends. According to Berger, "the conditions of capital defense work virtually guarantee ineffectiveness . . . in an alarming number of cases." In addition, the doctrinal demands of *Strickland* "make most sixth amendment challenges hopeless," and the practical impediments to unearthing and establishing trial counsel's failings are severe. Berger raises the distressing possibility that our nation "lacks the political will to stop" the travesties that routinely occur but maintains that they must be stopped if the constitutional promise of counsel is to be honored. Her portrayal of the poor quality of representation in capital cases, her explanation of the reasons for that state of affairs, and her suggestion that *Strickland* offers no hope for those victimized by ineffective representation are convincing and deeply disturbing.

Ellen Kreitzberg has similar views. She asserts that the death penalty is not being imposed in a manner that comports with constitutional mandates and that *Strickland* is largely to blame. She calls upon the judiciary either to employ more demanding standards of performance for capital cases or to adopt a presumption of ineffectiveness when counsel fails to investigate thoroughly and look for mitigating evidence. She urges legislators to enact appointment guidelines that will ensure adequate representation and to provide the resources necessary to defend against capital charges. Those concerned with *Strickland*'s implications for and impact upon capital cases will find Kreitzberg's piece helpful. The article is: Ellen Kreitzberg, "Death Without Justice," 35 *Santa Clara Law Review* (1995) 485.

As part of a colloquium on the effective assistance of counsel, Gary Goodpaster has published a paper focusing on the constitutional standard for ineffectiveness. He examines the *Strickland* standard and its implications, concluding that it provides relief for some of the defendants who receive inadequate representation and that it helps lower courts resolve ineffectiveness claims. He maintains that the *Strickland* rules "do not solve the systemic problem of ineffective assistance, . . . provide no practical guidance to criminal defense attorneys, and do nothing to improve the quality of criminal defense." Goodpaster argues that the *Strickland* Court erred insofar as it "recognized only the due process aspects of the effective assistance guarantee" and neglected the "equal protection" demand of "roughly equal treatment between defendants." In his view, the "equal protection component of the adversary system can only be realized through an advocacy model." According to that model, a defense lawyer can serve all four adversary system goals (i.e., truth-finding, achieving publicly acceptable results, fairness to the accused, and protecting constitutional rights) by "zealously and singlemindedly serv[ing] the interests of her client, attempting to obtain the best possible result under the circumstances." According to Professor Goodpaster, constitutional ineffective assistance standards should "be based on advocacy norms . . . and not on system purposes." His summary and critique of *Strickland* are well conceived and insightful. His contention that the Court ignored an important constitutional perspective is thought-provoking. While he adopts a distinctive theoretical approach, it leads him to some of the same criticisms of *Strickland* that others have launched from different directions. The article is: Gary Goodpaster, "The Adversary System, Advocacy, and Effective Assistance of Counsel in Criminal Cases," 14 *New York University Review of Law & Social Change* (1986) 59.

Effective assistance in the plea process is the concern of Steven Zeidman, "To Plead or Not to Plead: Effective Assistance and Client-Centered Counseling," 39 *Boston College Law Review* (1998) 841. Zeidman identifies a "critical," but neglected, question: "What does the Constitution require with respect to counseling a defendant during the plea bargaining process and the decision whether to plead guilty?" His focus is not on whether the *Strickland* standards should be applicable but, instead, on the particular conduct that constitutes effective assistance in this important context. After describing the relevant doctrine and its significance for client counseling, Zeidman explains "the concept of client-centered counseling and its implications for an attorney's role in advising clients." According to Zeidman, unlike the "traditional view of lawyering," which assumes passive clients who delegate decision-making authority to their counsel, client-centered counseling "requires that attorneys listen to their clients and ensure that clients assume an active and primary role in making decisions about their cases." Zeidman engages in a detailed analysis of Boria v. Keane, a decision in which an attorney was deemed ineffective for failing to adequately counsel his client regarding a potential plea. In his view, *Boria* "mandates a reevaluation of the applicability of client-centered counseling to criminal cases." His reevaluation leads him to conclude that a client-centered approach is inconsistent with defense counsel's constitutional obligations. Neutrality cannot fulfill a lawyer's constitutional obligations. Instead, defense attorneys must offer their opinions and advice, explaining how they arrived at them. They must also try to persuade their clients to accept recommended courses of action while not usurping decisions that ultimately belong to the clients. Zeidman's exploration of the debate over attorneys' responsibilities to defendants in plea contexts makes an important, pragmatic contribution. Some might question whether Zeidman's view adequately accounts for unfortunate realities of our criminal justice system, in particular, the enormous pressures on defense counsel to accept plea bargains and the frequently deficient investigation and preparation undertaken by counsel appointed for indigent defendants. Nonetheless, the position that he endorses—requiring an active, involved lawyer who offers her expertise and endeavors to influence an accused to accept her best judgment—is amply defended and seems logically reconcilable with the purposes of the Sixth Amendment right to effective assistance.

The Entitlement to Competent Representation by Counsel on Appeal

As noted in the analysis, the Sixth Amendment does not guarantee a right to counsel on appeal. The Due Process and Equal Protection Clauses of the Fourteenth Amendment, instead, are the wellsprings of the entitlement to legal assistance at the appellate stage. Principles of due process also guarantee that the right to appellate counsel, like the Sixth Amendment right to trial counsel, includes an entitlement to "effective" assistance. An article by Lissa Griffin explains the constitutional roots of the right to effective appellate assistance. Griffin takes issue with the lower courts' unanalyzed decisions to apply the *Strickland* standards to appellate ineffectiveness claims. Based on significant differences both in the *functions* of trial and appellate counsel and in the trial and appellate *forums*, she constructs an engaging argument against applying *Strickland* to appellate ineffectiveness claims. She proposes redefinitions of the "reasonable competence" standard "to fit the role of appellate counsel" and the appellate forum and argues that there should be no "prejudice" requirement for establishing appellate ineffectiveness. As the discussion in this text makes clear, recently the Supreme Court has indicated that *Strickland* does govern determinations of ineffectiveness at the appellate stage. Griffin's straightforward analysis of the right to effective legal representation on appeal and her case against a simplistic adoption of *Strickland* for appellate purposes will prove valuable for those who wish to explore more fully the debate over the proper constitutional standards for judging appellate counsel's efficacy. The article is: Lissa Griffin, "The Right to Effective Assistance of Appellate Counsel," 97 *West Virginia Law Review* (1994) 1.

Relief for Deprivations of the Right to the Assistance of Counsel: Automatic Reversal and Harmless Error

There are a number of solid analytical treatments of the harmless error doctrine. Each of them makes a cognizable contribution to our understanding of the issues raised by and the potential deficiencies in the current law governing harmless error determinations. James Wicht and David McCord both focus their analyses upon the dichotomy between trial errors and structural errors that governs constitutional harmlessness analysis since the Court's decision in Arizona v. Fulminante. Wicht explores the history of harmless error jurisprudence and highlights the common ground that all constitutional violations share. In his view, constitutional transgressions *cannot* be divided into "trial" and "structural" errors. Moreover, there are inherent difficulties in subjecting any constitutional violations to harmlessness analysis. For one thing, a realistic assessment of the impact of such an error on the trier of fact is impossible. In addition, the effect of applying harmless error analysis to constitutional rights is a "lowering of the inherent value attached to those rights." Wicht finds "compelling reasons" for turning back the legal clock to the pre-*Chapman* era, when all constitutional violations resulted in automatic reversal. In his view, "criminal defendants . . . deserve proceedings free from Constitutional infirmity." His analysis is plausible, while his conclusion and proposal are radical, provocative, and somewhat idealistic.

David McCord is also highly critical of the trial error–structural error dichotomy, deeming it "doomed to fail" and "analytically flawed from the outset." He discusses the pre-*Fulminante* precedents, the formulation of the *Fulminante* dichotomy, the flaws that were "immediately apparent" in that dichotomy, and the problems that it has caused the lower courts and the Supreme Court in subsequent cases. In his view, the division of constitutional errors into two categories has bred "rampant confusion," has made the law unnecessarily complex, and has distracted courts from the real issue—whether a constitutional error is serious enough to require reversal. The dichotomy has had "minimal benefits" and takes "a meat-axe approach to what necessarily must be a highly nuanced, case-by-case inquiry." McCord identifies eight factors that should play a role in case-by-case harmlessness analysis. McCord's criticisms of the *Fulminante* Court's division of constitutional errors into two categories are well conceived. His proposal is less extreme than Wicht's and would be less costly to the criminal justice system insofar as it permits constitutional errors to be declared harmless. The case-by-case, multifactor approach that he proposes, while analytically defensible, could prove extremely manipulable in the hands of appellate courts, incredibly inconsistent in application, and quite cumbersome in operation. The two articles are: James Edward Wicht III, "There Is No Such Thing as a Harmless Constitutional Error: Returning to a Rule of Automatic Reversal," 12 *Brigham Young University Journal of Public Law* (1997) 73; and David McCord, "The 'Trial'/'Structural' Error Dichotomy: Erroneous and Not Harmless," 45 *University of Kansas Law Review* (1997) 1401.

Tom Stacy and Kim Dayton construct a somewhat novel approach to constitutional harmless error analysis in a pre-*Fulminante* article published in the *Columbia Law Review*. After evaluating the doctrine that was controlling at the time, Stacy and Dayton offer the simple, yet revolutionary, suggestion that harmless error doctrine should be responsive "to constitutional values unrelated to truth determination." Their careful consideration of the principles and concerns underlying harmlessness doctrine and of the different values that underlie various constitutional provisions leads them to propose a harmless error approach that focuses closely "on the purpose of the particular right violated." In their view, the extant harmlessness doctrine reflects the Supreme Court's "obsession with the truth-determination function of the criminal process." By dissecting the controlling rules and offering a values-based alternative, Stacy and Dayton boldly seek to "confront[] the Court with the question of whether it is serious about protecting rights that do not enhance, and may hinder, the search for the truth." The article is: Tom Stacy and Kim Dayton, "Rethinking Harmless Constitutional Error," 88 *Columbia Law Review* (1988) 79.

In Harry T. Edwards, "To Err is Human But Not Always Harmless: When Should Legal Error Be Tolerated?" 70 *New York University Law Review* (1995) 1167, a distinguished judge on the federal court of appeals offers his perspectives on the harmless error doctrine. Judge Edwards asserts that harmlessness law is plagued by "confusing" and "artificial distinctions" that have provided "excuses for appellate judges to opt in favor of guilt-based decisionmaking," that is, resolutions based on the likelihood of a defendant's factual guilt or innocence. He quite clearly believes that such decision making is misguided. While Judge Edwards remains somewhat "skeptical," he finds reasons to be "optimistic" about "a recent trend in the Supreme Court's case law toward a more constrained approach to harmless error." His analysis of the most recent precedents reveals an emphatic rejection of "the guilt-based approach to harmless error" and movement toward "a common-sense view of harmless error focused not on artificial categories of cases, but on notions of fundamental fairness." Judge Edwards' distinction between harmless error analysis that is "guilt-based" and harmless error analysis that emphasizes "fundamental fairness" raises core questions about the rationales for and objects of harmless error review. Whether his optimism concerning a trend toward the "fundamental fairness" approach is justified remains to be seen.

Daniel Meltzer undertakes a more theoretical treatment of the subject of harmless constitutional error. Meltzer endeavors to explore the "conceptual uncertainties that underlie the federal harmless error rule" in the hope of developing an "understanding of the basis for the doctrine in general." His goal is to uncover the constitutional foundations, if any, for Chapman v. California's decision to subject states to the control of federal harmless error standards. Ultimately, he concludes that whether or not there is a constitutional right to appeal a criminal conviction, the *Chapman* decision cannot be explained "as a simple constitutional decision." Instead, "*Chapman* is best viewed as a rule of constitutional common law, born of concern that state courts, if left free to apply their own harmless error standards, would dilute federal constitutional norms." Meltzer defends this interpretation of *Chapman* and explains its implications—including the consequence that harmless error standards are subject to modification by Congress. His thesis and analyses appear in: Daniel J. Meltzer, "Harmless Error and Constitutional Remedies," 61 *University of Chicago Law Review* (1994) 1. Those interested in the dispute over the underpinnings of constitutional harmless error analysis will find the piece enlightening.

William Geimer, in a far-reaching critique of the ineffective assistance standards of Strickland v. Washington, discusses the relationship between *Strickland*'s prejudice requirement and harmless error analysis. According to Geimer, despite the Supreme Court's "pronouncement that *Strickland*'s approach does not involve harmless error analysis, the contrary is obviously true. *Strickland* involves 'unarticulated harmless error.' " Geimer proffers a cynical, albeit plausible, explanation for the Court's refusal "to acknowledge that its *Strickland* rules turn harmless error on its head." He cogently argues that the Court's decision to create an "exception to the reach of harmless error analysis" is entirely unjustified and undermines the substance of the right to counsel. In Geimer's view, "ineffective assistance of counsel claims ought at the very least be included in the ambit of harmless error." Thus, once a defendant shows a harmfully deficient performance, a violation of the right to counsel should be found and a conviction should be overturned unless the government demonstrates harmlessness beyond a reasonable doubt.

Geimer's arguments and conclusion have much to commend them. As the textual analysis suggests, the prejudice requirement of *Strickland* seems intimately related to the concept of harmless error but places the burden of proving harm on the defendant. Those hostile to *Strickland* will find Geimer's efforts to unmask the prejudice demand persuasive. Those who believe that the prejudice requirement is a reflection of the Court's pragmatism could logically contend that Geimer's analysis is one-sided and oblivious to the realities of the criminal justice system. His article is: William S. Geimer, "A Decade of *Strickland*'s Tin Horn: Doctrinal and Practical Undermining of the Right to Counsel," 4 *William & Mary Bill of Rights Journal* (1995) 91.

Table of Cases

Adams v. United States *ex rel.* McCann, 317 U.S. 269 (1942)
Anders v. California, 386 U.S. 738 (1967)
Argersinger v. Hamlin, 407 U.S. 25 (1972)
Arizona v. Fulminante, 499 U.S. 279 (1991)
Arizona v. Washington, 434 U.S. 497 (1978)
Ash, United States v., 413 U.S. 300 (1973)
Avery v. Alabama, 308 U.S. 444 (1940)
Baldasar v. Illinois, 446 U.S. 222 (1980)
Barron v. Baltimore, 32 U.S. 243 (1833)
Betts v. Brady, 316 U.S. 455 (1942)
Blanton v. City of Las Vegas, 489 U.S. 538 (1989)
Blockburger v. United States, 284 U.S. 299 (1932)
Brecht v. Abrahamson, 507 U.S. 619 (1993)
Brewer v. Williams, 430 U.S. 387 (1977)
Brookhart v. Janis, 384 U.S. 1 (1966)
Brooks v. Tennessee, 406 U.S. 605 (1972)
Calandra, United States v., 414 U.S. 338 (1974)
California v. Trombetta, 467 U.S. 479 (1984)
Caplin & Drysdale v. United States, 491 U.S. 617 (1989)
Chambers v. Maroney, 399 U.S. 42 (1970)
Chambers v. Mississippi, 410 U.S. 284 (1973)
Chandler v. Fretag, 348 U.S. 3 (1954)
Chapman v. California, 386 U.S. 18 (1967)
Coleman v. Alabama, 399 U.S. 1 (1970)
Colorado v. Connelly, 479 U.S. 157 (1986)
Crane v. Kentucky, 476 U.S. 683 (1986)
Cronic, United States v., 466 U.S. 648 (1984)
Cuyler v. Sullivan, 446 U.S. 335 (1980)

Davis v. United States, 512 U.S. 452 (1994)
Douglas v. California, 372 U.S. 353 (1963)
Duncan v. Louisiana, 391 U.S. 145 (1968)
Estelle v. Smith, 451 U.S. 454 (1981)
Evitts v. Lucey, 469 U.S. 387 (1985)
Ex Parte, ———. See name of party
Faretta v. California, 422 U.S. 806 (1975)
Ferguson v. Georgia, 365 U.S. 570 (1961)
Fuller v. Oregon, 417 U.S. 40 (1974)
Geders v. United States, 425 U.S. 80 (1976)
Gideon v. Wainwright, 372 U.S. 335 (1963)
Gilbert v. California, 388 U.S. 263 (1967)
Glasser v. United States, 315 U.S. 60 (1942)
Godinez v. Moran, 509 U.S. 389 (1993)
Gouveia, United States v., 467 U.S. 180 (1984)
Griffin v. Illinois, 351 U.S. 12 (1956)
Hamilton v. Alabama, 368 U.S. 52 (1961)
Henry v. Mississippi, 379 U.S. 443 (1965)
Henry, United States v., 447 U.S. 264 (1980)
Herring v. New York, 422 U.S. 853 (1975)
Hill v. Lockhart, 474 U.S. 52 (1985)
Holloway v. Arkansas, 435 U.S. 475 (1978)
Illinois v. Perkins, 496 U.S. 292 (1990)
Johnson v. Zerbst, 304 U.S. 458 (1938)
Jones v. Barnes, 463 U.S. 745 (1983)
Kimmelman v. Morrison, 477 U.S. 365 (1986)
Kirby v. Illinois, 406 U.S. 682 (1972)
Kotteakos v. United States, 328 U.S. 750 (1946)
Kuhlmann v. Wilson, 477 U.S. 436 (1986)
Lockhart v. Fretwell, 506 U.S. 364 (1993)
Maine v. Moulton, 474 U.S. 159 (1985)
Martinez v. Court of Appeal of California, 528 U.S. 152 (2000)
Massiah v. United States, 377 U.S. 201 (1964)
Matthews v. United States, 485 U.S. 58 (1988)
McCoy v. Court of Appeals of Wisconsin, 486 U.S. 429 (1988)
McKane v. Durston, 153 U.S. 684 (1894)
McKaskle v. Wiggins, 465 U.S. 168 (1984)
McMann v. Richardson, 397 U.S. 759 (1970)
McNeil v. Wisconsin, 501 U.S. 171 (1991)
Mempa v. Rhay, 389 U.S. 128 (1967)
Michigan v. Harvey, 494 U.S. 344 (1990)
Michigan v. Jackson, 475 U.S. 625 (1986)
Michigan v. Tucker, 417 U.S. 433 (1974)
Mickens v. Taylor, ___ U.S. ___, 122 S.Ct. 1237 (2002).
Milligan, *Ex Parte*, 71 U.S. 2 (1866)
Milton v. Wainwright, 407 U.S. 371 (1972)
Miranda v. Arizona, 384 U.S. 436 (1966)
Monsanto, United States v., 491 U.S. 600 (1989)

Montana v. Egelhoff, 518 U.S. 37 (1996)
Moore v. Illinois, 434 U.S. 220 (1977)
Moore v. Michigan, 355 U.S. 155 (1957)
Moran v. Burbine, 475 U.S. 412 (1986)
Morris v. Slappy, 461 U.S. 1 (1983)
Morrison, United States v., 449 U.S. 361 (1981)
Murray v. Giarratano, 492 U.S. 1 (1989)
New York v. Hill, 528 U.S. 110 (2000)
Nichols v. United States, 511 U.S. 738 (1994)
Nix v. Whiteside, 475 U.S. 157 (1986)
Nix v. Williams, 467 U.S. 431 (1984)
Nixon, United States v., 418 U.S. 683 (1974)
Oregon v. Bradshaw, 462 U.S. 1039 (1983)
Palko v. Connecticut, 302 U.S. 319 (1937)
Patterson v. Illinois, 487 U.S. 285 (1988)
Pennsylvania v. Finley, 481 U.S. 551 (1987)
Penson v. Ohio, 488 U.S. 75 (1988)
Perry v. Leeke, 488 U.S. 272 (1989)
Polk County v. Dodson, 454 U.S. 312 (1981)
Powell v. Alabama, 287 U.S. 45 (1932)
Rhode Island v. Innis, 446 U.S. 291 (1980)
Rock v. Arkansas, 483 U.S. 44 (1987)
Roe v. Flores-Ortega, 528 U.S. 470 (2000)
Ross v. Moffitt, 417 U.S. 600 (1974)
Satterwhite v. Texas, 486 U.S. 249 (1988)
Scott v. Illinois, 440 U.S. 367 (1979)
Singer v. United States, 380 U.S. 24 (1965)
Smith v. Robbins, 528 U.S. 259 (2000)
Stone v. Powell, 428 U.S. 465 (1976)
Strickland v. Washington, 466 U.S. 668 (1984)
Taylor v. Illinois, 484 U.S. 400 (1988)
Texas v. Cobb, 532 U.S. 162 (2001)
Townsend v. Burke, 334 U.S. 736 (1948)
Ungar v. Sarafite, 376 U.S. 575 (1964)
United States v. ———. *See opposing party*
Van Duzee, United States v., 140 U.S. 169 (1891)
Von Moltke v. Gillies, 332 U.S. 708 (1948)
Wade, United States v., 338 U.S. 218 (1967)
Wainwright v. Sykes, 433 U.S. 72 (1977)
Wainwright v. Torna, 455 U.S. 586 (1982)
Weatherford v. Bursey, 429 U.S. 545 (1977)
Wheat v. United States, 486 U.S. 153 (1988)
White v. Maryland, 373 U.S. 59 (1963)

Index

About the Author

JAMES J. TOMKOVICZ is a Professor of Law at the University of Iowa College of Law. He served as a judicial clerk for the Honorable Edward J. Schwartz and the Honorable John M. Ferren and as an attorney with the United States Department of Justice. Professor Tomkovicz is co-author of a casebook on criminal procedure, has written a number of scholarly articles pertaining to the Fourth Amendment, the Sixth Amendment, and other topics of criminal law and procedure, and has authored *amicus curiae* briefs in three cases before the United States Supreme Court.